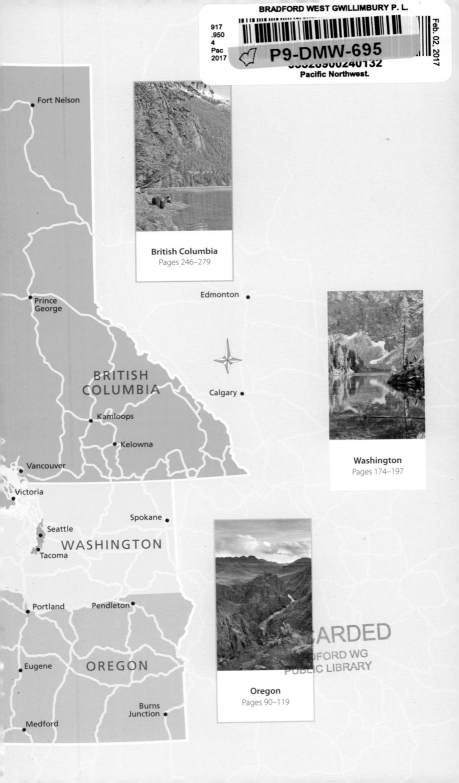

Fort Nelson

British Columbia
Pages 246–279

Prince
George

Edmonton

BRITISH
COLUMBIA

Calgary

Kamloops

Kelowna

Washington
Pages 174–197

Vancouver

Victoria

Spokane

Seattle

WASHINGTON

Tacoma

Portland

Pendleton

OREGON

Eugene

Oregon
Pages 90–119

Burns
Junction

Medford

EYEWITNESS TRAVEL

PACIFIC
NORTHWEST

EYEWITNESS TRAVEL

PACIFIC
NORTHWEST

Main Contributors **Stephen Brewer,
Constance Brissenden, Anita Carmin**

Produced by International Book Productions Inc.,
Toronto, Ontario, Canada

Project Editor Barbara Hopkinson

Art Editors James David Ellis, Barbara Hopkinson

Editors Judy Phillips, Sheila Hall, Debbie Koenig, Tara Tovell

DTP Designers Dietmar Kokemohr, Nicola Lyon

Picture Research and Permissions Diana Bahr

Main Contributors

Stephen Brewer, Constance Brissenden, Anita Carmin

Photographers

Bruce Forster, Gunter Marx, Scott Pitts

Illustrator

William Band

Production Controller

Shane Higgins

Printed in China

First American Edition, 2003

16 17 18 19 10 9 8 7 6 5 4 3 2 1

Published in the United States by Dorling Kindersley Limited,

345 Hudson Street, New York, NY 10014

Reprinted with revisions 2006, 2008, 2010, 2012, 2015, 2017

Copyright 2003, 2017 © Dorling Kindersley Limited, London

A Penguin Random House Company

All rights reserved. Without limiting the rights under copyright reserved above, no part of this publication may be reproduced, stored in or introduced into a retrieval system, or transmitted, in any form, or by any means (electronic, mechanical, photocopying, recording, or otherwise), without the prior written permission of both the copyright owner and the above publisher of this book.

A catalog record for this book is available from the Library of Congress.

ISSN 1542-1554

ISBN 978-1-4654-5712-7

MIX
Paper from
responsible sources
FSC
www.fsc.org   FSC™ C018179

**The information in this
DK Eyewitness Travel Guide is checked regularly.**
Every effort has been made to ensure that this book is as up to date as possible at the time of going to press. Some details, however, such as telephone numbers, opening hours, prices, gallery hanging arrangements and travel information, are liable to change. The publishers cannot accept responsibility for any consequences arising from the use of this book, nor for any material on third-party websites, and cannot guarantee that any website address in this book will be a suitable source of travel information. We value the views and suggestions of our readers very highly. Please write to: Publisher, DK Eyewitness Travel Guides, Dorling Kindersley, 80 Strand, London, WC2R 0RL, UK, or email: travelguides@dk.com.

Front cover main image: Mount Shuksan in North Cascades National Park, Washington

◄ Lake McArthur in Yoho National Park, BC

Sailboats on the waters of Burrard Inlet, BC

Contents

How to Use this Guide **6**

Introducing the Pacific Northwest

Emmons Glacier, Mount Rainier National Park, Washington

Freshly caught crab

Sea kayaks at Snug Harbor, San Juan Island, Washington

Guitar from the collection at the EMP Museum, Seattle

Victorian home in Portland's neighborhood of Nob Hill

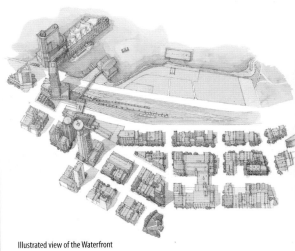

Illustrated view of the Waterfront and Gastown, Vancouver

HOW TO USE THIS GUIDE

This guide helps you to get the most from your visit to the Pacific Northwest. It provides detailed information and expert recommendations. *Introducing the Pacific Northwest* maps the region and sets it in its historical and cultural context. Features cover topics from wildlife to geology. The three area sections, as well as the three city sections, describe important sights, using maps, photographs, and illustrations. Restaurant and hotel listings can be found in *Travelers' Needs*. The *Survival Guide* offers tips on everything from public transport to using the telephone system.

Portland, Seattle, and Vancouver

The center of each of these cities is divided into several sightseeing areas, each with its own chapter. A last chapter, *Farther Afield*, describes sights beyond the central areas. All sights are numbered and plotted on the chapter's area map. Information on each sight is presented in numerical order, making it easy to locate within the chapter.

Sights at a Glance lists the chapter's sights by category, such as Museums and Galleries; Historic Buildings and Churches; Parks and Squares; Gardens and Viewpoints; and Shops.

2 Street-by-Street map
This gives a bird's-eye view of the heart of each sightseeing area.

A star indicates a sight that no visitor should miss.

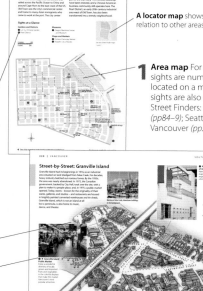

All pages about Portland have orange thumb tabs. Seattle's are purple, and Vancouver's are green.

A locator map shows where you are in relation to other areas of the city center.

1 Area map For easy reference, sights are numbered and located on a map. City center sights are also marked on Street Finders: Portland *(pp84–9)*; Seattle *(pp168–73)*; Vancouver *(pp240–45)*.

A suggested route for a walk is shown in red.

3 Detailed information The sights in the three main cities are described individually. The address, telephone number, opening hours, and information on admission charge, tours, wheelchair access, and public transport are provided. The key to the symbols is on the back flap.

1 **Introduction** The landscape, history, and character of each state or province is outlined here, showing how the area has developed over the centuries and what it has to offer to the visitor today.

Pacific Northwest Area by Area

In this book, the Pacific Northwest has been divided into the two states and one province, each of which has its own chapter. Portland, Seattle, and Vancouver are dealt with in separate chapters. Interesting sights to visit are numbered on a regional map.

2 **Regional map** This shows the road network and gives an illustrated overview of the region. Interesting places to visit are numbered, and there are also useful tips on getting to, and around, the region by car and public transport.

Each area of the Pacific Northwest can be quickly identified by its color coding, shown on the inside front flap.

3 **Detailed information** Noteworthy towns, cities, and other places to visit are described individually. They are listed in order, following the numbering on the regional map. Within each sight there is detailed information on interesting buildings and other attractions.

A visitors' checklist provides all the practical information needed to plan your visit.

4 **Top sights** These are given two or more pages. The most interesting town or city centers are shown with sights picked out and described; parks have maps showing facilities, major exhibits, and the main roads and trails.

INTRODUCING THE PACIFIC NORTHWEST

DISCOVERING THE PACIFIC NORTHWEST

These tours have been designed to take in as many of the region's highlights as possible, while keeping long-distance travel to a minimum. Three 2-day tours cover the Pacific Northwest's most notable cities: Portland, Seattle, and Vancouver. With abundant natural beauty and thriving cultural scenes, all three consistently rank among North America's most popular cities for visitors. Next are two 7-day tours covering the southern region of British Columbia and the western regions of Washington and Oregon. Both are filled with activities and attractions, including some of North America's most decorated wine regions. These two routes can be combined to make a superb 2-week tour of the whole region.

1 Week in Western Washington and Western Oregon

- Shop, dine, and feel the energy of lively **Seattle**.

- Admire the magisterial beauty of the imposing **Mt. Rainier National Park** and **Mt. St. Helens Volcanic Monument**.

- Enjoy the historic atmosphere of Oregon coast towns such as **Astoria** and **Newport**.

- Dip your toes into the surf at **Cannon Beach**, then gawk at the mighty mounds of the **Oregon Dunes National Recreation Area**.

- Marvel at stunning scenery on a drive along the rim of one of the world's deepest lakes at **Crater Lake National Park**.

- Tour the **Wine Country of the North Willamette Valley** and indulge in some of the best wines in the US.

- In fun, funky **Portland** immerse yourself in current cultural trends in the Pearl District.

Seattle
The city skyline forms a dramatic backdrop to Pier 66, a lively area home to a pleasure boat marina and various restaurants.

◀ A print by Paolo Fumagalli from a painting of the George III Archipelago near Vancouver

Whistler
Famous for its reliable snow and fantastic ski runs, Whistler offers a varierty of winter activities.

Stanley Park
Totem poles are just one of the many things to see at Vancouver's top attraction.

Key

— Western Washington and Western Oregon

— Southern British Columbia

0 kilometers 100

0 miles 100

1 Week in Southern British Columbia

- Visit the main sights of charming **Victoria**, British Columbia's capital: the scenic **Inner Harbour**, handsome **Parliament Buildings**, and informative **Royal BC Museum**.

- Explore **Vancouver Island's** natural beauty with a visit to the **Butchart Gardens** or one of the Gulf Islands, such as **Saltspring Island**.

- Discover **Vancouver**'s historic neighborhood of **Gastown** and go shopping in **Yaletown**.

- Hit the slopes at **Whistler**, where you can also shop and dine the day away in inviting **Whistler Village**. In warmer weather, enjoy the scenery at **Alta Lake**.

- Use **Kelowna** as your base from which to explore the **Okanagan Valley**. Before leaving the city, be sure to visit the **Father Pandosy Mission** for a peek into the region's past. Lose track of time at one, or two, of the region's acclaimed wineries.

2 Days Each in Portland, Seattle, and Vancouver

Portland
- Explore inviting shops and cafés in the hip **Pearl District**.

- Stroll through historic **Old Town**, stopping at the **Lan Su Chinese Garden** or the **Oregon Maritime Center and Museum**.

Seattle
- Indulge in a tasty treat at the original **Starbucks®** and the famous **Pike Place Market**.

- Take a ride on one of the **Washington State Ferries** to appreciate the city's watery setting.

- Visit the **Seattle Center**, home to the **EMP Museum** and the beloved **Space Needle**.

Vancouver
- Enjoy the trendy shops and cafés housed in the restored 19th-century buildings of **Gastown**.

- Lose track of time in **Stanley Park**, home to colorful totem poles and a stunning seawall.

- Hop on the **Granville Island Market Ferries** to reach **Granville Island** and its acclaimed **Public Market**.

2 Days in Portland

Rugged Portland offers a mix of trendy city life and stunning natural beauty, and sits at the forefront of numerous cultural trends.

- **Arriving** Portland International Airport is located 9 miles (15 km) northeast of downtown. The MAX light rail red line takes roughly 30 minutes to reach downtown; taxis are quicker but more expensive.

Day 1
Morning Start the day with a coffee and pastry in one of **Pearl District**'s *(pp58–9)* numerous coffee shops. Explore the inviting stores that populate the area, stopping to note the architectural details revealing the neighborhood's industrial past. Continue on foot through the city's original namesake port, known as **Old Town** *(pp56–7)*. The neighborhood's diverse history can be appreciated by visiting one of its two most popular sights: the breathtaking **Lan Su Chinese Garden** *(p58)* or the informative **Oregon Maritime Center and Museum** *(p58)*. If visiting the area on a weekend, be sure to check out the **Portland Saturday Market** *(p58)*, one of the oldest of its kind in the US.

Afternoon After grabbing lunch in one of the hip cafés that dot the area, hop aboard one of the **streetcars** *(p67)* that link Old Town to **Downtown** *(pp61–9)*, then idle the afternoon away at

the **Portland Art Museum** *(p66)*. Before darkness falls, head over to **Pioneer Courthouse Square** *(p64)* and watch the city's worker bees cross paths with trendy youths during the after-work rush hour. Grab a happy hour drink at one of the area's award-winning microbreweries, then have a bite to eat at one of the city's numerous nationally renowned eateries.

Day 2
Morning Start your day by taking the MAX red or blue line to reach the sprawling **Washington Park** *(pp74–7)*, where you can spend a full day exploring attractions such as the popular **Oregon Zoo** *(p77)*, the calming **Japanese Garden** *(p76)*, and the astounding **International Rose Test Garden** *(p76)*.

Afternoon Head back to the city center, stopping for a late lunch or early dinner before diving into the world's largest independent bookstore, **Powell's City of Books** *(p59)*, which has more than a million volumes on hand. Grab a free city events calendar at the store and plan the rest of your evening around Portland's thriving performing arts community.

To extend your trip…

Visit one of the city's outer neighborhoods, such as the **Hawthorne District** *(p78)*, which has many boutique clothes stores, and the **Sellwood District**, which is good for antiques *(p78)*. Indulge in excellent food on **Southeast Division Street** *(p78)*, home to Portland's hottest dining scene.

The sign for Pike Place Market, high above the market's rooftop.

2 Days in Seattle

Ringed by breathtaking natural beauty and scenic bodies of water, the Emerald City itself is a blur of urban activity, with young residents packing legendary coffee shops, microbreweries, and music clubs.

- **Arriving** Seattle-Tacoma International Airport is located 13 miles (21 km) south of the city. The public light rail service connects the airport directly to downtown in about 35 minutes. Shuttle buses and taxis are available as well.

Day 1
Morning Start your day with a coffee at the original **Starbucks®** *(p139)*, then grab breakfast at the city's most popular attraction, **Pike Place Market** *(pp136–9)*. Watch chefs peruse the day's catch at the market's famous fish vendors, and finish up your visit before the lunchtime crowds arrive. A short walk away is the **Seattle Aquarium** *(pp142–3)*, which offers up-close views of the region's aquatic species.

Afternoon Take a **Washington State Ferry** *(p141)* for an inexpensive leisure cruise to **Bainbridge Island** *(p185)*, where you can disembark to enjoy lunch in a quaint café. Back in the city, end the afternoon either in the **Central Library** *(p133)*, browsing through the many books and admiring

The tranquility of Lan Su Chinese Garden

the art collection, or the popular **Seattle Art Museum** *(pp132–3)*. Finish your day with an evening stroll around lively **Capitol Hill** *(p157)*, home to numerous eclectic shops, bars, and eateries.

Day 2
Morning Give yourself an impromptu history lesson by strolling around **Pioneer Square** *(pp126–7)*, carefully navigating the cobblestone streets while stopping to peruse the square's numerous historic markers.

Afternoon Grab lunch in one of the area's inviting restaurants, then hop on the **Monorail** *(p149)* and cross the city to the **Seattle Center** *(pp146–7)*, home to the **EMP Museum** *(pp150–51)*. A must for music fans, the EMP is one of the world's leading museums of popular contemporary music. Nearby is the world-famous **Space Needle** *(pp148–9)*, where, if you time your visit correctly, you'll be rewarded with breath-taking sunset views of the city, **Mount Rainier** *(p188)*, and beyond. Sports fans should catch an evening baseball game at the impressive **Safeco Field** *(p156)*, while trend-seekers can explore the funky **Ballard** and **Fremont neighborhoods** *(p162)*.

> **To extend your trip...**
> Explore the **Woodland Park Zoo** *(pp160–61)*, enjoy a hike along the **Burke-Gilman Trail**, take a stroll in **Gas Works Park**, or canoe on **Green Lake** *(all p159)*.

Seattle's Space Needle, with rotating views at 500 ft (152 m) in SkyCity restaurant

City skyline of Vancouver, with the North Shore Mountains in the background

2 Days in Vancouver

Vancouver consistently tops annual rankings of the world's most livable cities. It is full of intriguing neighbor-hoods, colorful diversity, and natural beauty.

- **Arriving** Located 9 miles (14 km) south of Downtown, Vancouver International Airport is linked by the efficient SkyTrain Canada Line, which takes 25 minutes to reach the city center. Taxis are also available.

Day 1
Morning One of Vancouver's oldest neighborhoods, historic **Gastown** *(pp204–5)* provides an atmospheric welcome to the city. Explore the area's cobblestone streets and restored 19th-century storefronts, stopping for a bite in a funky café along the way. Continue along the attractive harborfront and take in the attractive architecture of **Canada Place** *(p206)*. Next, turn away from the water to stroll through the city's **Downtown** *(pp211–17)* key attractions including **Christ Church Cathedral** *(p214)*.

Afternoon After you've had your fill of the bustling cityscape, use the efficient bus system to travel to Vancouver's most popular attraction, the gorgeous **Stanley Park** *(pp230–31)*. One could easily spend an entire day exploring the park, so take your pick from attractions such as the stunning seawall, colorful totem poles, rose gardens, and the **Vancouver Aquarium** *(p231)*. As darkness approaches, venture back to the city center to finish your day with an authentic dinner in the city's historic **Chinatown** *(p208)*.

Day 2
Morning Hop on one of the **Granville Island Market Ferries** *(p223)* to idyllic **Granville Island** *(pp220–23)*, a must for any foodie thanks to its acclaimed **Public Market** *(p223)*. Enjoy tastes of local produce, fresh seafood, and artisan products, then burn off the calories by strolling through the island's artist studios or the acclaimed **Emily Carr University of Art & Design** *(p222)*.

Afternoon Shopaholics should make the short jaunt to **Yaletown** *(pp224–5)*, home to dozens of inviting shops; nature lovers can head in the opposite direction to lovely **Vanier Park** *(pp224–5)*, home of the **Museum of Vancouver** *(p225)*. No visit is complete without sampling the city's nightlife, from street performers to live jazz to raucous dance clubs.

> **To extend your trip...**
> Venture to the city's western coast to visit the **Museum of Anthropology** *(pp234–5)*. Thrill-seekers should head north to the **Capilano Suspension Bridge** *(p228)*.

1 Week in Western Washington and Western Oregon

- **Airports** Arrive at Portland International Airport and depart from Seattle-Tacoma International Airport.

- **Transport** Hiring a car is essential for this itinerary. Travelers may opt to use bus and rail connections for longer journeys where available.

Day 1: Seattle
Pick a day from the Seattle itinerary on pp12–13.

Day 2: Seattle to Astoria
Head south from Seattle, stopping to visit two of the Pacific Northwest's most famous sights. **Mount Rainier National Park** (pp188–9) offers several days' worth of attractions; depending on the season, you can choose from the likes of **Nisqually Glacier** (p188) and **Narada Falls** (p188). Alternatively, simply admire the majestic mountain from the roadside. Continue on your way to **Mount St. Helens National Volcanic Monument** (pp196–7), which has been a popular attraction since it erupted in 1980. Once darkness approaches, make the short drive to **Astoria** (pp96–7) for dinner and a good night's rest.

Day 3: Astoria to Cannon Beach
Astoria, the oldest American settlement west of the Rocky Mountains, offers numerous historic attractions. Climb atop the **Astoria Column** (p96) for scenic views of the region, then head south toward **Cannon Beach** (p97). Take in the natural beauty at **Ecola State Park** (p97), and visit the beach around sunset for gorgeous photo opportunities while dipping your feet in the chilly Pacific waters. Enjoy dinner in one of the town's inviting bistros.

Day 4: Cannon Beach to Newport
Continue your journey south, stopping in **Tillamook** (p97) to visit its famous **Creamery** (p97), where you can sample award-winning cheeses and other dairy products. Next, take a detour along the scenic **Three Capes Scenic Route** (p97). Keep heading south until you reach **Lincoln City** (p98), where you can visit the steep cliffs and misty rainforests of **Cascade Head Preserve** (p98). Finish your day in **Newport** (pp98–9), an atmospheric fishing town full of convivial bars and seafood restaurants. If time allows, visit either the **Oregon Coast Aquarium** (p99) or the **Hatfield Marine Science Center** (p99).

Day 5: Newport to Crater Lake
Rise early and begin your day by driving south to the incredible **Oregon Dunes National Recreation Area** (p100). Take it all in from the scenic overlook point or, if you have time, see the tallest dunes by visiting the Umpqua Scenic Dunes Trail. Next, drive 3 hours inland until you reach **Crater Lake National**

Aptly named Paradise Meadows in autumn colors, Mount Rainier National Park

Park (pp110–11). Do the 33-mile (53-km) **Rim Drive** (p111) to take in the lake in all its glory, then unwind with a well-deserved quiet evening at the **Crater Lake Lodge** (p110).

Day 6: Crater Lake to McMinnville
Begin your day communing with nature, then break up the lengthy drive to Oregon's famous wine region by stopping for a meal in **Eugene** (p105) or the state capital, **Salem** (pp104–5). Soon you will approach the heart of the **Wine Country of the North Willamette Valley** (pp102–3), where you can tour the wineries and enjoy tasting some excellent wines. Finish your day in the charming town of **McMinnville** (p104).

Day 7: McMinnville to Portland
Visit any wineries left on your to-do list, then make the short drive north to Portland. On the way, consider a stop in historic **Oregon City** (p79), where you can visit the **End of the Oregon Trail Interpretive Center** (p79) or the **Museum of the Oregon Territory** (p79). Arriving in Portland, depending on the time you have, pick and choose sights and activities from the Portland itinerary on p12.

To extend your trip…
Wine lovers can self-drive the 14-mile (22.5-km) **Walla Walla Valley Wine Tour** (pp196–7), located in southeastern Washington, about a 4-hour drive from Portland or Seattle.

Stunning Cannon Beach, on the rugged and uncrowded Oregon coast

1 Week in Southern British Columbia

- **Airports** Arrive at Victoria International Airport, located north of the city, and depart from Kelowna International Airport.

- **Transport** Although hiring a car will make for an easier journey, various bus and boat services connect major British Columbia cities and towns. Travelers may opt to use bus and boat connections for longer journeys, then hire rental cars within particular destinations.

British Columbia's Parliament Buildings, located in Victoria

Day 1: Victoria

Explore British Columbia's capital, **Victoria** (p250–55). Begin your visit on the scenic **Inner Harbour** (p250), snapping pictures of the attractive waterfront, and continue to the imposing **Parliament Buildings** (p254). One can easily lose oneself in the buildings, some of which date back to 1897. Enjoy lunch or afternoon tea at one of British Columbia's most famous hotels, the **Fairmont Empress** (see p253). Finish the day with a visit to the **Royal BC Museum** (pp256–7), which tells the story of the province through its natural history, geology, and peoples.

Day 2: Vancouver Island

Take your pick from numerous outdoorsy activities and destinations on Vancouver Island, all of which are accessible from Victoria. Amateur horticulturists should make a beeline to **Butchart Gardens** (p258). In the summer, the gardens often host special programs such as live classical music and fireworks. To best appreciate the area's rugged landscape and breathtaking natural beauty, spend the afternoon visiting one or two of the **Gulf Islands** (p259). Depending on one's interests, there's something for everyone: **Saltspring** has inviting shops and cafés; **Galiano** is ideal for hikers, and **Mayne** is best

for history lovers. As nightfall approaches, retreat to Victoria to enjoy a dinner of bountiful local produce and seafood at one of the city's award-winning restaurants.

Days 3 and 4: Vancouver

See the Vancouver itinerary on p13.

Day 5: Whistler

North of Vancouver, the year-round resort town of **Whistler** (pp260–61) lures visitors drawn to its world-class skiing and inviting summertime activities. The neighboring Whistler and Blackcomb Mountains house some of North America's most challenging ski runs. In warmer weather, visitors can enjoy a bevy of activities on **Alta Lake** (p261). The shops, cafés, and bars of **Whistler Village** (p261) are constantly packed. Splurge on an overnight stay (or afternoon tea) at the **Fairmont Chateau Whistler** (p260).

Verdant vineyards in the Okanagan Valley wine region

Day 6: Whistler to Kamloops

Make the drive to **Kamloops** (p262), located at the confluence of the North and South Thompson Rivers. The attractive city holds a pair of must-sees: the **Secwepemc Museum and Heritage Park** (p262), which provides a peek into the region's history, and the **British Columbia Wildlife Park** (p262), perfect for animal lovers.

Day 7: Okanagan Valley/Kelowna

Continue east, then south, and you'll arrive in **Kelowna** (p262). The city, which lies on the eastern shore of Okanagan Lake, provides an ideal base for exploring the **Okanagan Valley** (p263). Learn about the area's history with a visit to the **Father Pandosy Mission** (p262), then end the afternoon with a visit to one of the acclaimed wineries that make up Canada's second-largest wine region.

To extend your trip...
Further immerse yourself in the Okanagan Valley by visiting two of its charming small towns. **Summerland** (p262) is filled with 19th-century buildings, and visitors can take in breathtaking views by scaling Giant's Head Mountain. Nearby, tiny **Penticton** (p263) lures wine lovers with several wineries. Take a stroll along the town's Okanagan Beach, where the adventurous can enjoy water sports.

Putting Oregon and Washington on the Map

Nestling in the northwest corner of the United States and containing pristine expanses of forest, mountains, and desert, Oregon and Washington are two of the country's most beautiful states. Oregon's population of 3.9 million, and Washington's of over 7 million, are concentrated in and around the major cities. The region's economic base is as diverse as its landscape, with manufacturing, retail and services, tourism, agriculture, and forestry particularly strong industries.

North America

GREENLAND

USA

CANADA

USA

Pacific Ocean

MEXICO

PACIFIC OCEAN

0 kilometers 100
0 miles 50

Key

═══ Freeway

─── Major highway

┈┈┈ Major road

─── Railway

─── State border

▬▬▬ International border

☐ Urban area

For keys to symbols *see back flap*

Putting British Columbia on the Map

British Columbia, Canada's westernmost province, and the country's gateway to the Asia-Pacific region, is home to over 4.6 million people. Traditionally strong industries such as forestry, mining, and fishing remain vital to the province's economy, though recent years have seen a boom in the high-tech, film, and eco-tourism areas. Hydroelectricity and natural gas are other important resources. The beauty of the British Columbian wilderness – from the rugged coastline to the commanding mountain ranges – is preserved in the province's 830 parks and protected areas.

YUKON

Pelly Mountains

Atlin Lake

Juneau

Stikine

BRITISH COLUMBIA

ALASKA (USA)

Terrace

Prince Rupert

Skeena

Kitimat

PACIFIC OCEAN

0 kilometers 150
0 miles 100

Haida Gwaii (Queen Charlotte Islands)

Greater Vancouver

0 km 15
0 miles 10

BRITISH COLUMBIA

North Vancouver

Burnaby

Vancouver

Port Moody

Port Coquitlam

Richmond

Surrey

Langley

Mission

White Rock

Abbotsford

Lynden

WASHINGTON

Key

═══ Freeway

─── Major highway

┈┈┈ Major road

─── Railway

─── State border

▬▬▬ International border

Urban area

Vanco Islar

Vancc Islan

For keys to symbols *see back flap*

A PORTRAIT OF THE PACIFIC NORTHWEST

Some of North America's most rugged and spectacular terrain unfolds across the Pacific Northwest. Settled by Europeans barely 150 years ago, the region has cradled Native cultures for thousands. The region is now also home to three of the continent's most sophisticated cities – Portland, Seattle, and Vancouver – all of them surrounded by soaring mountains, dense forests, and sparkling water.

The Pacific Northwest, comprising Oregon, Washington, and British Columbia, is richly varied – with its desert, mountain, and seashore landscapes, its mild and extreme climates, and a cosmopolitan mix of cultures and ethnicities. The region straddles two nations – the US and Canada – and comprises 526,000 sq miles (1,362,240 sq km), making it larger than France, Germany, and Italy combined. The one quality that characterizes all of the Pacific Northwest is its natural beauty, the result of eons of geological activity that has left the region with lofty mountains, deep gorges, rocky shorelines, and mighty rivers.

Natural Wonders

The call of the wild is the draw for many travelers to the Pacific Northwest. Although highways, suburban sprawl, large-scale ranching, logging, dams, and other encroachments have all had a negative impact on this great wilderness, enough of its many natural wonders – such as 800-year-old Sitka spruce in the coastal rainforests – remains intact to offer a welcome escape from the stresses of the 21st century.

Another characteristic of the Pacific Northwest is its infamous weather. It can indeed rain for days on end here, but the weather varies as much as the topography does. Whereas west of the mountains the north Pacific Ocean currents ensure wet and mild winters and pleasant summers, an entirely different climate prevails east of the mountains. On the eastern plateaus and steppes, temperatures dip to well below freezing in the winter, often accompanied by heavy snow, and soar in the summer. In the central mountain region, inland deserts experience harsh winters – resulting in frequent road closures – and dry hot summers.

Outdoor Activities

Pacific Northwesterners claim to enjoy their cloudy skies and drizzly days. In defiance of the elements, many residents adopt a rugged look (hiking boots and

Sailboats in a regatta held on the waters of Burrard Inlet, British Columbia

◄ The gorgeous Crater Lake on a summer day, Oregon

Local hikers on a trail near Bellingham, Washington

incorporated striking new architecture into a landscape dominated by mountains and inlets.

Of course, the residents of each city tend to claim that theirs is the most beautiful and livable in the Pacific Northwest, if not in all of North America. Each has its own unique virtues. Portland takes first place for careful urban planning, for containing urban sprawl, and for preserving a charming small-town atmosphere. Seattle, with its imposing skyline, is the largest of the three cities. Well-known for its high-tech industries, it also offers a vibrant music and theater scene. Cosmopolitan Vancouver, nestled between the Strait of Georgia and the Coast Mountains, arguably enjoys the best setting.

heavy socks, khaki shorts, and flannel shirt) year-round and enthusiastically embrace the outdoors. The region offers some of the world's best white-water rafting, kayaking, hiking, skiing, fishing, scuba diving, windsurfing, and rock climbing. For those who prefer more placid pursuits, such as sitting beside a still mountain lake or a rushing stream, or strolling along a remote surf-pounded beach, the opportunities here are seemingly endless.

Art and Culture

Long gone are the days when the Pacific Northwest was considered a poor country cousin in terms of the arts. Highly regarded and wide-ranging collections of art now hang in many museums throughout the region, and excellent concert halls and other venues play host to world-renowned orchestras and performing artists, and to stellar home-grown talent. Unforgettable experiences such as a classical concert beneath a canopy of ponderosa pines at the annual Britt Festivals in Jacksonville, Oregon; an evening of jazz with a sunset backdrop of Seattle's Elliott Bay; or a Shakespeare play at a waterfront park in Vancouver, bring artistic flair to some of the most spectacular settings in the world.

City Life

All this natural beauty provides a backdrop for the urban sophistication of the Pacific Northwest's three major cities, Portland, Seattle, and Vancouver. Here residents have worked together to preserve the scenic virtues and old quarters of their cities while accommodating new growth. Portland has converted much of its downtown riverfront into parkland and laid the tracks of an efficient rapid transit system. Due to the efforts of residents, Seattle has restored its historic Pike Place Market, the colorful and quirky heart of the city, and Vancouver has

Portlanders relaxing at a local café and wine bar

Economy and Industry

While the economies of the major cities are healthy, the interior regions are suffering from high unemployment as traditional industries

Tourists at the top of Seattle's Space Needle

such as mining and logging decline and the economy shifts to one based largely on services and technology. In coastal areas, the fishing industry too has seen increasingly hard times. Fruit cultivation remains a major Pacific Northwest industry, its orchards yielding some of the most prized fruit in the world.

The emergence of high-tech companies in the region (some 3,000 software and e-commerce businesses are in the Seattle area alone) began with the rise in the 1980s of Microsoft, which now employs 40,000 Washingtonians. In 1995, entrepreneur Jeff Bezos opened the doors to the online shopping business, founding Amazon.com in his Seattle home. Aerospace giant Boeing operates several plants in western Washington. Manufacturing facilities for computer industry giants Intel, Epson, and Hewlett-Packard are located in Oregon's Willamette Valley; sportswear chain Nike is also based in Oregon.

Vancouver has benefited from its incarnation as Hollywood North: movie companies inject $3 billion annually into the local economy.

The increase in white-collar jobs has led to an influx of professionals into the three cities, not only expanding the urban areas but also raising the standard (and the cost) of living within them.

Amid this economic transformation, the tourist industry has consistently thrived. Increasing numbers of tourists come to enjoy what locals have long considered their greatest resource: the Pacific Northwest's natural beauty.

People and Politics

Some 15 million people call the Pacific Northwest home. Portland, Seattle, and Vancouver are among the fastest-growing cities in North America. After a US-wide spike in growth in the 1990s, the Hispanic population is today Oregon's largest ethnic group, representing nearly 12 percent of that state's population. And Hispanics now represent 11 percent of Washington's population. Vancouver has swelled in size and prosperity since the 1980s with the arrival of Asian immigrants, particularly from mainland China, Hong Kong, India, Philippines, and South Korea. The First Nations and bands of the Pacific Northwest, many continuing to live in traditional communities, are recovering from a decline in population that occurred after European settlement.

Portland, Seattle, and Vancouver tend to be liberal in their politics; other areas of the region, conservative. Even so, a unique political climate emerges in the Pacific Northwest. Oregonians are the first in the US to have approved assisted suicide for the terminally ill; Washingtonians elected the US's first Asian-American governor; and British Columbians have bounced between right- and left-leaning parties, often bucking the national trend.

Pioneer Courthouse houses the US Court of Appeals, Portland

Geology of the Pacific Northwest

No small amount of geological activity has shaped the present-day Pacific Northwest. One hundred and fifty million years ago, much of the western part of the region was at the bottom of the sea. Over the eons, the North American continental landmass crept westward and collided with the landmass moving eastward across the Pacific Ocean, forcing the Earth's crust upward and creating the coastline of the Pacific Northwest as we know it today. Meanwhile, the eruption of volcanoes thrust up mountain peaks, and glaciers and ice sheets advanced and retreated, carving out deep gorges and canyons. As recent volcanic eruptions and earthquakes in the area attest, the Pacific Northwest is still a geologically active region, and its topography will continue to change as a result.

Washington's Mount Rainier – the most active volcano of the Cascades

Fossil records are found throughout the Pacific Northwest, with its sedimentary rock bearing traces of plant, marine, and animal life from as long ago as 136 million years. The world-renowned John Day Fossil Beds National Monument in Kimberly, Oregon, and the fossil beds at Burgess Shale near Field, British Columbia, are both extensive repositories of this ancient past.

Sedimentary Rock

As the Pacific plate periodically lurched eastward, sedimentary rock from older coastal mountains was uplifted to form the peaks of the Rocky and Cascade mountain ranges. Layers of the sedimentary rock, such as sandstone and shale, that were formed about 15 to 20 million years ago can be seen when visiting the ranges.

Volcanoes such as Mount St. Helens are formed when a plate descends (subducts) beneath another plate and it begins to melt. The molten rock rises to the surface to form a volcano. In the Pacific Northwest, volcanoes began erupting about 55 million years ago. The Cascade Mountains in Oregon and Washington, the Blue Mountains in Oregon, and the Olympic Mountains in Washington are in the Ring of Fire, a zone of volcanic activity that partially encircles the Pacific Ocean.

Glaciers are masses of ice that advance and retreat, scooping out deep gorges and sculpting jagged mountain peaks. Continent-sized glaciers are known as ice sheets. About 15,000 years ago, the Cordilleran ice sheet covered much of Washington and British Columbia; it was 4,000 ft (1,219 m) thick in places. When it melted, the raised water levels of the Pacific Ocean filled two of the deepest gouges, creating Puget Sound and the Strait of Juan de Fuca.

Plate Tectonics

Three main forces are responsible for the formation of mountain ranges such as the Rockies or the Cascades. First, large areas of the Earth's crust (known as tectonic plates), constantly moving together and apart, created uplift. Second, the North American plate, subducted by the Pacific plate, caused a chain of volcanoes to form from the molten rock of the oceanic crust. Third, erosion caused by ice ages deposited sedimentary rocks on the North American plate, which was then folded by more plate movement between 50 and 25 million years ago.

Volcanoes   North America plate

Pacific plate

1 Some 150 million years ago, the Pacific plate moved east, adding to the molten rock from great depths of the North American plate. This then rose up to form the Western Cordillera Mountains.

Pacific   Sediments
plate

2 The Cordilleras were eroded over millions of years and during various ice ages. This led to sediments being deposited in the sagging, wedge-shaped crust east of the mountain range.

Cordillera   Rockies
Mountains

3 Around 50 million years ago, the Pacific plate continued to push east, forcing the Cordillera range eastward, compressing sedimentary rocks, folding and uplifting them to form the Rockies.

Gorges were formed at the end of the last ice age, when massive floods were triggered periodically by melting glaciers. These floods etched out deep narrow chasms such as the one shown here, or much wider ones such as the Columbia River Gorge, which forms the boundary between Washington and Oregon.

Wildlife of the Pacific Northwest

The landscapes of the Pacific Northwest are the most varied in North America. The cold waters of the Pacific Ocean fill sheltered bays and wash onto great lengths of sandy beach, dense old-growth forests carpet the Coast and Cascade Mountains, and arid plateaus and high deserts spread across the eastern parts of the region. Over the past 150 years, settlers have created new landscapes, including the fertile farmland of Oregon's Willamette Valley and the expanses of orchards and wheatfields in eastern Washington and British Columbia. These landscapes – lush river valleys and harsh deserts alike – provide rich habitats for a great diversity of wildlife, and viewing these animals is a rewarding part of a visit to the Pacific Northwest.

Sea lions make their homes on rocky outcroppings along the Pacific shore.

Pacific salmon migrate from cold ocean waters, where they feed until maturity, into the inland streams, rivers, and lakes of their birth where they spawn, then die. Once they have reached fresh water, they stop feeding and live on their stored body fats. The fish often make journeys of more than 1,000 miles (1,600 km), swimming up rapids and bypassing dams. Each of the five species of Pacific salmon – sockeye, pink, chum, coho, and chinook – has a distinct appearance and life cycle. The pinks, for example, live up to two years and weigh little more than 5 lb (2.3 kg), while the chinook can reach 120 lb (54 kg) in weight and live up to seven years.

Elk

Elk reside in the subalpine forests of the Rockies and eastern Oregon mountains. During the mating season in the fall, males become aggressive and fight for herd domination. The nasal, whining sound they emit, known as "bugling," should be taken by humans as a warning. Approaching a mother elk and her calf is dangerous.

Sea otters were rendered almost extinct in the 19th century by trappers who obtained enormous prices for their pelts, but they are now making a comeback along the Pacific Northwest coast. These creatures eat the equivalent of a third of their weight a day, providing quite a show as they feed. A sea otter lies on its back and, using its paws, smashes crabs, mussels, and other shellfish against a rock it has placed on its chest. Otters can be easily spotted, lolling on rocks or floating asleep on the water, their bodies entwined in kelp to keep them from drifting.

Whales belonging to over 20 species pass Vancouver Island, the Olympic Peninsula, and the Oregon coast as they travel between the Arctic and their breeding grounds off southern California and Mexico. It is estimated that 20,000 gray whales and 2,000 orcas make the 5,500-mile (8,850-km) trip each year. The whales migrate south from December to early February and return north from March through May.

Bald eagles, once common thoughout North America, are now mainly found in the Pacific Northwest, in coastal areas or near large inland lakes. The bald eagle is regarded as a symbol of strength and independence, and was designated as the national bird of the US in 1782. Contrary to what its name implies, this eagle is not actually bald; the term comes from the Old English word *balde*, meaning "white."

Beavers are very industrious, using their sharp upper teeth to fell small trees, which they then float to a chosen dam site. The lodges they build within the dam can be as wide as 16 ft (5 m).

Moose, distinguishable by their magnificient spreading antlers, are often spotted grazing by streams, ponds, and other marshy areas.

Grizzly bears, weighing up to 800 lb (350 kg) and standing as tall as 8.8 ft (2.68 m), roam remote parts of the northern Cascades and the Rockies. Far more common is the black bear, smaller than the grizzly but imposing nonetheless.

Flora of the Pacific Northwest

Deep forests, wildflower-filled alpine meadows, and grass-covered steppes are all typical of the Pacific Northwest. Although vastly different, these landscapes are often found in close proximity to one another. The moist, temperate climate of the region's coastal areas fosters an abundance of plant life, including the towering trees, mosses, and shrubs that thrive in centuries-old forests, such as the rainforest in British Columbia's Pacific Rim National Park Reserve. In Washington's Skagit Valley, tulips covering thousands of acres bloom each spring. In the Cascade and Rocky Mountains, and in the deserts and steppes east of the mountains, the terrain is less hospitable and only the hardiest plants survive. But even here, alpine meadows and stands of juniper that scent the high desert attest to the rich diversity of the region's flora.

Mountain Forests
Many of the trees in the rugged mountain forests are several centuries old. Douglas firs can live as long as 1,200 years and grow to be 260 ft (79 m) tall. Fallen logs that foster young trees are known as "nurse logs," which, if they survive 200 years, will earn "old-growth" status.

Wildflowers
The moist climate of the coastal forests and high-country meadows provide perfect growing conditions for colorful wildflowers, such as wood lilies, asters, Jacob's ladder, and purple mountain saxifrage.

Lichens
Hardy lichens – along with mosses, liverworts, ferns, skunk cabbage, and orchids – flourish in the dampness of rainforests that grow along the coast of the Pacific Ocean.

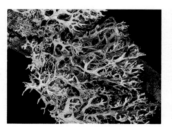

Sagebrush
The arid environment of the Columbia River basin and the high plateaus of Oregon and Washington support only vegetation that can survive with little moisture, such as sagebrush.

Deciduous Forests

Deciduous trees grow in river valleys in the Pacific Northwest. In the fall, these trees provide a brilliant show of color, all the more dramatic because the multihued leaves are usually set against a backdrop of evergreen trees.

Ferns

Lady's fern, maidenhair fern, and deer fern are among the many species that grow in the region. In the Hoh Rainforest, ferns grow taller than the hikers.

Pines and Junipers

Ponderosa pines, lodgepole pines, and junipers have long roots that tap subterranean water tables. With flat needles that retain moisture, junipers can survive on just 8 inches (20.5 cm) of precipitation a year.

Rainforests

Rainforests carpet much of the Pacific Northwest, on British Columbia's Vancouver Island and Haida Gwaii archipelago, and along the Pacific coast. These lush green forests of Sitka spruce, Douglas fir, red cedar, Pacific silver fir, western hemlock, and yew can receive more than 150 inches (381 cm) of rain per year.

First Nations Peoples of the Pacific Northwest

For the First Nations peoples of the Pacific Northwest, 15,000 years of a bountiful life and rich cultural tradition were abruptly upset when European traders and settlers began arriving in the late 18th century. Diseases introduced by these newcomers all but obliterated many First Nations. Those who survived were forced to surrender their lands and ways of life, and move to government-designated reservations. Today, although indigenous people continue to fight against racism and for their self-determination, Native traditions are increasingly recognized as a vital part of the region's rich heritage. Native cultures and history can be explored in such places as the Royal BC Museum, in Victoria *(see pp256–7)*; Whatcom Museum, in Bellingham, Washington *(see p184)*; and Oregon's Museum at Warm Springs *(see p106)*.

A stone inukshuk, sign of friendship

Totem poles are among the best-known artifacts created by the First Nations peoples of the Pacific Northwest. Each pole depicts a legend; magical birds and beasts mix with semi-human figures to tell a story in carved panels arranged in sequence up the pole. Other elaborate carvings, such as those on masks, ornaments, and utensils, often also represent real and supernatural beings.

Artisans and Builders

The trunks of cedar trees were used by Pacific Northwest First Nations peoples to make masks, cooking utensils, wooden chests, elaborate dwellings up to 500 ft (150 m) long and aptly called longhouses, and magnificent dugout canoes, used for transportation, hunting, and fishing.

Respect for the land underpins the spirituality and way of life of First Nations peoples of the Pacific Northwest. Nature provides all, so long as nature's balance is not disturbed. Chief Seattle once said: "We are part of the Earth and it is part of us. The perfumed flowers are our sisters; the deer, the horse, the great eagle, these are our brothers. The rocky crests, the juices in the meadows, the body heat of the pony, and man – all belong to the same family."

Canoes made of birch bark or dug out of massive cedar logs provided an essential mode of transportation on the many rivers that formed a network of trade routes throughout the Pacific Northwest. Canoes ranged in size from small vessels for personal use to large and elaborately decorated ceremonial canoes.

Wigwams were built as dwellings by tribes living in the interior, such as the Nez Perce, Yakama, Cayuse, Shoshone, and Modoc. More permanent longhouses were preferred by many of the tribes that settled along the Pacific Northwest coast from southern Alaska down to Oregon. They include the Tlingit, the Tsimshian, the Haida, the Kwagiutl, the Makah, and the Coast Salish.

Noteworthy Chiefs

Chief Seattle (1786–1866), leader of the Duwamish and Squamish tribes, was just six years old when he witnessed the arrival of Captain Vancouver in Puget Sound. He frequently petitioned American and British authorities for Indian rights and urged peaceful coexistence with settlers.

Chief Joseph (1840–1904) was the renowned leader of the Nez Perce tribe. In 1877, his tribe was forced out of its beloved Wallowa Valley in Oregon. The tribe fled, fighting, and Chief Joseph showed great skill leading his warriors in battle against the American troops until his defeat the same year.

Chief Joe Capilano (1850–1910) was born on what is now Vancouver's North Shore. An esteemed Squamish chief, he and his wife Mary, known as the "Indian Princess of Peace," visited King Edward VII in Great Britain in 1906 to present a petition for Indian rights.

Landscapes of the Pacific Northwest

The Pacific Northwest is blessed with an abundance of dramatically different landscapes. Seashores give way to coastal mountains, which drop into the Fraser Plateau in British Columbia, into Puget Sound in Washington, and into the Willamette Valley in Oregon. The peaks of the Cascade Mountains bisect both Oregon and Washington, and the majestic Rockies rise in eastern British Columbia. Other distinct landscapes are the Columbia Plateau's layers of ancient lava that spread across eastern Oregon and Washington, and the high deserts of central and southern Oregon.

Sea Stacks
Portions of wave-eroded headlands that remain as offshore mounds rise majestically from the surf of the Pacific Ocean. The stacks are most numerous along the southern Oregon coast near Cape Blanco and off Washington's Olympic Peninsula.

Coasts
In Oregon and southern Washington, sandy beaches and rocky headlands extend for more than 450 miles (725 km) along the coast. The Strait of Juan de Fuca etches Washington's northern coastline with a succession of bays and inlets, while in British Columbia, 10,340 miles (16,640 km) of shoreline wrap around inlets, fjords, and islands.

Mountain Ranges
The Coast and Cascade ranges form a spine of mountains that rises almost continuously from southern Oregon to northern British Columbia. Much of the lower slopes of the mountains are carpeted with forests that give way to alpine meadows, then to glaciers.

The Canadian Rockies
With their dominating peaks and vast ice fields, the Rocky Mountains cover a large part of British Columbia. Thirty mountains of this immense range are more than 10,000 ft (3,048 m) high.

Mountain Areas
The mountains in the Pacific Northwest form a barrier that traps great amounts of moisture, which in winter can cause heavy snowfall on peaks such as Oregon's Diamond Peak.

Gorges
Gorges reveal the dramatic geological history of the region. Over the course of thousands of years, rushing rivers have carved away rock and earth, leaving behind huge gorges as well as long and narrow chasms, such as Oregon's Oneonta Gorge in the Columbia River Gorge National Scenic Area.

Waterfalls
The spectacular Lower Kentucky Falls in Oregon's Siuslaw National Forest is one of thousands of waterfalls in the Pacific Northwest. The Kentucky Creek runs through old-growth forest before spilling over a cliff, plummeting 75 ft (23 m), then an additional 25 ft (8 m), to the rocky slopes below.

Dry Lands and Desert Country
East of the mountains, the terrain tends to be flat, and precipitation can average as little as 12 inches (30.5 cm) a year. As a result, the landscape here is vastly different from that found in the mountain and coastal regions. In eastern Oregon, steppes and deserts are covered with juniper and sagebrush. Rocky outcroppings, usually composed of volcanic basalt, are also common here, and vegetation is often sparse.

THE PACIFIC NORTHWEST THROUGH THE YEAR

The image of the Pacific Northwest's weather as consistently wet is rooted as much in myth as in fact. Rain is a distinctive presence in only half of the Pacific Northwest – the part west of the mountains that divide the region. The weather in this western, coastal section remains mild throughout the year, and snow is rare in all but the higher elevations. In the mountains, winter snowfall is heavy, much to the delight of skiers. East of the mountains, where cold and heat reach extreme levels, winter snowfall can be heavy but summers can be bone dry. In spite of the variable weather throughout the Pacific Northwest, the unique rewards of living and traveling in the region are many. Even in the damp and most heavily populated western sections, rain doesn't prevent residents and visitors alike from heading outdoors to enjoy a large variety of entertaining festivals and events.

Spring

March and April bring the signs of spring to the lower elevations of the Pacific Northwest. A number of festivities celebrate the region's lush gardens as they come into bloom in an array of glorious colors.

March

Vancouver International Wine Festival *(Feb or Mar)*, Vancouver, BC. A week of wine tastings held at the Vancouver Convention Centre *(p206)* and other locales.
Oregon Cheese Festival *(mid-Mar)*, Central Point, OR. Artisan cheesemakers from Oregon and Northern California dairies show their wares, along with local wines.
Othello Sandhill Crane Festival *(late Mar)*, Othello, WA. Witness the sounds and rituals of 25,000 migrating cranes.

Blossoming fruit trees in April, the Hood River Valley, Oregon

Victorian Heritage Festival *(late Mar)*, Port Townsend, WA *(pp180–81)*. All things Victorian are celebrated in this fine historic seaport.

April

Skagit Valley Tulip Festival *(Apr)*, Skagit Valley, WA. A month-long festival of arts and crafts fairs, barbecues, and walking tours amid thousands of tulips.
Hood River Valley Blossom Festival *(third weekend)*, Hood River Valley, OR. Arts and crafts fairs and tours of orchards and wineries in towns along the Hood River.
Washington State Apple Blossom Festival *(late Apr–early May)*, Wenatchee, WA. Parades, a carnival, and concerts to usher in spring.

May

Bloomsday Run *(first Sun)*, Spokane, WA. Every year, this 7.5-mile (12-km) race through downtown attracts more than 50,000 runners.
Cinco de Mayo Fiesta *(early May)*, Portland, OR. Three days of Mexican food, art, music, and dance on the Portland waterfront.
Annual Rhododendron Festival *(third weekend)*, Florence, OR. A parade and carnival to celebrate the rhododendron blossoms.
Northwest Folklife Festival *(Memorial Day weekend)*, Seattle, WA. Enjoy dance, exhibits, and workshops at one of the largest free events in the US.

A perfect rose on show at the Portland Rose Festival in June

Brookings-Harbor Azalea Festival *(Memorial Day weekend)*, Brookings, OR. Blossoms and food in a coastal town famous for its azaleas.
Seagull Calling Festival *(late May)*, Port Orchard, WA. This waterfront festival is centered on a seagull-calling contest.
Blessing of the Fleet *(late May)*, Westport, WA. A parade and a blessing of the town's famous fishing fleet.
Vancouver International Children's Festival *(late May)*, Granville Island, Vancouver, BC. Local, national, and international performing artists present theater and music for children.

Summer

Summer in much of the Pacific Northwest is not assuredly sunny. But locals do not hesitate to venture outdoors for a variety of activities and events, including wine festivals, rodeos and plays.

June

Portland Rose Festival *(Jun)*, Portland, OR. Parades, concerts, races, and a carnival in honor of the rose.

Bard on the Beach Shakespeare Festival *(Jun–Sep)*, Vancouver, BC. Lively plays at Vanier Park *(pp224–5)*.

Sisters Rodeo *(mid-Jun)*, Sisters, OR *(p106)*. Rodeo held every year since 1940.

Britt Festivals *(mid-Jun–early Sep)*, Jacksonville, OR *(p112)*. Music concerts from classical to pop under the ponderosa pines and stars.

First Peoples Festival *(late Jun)*, Victoria, BC. Three days of art, food, and performances by First Nations peoples.

TD Victoria International JazzFest *(late Jun)*, Victoria, BC. Jazz and blues concerts at venues all over town.

Pi-Ume-Sha Treaty Days *(late Jun)*, Warm Springs, OR *(p106)*. A powwow, parade, and rodeo mark the treaty that formed the Confederated Tribes of Warm Springs.

Oregon Bach Festival *(late Jun–mid-Jul)*, Eugene, OR *(p105)*. A series of concerts honoring J. S. Bach.

Summer Nights at South Lake Union *(late Jun–Aug)*, Seattle, WA. Concert series at South Lake Union Park with beautiful views.

Hoopfest *(last weekend)*, Spokane, WA. The largest three-on-three basketball tournament in the US.

Seafair *(Jun–Jul)*, Seattle, WA. This month-long festival, with a torchlight parade, hydroplane races, and an air show, takes place in several spectacular venues around the city.

July

Vancouver Folk Music Festival *(Jul)*, Vancouver, BC. Annual folk festival, in Jericho Beach Park.

Costumed dancer, Caribbean Days Festival, North Vancouver, July

Canada Day *(Jul 1)*, across British Columbia. Parades, live music, and evening fireworks are held.

Williams Lake Stampede *(Jul 1 weekend)*, Williams Lake, BC. Rodeo fun at one of North America's largest stampedes.

Waterfront Blues Festival *(early Jul)*, Portland, OR. Four days of blues from local and nationally acclaimed artists.

Independence Day *(Jul 4)*, Seattle, WA. A spectacular fireworks display takes place over Gas Works Park *(p159)*.

Ripe peaches in the Okanagan Valley, BC

Bite of Seattle *(mid-Jul)*, Seattle, WA. A popular two-day food festival, with edibles and delectables from more than 60 participating restaurants.

Oregon Coast Music Festival *(mid–late Jul)*, Charleston, Coos Bay, and North Bend, OR. Classical music and jazz performed next to the ocean.

Caribbean Days Festival *(late Jul)*, North Vancouver, BC. A celebration of all things Caribbean.

International Pinot Noir Celebration *(late Jul)*, McMinnville, OR *(p104)*. Pinot noirs paired with food from noted local chefs.

Celebration of Light *(late Jul–early Aug)*, Vancouver, BC. Fireworks competition at English Bay.

August

Penticton Peach Festival *(early Aug)*, Penticton, BC. A charming festival celebrating the local peach harvest.

Mt. Hood Jazz Festival *(early Aug)*, Gresham, OR. Two days of jazz, food, and local wines.

ExtravaGAYza! Parade and Festival *(early Aug)*, Vancouver, BC. Fun and fanciful events for Gay Pride Week.

Omak Stampede and World Famous Suicide Race *(mid-Aug)*, Omak, WA. A rodeo, stampede, and daredevil horse race.

Pacific National Exhibition *(mid-Aug–early Sep)*, Vancouver, BC. Entertainment, rides, pavilions, and agricultural exhibits.

Oregon State Fair *(late Aug–early Sep)*, Salem, OR *(p104)*. Twelve days of Oregon produce and livestock, rides, concerts, and food.

Evergreen State Fair *(late Aug–early Sep)*, Monroe, WA. Arts and crafts, rides, races, and rodeo events.

Steer roping at the Sisters Rodeo, held mid-June in Sisters, Oregon

People admiring the boats at the Victoria Classic Boat Festival, Victoria, BC

Fall

Fall foliage can be quite spectacular in the Pacific Northwest, as brilliant reds and yellows stand out against evergreens. Colorful landscapes are the backdrop for events celebrating the harvest of cranberries, oysters, and other regional specialties.

September
Great Canadian Beer Festival *(Sep)*, Victoria, BC. Forty craft breweries from Canada and the Pacific Northwest take part and offer beer samples.
Bumbershoot *(Labor Day weekend)*, Seattle, WA. A mix of music and film at the Seattle Center *(pp146–7)*.

Victoria Classic Boat Festival *(late Aug–early Sep)*, Victoria, BC. Racing of classic sailboats, steam boats, and powerboats in the Inner Harbour.
Washington State Fair *(early Sep)*, Puyallup, WA. A 17-day state fair with rides, exhibits, a rodeo, and live music.
Oktoberfest *(mid-Sep)*, Mount Angel, OR. Bavarian food and plenty of beer.
Pendleton Round-Up *(mid-Sep)*, Pendleton, OR *(p115)*. A rodeo featuring calf-roping, bull-riding, and a town full of real cowboys.
Autumn Leaf Festival *(last weekend)*, Leavenworth, WA. One of the state's oldest festivals, which celebrates the arrival of autumn with a Grand Parade, contests, and live music.

October
Okanagan Wine Festival *(early Oct)*, Okanagan Valley, BC. Vineyard tours and wine tastings, as well as gourmet food, at grape harvest time.
OysterFest *(early Oct)*, Shelton, WA. A weekend of oyster shucking, wine tastings, and cooking contests.
Annual Cranberrian Fair *(mid-Oct)*, Ilwaco, WA. Cranberry tastings, music, and dancing to celebrate the local harvest.
Vancouver Writers Fest *(third week)*, Granville Island, Vancouver, BC. Readings by Canadian and international writers.
Earshot Jazz Festival *(mid-Oct– early Nov)*, Seattle, WA. This celebrated jazz festival draws big names at various venues around the city.

November
Cornucopia *(mid-Nov)*, Whistler, BC *(pp260–61)*. A festival featuring fine dining, wine tastings, and seminars.
Christkindlmarkt *(Thanksgiving weekend)*, Leavenworth, WA *(p190)*. An open-air market selling German treats, such as bratwurst.
Seattle Marathon *(Sun after Thanksgiving)*, Seattle, WA. More than 10,000 participants run off Thanksgiving excesses.

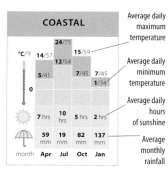

COASTAL				
°C/°F	14/57	24/75	15/59	
	5/41	12/54	7/45	7/45
0				1/34
hrs	7 hrs	10 hrs	5 hrs	2 hrs
mm	59 mm	19 mm	82 mm	137 mm
month	Apr	Jul	Oct	Jan

Average daily maximum temperature

Average daily minimum temperature

Average daily hours of sunshine

Average monthly rainfall

Climate
Climate varies widely across the Pacific Northwest. Coastal areas, such as Portland, Seattle, and Vancouver, are mild and wet, while inland deserts, such as the areas around Spokane and Kamloops, have seasonal extremes. Climates of mountain ranges in the Pacific Northwest, represented here by the Cascade Mountains, have divergent microclimates.

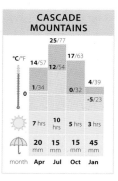

CASCADE MOUNTAINS				
°C/°F	14/57	25/77	17/63	
	1/34	12/54	0/32	4/39
0				−5/23
hrs	7 hrs	10 hrs	5 hrs	3 hrs
mm	20 mm	15 mm	15 mm	45 mm
month	Apr	Jul	Oct	Jan

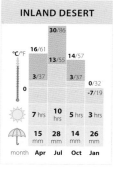

INLAND DESERT				
°C/°F	16/61	30/86	14/57	
	3/37	13/55	3/37	0/32
0				−7/19
hrs	7 hrs	10 hrs	5 hrs	3 hrs
mm	15 mm	28 mm	14 mm	26 mm
month	Apr	Jul	Oct	Jan

In December, a cheering Christmas Lighting Festival in Bavarian-themed Leavenworth

Winter

When snow covers the region's mountains, many Pacific Northwesterners take to downhill ski slopes or cross-country trails. In mild coastal areas, where winter days are short and rainy, unique Christmas celebrations provide a cheerful glow.

December

Portland's Christmas Ships Parade *(Dec)*, Portland, OR. Gaily decorated boats sail down the Willamette River.

VanDusen Botanical Gardens' Festival of Lights *(Dec)*, Vancouver, BC. Thousands of lights glitter throughout

One of many ski competitions held in the region during winter

the lush plantings in this botanical garden.

Christmas Lighting Festival *(first three weekends)*, Leavenworth, WA. Visitors enjoy roasted chestnuts, bratwurst, strolling carolers, and twinkling lights against the snowcapped Cascade Mountains in a Bavarian-style town.

Carol Ships Parade of Lights *(first three weekends)*, Vancouver, BC. Beautifully decorated vessels light up local waters.

January

Eagle Festival and Count *(early Jan)*, Brackendale, BC. Festival centered on a competition to count the number of bald eagles settling for the winter on the Squamish River.

Chinese New Year *(late Jan or early Feb)*, Vancouver, BC. Almost two weeks of colorful festivities, including dance, music, and a parade, celebrate the new lunar year.

February

Northwest Flower and Garden Show *(third week of Feb)*, Seattle, WA. Full-scale landscaped garden displays and a flower show featuring creative designs attract flower lovers to this event.

Oregon Shakespeare Festival *(mid-Feb–Oct)*, Ashland, OR *(p112)*. Classic and contemporary plays draw actors and spectators from around the world to this highly acclaimed drama festival.

The FisherPoet's Gathering *(last weekend)*, Astoria, OR.

Various events celebrate the commercial fishing industry and its people through stories, poetry, and song.

Public Holidays

United States

New Year's Day (Jan 1)

Martin Luther King Day (3rd Mon in Jan)

Presidents' Day (3rd Mon in Feb)

Memorial Day (last Mon in May)

Independence Day (Jul 4)

Labor Day (1st Mon in Sep)

Columbus Day (2nd Mon in Oct)

Veterans' Day (Nov 11)

Thanksgiving Day (4th Thu in Nov)

Christmas Day (Dec 25)

Canada

New Year's Day (Jan 1)

Family Day (BC only; 2nd Mon in Feb)

Good Friday (Mar/Apr)

Victoria Day (Mon before May 25)

Canada Day (Jul 1)

Civic holiday (BC Day) (1st Mon in Aug)

Labor Day (1st Mon in Sep)

Thanksgiving Day (2nd Mon in Oct)

Remembrance Day (Nov 11)

Christmas Day (Dec 25)

THE HISTORY OF THE PACIFIC NORTHWEST

The vast landscapes of the Pacific Northwest bear the imprint of the geological forces that carved deep gorges and thrust up soaring mountain peaks. The imprint left by First Nations peoples who lived in harmony with the land for thousands of years is less visible. In the early 19th century, after explorers had opened up the territory, settlers began to arrive and the modern Pacific Northwest was born.

Enough is known about the early inhabitants of the region to suggest that many enjoyed a good life among the natural riches. The earliest inhabitants were likely nomadic hunters who, 15,000 to 25,000 years ago, crossed a land bridge across the then-dry Bering Strait from Russia to North America.

These early societies left various traces of their presence. Among intriguing finds is a 14,000-year-old spear point left embedded in fossilized mastodon bones. Sagebrush sandals, on display at the University of Oregon Museum of Natural and Cultural History, are possibly the world's oldest shoes, revealing that 10,000 years ago the art of shoemaking was practiced. Other signs that the region was long settled can be found in oral traditions, rife with tales of the eruption of Mount Mazama, some 8,000 years ago. Rock carvings and paintings in Petroglyph Provincial Park, near Nanaimo, BC, are thought to be at least 1,000 years old.

Early Life

Food and other resources were abundant for tribes living in the forests west of the Cascade Mountains and along the Pacific coast. Many tribes lived in well-established settlements, fished the rivers for salmon, and, in long dugouts, set out to sea in search of whales. They also cut timber for longhouses – massive dwellings that could house as many as 50 to 60 people. Tribes living in the harsher landscapes east of the mountains had fewer resources at hand and migrated across high-desert hunting grounds in search of bison, deer, and other game. In spring and summer, they moved up mountain slopes to pick berries and dig roots. By the 19th century, tribes living in the high deserts had acquired horses and rode them east to the Great Plains to hunt bison, which had become extinct farther west.

Illustration of First Nations people of the Pacific Northwest

◀ A 1946 illustration of Captain George Vancouver's ship, HMS *Discovery*

A Shoshone hunting elk with bow and arrow

For many tribes, life was so bountiful that a tradition of potlatch evolved. At these elaborate ceremonies, which marked important occasions and which were centered around a feast, the host chief would offer gifts with the expectation that the recipients would eventually repay the gesture with loyalty and gifts at a subsequent potlatch.

Arrival of Explorers

First Nations peoples thrived in the Pacific Northwest until the 18th century, disturbed only by occasional incursions by explorers and traders. In the 16th century, the first Europeans began exploring the coastline in search of the Northwest Passage, a sea route that would provide a passage between Europe and the Far East.

The first European to sight the Pacific Northwest was Spanish explorer Juan Rodriguez Cabrillo, who sailed with his crew from Mexico to southern Oregon in 1543. Once the Spanish had gained a stronghold in the New World, the British, too, wanted a share of the riches. The mission of Sir Francis Drake (1540–96), financed by Queen Elizabeth I, was to sail up the west coast of North America, plundering gold from Spanish galleons. After claiming the land around San Francisco Bay for Britain, Drake sailed up the Oregon coast, as far north as the Strait of Juan de Fuca, first navigated by Juan de Fuca in 1592. Drake then traveled across the Pacific Ocean back to England.

In the 1770s, Captains George Vancouver (1758–98) and Peter Puget (1765–1822) accompanied Captain James Cook (1728–79) on a voyage along the Pacific Northwest coast in search of the fabled Northwest Passage. The explorers sailed up the coasts of Oregon, Washington, and British Columbia. In 1791, Vancouver and Puget also charted what are now Puget Sound (Washington) and Vancouver (British Columbia). However, they did not notice the Columbia River, discovered the following year by Captain Robert Gray, an American fur trader from the East Coast,

Ship caught in the ice along the northern Pacific coast

25,000–15,000 BC Nomadic hunters arrive in North America across a land bridge from Asia	1492 Christopher Columbus arrives in America	1534–5 Cartier explores the Canadian east coast, sailing up the St. Lawrence River as far as Hochelaga (Montreal)	1579 Sir Francis Drake sails up the west coast of North America during his second journey around the world (1577–80)
25,000 BC	**1500**	**1550**	**1600**
13,000 BC Massive floods carve the Columbia River Gorge	*Totem pole*	**1543** Juan Rodriguez Cabrillo, a Spaniard, sails from Mexico to the coast of southern Oregon	**1592** Juan de Fuca sails from Mexico to Vancouver Island and is the first to navigate the strait later named for him

Simon Fraser and companions on the Fraser River

who named the river after his ship, the *Columbia Rediviva*. Other American vessels soon arrived in search of animal pelts and other bounty. The Spanish, who had been attempting to establish strongholds along the Pacific coast for centuries, retreated to their claims in California.

In 1793, Scotsman and Montreal fur trader Alexander Mackenzie crossed Canada to British Columbia, proving that an overland trade route was feasible. Mackenzie was also the first European to navigate the Peace River, the only river in British Columbia that drains into the Arctic Ocean.

From 1805 to 1808, Simon Fraser (1776–1862), a partner in the fur-trading North West Company, was charged with extending the company's trading activities west of the Rocky Mountains to the Pacific Ocean, and exploring a river thought to be the Columbia. In this capacity, Fraser established Fort McCleod, Fort St. James, Fort Fraser, and Fort George, all in British Columbia. Fraser's major accomplishment, though, was to be the first to navigate the longest river in British Columbia, now known as the Fraser River, which courses through the rugged BC interior to the Pacific Ocean.

Lewis and Clark

US president Thomas Jefferson called on his former secretary, Meriwether Lewis, and Lewis's friend, William Clark, to find an overland route to the Pacific Ocean. The pair and an entourage of 33 set out from St. Louis, Missouri, in May 1804 and walked, rode horseback, and canoed to the Oregon coast, which they reached a year and a half later, in November 1805. The only female member of the expedition was Sacagawea, a young Shoshone woman who proved to be an invaluable guide and translator. The famed expedition set the stage for the rapid settlement of the Pacific Northwest. The expedition members not only plotted the first overland route across the US, mapping unexplored territory and collecting data on First Nations peoples and wildlife, but they also published journals that sparked a wave of migration from the east.

A Battle for the Spoils

The battle to control the Pacific Northwest was waged by the British and the Americans not with gunfire but through trade. The expedition of Lewis and Clark opened up the region to US fur traders. They could now compete with the British, who dominated the lucrative pelt trade.

Pioneer log cabin, Champoeg State Heritage Area, Oregon

1663 France proclaims Canada a French colony

1765 Robert Rogers maps the vast territory he refers to as "Ouragon"

1763 Canada becomes a British Crown colony

1778 Captain James Cook explores the Pacific coast

1804–1806 Expedition of Meriwether Lewis and William Clark

1650 **1700** **1750** **1800**

1670 Hudson's Bay Company founded

The Willamette Valley before the arrival of settlers

1791 Captain George Vancouver and Peter Puget circumnavigate Vancouver Island

1793 Alexander Mackenzie forges an overland route across Canada

1792 Captain Robert Gray is the first non-Native to navigate the Columbia River

In 1811, the American John Jacob Astor established a fur-trading post, Astoria, at the mouth of the Columbia River. Although US president Jefferson had hoped that Lewis and Clark's expedition would displace the British, the British-owned Hudson's Bay Company effectively continued to rule the Pacific Northwest until the middle of the 19th century. The company controlled both the growing population of settlers and much of the trade activity. Company headquarters at Fort Vancouver, overlooking the confluence of the Columbia and Willamette Rivers, and at Fort Victoria, on Vancouver Island in British Columbia, were the region's major settlements. Hudson's Bay Company trading posts became such common sights in the wilderness that it was quipped that the initials "HBC" stood for "Here Before Christ."

Territorial tensions between Britain and the US erupted in the War of 1812. Although neither side "won" this war, the dominance of the British was later undermined when thousands of American farmers migrated westward along the Oregon Trail. Britain and America divided the spoils of the Pacific Northwest in 1846, using the 49th parallel as the new boundary, with the land to the north (British Columbia) being claimed by Britain, and that to the south (Oregon) by the US. Oregon, which included the present-day states of Oregon, Washington, and Idaho, became a US territory in 1848. The Oregon Territory was itself divided in 1852, with lands north of the Columbia River forming the new Washington Territory.

Oregon gained statehood in 1859, Washington in 1889. British Columbia and Vancouver Island joined to become one colony in 1866, and joined the Dominion of Canada in 1871.

Those who profited least from the division of spoils were the First Nations peoples. Already decimated by diseases introduced by settlers, such as smallpox, measles, and influenza, they were forcibly removed from the lands they had inhabited for millennia and resettled on reservations.

The Great Migrations

Between 1843 and 1860, more than 60,000 settlers embarked on a 6-month, 2,000-mile (3,218-km) trek from Independence, Missouri, across the US along the Oregon Trail mapped by Lewis and Clark in 1804–05. Many settlers left the trail in Idaho and headed south to California. Most of those who continued west to Oregon followed the Snake River to the Columbia River, where they put their wagons on rafts. The downstream trip across dangerous rapids led to the mouth of the Willamette River and, just upstream, the trail's end at Oregon City. Rather than pay the exorbitant fee of $50 to float a wagon down the river, some

Astoria, founded by John Jacob Astor in 1811

| 1810 | 1820 | 1830 | 1840 |

1811 John Jacob Astor establishes Astoria, a trading post at the mouth of the Columbia River

1829 Oregon City is the first town west of the Rocky Mountains to be incorporated

1843 James Douglas, of the Hudson's Bay Company, founds Fort Victoria, later renamed Victoria, in British Columbia; a wagon train transporting 900 settlers blazes the Oregon Trail to the Willamette Valley

1812–14 War of 1812 between Britain and the US

A French-Canadian woodsman

1824 Fort Vancouver is established by the Hudson's Bay Company

Watercolor of Mount Baker, Washington, 1848

Fort Vancouver, a strategically located trading post, in 1848

and Vancouver in 1886, opening up British Columbia to mass settlement.

In the US the arrival of the railroad was especially beneficial to the tiny settlement of Alki-New York in Washington, which soon burgeoned into Seattle, and eventually outstripped Portland as the Pacific Northwest's major port and center of trade.

settlers opted for the treacherous climb across Barlow Pass on the flanks of Mount Hood, one of the peaks of the Cascade Mountains.

The reward for those who made the arduous trek to Oregon's fertile Willamette Valley was a land grant of 350 acres (140 ha). Many settlers staked their claims in Oregon, while others made their way farther north and settled in Washington. With its strategic location at the confluence of the Columbia and Willamette Rivers, Portland became the region's major port and most important city.

By the 1870s, transcontinental railroads were steaming across the US and Canada, making the Pacific Northwest accessible to hundreds of thousands more settlers. Trains began crossing Canada between Montreal

Gold Rushes

Gold fever gripped the Pacific Northwest in 1848, when gold was discovered in California's Sierra Nevada mountains. Many of the new settlers who had staked land claims in Oregon headed south, lured by the hope of making their fortune.

In fact, two-thirds of the male population of Oregon followed the lure of gold. Many returned soon afterward with gold nuggets in their pockets.

Romantic vision of the westward trek, painted c.1904

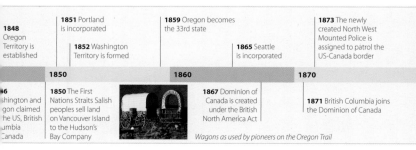

1848 Oregon Territory is established

1851 Portland is incorporated

1852 Washington Territory is formed

1859 Oregon becomes the 33rd state

1865 Seattle is incorporated

1873 The newly created North West Mounted Police is assigned to patrol the US-Canada border

1850

1860

1870

46 shington and gon claimed he US, British umbia Canada

1850 The First Nations Straits Salish peoples sell land on Vancouver Island to the Hudson's Bay Company

1867 Dominion of Canada is created under the British North America Act

1871 British Columbia joins the Dominion of Canada

Wagons as used by pioneers on the Oregon Trail

Government House, New Westminster, BC, in 1870

The Gold Rush moved north in 1851, when prospectors found gold in southern Oregon, and farther north again, to British Columbia's Fraser River, in 1858. Canadian prospectors also struck it big in 1860 in the Cariboo Mountains, in the BC Interior.

The Klondike, in Canada's Yukon Territory, was the stage for the next frenzy of gold fever. Once prospectors stepped off ships in Seattle and San Francisco, in 1896, with gold they had found along Bonanza Creek, the word was out. More than 100,000 prospectors flooded into the Klondike gold fields, and Vancouver and Seattle prospered by supplying and housing the miners and banking their finds.

Modern Times

By the early 20th century, the Pacific Northwest was celebrating its prosperity. Portland hosted the Lewis and Clark Exposition in 1905, honoring the pair's voyage 100 years earlier. The city put up new buildings downtown, planted thousands of roses, and laid out new parks for the event. Many of the

thousands of exposition visitors stayed in the newly dubbed "City of Roses," and the population doubled to more than 250,000 by 1910. Seattle, having quickly rebounded from an 1889 fire that leveled all of downtown, followed suit in 1909 with the Alaska-Yukon-Pacific Exposition.

These expositions set the stage for the region's growth throughout the 20th century. The Boeing Airplane Company, founded in Seattle in 1916 and rivaling the state's timber industry in economic importance, created tens of thousands of jobs through its military and commercial aircraft contracts. During World War II (1939–45), factories in the Pacific Northwest produced aircraft, weapons, and warships for the Allies' war effort. When Seattle-based Microsoft took off in the 1980s, this ushered in a wave of high-tech business.

Vancouver became the focus of world attention when 21 million visitors attended festivities at Expo '86 to celebrate the city's 100th anniversary. In the years immediately following, there was a huge surge in population growth, business development, and cultural diversification.

In the late 1990s, trade liberalization and the globalization of goods manufacturing increasingly became topics for public

Historic cannery along the British Columbia coast

Mount St. Helens before its cataclysmic explosion

debate. On the streets of Seattle, in December 1999, more than 30,000 protested against the World Trade Organization and its policies on multinational corporations, environmental and labor laws, and subsidies for developing countries.

The Pacific Northwest has also had its share of natural disasters in modern times. Washington's Mount St. Helens *(see pp196–7)* erupted violently in 1980, and the accompanying earthquake triggered the largest avalanche in recorded history, killing 57 people as well as millions of birds, deer, elk, and fish. Floods and avalanches devastated parts of Oregon and Washington in February 1996, as a result of heavy rains and melting snow caused by unusually mild temperatures; the swelling of the Willamette River and its tributaries forced the evacuation of residents in low-lying areas, stranded hundreds of drivers, and resulted in at least one fatality. On the evening of February 28, 2001, Seattle was rocked by a Mardi Gras riot and then a 6.8-magnitude earthquake. The façades of many of the historic red-brick buildings in Pioneer Square were destroyed by a combination of the rioters' violence and the effects of the quake.

For the First Nations peoples of the Pacific Northwest, the 20th century brought gains as well as losses. Fishing rights were restored, but the construction of dams along many rivers destroyed some traditional fishing grounds and greatly diminished salmon runs. The casinos on Native lands brought economic benefits to some tribes but not to others. With the Nisga'a Treaty, drawn up in 2000, the Canadian and BC governments acknowledged that 744 sq miles (1,927 sq km) of Crown land in northern British Columbia belongs to the Nisga'a Nation.

Keeping the landscape pristine in the Pacific Northwest continues to be both a source of pride and an ongoing bone of contention. Conservationists fight to curtail lumbering operations and limit growth, while loggers and ranchers often resist government intervention in their affairs. This conflict between the need to protect the environment and interests in capitalizing on the region's natural resources shows no sign of slowing.

Airplanes on the Boeing assembly line, Seattle

THE PACIFIC NORTHWEST REGION BY REGION

The Pacific Northwest at a Glance

An area of many contrasts,
the Pacific Northwest has much to
offer visitors. From Portland, Seattle, and
Vancouver, its vibrant and attractive cities,
many of the region's impressive natural wonders
are only a short excursion away. Imposing
mountain ranges, vast stretches of deserts, deep,
wild canyons, crystal-clear lakes, and a magnificent
coastline ensure that there is a sight or activity to
suit every taste. While in summer wildflowers carpet
alpine meadows, in winter, visitors and locals take
advantage of the snow-covered slopes to enjoy winter
sports. On the West Coast, whale-watching enchants
visitors year-round.

Smithers

Alta Lake, in Whistler, British Columbia,
offers many summer activities in a town
which, in winter, is one of the world's most
popular ski destinations *(see pp260–61)*.

*North Pacific
Ocean*

Vanco

Vict

Cannon Beach is
just one of the many
beautiful stops along
the Oregon coast
offering breathtaking
vistas of sand, sky, and
sea stacks that rise out
of the ocean *(see p97)*.

S

Deepwood Estate (1894),
one of Salem's many historic
buildings, is now a museum
showcasing period pieces that
offer a glimpse of what life was
once like in this city, Oregon's
capital since 1851 *(see pp104–5)*.

Eu

0 kilometers   150

0 miles   100

Me

◀ Stunning aerial view of Vancouver, British Columbia

Sinclair Pass, located on the parkway that cuts through British Columbia's Kootenay National Park, is surrounded by the high walls of Sinclair Canyon, a red limestone gorge. It is just one of many natural wonders that attracts visitors to this national park, which covers 543 sq miles (1,406 sq km) of diverse terrain *(see p269)*.

Fort Steele Heritage Town is a re-created BC mining town. The original town of Fort Steele was established in 1864 after gold was discovered nearby. When its fortunes faded, it became a ghost town – until reconstruction began in 1961 *(see p268)*.

Nelson

Kamloops

Kelowna

Whatcom Museum, in Bellingham, Washington, houses many excellent exhibits on the First Nations peoples of the Pacific Northwest coast *(see p184)*.

Spokane

Vineyards on Canoe Ridge supply the well-known Washington winery Chateau Ste. Michelle, the oldest winery in the state *(see p185)*.

Pendleton

Burns Junction

Granite, in Oregon, once a thriving Gold Rush town, is now a ghost town *(see p116)*.

PORTLAND

Portland at a Glance

Portland enhances its beautiful natural surroundings with a healthy dose of urban vitality and a relaxed yet sophisticated lifestyle. Spectacular parks and gardens flourish throughout the City of Roses. Historic landmarks and neighborhoods show off the city's commitment to preserving its rich past, while Pioneer Courthouse Square, a bustling pedestrian-only space in the heart of what is now the city center, reflects the effective urban planning that makes Portland so pleasant. Meanwhile, the city continues to enhance its many charms with locales such as the Pearl District, a neighborhood that has emerged out of an old industrial area.

Pearl District
Portland has reclaimed this former industrial district as its neighborhood for art galleries, boutiques, restaurants, and sophisticated urban living (see pp58–9).

Portland Streetcar
Modern, low-slung trams link Nob Hill, the Pearl District, and downtown Portland. Not only is a ride a handy way to get around town, it's also one of the most economical (see p67).

Sentinel Hotel
Early 20th-century grandeur prevails at the Sentinel Hotel. Murals in the ground-floor Jake's Grill honor an earlier chapter of local history – the Lewis and Clark Expedition (see pp64–5).

Portland Art Museum
The holdings of the oldest art museum in the Pacific Northwest include European paintings, Asian ceramics, and Native American basketry (see p66).

SOL

SOUTHWEST 1st

SOUTHWEST

South Park Blocks
A farmers' market takes place every Saturday in Portland State University's elm-shaded lawns, laid out in 1852 (see p66).

◀ South Waterfront Park and downtown Portland bathed in morning light

0 meters	300
0 yards	300

Powell's City of Books
The largest independent bookstore in the world houses more than a million volumes (maps of the store are provided) and is one of Portland's most popular spots (see p59).

Lan Su Chinese Garden
This Ming Dynasty-style walled garden, with its tile-roofed pavilions, embodies traditional Chinese concepts of harmony and tranquility (see p58).

OLD TOWN AND THE PEARL DISTRICT
(See pp54–59)

NORTHWEST NAITO PARKWAY

THWEST GLISAN STREET

NORTHWEST EVERETT STREET

WEST BURNSIDE STREET

ASHINGTON
REET

STREET

DOWNTOWN
(See pp60–69)

SOUTHWEST 4TH AVENUE

SOUTHWEST MADISON STREET

LUMBIA STREET

EET

Pioneer Courthouse Square
At the city center is a welcoming expanse of brick paving where Portlanders gather, come rain or shine (see p64).

Governor Tom McCall Waterfront Park
Portland has reclaimed this 1.5-mile- (2.5-km-) long stretch of Willamette River waterfront as a park, waterside promenade, and locale for the Rose Festival and other public celebrations (see pp68–9).

Keller Auditorium
Keller Auditorium hosts operas and Broadway shows; the adjacent Ira Keller Memorial Fountain suggests the waterfalls of the Cascade Mountains (see p69).

OLD TOWN AND THE PEARL DISTRICT

Portland grew up along the west bank of the Willamette River. Following its establishment in 1843, it became a major port, and docks in the riverfront quarter now known as Old Town were often lined with schooners that sailed across the Pacific Ocean to China and around Cape Horn to the east coast of the US. Old Town was the city's commercial center and home to many Asian immigrants who came to work at the port. The city center moved inland in the late 19th century, when the arrival of the railroad reduced river trade. Declared a National Historic Landmark in 1975, Old Town is now once again a popular part of the city. Many 19th-century buildings have been restored, and a Chinese-American business community still operates here. The Pearl District, an early 20th-century industrial area west of Old Town, has also been transformed into a trendy neighborhood.

Sights at a Glance

Gardens and Districts
❸ Lan Su Chinese Garden
❹ Pearl District

Museums
❶ Oregon Maritime Center and Museum

Shops and Markets
❷ Portland Saturday Market
❺ Powell's City of Books

0 meters   200
0 yards   200

See also Street Finder maps 1 and 2

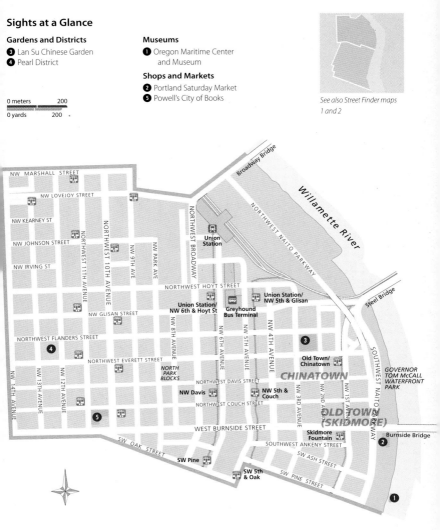

◀ One of the many bars in the trendy neighborhood of Old Town

For keys to symbols *see back flap*

Street-by-Street: Old Town

Elegant brick façades and quiet streets belie Old Town's raucous, 19th-century frontier-town past, when the district hummed with traders, dockworkers, shipbuilders, and sailors from around the world. While the saloons and bordellos that once did a brisk business are long gone, Old Town is still known for harboring some of the city's wilder nightlife. The street life here can be colorful, too, especially on weekends, when the Saturday Market takes over several blocks, as well as during the many festivals held year-round on the nearby waterfront.

Chinatown Gate
This multicolored, five-tiered, dragon-festooned gate is the official entryway to Chinatown, home to many immigrants from Asia for more than 135 years.

Pine Street Market
Portland's modern food hall opened in 2016 and features several big-name restaurants, cafés, bars, and more. It spans the ground floor of a historic building, built in 1886, located at 126 SW 2nd Avenue.

The New Market Block
This group of Italianate buildings is typical of the cast-iron and brick structures built after fire destroyed much of Portland in the 1870s.

Key

— Suggested route

Skidmore Fountain
Built in 1888 as a place for citizens and horses to quench their thirst, this elegant fountain and the adjacent plaza are at the center of Old Town.

0 meters 100
0 yards 100

N W FLANDERS

WEST 2ND AVENUE

NORTHWEST 1ST AVENUE

SOUTHWEST FRONT

BURNSIDE STREET

Locator Map
See Street Finder map 2

OLD TOWN & THE PEARL DISTRICT

DOWNTOWN

❸ ★ Lan Su Chinese Garden
In this one-block-square walled enclave, stone paths wind through a beautiful landscape of water, stone, plantings, and Chinese pavilions.

❷ ★ Portland Saturday Market
On Saturdays and Sundays, over 250 vendors gather here for America's largest handicrafts market.

Governor Tom McCall Waterfront Park Walkway
This path extends along the west side of the river from Burnside Bridge to RiverPlace Marina *(see p69).*

❶ ★ Oregon Maritime Center and Museum
One of the best things about this informative little maritime museum is where it's housed – aboard the tugboat Portland, which is docked in the Willamette River alongside the waterfront.

❶ Oregon Maritime Center and Museum

113 SW Naito Pkwy. **Map** 2 E5. **Tel** (503) 224-7724. 🚋 Skidmore Fountain (red, blue lines). **Open** 11am–4pm Wed–Sat, 12:30–4:30pm Sun. **Closed** major hols. 🏛 **w oregonmaritimemuseum.org**

This small but colorful museum is housed aboard the *Portland*, a stern-wheel, steam-powered tugboat – the last to be in operation in the US when it was decommissioned in 1982. The ship is now permanently moored alongside Governor Tom McCall Waterfront Park *(see pp68–9)*, where docks once bustled with seafaring trade.

Visits include a climb up to the captain's quarters and the wheelhouse, which provides a captivating view of the river, the downtown waterfront, and the bridges that span the Willamette River. Visitors can also descend into the huge below-decks engine room.

In the main cabin, photographs, paintings, models of ships, navigation instruments, and other marine memorabilia record the pre-railroad days when Portland, with its key position at the confluence of the Willamette and Columbia Rivers, flourished as a major seaport. Visitors also get a glimpse of maritime life in Portland throughout the 20th century, during which the city was an important shipping center and its shipyards were some of the largest in the world. Portland continues to be a major port today.

Ship's wheel on board the Oregon Maritime Center and Museum

An intricately carved pavilion at the Lan Su Chinese Garden

❷ Portland Saturday Market

2 SW Naito Pkwy. **Map** 2 E4. 🚌 16. 🚋 Skidmore Fountain (red, blue lines). **Open** Mar–Dec 24: 10am–5pm Sat, 11am–4:30pm Sun. **w portlandsaturdaymarket.com**

Founded by craftspeople Sheri Teasdale and Andrea Scharf, the bustling Portland Saturday Market is the largest weekly open-air arts and crafts market in the US. It shifted to its present location in Governor Tom McCall Waterfront Park and Ankeny Plaza in 2009.

Operating since 1974, the market features hand-crafted goods made by the people who sell them, local and international food, and entertainment ranging from live music to colorful street performances. Every participating member is chosen by a jury, and each item is reviewed to ensure it meets the market's standards.

With a variety of products on offer, including clothes, jewelry, ceramics, and art, this is a great place to buy gifts and souvenirs. It is open only on weekends, except in the week prior to Christmas, when it holds its "Festival of the Last Minute."

❸ Lan Su Chinese Garden

239 NW Everett St. **Map** 2 D3. **Tel** (503) 228-8131. 🚌 4, 8, 12, 16, 17, 19, 20, 35, 44, 77. 🚋 Old Town/Chinatown (red, blue lines). **Open** Apr 15–Oct 14: 10am–6pm daily; Oct 15–Apr 14: 10am–5pm daily. **Closed** Jan 1, Thanksgiving, Dec 25. 🏛 ♿ 🎁 💻 📷 **w lansugarden.org**

Artisans and architects from Suzhou, Portland's sister city in China, built this walled garden

in the late 1990s. The garden, which covers one entire city block, or 40,000 sq ft (4,000 sq m), is located in Portland's Chinatown.

The landscape of pavilions, waterfalls, lily pads, bamboo, a bridged lake, and stone paths, is classic Ming Dynasty style and provides a tranquil glimpse of nature amid urban surroundings. Hundreds of plants grow in the garden, many of which are indigenous to China. Traditional Taihu rocks mimic mountain peaks, while the mirror-like surface of the central Lake Zither reflects the plants and architecture of the garden. Mosaic-patterned footpaths, winding through stands of bamboo and across bridges, lead to several pavilions intended to be places for rest and contemplation. The ornate Tower of Cosmic Reflection pavilion houses a traditional teahouse that serves tea and Chinese delicacies.

Throughout the garden, poems and literary allusions are inscribed on rocks, entryways, plaques, and above doors and windows.

❹ Pearl District

W Burnside to the Willamette River (N), from NW 8th to NW 15th Aves. **Map** 1 B3. 🚋 to NW Glisan St.

One of Portland's most desirable neighborhoods occupies an old industrial district on the north side of Burnside Street, between Chinatown to the east and Nob Hill *(see p72)* to the west. Galleries, shops, design studios, breweries, cafés, restaurants, and clubs – especially hip and trendy ones – occupy former

The Pearl District's First Thursday, showcasing the work of local artists

factories, warehouses, and garages. Meanwhile, buildings are being renovated as condos and apartments, and modern residential blocks are going up all the time. Visitors may notice many similarities to urban renewal projects in other cities such as Boston, New York, and London, but the Pearl District is still relatively free of large-scale commercialism. Some big-name stores, such as REI, Patagonia, and North Face, have moved in; a sign that the neighborhood is changing.

One of the most enjoyable times to visit the Pearl District neighborhood is during a First Thursday event (the first Thursday of every month), when the many art galleries in the area remain open late to show the latest pieces. The collections feature a broad range of contemporary art and artists. The gallery receptions are open to the public and are free of charge.

Art galleries have played such an important role in the development of the Pearl District that Jamison Square Park is named after William Jamison, the first art dealer to set up shop in the area. Jamison Square, the first of three new parks built in the area, includes a water feature that fills and recedes over a central plaza. When the fountain is not in use, the plaza is used as an amphitheater for small performances. The park also features a wooden boardwalk, lawns, and colorful public art. It is an excellent place to begin a walk around the area, taking in the contemporary and historical buildings, and the district's ongoing regeneration.

The name of the district itself is said to have been coined by a local gallery owner, Thomas Augustine. He suggested that the buildings in the Warehouse District were like gray, dull oysters, and that the galleries within were like pearls.

❺ Powell's City of Books

1005 W Burnside St. **Map** 1 B4. **Tel** (503) 228-4651. 🚌 20. **Open** 9am–11pm daily. ♿ See Shopping in Portland *p80*. 🌐 **powells.com**

The largest independent bookstore in the world houses more than one million volumes, including new, old, used, rare, and out-of-print books, on a wealth of subjects. The store welcomes 6,000 shoppers each day, and has become one of Portland's most beloved cultural institutions since its establishment in 1971.

Despite its size, Powell's is easy to browse in: the 3,500 sections are divided into nine color-coded and well-marked rooms, and knowledgeable staff at the information desks possess the remarkable ability to lay their hands on any book in the store. The in-store coffee shop allows browsers to linger for hours, making Powell's a popular hangout any day of the year. Indeed, it's open all 365 of them.

During the first half of 2014, Powell's City of Books underwent a major remodeling project that focused on the Green and Blue rooms. Changes included a new roof, entrance porch, lighting, skylights and energy-efficient windows. These alterations have modernized the space while respecting the store's history and preserving a number of important elements such as the iconic Powell's Books marquee.

City of Bridges

Portland, the City of Roses, is also called the City of Bridges because the east and west banks of the Willamette River are linked by more than 10 bridges. The first to be built was the Morrison, in 1887, though the original wooden crossing has long since been replaced. Pedestrian walkways on many of the bridges connect the Eastbank Esplanade on the east side of the river with Governor Tom McCall Waterfront Park on the west side. The Steel Bridge affords the most dramatic crossing: a pedestrian path on the lower railroad deck seems to be almost at water level; when a ship needs to pass, the entire deck is lifted into the bottom of the roadway above. The latest addition is the striking Tilikum Crossing, which opened in 2015 and is for pedestrians, cyclists, and public transport only.

St. Johns Bridge, completed in 1931

DOWNTOWN

With the decline of river traffic in the late 19th century, Portland's center moved inland to the blocks around the intersection of Morrison Street and Broadway. The 1905 Lewis and Clark Exposition brought new prosperity and new residents to the city: downtown became a boomtown. Steel-frame buildings with façades of glazed, white terracotta tiles (Macy's department store is a fine example) began to rise; they continue to give the downtown a bright, distinctive look. Since the 1970s, urban planning efforts have earned Portland's downtown a reputation as one of the most successful city centers in the US. The area around Pioneer Courthouse Square is the city's commercial and cultural hub, while many government offices are housed in innovative new buildings to the east, near historic Chapman and Lownsdale Squares.

Sights at a Glance

Buildings and Churches
- ❷ Pioneer Courthouse
- ❹ Sentinel Hotel
- ❺ Multnomah County Library
- ❾ The Old Church
- ❷ Portland Building
- ❿ Mark O. Hatfield US Courthouse
- ⓰ KOIN Center

Museums, Galleries, and Theaters
- ❸ Portland Institute for Contemporary Art
- ❻ Portland'5 Centers for the Arts
- ❼ Oregon Historical Society
- ❽ Portland Art Museum
- ⓱ Keller Auditorium

Parks and Squares
- ❶ Pioneer Courthouse Square
- ❿ South Park Blocks
- ⓭ Chapman and Lownsdale Squares
- ⓯ Governor Tom McCall Waterfront Park
- ⓲ RiverPlace Marina

Other Attractions
- ⓫ Portland Streetcar

See also Street Finder maps 1, 2, 3, and 4

◄ A mural on the façade of the Oregon Historical Society, Portland

For keys to symbols see back flap

Street-by-Street: Downtown

One of the most appealing characteristics of Portland is the way the city combines cosmopolitan sophistication with a relaxed, low-key ambience. Nowhere is this more in evidence than on the attractive downtown blocks that surround Pioneer Courthouse Square. Broadway and the streets that cross it here are lined with department stores and boutiques, office complexes, hotels, restaurants, theaters, and museums, many occupying well-restored century-old buildings. Busy and vital as these downtown blocks are, sidewalks are shaded, parks are plentiful, and glimpses of the hills and mountains that encircle the city are easy to come by.

❽ ★ Portland Art Museum
The holdings of the oldest art museum in the Pacific Northwest range from Monet paintings to Native American crafts.

❼ Oregon Historical Society
Huge murals on the façades of this complex depict scenes from the Lewis and Clark expedition and other great moments in Oregon history. Inside is a wealth of memorabilia from the early days of the state.

❿ ★ South Park Blocks
Daniel Lownsdale laid out these city blocks as parkland in 1848. A local farmer's market is held here Saturdays in spring through fall.

SOUTHWEST PARK AVENUE

SOUTHWEST SALMON STRE

SOU

SW PARK AVE STRE

SW PARK AVE STRE

SOUTHWEST MAIN STREET

SOUTHWEST MADISON STREET

SOUTHWEST BROADWAY

SOUTHWEST JEFFERSON STREET

SOUTHWEST STREET

Key

— Suggested route

❻ Portland'5 Centers for the Arts
This organization operates some of Portland's major venues for theater, music, and dance. One of these is the Arlene Schnitzer Concert Hall, which lights up a stretch of Broadway. Its marquee has been shining brightly since 1927, when the theater opened as the city's foremost movie palace and vaudeville house.

PORTLAND

0 meters	80
0 yards	80

For hotels and restaurants see p286 and pp294–6

Weather Machine
A whimsical, 25-ft- (8-m-) tall sculpture comes to life every day at noon, when figures emerge from its top to announce the weather for the next 24 hours.

Jackson Tower, built by the Reid brothers in 1912 for a newspaper magnate, features glazed terracotta as a decorative element for its steel frame.

Locator Map
See Street Finder map 1

American Bank Building
This neo-Classical building, finished in 1914, features Corinthian columns at its base and is decorated with terracotta eagles and griffins.

❶ ★ **Pioneer Courthouse Square**
This one-block-square open space is the heart of Portland, where fountains splash and Portlanders gather for free lunchtime concerts, flower shows, and other events, or simply for a chance to sit and enjoy their city.

❷ **Pioneer Courthouse**
The octagonal tower of the first federal building in the Pacific Northwest has been a fixture of the Portland skyline since 1873.

Pioneer Courthouse Square, a popular public gathering place

❶ Pioneer Courthouse Square

SW Broadway & Yamhill St. **Map** 1 C5. **Tel** (503) 223-1613. 🚊 Pioneer Square (red, blue, green, yellow lines). ♿
🌐 **thesquarepdx.org**

Pioneer Courthouse Square resembles the large central plazas of many European cities, which was the intent of the city planners who designed this brick-paved pedestrian-only square in the mid-1980s. Despite its recent vintage, the square stands on hallowed Portland ground: the city's first schoolhouse was erected on this site in 1858, and the much-admired Portland Hotel stood here from 1890 to 1951, when it was demolished to make way for a parking lot.

According to plan, Pioneer Courthouse Square has become the center of the city, a friendly space where Portlanders gather to enjoy a brown-bag lunch or free outdoor concert. Architectural flourishes include a graceful, amphitheater-like bank of seats, a fountain that resembles a waterfall, and a row of 12 columns crowned with gilt roses.

Underground spaces adjoining the square accommodate offices and businesses, including the Travel Portland Visitors Information Center, Portland Walking Tours, Trimet Transit Planning Center, and a Starbucks®. The most compelling aspect of the square, though, is the lively presence of the many residents who use the space.

❷ Pioneer Courthouse

700 SW 6th Ave. **Map** 1 C5. **Tel** (503) 833-5311. 🚊 Pioneer Square (red, blue, green, yellow lines). **Open** 8am–5pm Mon–Fri. **Closed** Sat, Sun & major hols. ♿

Completed in 1873 and restored in 2005, Pioneer Courthouse was the first federal building to be constructed in the Pacific Northwest and is the second oldest federal building west of the Mississippi River. The trees planted here at that time are still standing. The Italianate structure, faced with freestone and topped by a domed cupola, houses the US Court of Appeals. Visitors can wander the grand hallways and public areas, where exhibits explore the building's history. There are panoramic views of Portland from the cupola, and historic photographs next to each window show the same view as it was in the city's early years.

❸ Portland Institute for Contemporary Art

415 SW 10th Ave, Ste 300. **Map** 1 B4. **Tel** (503) 242-1419. 🚌 to NW Everett St. **Open** 11am–6pm Tue–Fri. **Closed** major hols. ♿ 🌐 **pica.org**

Portland's venue for the latest trends in art does not have a permanent collection but hosts a variety of exhibitions, lectures, and residencies culminating in the annual Time-Based Art (TBA)

festival every July and August. The institute also provides a stage for performing artists from around the world, and has sponsored appearances of contemporary classical composer Philip Glass and the experimental performance-art troupe Dumb Type.

❹ Sentinel Hotel

614 SW 11th Ave. **Map** 1 B5. **Tel** (503) 224-3400. 🚊 Galleria/SW 10th Ave (red, blue lines). 🚌 to SW Alder St. ♿ See Where to Stay p286. 🌐 **sentinelhotel.com**

Originally opened as the Seward Hotel in 1909, and later the Governor Hotel in 1991, this extensively renovated hotel now bears the moniker of the Sentinel. The expedition of Meriwether Lewis and William Clark (see p41), whose 1804–1806 journey across the US and down the Columbia River put Oregon on the map, figures prominently in the hotel.

A sepia-colored, four-section mural in the restaurant shows a map of the Lewis and Clark expedition and depicts scenes from the explorers' journey: Native Americans fishing at Celilo Falls on the Columbia River, Meriwether Lewis trading with members of the Nez Perce tribe in present-day Idaho, and the guide Sacagawea (see p41) surveying the Pacific Ocean. Even the lampshades pay tribute to the pair – they are decorated with excerpts from the explorers' journals.

Façade of the stately Sentinel Hotel

The light-filled stairwell of the Multnomah County Library

The hotel incorporates the ornate former headquarters of the Elks Lodge as its west wing, built in the luxuriant style of the pre-Depression early 1920s to resemble the Palazzo Farnese in Rome. Mahogany detailing, leather chairs, fireplaces, and warm tones create an atmosphere of old-fashioned opulence.

❺ Multnomah County Library

801 SW 10th Ave. **Map** 1 B5.
Tel (503) 988-5123. 🚇 Library/SW 9th Ave (red, blue lines). 🚋 to SW Taylor St.
Open 10am–8pm Mon, noon–8pm Tue & Wed, 10am–6pm Thu–Sat, 10am–5pm Sun. **Closed** major hols.
♿ 📷 Ⓦ multcolib.org

Alfred E. Doyle, the architect whose work in Portland includes such landmarks as the Meier and Frank department store and the drinking fountains that grace downtown streets, chose limestone and brick for this distinctive Georgian structure. The building, completed in 1913, is the headquarters of the county library system, established in 1864 and the oldest library system west of the Mississippi.

Construction and furnishing of the building cost $480,000. The interior has undergone a few renovations over the years, the most major of which was completed in 1997 and cost $27 million.

Notable holdings of the collection, which is valued at $18 million, include one of the two known copies of the original Portland charter, housed in the John Wilson Rare Book Room. The library's most valuable possession, worth millions, is *The Birds of America* by John James Audubon, in a full-size multi-volume folio edition.

❻ Portland'5 Centers for the Arts

1111 SW Broadway. **Map** 3 B1.
Tel (503) 248-4335. 🚋 to SW Broadway. ♿ 📷 Ⓦ portland5.com

Since the mid-1980s, Portland'5 Centers for the Arts has been the city's major venue for theater, music, and dance. The complex consists of the Arlene Schnitzer Concert Hall and the , on Broadway, and the Keller Auditorium, a few blocks east at Southwest 3rd Avenue and Clay Street *(see p69)*. In the Antoinette Hatfield Hall, the Newmark Theatre, the Brunish Theatre, and the Dolores Winningstad Theatre open off a dramatic, five-story, cherry-paneled rotunda capped by a dome designed by glass artist James Carpenter.

The Arlene Schnitzer Concert Hall occupies a former vaudeville house and movie palace built in 1927. Its ornate, Italian Rococo Revival interior has been restored, and it is now the home of the Oregon Symphony. The marquee continues to illuminate Broadway with 6,000 lights, and it now props up a 65-ft- (20-m-) high sign that screams "Portland" in bright white lights.

❼ Oregon Historical Society

1200 SW Park Ave. **Map** 3 B1.
Tel (503) 222-1741. 🚇 Library/SW 9th Ave (red, blue lines). 🚋 to Jefferson St. Museum:
Open 10am–5pm Mon–Sat, noon–5pm Sun. Library: **Open** 1–5pm Tue, 10am–5pm Wed–Sat. 📷 ♿ 📷
Ⓦ ohs.org

Eight-story murals by Richard Haas on the west and south façades of the Oregon Historical Society depict the Lewis and Clark expedition *(see p41)*, fur trading, and other important events that have shaped the history of Oregon. On display in the galleries, which extend through three buildings, are some of the 85,000 objects that make this museum the largest repository of Oregon historical artifacts. The exhibits, which include maps, paintings, photographs, and historical documents, change frequently, since space does not allow for the display of the entire collection at once.

On permanent display is "Oregon My Oregon", a remarkable exhibition that includes 50 separate displays recounting the history of the state. There are 12 distinct sections depicting Oregon's rich past, including Native American languages and culture, memorabilia tracing the state's maritime history, and the region's varied geography. Journals of pioneers and millions of other items can also be viewed in the society's research library.

Decorative murals on the façade of the Oregon Historical Society

Portland Art Museum's gallery of late 19th-century European art

❽ Portland Art Museum

1219 SW Park Ave. **Map** 3 B1.
Tel (503) 226-2811. 🚊 Library/SW 9th
Ave (red, blue lines). 🚌 to Jefferson St.
Open 10am–5pm Tue, Wed & Sat,
10am–8pm Thu & Fri, noon–5pm Sun.
Closed major hols. 🅿️ ♿ 🚻 📷
🌐 **portlandartmuseum.org**

The oldest art museum in the
Pacific Northwest opened in
1892, introducing the citizenry
to classical art with a collection
of plaster casts of Greek and
Roman sculpture. Today, the
42,000-piece-strong collection,
which places the museum
among the 25 largest in the
country, is housed in a building
designed by modernist
architect Pietro Belluschi. In
2005, the North Building was
extensively renovated in order
to house the Center for Modern
and Contemporary Art.

A sizable collection of
European paintings, including
works by Van Gogh, Picasso,
Italian Renaissance masters,
and French Impressionists,
hang in the galleries. Works
by Rodin and Brancusi fill the
sculpture court; further galleries
house works by Frank Stella and
Willem de Kooning; and there
is a wing devoted to historical
and contemporary photo-
graphs, prints, sculptures, and
drawings by artists from the
region. The Grand Ronde
Center for Native American
Art displays masks, jewelry,
totem poles, and works by
artists from 200 North
American indigenous groups.

The museum is an important
stop for traveling exhibitions.

❾ The Old Church

1422 SW 11th Ave. **Map** 3 A1.
Tel (503) 222-2031. 🚌 to SW Clay St.
Open 11am–3pm Tue–Fri.
🔲 self-guided. 🌐 **oldchurch.org**

Built in 1882, this church reflects
a Victorian Gothic Revival style,
also known as Stick or Carpenter
Gothic style, with exaggerated
arches, a tall steeple, and sleek
windows. The rough-hewn wood
exterior lends it a distinctly
Pacific Northwestern flavor. On
Wednesdays at noon, the original
Hook and Hastings pipe organ is
put into service for free concerts.

The Gothic Revival-style Old Church, with
an intricately detailed wood exterior

❿ South Park Blocks

Bounded by SW Salmon St & I-405, SW
Park & SW 9th Aves. **Map** 3 B1. 🚌 to
stops between SW Salmon & SW Mill Sts.

In 1852, frontier businessman
and legislator Daniel Lownsdale
set aside the blocks between
Park and 9th Avenues as
parkland. After the city council

authorized the landscaping of
these blocks, landscape designer
Louis G. Pfunder planted 104
Lombardy poplars and elms
between Salmon and Hall. The
so-called South Park Blocks
continue to form a 12-block
ribbon of tree-shaded lawns
through the central city, running
past the Portland Art Museum
and Portland's Centers for
the Arts *(see p65)* and into
the campus of Portland State
University. In this city forested
by so many evergreens, the
blocks of deciduous trees are
refreshingly pleasant in the fall,
when the foliage turns vibrant
colors. Particularly vivid is the
area around Madison Street,
where the First Congregational
Church rises above the trees.

Notable statuary along the
blocks includes, between
Madison and Main Streets,
a dour-looking US president
Abraham Lincoln (1861–5) by
George Fite Waters, who was
a student of Rodin. One block
south is the 18-ft- (5.5-m-) tall
bronze equestrian *Rough Rider*,
a statue of President Theodore
Roosevelt (1901–9), by his friend
and hunting partner Alexander
Phimister Proctor.

Among the most distinctive
ornaments are the Benson
drinking fountains. In 1917,
lumber baron Samuel Benson
commissioned prominent architect A. E. Doyle to design these
graceful, four-bowled fountains.
He placed 20 of them throughout the South Park Blocks and
the rest of downtown to quench
the thirst of residents who might
otherwise be tempted to visit
saloons. Since then, 20 more
fountains have been added.

Offerings at the Saturday farmers' market,
South Park Blocks

⓫ Portland Streetcar

East- & southbound on NW Lovejoy St & 11th Ave, north- & westbound on 10th Ave & NW Northrup St. **Map** 1 A2–3 B2. **Tel** (503) 222-4200. **Open** 5:30am–11:30pm Mon–Fri, 7:15am–11:30pm Sat, 7:15am–10:30pm Sun. portlandstreetcar.org

Horse-drawn streetcars began running in the 1870s. By the early 20th century, electric streetcars were rumbling all across Portland, bringing downtown within reach of newly established residential neighborhoods. Cars had put the streetcars out of service by the 1950s, but in the late 1990s, city planners turned to streetcars again as part of a scheme to reduce congestion and ensure the vitality of the central business district.

The Czech- and Oregon-built street- cars travel along three lines. The first, the North/South (NS) line, runs from NW 23rd Avenue to the South Waterfront, where it connects with the Aerial tram to Oregon Health and Science University. The other two lines run in loops around the Central City, connecting the four quadrants over the Broadway Bridge and the new Tilikum Crossing. Single rides and day passes can be purchased, including via a smartphone app.

Portland streetcars, environmentally sound transit

⓬ Portland Building

1120 SW 5th Ave. **Map** 3 C1. Gallery: **Tel** (503) 823-5252. Transit Mall. **Open** 8am–5pm Mon–Fri. **Closed** major hols.

The Portland Building, designed by New Jersey architect Michael Graves, has been featured on the covers of both *Time* and *Newsweek* and was called Portland's "Eiffel Tower" by the city's former mayor Frank Ivancie. The building has been controversial ever since it was completed in 1982. Displaying an experimental combination of architectural styles, this first large-scale post- modern office building in the US has been hailed as a major innovation in contemporary urban design and a credit to forward-thinking Portland. It has also been denounced

Portlandia watching from the Portland Building

as just plain ugly. The use of muted colors and ornamental swags and pilasters lends a certain playfulness to the exterior, while the 15-story building's relatively modest height and multiple rows of small square windows suggest

The landmark Portland Building, home to City of Portland offices

practicality and a lack of pretension, as befits the home of government offices.

More ostentatious is *Portlandia*, a 36-ft- (11-m-) tall statue fashioned from 6.5 tons of copper that emerges from a second-floor balcony above the main doors. The figure crouches, with one hand extended and the other brandishing a giant trident. Completed by sculptor Raymond Kaskey in 1985, *Portlandia* is modeled on Lady Commerce, the symbolic figure that appears on the city seal and that supposedly welcomed traders into the city's port. After New York City's Statue of Liberty, *Portlandia* is the largest copper statue in the US.

A small gallery on the second floor of the building displays public art of the region. There are also plans and models related to the design and construction of the building and the *Portlandia* statue.

Portland the Green

Justifiably, Portland's abundant parks and gardens are often described in superlatives. The city can make claim to one of the largest forested city parks in the US, 8-sq-miles (21-sq- km) Forest Park, and the smallest park in the world, 452-sq-inch (0.3-sq-m) Mill Ends Park (*see p69*). The city boasts some of the nation's largest and most extensive rose test gardens (*see p76*), one of the world's most renowned rhododendron gardens (*see p78*), one of the finest Japanese gardens outside Japan (*see p76*), and the largest classical Chinese garden outside China (*see p58*). Many of the other parks and gardens included in the city's 56 sq miles (145 sq km) of green space have no such claims attached, but they are nonetheless pleasant places in which to enjoy the great outdoors.

Mill Ends Park, the world's tiniest park

⑬ Chapman and Lownsdale Squares

Bounded by SW Salmon & SW Madison Sts, SW 3rd & SW 4th Aves. **Map** 3 C1. 🚋 Mall/SW 4th Ave (red, blue lines), City Hall/SW Jefferson St (green, yellow lines).

It is only fitting that Daniel Lownsdale should have a one-block-square park named for him. The tanner who became one of Oregon's early legislators had the foresight to set aside a parcel of downtown for the South Park Blocks (see p66), and he did much to encourage trade on the nearby waterfront by building a wood-plank road into the countryside so that lumber and other goods could be transported to the Portland docks.

Judge William Chapman, for whom the adjoining square is named, was one of the founders of the *Oregonian* newspaper. Along with Terry Schrunk Plaza – a third, adjacent park-like block – the squares provide a soothing stretch of greenery in Portland's quiet courthouse and government-building district. The neighborhood was not always so sedate, though: anti-Chinese riots broke out here in the 1880s, and the area was raucous enough in the 1920s that Chapman Square was declared off-limits to men so that women could enjoy the space in safety.

Portland's popular Elk Fountain, built in 1852, near the courthouse

The limestone, aluminum, and glass Mark O. Hatfield US Courthouse

⑭ Mark O. Hatfield US Courthouse

1000 SW 3rd Ave. **Map** 3 C1. **Tel** (503) 326-8000. 🚋 Transit Mall. **Open** 7am–5pm Mon–Fri. **Closed** major hols. ♿

Named for a popular Oregon governor and senator, the Mark O. Hatfield US Courthouse defies any preconceived notion that a government building is by definition unimaginative. Designed by the New York firm of Kohn Pedersen Fox and completed in 1997, the courthouse presents a handsome and bold façade of glass, aluminum, and limestone. A ninth-floor sculpture garden provides excellent views of both the river and one of Portland's most beloved pieces of statuary, the **Elk Fountain**, which stands across the street.

Erected in 1852 on land where elk once roamed freely, for many years the Elk Fountain provided citizens' horses with a place to drink. When automobile traffic began to increase in the early 20th century, the fountain stood in the path of a proposed extension of Main Street. Angry citizens protested plans to move the fountain; it now stands in the middle of the street.

⑮ Governor Tom McCall Waterfront Park

Bounded by SW Harrison & NW Glisan Sts, SW Naito Pkwy & Willamette River. **Map** 4 D1. 🚋 Skidmore Fountain, Morrison/SW 3rd Ave, Yamhill District (red, blue lines).

This 1.5-mile- (2.5-km-) long park on the west bank of the Willamette River covers land that once bustled with activity on the Portland docks and which, from the 1940s to the 1970s, was buried beneath an expressway. The city converted the land to a park as part of an urban renewal scheme and named it for the environmentally minded Tom McCall, Oregon's governor, 1967–75.

The park is a much-used riverside promenade and the locale for many festivals. One of its most popular attractions is **Salmon Street Springs**, a fountain whose 100 jets splash water directly onto the pavement, providing easily accessible relief on a hot day. The foot of nearby Southwest Salmon Street was once the roughest part of town. Here, drunken revelers were routinely knocked unconscious and then taken aboard ships as involuntary crew members. A block away, at the foot of

The Battleship Oregon Memorial, Governor Tom McCall Waterfront Park

Southwest Taylor Street, is **Mill Ends Park**, measuring only 452 sq inches (0.3 sq m). The park is the former site of a telephone pole, removed in the late 1940s. Local journalist Dick Fagan began planting flowers on the patch of earth and writing articles about what he dubbed the "World's Smallest Park," which it officially became when the City of Portland adopted it as part of the park system in 1976.

The **Battleship Oregon Memorial**, built in 1956, honors an 1893 US Navy ship. A time capsule sealed in its base in 1976 is due to be opened in 2076.

Keller Auditorium, part of the Portland'5 Centers for the Arts

The multifunctional KOIN Center, rising 29 stories above Portland

⓰ KOIN Center

222 SW Columbia St. **Map** 3 C2.
🚋 Transit Mall.

Like the Portland Building (see p67), the KOIN Center is designed in the postmodern style, which incorporates a plurality of architectural styles in one structure. However, this 29-story blond-brick tower capped by a pyramidal blue steel roof has elicited none of the controversy that the Port-land Building has. Instead, the KOIN Center, designed by the Portland firm of Zimmer Gunsul Frasca and completed in 1984, is considered a model urban complex. The building houses residences, offices – including those of the television station for which it is named – and shops, as well as a popular steakhouse.

⓱ Keller Auditorium

222 SW Clay St. **Map** 3 C2. **Tel** (503) 248-4335. 🚋 Transit Mall. ♿

When a Broadway roadshow or other big production comes to Portland, the 3,000-seat Keller Auditorium often plays host. Built in 1917 on the former site of an exhibition hall and sports arena known as the Mechanics' Pavilion, the auditorium was completely remodeled in the late 1960s, gaining clean sightlines as well as excellent acoustics. The auditorium is part of the Portland'5 Centers for the Arts (see p65) and is home to the Portland Opera, the Oregon Ballet, and sometimes the Oregon Children's Theatre.

Across the street is the **Ira Keller Memorial Fountain**, a waterfall cascading over 18-ft (5.5-m) concrete cliffs into a pool crisscrossed with platforms laid out like stepping stones. The fountain, enclosed by a delightful garden, successfully presents a typical Pacific Northwest experience – that of emerging from the shade of trees to the sight, sound, and spray of a plunging torrent. Completed in 1970, the fountain was designed by Angela Danadjieva. Originally called the Forecourt Fountain, it was renamed in 1978 to honor civic leader Ira C. Keller.

⓲ RiverPlace Marina

SW Clay St & Willamette River.
Map 4 D3. 🚌 95X, 96. 🚢 RiverPlace.
🚲 📷

RiverPlace Marina is located on the west bank of the Willamette River, situated at the southwest end of Governor Tom McCall Waterfront Park.

Among the amenities here are upscale shops, several restaurants, including Portland's only floating restaurant, and one of the city's higher-end hotels, RiverPlace Hotel. The complex also has sloping lawns, riverside walks, and a large marina. Sea kayaks are available for rental, providing an alternative way to view the river and city.

Ira Keller Memorial Fountain, across from the Keller Auditorium

FARTHER AFIELD

By the late 19th century, Portland was fast growing from a small riverfront settlement surrounded by forests into an important port city. It expanded westward into Nob Hill, where wealthy merchants settled, and eastward across the Willamette River. In 1871, the City created Washington Park, now Portland's favorite green retreat. Crystal Springs Rhododendron Garden, to the south, is another tranquil spot. Numerous important events in Oregon's history transpired just south of Portland. Oregon City, at the end of the Oregon Trail, was the site of the first meeting of the territory's provisional legislature, in 1843. At Aurora, a Utopian society once thrived, and at nearby Champoeg State Heritage Area pioneers voted to break from Britain.

Sights at a Glance

Towns and Neighborhoods
❹ Nob Hill
❺ Rose Quarter
❽ Hawthorne District
❾ Southeast Division Street
❿ Sellwood District
⓮ Oregon City
⓯ Aurora

Institutions
⓬ Reed College

Museums
❼ Oregon Museum of Science and Industry

Historic Buildings
❸ Pittock Mansion

Historic Sites
⓭ End of the Oregon Trail Interpretive Center

Parks, Gardens, and Natural Areas
❶ Sauvie Island
❷ *Washington Park pp74–7*
❻ Eastbank Esplanade
⓫ Crystal Springs Rhododendron Garden

Key
Central Portland
Urban area
Major highway
Highway
Minor road

| 0 kilometers | 10 |
| 0 miles | 10 |

◀ Colorful trees and lush greenery in the Strolling Pond Garden, Japanese Garden, Washington Park   **For keys to symbols** *see back flap*

One of several beaches along Sauvie Island's Columbia River side

❶ Sauvie Island

ℹ️ 18330 NW Sauvie Island Rd, (503) 621-3488. 🚌 17 NW 21st Ave/ St. Helens Rd. Sauvie Island Wildlife Area: **Open** mid-Apr–Sep: 4am–10pm daily. 🆆 sauvieisland.org

Sauvie Island comprises of low-lying land at the confluence of the Willamette and Columbia Rivers, just 10 miles (16 km) from downtown Portland. With rich soil that supports many berry farms and orchards, the southern half of the island is primarily agricultural. The northern half is set aside as the **Sauvie Island Wildlife Area**, managed by the Oregon Department of Fish and Wildlife. Bird-watchers come to see some of the estimated quarter of a million birds – including swans, ducks, and cranes – that stop here on their spring and fall migrations.

During the summer, swimmers and sunbathers enjoy beaches on the island's Columbia River side, and anglers fish for sturgeon and salmon in nearby channels.

The island's **Bybee-Howell House**, a Greek Revival-style house built in 1858 by James Y. Bybee, is surrounded by fruit orchards, brought by pioneers on the Oregon Trail. The house is no longer open to the public, but visitors can tour the grounds.

🏛️ **Bybee-Howell House**
Howell Territorial Park. **Tel** (503) 222-1741. **Open** dawn–dusk (grounds only).

❷ Washington Park

See pp74–7.

❸ Pittock Mansion

3229 NW Pittock Dr. **Tel** (503) 823-3623. 🚌 20 (to W Burnside Rd, then 20-min walk), 77. **Open** Feb–Jun & Sep–Dec: 11am–4pm daily; Jul–Aug: 10am–5pm daily. **Closed** Jan, Thanksgiving weekend, Thanksgiving, Dec 25 & major hols. 🎟️ 👶 (partial; call 48 hrs ahead). 🎥 📷
🆆 pittockmansion.org

Henry Pittock, who came west on the Oregon Trail as a young man and published the *Oregonian* newspaper, commissioned this mansion in 1909. Designed by San Francisco architect Edward T. Foulkes, the house is still the grandest residence in Portland. Perched on a 1,000-ft (305-m) summit in the West Hills, it commands superb views of the city and snowcapped mountain peaks. The mansion's gardens are a good picnic spot.

Guided tours, including self-guided tours, show off the mansion's remark-

A turn-of-the-19th-century house in Nob Hill

able embellishments. Among them are a marble staircase, elliptical drawing room, and circular Turkish-style smoking room. Historic artifacts decorate the home. The furnishings, though not original to the house, reflect the finest tastes of Pittock's time.

The sweeping entrance of the imposing Pittock Mansion

A Nob Hill mansion, typical of those in the fashionable district

❹ Nob Hill

W Burnside to NW Pettygrove Sts, from NW 17th to NW 24th Sts. 🚊 to NW 23rd St.

Also known as Northwest 23rd in reference to its main business street, Nob Hill is a gracious, late 19th-century neighborhood of shady streets, large wooden houses, and apartment buildings. With its proximity to downtown and its inherent charms, Nob Hill has become one of the city's most popular commercial and residential neighborhoods. A slightly bohemian atmosphere, together with upscale shops and restaurants, make Nob Hill a pleasant place to stroll.

Northwest 23rd Street from West Burnside to Northwest Lovejoy Streets is the neighborhood's commercial core. The side streets are lined with lovely old houses. The 1892 Victorian gingerbread **Pettygrove House** (2287 Northwest Pettygrove Street) was the home of Francis Pettygrove, the city founder who flipped a coin with fellow founder Asa Lovejoy to determine the city's name. Pettygrove won and chose the name of a city in his native Maine (Lovejoy preferred "Boston"). Northwest Johnson Street between Northwest 22nd and 23rd Streets is lined with many fine houses from the 1880s, when Nob Hill first became fashionable.

❺ Rose Quarter

1 Center Ct. 🚇 Rose Quarter (red, blue lines). See Entertainment in Portland *p81*. 🆆 **rosequarter.com**

Portland's major venues for sports, big-ticket entertainment events, and conventions are clustered in the Rose Quarter, a commercial riverside area on the east bank of the Willamette River. Portlanders come in droves to the otherwise quiet neighborhood to attend Portland Trail Blazer basketball games, Portland Winterhawks ice hockey games, and major pop and rock concerts by the likes of Paul McCartney and Bruce Springsteen at the **Moda Center**. Designed by the Kansas City firm of Ellerbe Becket, the arena was completed in 1996. It features a unique "acoustical cloud" made up of 160 rotating acoustic panels which can be tailored to the needs of the specific event.

The smaller, nearby **Veterans Memorial Coliseum** (300 Winning Way) once hosted these events. Its glass-fronted hall, designed by New York firm Skidmore, Owens and Merrill and completed in 1960, is now used for conventions and trade shows. It also serves as the primary home for the Portland Winterhawks WHL team.

The **Lloyd Center**, just east of the Rose Quarter, is recognized as the US's first covered shopping center. Although such malls are now ubiquitous, the Lloyd Center retains an old-fashioned charm, with more than 200 shops and restaurants lining handsome, well-planted walkways that radiate from a skating rink.

Portland's cityscape, the Eastbank Esplanade in the foreground

❻ Eastbank Esplanade

Bounded by Willamette River & I-5, Steel & Hawthorne Bridges. 🚇 Rose Quarter (red, blue lines). 🚌 4, 5, 6, 8, 10, 14.

This pedestrian and bicycle path following the east bank of the Willamette River between the Hawthorne and Steel Bridges was part of a massive riverfront redevelopment. While the esplanade's unobstructed views of downtown Portland and the opportunity it provides to enjoy the river are compelling reasons to visit, the walkway is an attraction in its own right. A 1,200-ft (365-m) section floats on the water, and another cantilevered portion is suspended above one of the city's original commercial piers.

The esplanade provides access to four of the city's major downtown bridges, linking the walkway to Governor Tom McCall Waterfront Park *(see pp68–9)* on the west bank of the river. The most dramatic crossing is via the Steel Bridge Riverwalk, perched just 30 ft (9 m) above the water.

❼ Oregon Museum of Science and Industry

1945 SE Water Ave. **Tel** (503) 797-4000. 🚇 OMSI/SE Water Ave (orange line). 🚋 A Loop. 🚌 17. **Open** 9:30am–5:30pm Tue–Sun (mid-June–Sep: to 7pm). **Closed** major hols. ♿ 🅿 (partial). 🎟 of submarine. 📷 🆆 **omsi.edu**

Commonly referred to as OMSI, the Oregon Museum of Science and Industry is one of the top science museums in the US. The multiple exhibition halls and science labs of this world-class tourist attraction house hundreds of interactive exhibits. Visitors may enjoy hands-on experiences in subjects such as space exploration, computers, physics, chemistry, and mathematics. A favorite is the earthquake simulator, in which visitors are shaken and rattled while learning about the tectonic plates that continue to shift beneath Portland.

The **Kendall Planetarium**, a state-of-the-art facility, places OMSI at the forefront of astronomical education. For kids under nine, the Science Playground is a wonderland with interactive zones. The **Empirical Theater**, four stories tall, is the largest screen in Portland and shows various science-themed documentaries and feature films.

Moored alongside the museum is the USS *Blueback*, first launched in 1959 and the last diesel submarine to be used by the US Navy. Guided tours provide a chance to look at downtown through a periscope and to experience the claustrophobic conditions in which 85 submariners lived.

An interactive exhibit at the Oregon Museum of Science and Industry

❷ Washington Park

Though a park first took shape in the western hills of downtown Portland in 1871, it was not until 1903 that Washington Park acquired much of its present appearance. This was the year Boston landscape architect John Olmsted came to Portland to help plan the Lewis and Clark Exposition and lay out a parks plan for the young city. Reflecting Olmsted's suggestions, Washington Park has developed, over the years, to encompass gardens, open spaces, great groves of evergreens, a zoo, and recreational facilities. Today, the park is one of Portland's most popular outdoor playgrounds.

The iconic totem pole at Washington Park's Oregon Zoo

★ Hoyt Arboretum
More than 8,000 trees and shrubs from around the world grow in this arboretum; they can be appreciated along the 12 miles (19 km) of well-marked hiking trails.

World Forestry Center
This renowned center includes a discovery lab and a museum, with its "talking" 70-ft (21-m) Douglas fir that explains how trees grow and excellent exhibits on rain- and old-growth forests.

KEY

① **Portland Children's Museum** is an exciting interactive museum designed for children from ages six months to 10 years.

② **Vietnam Veterans of Oregon Memorial**, a ring of dramatic black granite blocks, honors Oregonians who served in the Vietnam War.

③ **Wildwood Trail**, a 30-mile (48-km) portion of the 40-Mile Loop, runs the length of Washington Park and into Forest Park to the north, winding past Douglas firs and wildflowers.

0 meters 400
0 yards 500

★ Oregon Zoo
Oregon's most-visited attraction, famous for its elephants, is a noted research institute, harboring over 50 threatened and endangered species on forested hillside.

For hotels and restaurants see p286 and pp294–6

★ Japanese Garden
Plants, stones, and water are arranged to reflect the essence of nature in five distinct traditional Japanese gardens.

Key

— Trail

 Train route

★ International Rose Test Garden
Award-winning roses from around the world, a grass amphitheater, and a walkway honoring every queen of the city's annual Rose Festival since 1907 are among the treasures of this garden, the oldest public garden of its kind in the US.

26

Washington Park and Zoo Railway
Three locomotives – the old-style Steamer, the sleek 1958 Zooliner, and a train known as the Oregon Express – meander through the park's lush landscape, offering great views of downtown Portland, Mounts Hood and St. Helens, and the zoo.

For keys to symbols *see back flap*

Exploring Washington Park

Hiking on a forest trail beneath a canopy of old-growth pine trees or coming upon a meadow filled with wildflowers, visitors may find it hard to believe that Washington Park is surrounded by the city. Wild as the hilly terrain is in places, however, the park also contains some of the city's best-tended gardens and the always busy zoo, as well as large expanses of manicured lawn. Scenic roadways, an extensive trail system, and even a miniature railway make it easy to explore the park and enjoy its diverse experiences.

Roses in full bloom in the International Rose Test Garden

International Rose Test Garden

400 SW Kingston Dr. **Tel** (503) 823-3636. **Open** 7:30am–9pm daily.

A magnificent treat for all those who love flowers, this garden is the oldest continuously operated rose test garden in the US. It can trace its beginnings to a summer day in 1888, when Georgiana Pittock, wife of pioneer publisher Henry Pittock (see p72), invited her friends to display their prize roses in a tent on the lawn of her mansion. The enthusiasts formed the Portland Rose Society in 1888, planted roses along city streets, and dubbed Portland the "City of Roses." In 1917, the society established the rose garden in Washington Park, on a terraced hillside commanding memorable views of the city and Mount Hood. Today, the garden's 8,000 bushes and 525 species come into bloom in a spectacle of color every June, in time for the annual Portland Rose Festival (see p34).

In the All-American Rose Test Garden, new varieties of roses are carefully observed for two years, as a panel of judges evaluates them for color, form, fragrance, and other criteria. The evaluations are then combined with those of judges at 23 other test gardens around the country to determine the best roses. The City of Portland also chooses its own favorites; these annual winners are on display in the Gold Medal Garden.

Only at the Shakespeare Garden do roses not take center stage – this pleasant bower is planted with flowers mentioned in the bard's plays.

The Rose Society also maintains gardens in Peninsula Park, in north Portland, and in the neighborhood of Ladd's Addition (see p78), in southeast Portland.

Japanese Garden

611 SW Kingston Dr. **Tel** (503) 223-1321. 63, 83. **Open** Apr–Sep: noon–7pm Mon, 10am–7pm Tue–Sun; Oct–Mar: noon–4pm Mon, 10am–4pm Tue–Sun. **Closed** Jan 1, Thanksgiving, Dec 25. check website for details.
w japanesegarden.com

This lovely, manicured landscape, spread across hilly terrain next to the International Rose Test Garden, is said to be one of the most authentic Japanese gardens outside of Japan and is certainly one of the most tranquil spots in Portland. Within the garden, designed by noted Japanese landscape architect Takuma Tono, meticulously tended plantings surround ponds, streams, and pavilions. Paths wind through five distinct landscapes: the Flat Garden, a typical urban garden design; the Tea Garden, built around a ceremonial teahouse; the Strolling Pond Garden, where zigzagging bridges cross carp-filled pools and iris beds; the Natural Garden, where shrubs, ferns, and mosses grow in their natural state alongside ponds, streams, and waterfalls; and the Sand and Stone Gardens, in which raked gravel simulates the sea and plantings depict a sake cup and gourd to wish the visitor happiness. The wood, tile-roofed entrance gate can be reached by a short uphill climb on a woodland path or via a shuttle bus departing every 25 minutes from the parking lot below.

Stone pagoda in the Japanese Garden

The authentic and tranquil Japanese Garden, designed by Takuma Tono

Stately conifers, part of the collection of trees in the Hoyt Arboretum

Hoyt Arboretum

4000 SW Fairview Blvd. **Tel** (503) 865-8733. **Open** 5am–10pm daily. 🔲 Apr–Oct: noon Sat (call ahead). 🅦 hoytarboretum.org

The groves and meadows of this arboretum contain more than 6,000 trees and plants from around the world, with over 2,000 species, 63 of which are vulnerable or endangered. The Hoyt Arboretum is a living museum where anyone can explore vegetation both familiar and unexpected, marked with identification labels.

The visitors' center – the departure point for tours – also provides maps of the many trails that crisscross the arboretum as well as suggested walking routes and detailed lists of the trees and plants to be found along the way.

At the south end, the **Vietnam Veterans of Oregon Memorial** – a subdued assemblage of lawns, gardens, and six granite slabs inscribed with the names of veterans – commemorates those Oregonians who were killed or reported missing during the Vietnam War.

Oregon Zoo

4001 SW Canyon Rd. **Tel** (503) 226-1561. 🔲 Washington Park (blue line). 🚌 63. **Open** Jan & Feb: 10am–4pm daily; Mar–May & Sep–Dec: 9am–4pm daily; Jun–Aug: 9am–6pm daily. **Closed** Dec 25. 🔲 ♿ 🔲 📷 🅦 oregonzoo.org

In 1887, pharmacist Richard B. Knight donated a grizzly bear and a brown bear to the city. A zoo has been located in Washington Park ever since, moving to its present location on the hillsides and ravines of the south side of the park in 1959. More than 1,000 birds, mammals, reptiles, and invertebrates – representing 200 species – live in the zoo, many in spacious, naturalistic habitats. The zoo, home to the largest breeding herd of elephants in captivity, is noted for its efforts to perpetuate some 21 endangered and 33 threatened species.

Among the zoo's most popular denizens are the Humboldt penguins from Peru that live in the Penguinarium; the sea otters in Stellar Cove; the African rock python and the lions in the Predators of the Serengeti exhibit; the impalas and giraffes that graze in the zoo's Africa Savanna exhibit; and the wolves and grizzly bears of the Alaskan Tundra exhibit. The Cascade exhibit provides a look at the goats, elk, otters, and other animals that roam the Pacific Northwest wilds.

World Forestry Center Discovery Museum

4033 SW Canyon Rd. **Tel** (503) 228-1367. **Open** 10am–5pm daily. **Closed** Thanksgiving, Dec 25. 🔲 ♿ 📷 🅦 worldforestry.org

Trees steal the show at this museum devoted to the world's forests. On the main floor of the stylishly designed timber building is a grove of trees native to the area. There is also an outstanding collection of petrified wood – wood that has been buried for thousands of years and transformed into mineral deposits.

Upstairs, photographs and text panels explore the importance of old-growth forests and tropical rainforests. The Forest Discovery Lab provides hands-on exhibits for kids.

The interactive Global Forest exhibit, featuring the sights, sounds, and smells of each different world forest, is definitely worth a visit.

The timbered exterior of the World Forestry Center Discovery Museum

Portland Children's Museum

4015 SW Canyon Rd. **Tel** (503) 223-6500. 🔲 Washington Park (blue line). 🚌 63. **Open** 9am–5pm daily. 🔲 🔲 📷 🅦 portlandcm.org

When it was established in 1949, the Portland Children's Museum was one of the first of its kind in the US. Today the museum attracts some 250,000 visitors yearly and offers a wide range of exhibits geared to kids under the age of 10.

"Play" is the operative word at the museum, as youngsters turn cranks and operate valves to send water cascading through Water Works, use giant rain sticks to make music in the Zounds! exhibit, perform medical operations in the Kids' Clinic, and in other creative, hands-on ways explore the world around them.

A lion in the Predators of the Serengeti exhibit at the Oregon Zoo

Street shopping in Portland's funky Hawthorne District

❽ Hawthorne District

NE Hawthorne Blvd, from SE 17th to SE 39th Sts.

An east-side residential and business area somewhat reminiscent of parts of Berkeley, California, the Hawthorne District is hip, funky, and bustling with young people, many of whom attend nearby Reed College. Hawthorne Boulevard is lined with coffee-houses, clothing boutiques, bookstores, bakeries, delis, and restaurants, several serving ethnic foods, including Vietnamese, Indian, Lebanese, and Ethiopian. Buskers add their sounds to the area's vibrant street scene.

The district's surrounding residential neighborhoods, dating from the early 20th century, were among Portland's first so-called "streetcar suburbs." Of these, Ladd's Addition is one of the oldest planned communities in the western US. Built in a circular grid of streets that surround five rose gardens, the plan was considered radical when it was laid out in 1939. Today, the area boasts many styles of 20th-century architecture: bungalow, craftsman, mission, Colonial Revival, and Tudor.

To the east, Hawthorne Boulevard ascends the slopes of Mount Tabor, an extinct volcano whose crater is now surrounded by a lovely forested park, popular with picnickers. Walking trails are to be found throughout the park.

❾ Southeast Division Street

SE Division Street corridor, from SE 19th St to SE 45th St.

Not long ago, Southeast Division Street was a thorough-fare known for hardware shops, auto-body repair and seedy blue-collar bars. However, a series of high-profile restaurants have opened, making this stretch the hottest area on the Portland dining scene. It began in 2005 with Andy Ricker's wildly popular Thai cocktail and snack shack, Pok Pok *(see p295)*, which has since expanded to NYC and inspired a bestselling cookbook. The culinary streak has intensified with exciting, quirky farm-to-table concept restaurants and cafés springing up one after another. From old-world Italian at Ava Gene's to small-batch ice cream in experimental, savory flavors at Salt & Straw, diners can restaurant-hop their way down this street full of "it" eats.

❿ Sellwood District

SE 13th to SE 17th Aves, from SE Tacoma St to SE Bybee Blvd.

Sellwood, a quiet residential neighborhood on a bluff above the Willamette River in the southeast corner of the city, has become the antiques center of Portland. Long gone are the days when Sellwood was a bargain-hunter's paradise, but shoppers continue to descend upon Sellwood's 30 or so antique shops – many of which occupy old Victorian houses along Southeast 13th Avenue, known as **Antique Row**. They may then enjoy a meal in one of the area's many restaurants or in the adjoining Westmoreland neighborhood.

The riverbank just below the Sellwood bluff is made festive by the presence of the Ferris wheel, roller coaster, roller-skating rink, and other attractions of **Oaks Park**, a shady amusement park that opened during the 1905 Lewis and Clark Exposition *(see p44)*.

⓫ Crystal Springs Rhododendron Garden

SE 28th Ave & SE Woodstock Blvd. **Tel** (503) 771-8386. 🚌 19. **Open** Apr–Sep: 6am–10pm daily; Oct–Mar: 6am–6pm daily. 🅿 (free Mon & Tue). ♿

This garden is laced with trails that cross streams, pass beneath misty cascades, and circle a spring-fed lake attracting ducks, geese, herons, and other waterfowl. The garden erupts into a breathtaking blaze of color during spring through to early summer, when hundreds of species of rare rhododendrons and azaleas – one of the world's leading collections of these woodland plants – are in bloom.

The serene lake at Crystal Springs Rhododendron Garden

⓬ Reed College

3203 SE Woodstock Blvd. **Tel** (503) 771-1112. 🚌 19. Grounds: **Open** dawn–dusk daily. 🅦 **reed.edu**

Founded in 1908 with a bequest from Oregon pioneers Simeon and Amanda Reed, Reed College occupies a wooded campus at the edge of Eastmoreland, one of Portland's most beautiful residential neighborhoods. Brick Tudor Gothic buildings, along with others designed in traditional Northwest timber style, are set amid rolling lawns surrounding the "canyon," a wooded wetland; shade is provided by 125 species of maples, cedars, and other trees. Reed has produced the second-highest number of Rhodes scholars of all US liberal arts colleges. The college also hosts several public events such as plays, lectures, and concerts.

Artifacts of early pioneers, End of the Oregon Trail Interpretive Center

⓭ End of the Oregon Trail Interpretive Center

1726 Washington St, Oregon City. **Tel** (503) 657-9336. **Open** 9:30am–5pm Mon–Sat, 10:30am–5pm Sun (last entry 1 hour before closing). **Closed** Jan 1, Thanksgiving, Dec 25. 🅿️ ♿ 📷 🆆 historicoregoncity.org

Although many of the pioneers who crossed the country on the Oregon Trail went their separate ways once they reached eastern Oregon, for those who continued west across the Cascade Mountains, Abernethy Green near Oregon City was the end of the trail. Here they stocked up on provisions and set up farmsteads in the fertile Willamette Valley.

The End of the Oregon Trail Interpretive Center tells the story of life on the trail in three oversized, 50-ft- (15-m-) high covered wagons that encircle Abernethy Green. Exhibits of heirlooms, the *Bound for Oregon* feature film, as well as hands-on experiences and pioneer crafts, such as packing a wagon and candle dipping, bring past hardships to life. Visitors can also take a guided walk of one-thousandth of the trail.

⓮ Oregon City

Road map 1 A3. 🅰️ 29,500. 🛈 1201 Washington St, (503) 656-1619.

Terminus of the Oregon Trail and capital of the Oregon Territory from 1849 to 1852, Oregon City's past prominence is largely due to its location beside the 40-ft (12-m) Willamette Falls, which powered flour and paper mills. The mills brought prosperity to the city, which was the site of the first meeting of the territory's provisional legislature, in 1843.

Museum of the Oregon Territory traces this history from the days when John McLoughlin, an Englishman sympathetic to the cause of bringing Oregon into the US, settled the town in 1829. In 1846, the "Father of Oregon" built the then-grandest home in Oregon, now the **McLoughlin House**, a unit of Fort Vancouver National Historic Site.

🏛 **Museum of the Oregon Territory**
211 Tumwater Dr. **Tel** (503) 655-5574. **Open** 11am–4pm Wed–Sat. **Closed** major hols. ♿ 🆆 clackamashistory.org

🏛 **McLoughlin House**
713 Center St. **Tel** (503) 656-5146. **Open** 10am–4pm Fri & Sat. **Closed** mid-Dec–Jan & major hols. 📷 🆆 mcloughlinhouse.org

The stately McLoughlin House (1846) in Oregon City

⓯ Aurora

Road map 1 A3. 🅰️ 650. 🛈 (503) 678-5754 (Old Aurora Colony Museum).

The town of Aurora traces its roots to the Aurora Colony, a Utopian community founded by Prussian immigrant William Keil in 1852. Similar to Shaker communities in the east, it was a collective society based on the principles of Christian fundamentalism and shared property. The colony thrived for more than a decade, until it was decimated by a smallpox epidemic. Exhibits tracing the colony's history fill the **Old Aurora Colony Museum**'s handsome white-frame buildings. Many of Aurora's other historic buildings now house antique shops.

Nearby **Champoeg State Heritage Area** is the site of an 1843 convention at which settlers voted to break from Britain and establish a provisional American government in Oregon. By that time, Champoeg was a thriving trading post on the banks of the Willamette River, having been established by the Hudson's Bay Company in 1813. The town that grew up around the trading post was abandoned as a result of devastating floods in 1861 and 1890; the park now comprises of meadows and stately stands of oaks and evergreens.

Displays in the visitor center pay tribute to the Calapooya Indians, who once lived here on the banks of the river, and to the traders and pioneers who came in the wake of the Hudson's Bay settlement. Its historic buildings include a jail, a schoolhouse, a barn, and several early dwellings.

🏛 **Old Aurora Colony Museum**
15018 2nd St NE. **Tel** (503) 678-5754. **Open** Feb–Dec: 11am–4pm Tue–Sat, noon–4pm Sun. **Closed** Jan, major hols. 📷 ♿ check website for details. 🆆 auroracolony.org

🏕 **Champoeg State Heritage Area**
Rte 99 W, 12 miles (7.5 km) west of Aurora. **Tel** (503) 678-1251. **Open** dawn–dusk daily. 📷 🅿️

Picturesque cottages in Aurora's National Historic District

Shopping in Portland

One of the many pleasures of shopping in Portland is the fact that no state sales tax is levied. Another is the convenient location of the city's commercial areas in or near downtown. Portland has its share of nationally known department stores and chains, but it also has many specialty shops, often selling locally manufactured goods.

Shopping Districts

Downtown, near Pioneer Courthouse Square, is the city's main shopping district. Major department stores are here, as are jewelry and clothing stores, and other specialty shops. In Nob Hill, Northwest 23rd Avenue west of Burnside is lined with an eclectic mix of chic and trendy shops specializing in home furnishings, clothing, gifts, and gourmet foods. The Pearl District (see pp58–9) has a concentration of commercial galleries, along with shops offering designer furniture and wares.

In Sellwood (see p78), antique stores line Southeast 13th Avenue. A funky counterculture holds sway on nearby Southeast Hawthorne Boulevard (see p78), with book, music, and vintage clothing shops. At Portland Saturday Market (see p58), over 300 artisans gather on weekends to sell their work.

Sign atop one of the unique Made in Oregon stores

established in Seattle in 1901 as a shoe store, is well-known for its quality clothing for men, women, and children and superb service, while **Bridgeport Village** has about 90 shops and restaurants, as well as a movie theater. More than 70 upscale retailers are housed in the three-level **Pioneer Place**. The 200 stores in **Lloyd Center** encircle an ice-skating rink.

Specialty Shops

Specializing in items "made, caught, or grown" in the state, such as local jams and preserves, and smoked salmon, **Made in Oregon** also stocks a selection of products from the Pendleton Woolen Mills (see p115), as does the **Portland Pendleton Shop**.

An excellent selection of wines produced from the bounty of the state's many acclaimed vineyards is to be found at **Oregon Wines on Broadway**. There is a wine bar adjacent to the shop. **Columbia Sportswear** specializes in athletic wear made in the Pacific Northwest. Portland's very own **Norm Thompson** carries classic casual and outdoor clothing with a Pacific Northwest look. It also has a highly successful worldwide mail-order business.

Powell's City of Books (see p59), with its inventory of over

Gallery art on a First Thursday

Department Stores and Shopping Centers

Founded in 1857, Meier & Frank is these days known as **Macy's**, an upscale store selling everything from beauty products to housewares. **Nordstrom**,

Wares of all kinds on display at the popular Portland Saturday Market

one million new and used books, is said to be the world's largest independent bookstore.

What to Buy

Wine connoisseurs will enjoy the offerings of Oregon's vineyards, and coffee lovers the artisan-roasted single origin beans by Portland's Stumptown. Smoked salmon and oysters from Oregon waters also rank high among local delicacies. A wool blanket or plaid shirt or scarf from Oregon's famed Pendleton Woolen Mills (see p115) is high on the list of popular gifts, as is Native American art, such as masks, carvings, and jewelry.

DIRECTORY

Department Stores and Shopping Centers

Bridgeport Village
7455 SW Bridgeport Rd.
Tel (503) 968-1704.

Lloyd Center
NE Multnomah St & NE 9th Ave.
Tel (503) 282-2511.

Macy's
621 SW 5th Ave. **Map** 1 C5.
Tel (503) 223-0512.

Nordstrom
701 SW Broadway. **Map** 1 C5.
Tel (503) 224-6666.

Pioneer Place
700 SW 5th Ave. **Map** 1 C5.
Tel (503) 228-5800.

Specialty Shops

Columbia Sportswear
911 SW Broadway. **Map** 1 C5.
Tel (503) 226-6800.

Made in Oregon
Suite 1300, 340 SW Morrison St.
Map 1 C5. **Tel** (503) 241-3630.
(One of several locations.)

Norm Thompson
Tel (503) 614-4600.
Ⓦ normthompson.com

Oregon Wines on Broadway
515 SW Broadway. **Map** 1 C5.
Tel (503) 228-4655.

Portland Pendleton Shop
900 SW 5th Ave. **Map** 3 C1.
Tel (503) 242-0037.

Powell's City of Books
1005 W Burnside St. **Map** 1 B4.
Tel (503) 228-4651.

Entertainment in Portland

Portland has a vibrant and growing cultural scene. The performing arts thrive in the many venues located throughout the city, with theater and music offerings being especially plentiful. And, of course, Portland has its fair share of big-ticket rock concerts and professional sports matches.

Information

Portland has become the first US city to launch a "Twisitor Center," a virtual visitor center, Travel Portland (www.travel portland.com). Twitter technology is used to connect travelers with those who can answer their questions and help plan their trips.

The free weekly *Willamette Week* newspaper runs comprehensive entertainment listings. The *Oregonian*, the city's major daily, prints listings in its Friday edition. The Travel Portland website also provides information on events around town.

Buying Tickets

Tickets for many events can be purchased by phone or in person from **Ticketmaster** and **Tickets West**.

Free Events

Every Wednesday at noon, **The Old Church** *(see p66)* hosts a free organ concert. Free noontime concerts are also held at **Pioneer Courthouse Square** *(see p64)*.

During summer, the Amphitheater at **Oregon Zoo** *(see p77)* is the setting for concerts several nights a week (tickets can be booked through Ticketmaster).

Theater

Topping the list of Portland's theater troupes are the **Artists**

The modern Moda Center, in the Rose Quarter complex

The façade of the Portland'5 Centers for the Arts

Repertory Theatre, the oldest theater group in the city; **Portland Center Stage**, with a repertoire of classic and contemporary plays; and the **Miracle Theatre Group**, which is dedicated to the Hispanic arts and community.

Dance

Based at the **Portland'5 Centers for the Arts**, the **Oregon Ballet Theatre** performs classical and contemporary pieces, including *The Nutcracker* during the holiday season and new works showcased in late spring.

Music

The oldest symphony orchestra on the West Coast, the **Oregon Symphony** has garnered considerable praise under conductor and music director Carlos Kalmar. The **Portland Baroque Orchestra** presents a program of early music, fall through spring, while the **Portland Opera** stages five works a year.

The **Crystal Ballroom**, opened in 1920, hosts popular musical acts; it is famous for its "floating" dance floor, which rests on ball bearings.

DIRECTORY

Ticket Outlets

Ticketmaster
Tel (503) 224-4400.

Tickets West
Tel (503) 224-8499.

Theater

Artists Repertory Theatre
Tel (503) 241-1278.

Miracle Theatre Group
Tel (503) 236-7253.

Portland Center Stage
Tel (503) 445-3700.

Dance

Oregon Ballet Theatre
Tel (503) 222-5538.

Portland'5 Centers for the Arts
Tel (503) 248-4335.

Music

Crystal Ballroom
Tel (503) 225-0047.

Jimmy Mak's Bar & Grill
Tel (503) 295-6542.

Oregon Symphony
Tel (503) 228-1353.

Portland Baroque Orchestra
Tel (503) 222-6000.

Portland Opera
Tel (503) 241-1802.

Sports Venues

Moda Center
Tel (503) 235-8771.

Providence Park
Tel (503) 553-5400.

A favored jazz haunt of locals is **Jimmy Mak's Bar & Grill** in the Pearl District, where world-class jazz can be enjoyed. Music can be accompanied by Greek and Middle Eastern cuisine.

Spectator Sports

The **Moda Center**, part of the Rose Quarter complex *(see p73)*, is home to the Portland Trail Blazers basketball team and Portland Winterhawks hockey team.

Fans can watch the Portland Timbers play soccer at the handsomely renovated **Providence Park**.

Getting Around Portland

The results of Portland's efforts to prevent urban sprawl and congestion are noticeable in the compact metropolis. It is easy to navigate Central Portland on foot, while public transportation is readily available. The extensive bus, light rail, and streetcar systems put most places within easy reach.

Old-fashioned streetcar near Jamison Square

Bicycle parked on a Portland downtown street, a common sight

Street Layout

The Willamette River, which is spanned by 12 downtown bridges, divides Portland into east and west. Burnside Street bisects the city into north and south. As a result, Portland is divided into quadrants, reflected in street addresses, most of which begin with a "Northwest," "North-east," "Southwest," or "Southeast."

Avenues in Portland are numbered and run north–south; streets are named and run east–west. The streets north of Burnside run alphabetically, making them easy to find – for example, Couch is next to Burnside and Davis is next to Couch. South of Burnside, however, street names run in a random order. Street numbers that are odd are usually on the west and north sides; even numbers, usually on the east and south.

Several highways crisscross Portland. The I-5, the main West Coast north–south route, runs through the city, while the I-84 runs from the east bank of the Willamette River east toward Idaho and beyond. The I-205 forms a perimeter around the city's outskirts and runs by the airport; the I-405 loops around the southern and western edges of downtown.

Walking

Portland's downtown is so compact that it is easy to get almost anywhere on foot, and walkways on some bridges make most eastside neighbor-hoods accessible to pedestrians. Powell's City of Books (see p59) offers a free walking map. Maps are also available at **Travel Portland**, at Pioneer Courthouse Square (see p64).

Bicycling

Portland is a bicycle-friendly city. Bikes are permitted on public transit, most public buses are equipped with bike racks, and many streets have designated bicycle lanes.

Helmets are mandatory for cyclists under 16 years of age, and all cyclists who ride after dark must equip their bicycles with a red reflector that can be seen from the rear and a flashing white light that is visible from ahead. The **Bicycle Transportation Alliance**, a cycling advocacy group, provides route maps and other useful cycling information.

Taxis

Taxis do not cruise the streets in Portland looking for fares as they do in many other cities. You can find a cab outside major downtown hotels or call one of the city's taxi companies. Fares can be paid with major credit cards.

Public Transit

The Portland transportation authority, **Tri-Met**, provides three types of public transit: light rail, buses, and streetcars.

All require a validated ticket, bus transfer receipt, or pass. Ticket machines and validators are located at the station. Before boarding, buy your ticket from a ticket machine or with the mobile ticketing app – or validate a previously purchased ticket in the validator located near the ticket machine. A validated ticket is good for 2 hours on MAX, buses, and Portland Streetcars.

The Metro Area Express (MAX) light rail system serves the Portland metropolitan area. Its blue-line trains run through downtown between Hillsboro in the west and Gresham in the east, while the red line connects downtown with the airport. The yellow line runs across north Portland, from the Rose Quarter to the Expo Center, while the orange line runs from Union Station to Milwaukee. The green line connects Union Station to Portland State University.

A MAX train servicing Portland's historic Old Town

Trains run roughly every 10 to 15 minutes, with a reduced late-night schedule.

Most Tri-Met bus routes include stops along the downtown transit malls on 5th and 6th Avenues, from which many downtown attractions are an easy walk.

The Portland Streetcar North/ South (NS) line travels through central Portland and makes many stops along 10th and 11th Avenues. At the south waterfront it connects with the Aerial tram, which takes passengers to Oregon Health and Science University. The other two lines run around the Central City in clockwise and counter-clockwise loops over the Broadway Bridge and the Tilikum Crossing *(see p67).*

The fare on MAX trains, buses, and streetcars varies depending on the distance traveled. There are three zones; the adult fare for one zone is $2.50, while a day pass is $5. The fare is reduced for seniors and for children aged 7 to 17. As many as three children under age 7 can ride for free when accompanied by an adult. Transfers are free and allow for interchangeable travel on the three forms of transit. Books of 10 tickets are available at a discount. All-day tickets offering unlimited rides anywhere in the system and 7-, 14-, and 30-day passes are also available. MAX tickets must be validated at one of the machines located throughout the trains.

Tri-Met buses, MAX trains, and Portland Streetcars all accommodate passengers with disabilities.

Driving

Compared with many other cities, Portland is relatively easy to drive in. Some of the major arteries out of downtown – such as US 26 West, I-84, I-85, and Macadam Boulevard – can become congested between 5 and 6pm, but at most other times, barring accidents and road work, traffic flows easily.

The many one-way streets downtown ease traffic congestion. Cars are prohibited

Portland Streetcar at the Portland State University Station

on parts of 5th and 6th Avenues designated as transit malls, which accommodate public trains and buses. It is legal to make a right turn on a red light, but only after coming to a full stop.

Speed limits are generally 25 mph (40 km/h) in residential areas, and 20 mph (32 km/h) in business and school districts. Drivers and passengers are required to wear seat belts and motorcyclists must wear helmets.

If you need assistance, maps, or guidebooks, contact the local office of the **American Automobile Association (AAA)**.

Parking

Metered street parking is available downtown, but the ease of finding a space greatly depends on the time of day. The parking time permitted varies from 15 minutes to 3 hours, 1 hour being the norm. An economical alternative is one of the many SmartPark garages.

On most downtown streets, the city has introduced a park-and-display system. Machines accept payment in cash or by credit card and issue a ticket – valid for up to 3 hours, depending

Union Station, with its prominent tower, welcoming train passengers

on the amount paid – to be displayed on the inside of the windshield. Metered parking is generally in effect Monday through Saturday, from 8am to 7pm, and Sunday from 1pm to 7pm, excluding state holidays.

Towing

Parking wardens are a vigilant presence on downtown streets. Check posted street parking rules, as they may limit parking during rush hours or specify other regulations, such as stopping being permitted only to load or unload. If your car has been towed, call the **Portland Police Auto Records Department**. A processing fee and towing charge will be levied.

DIRECTORY

Useful Numbers

American Automobile Association (AAA)
Tel (800) 222-4357. W aaa.com

Bicycle Transportation Alliance
Tel (503) 226-0676.
W btaoregon.org

Portland Police Auto Records Department
Tel (503) 823-0044.

Travel Portland
Tel (503) 275-9750 or (877) 678-5263. W travelportland.com

Tri-Met Customer Service
Tel (503) 238-7433.
W trimet.org

Taxis

Broadway Cab
Tel (503) 333-3333.

Radio Cab
Tel (503) 227-1212.

PORTLAND STREET FINDER

The key map below shows the area of Portland covered by the *Street Finder* maps, which can be found on the following pages. Map references for sights, hotels, restaurants, shops, and entertainment venues given throughout the Portland chapter of this guide refer to the grid on the maps. The first figure in the reference indicates which map to turn to (1 to 4), and the letter and number that follow refer to the grid reference on that map.

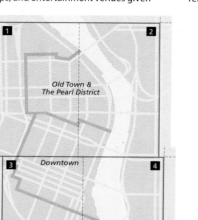

Key

- ▨ Sight
- ▨ Station building
- ▤ Train station
- ▤ Bus station – long-distance
- ▤ Streetcar stop
- ▤ MAX Light Rail stop
- *i* Information
- ✚ Hospital
- ✝ Church
- ══ Railroad line

Scale of maps 1–4

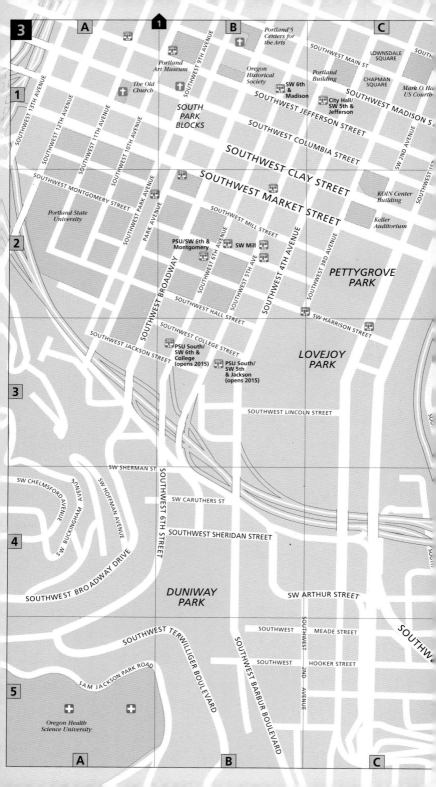

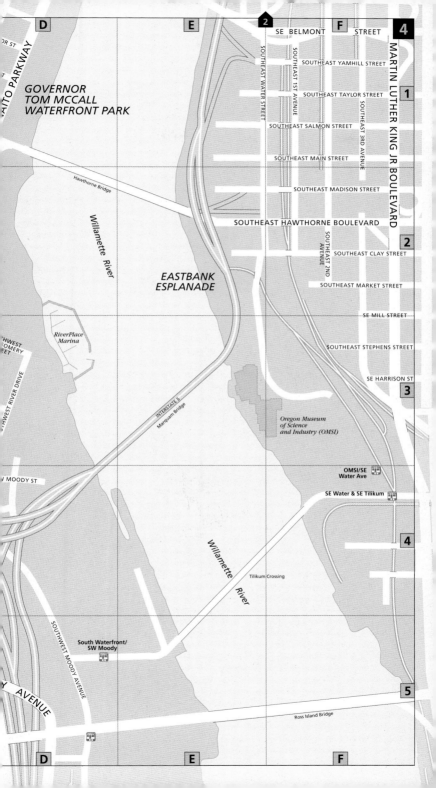

OREGON

Oregonians and their visitors alike run out of adjectives to describe the scenic wonders contained within the 97,000 sq miles (251,200 sq km) of the tenth largest US state. Here, snowcapped mountains pierce the clouds, waves break on rocky shores, rivers sprint through gorges, dense forests cling to ravines, and desert vistas stretch beneath skies that, indeed, are not cloudy all day.

A forest-cloaked headland, tidal estuary, or stretch of isolated beach appears around every bend of the 363-mile (584-km) Oregon coastline. In the north, the mighty Columbia River flows through a magnificent gorge where waterfalls plummet from cliffs. Those traveling alongside the river follow in the footsteps of explorers Lewis and Clark, who canoed the rushing waters in 1805. The Snake River, a tributary of the Columbia River, tumbles through inhospitable desert at the bottom of 8,000-ft (2,440-m) Hells Canyon, the deepest gorge in North America.

Looking at such rugged landscapes, it is easy to imagine the hardships hundreds of thousands of pioneers encountered as they migrated west along the Oregon Trail. Then, of course, there are the mountains – the Coast range taking shape above coastal headlands, the Cascades, peaks soaring above the central valleys, the Wallowas and Blues rising from high

desert country in the east. These landscapes provide more than memorable views. Hiking trails lace the forests, and rushing white-water rivers, such as the Rogue and Deschutes, brim with trout, salmon, and sturgeon, attracting white-water rafters and anglers. Lakes sparkle with crystal-clear water; the most awesome of them, Crater Lake, is the deepest in North America. And the slopes of Mount Hood are covered with snow – and skiers – all year.

Oregon serves up cosmopolitan pleasures, too. Portlanders are quick to claim their city as one of the most sophisticated and cultured anywhere. But even out-of-the-way places, such as Ashland, of Shakespeare Festival fame, stage notable events.

Wherever a traveler goes in Oregon, or whatever they do, the glimmer of a distant mountain peak and the scent of pine in the air will add an extra zest to the experience.

Cowboys in the sagebrush-dotted ranching settlement of Jordan Valley

◄ Imnaha River carving its way through Canyon, Hells Canyon Recreation Area, Oregon

Exploring Oregon

Travelers in Oregon will find that almost any drive inevitably takes them through beautiful landscapes. From Portland, day trips can easily be made to the Columbia River Gorge and Mount Hood, to the north and central coasts, and to the wine country and historic towns of the Willamette Valley. From the Pacific beaches, breathtakingly scenic drives lead across the Coast Range to Bend and central Oregon, and from there through pine forests and high desert country to such natural wonders as Crater Lake, Steens Mountain, and Hells Canyon.

Bybee-Howell House, a Sauvie Island landmark, northwest of Portland

Sights at a Glance

2. Astoria
3. Cannon Beach
4. Tillamook
5. Three Capes Scenic Route
6. Lincoln City
7. Newport
8. Yachats
9. Cape Perpetua Scenic Area
10. Florence
11. Oregon Dunes National Recreation Area
12. Bandon
14. McMinnville
15. Silverton
16. Salem
17. Eugene
18. Madras and Warm Springs
19. Sisters
20. Smith Rock State Park
21. Bend
22. Newberry National Volcanic Monument
25. Oregon Caves National Monument
26. Jacksonville
27. Ashland
29. Jordan Valley
30. Malheur National Wildlife Refuge
31. John Day Fossil Beds National Monument
32. Pendleton
34. Joseph
35. Wallowa Lake

Tours

1. *Columbia River Gorge and Mount Hood pp94–95*
13. *Wine Country of the North Willamette Valley pp102–3*
23. *Cascade Lakes Highway pp108–9*
24. *Crater Lake National Park pp110–11*
28. *Steens Mountain p113*
33. *Elkhorn Drive National Scenic Byway pp116–17*
36. *Hells Canyon National Recreation Area pp118–19*

tting Around

running north–south, and I-84, running
t to Idaho and the Midwest, are
gon's two major routes. Hwy 26 runs
ough lovely landscape from the coast
oss Mount Hood into eastern Oregon.
y 101 follows the coast; Hwy 97,
other scenic north–south route, skirts
Cascade Mountains and Crater Lake.
ving is the most convenient way to
vel in Oregon. Amtrak offers three train
tes: one east to Chicago, two along the
st. Bus service is limited.

Hood River, a small town on the Columbia River Gorge

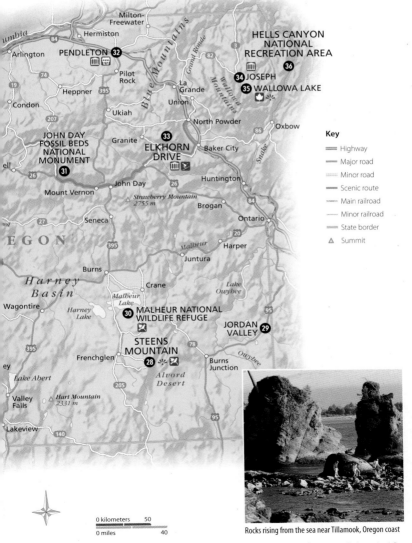

Key

- ▬▬ Highway
- ▬▬ Major road
- ▭▭▭ Minor road
- ▬▬ Scenic route
- ⌐⌐ Main railroad
- ‐‐‐ Minor railroad
- ▬▬ State border
- △ Summit

Rocks rising from the sea near Tillamook, Oregon coast

For keys to symbols *see back flap*

❶ Columbia River Gorge and Mount Hood Driving Tour

This easy outing from Portland encompasses a diverse sampling of Oregon scenery, including the banks of the Columbia River as it flows through a magnificent gorge and the spectacular summit of Mount Hood. Along the way, the route takes in five waterfalls, the bountiful orchards that surround the Hood River, and picturesque Timberline Lodge. Other features of this tour include scenic overlooks, rushing streams, mountain lakes, enormous glaciers, and dense forests.

③ **Oneonta Gorge**
Hardier hikers will enjoy walking through this dramatic gorge. It can also be viewed at the south end of a trail starting in Horsetail Falls.

④ **Bonneville Dam**
A tour of this 1930s dam reveals massive hydroelectric powerhouses, as well as underwater views of migrating salmon, and a fish hatchery.

② **Multnomah Falls**
The fourth-highest waterfall in the US tumbles 620 ft (188 m) in two picturesque cascades.

① **Vista House**
This historic, octagonal structure perched high above the river offers breathtaking views of the gorge and mountains.

⑪ **Timberline Lodge**
Artisans hired by the federal Works Project Administration crafted every detail of this beautiful 1930s ski lodge, from the wrought-iron door handles to its massive wood beams.

0 kilometers   15
0 miles   10

Key
= Tour route
= Other road

⑤ Ruthton Point
This cape situated in a small state park makes a perfect stopping-off point from which to view the mighty Columbia River Gorge and the surrounding Cascade mountain range.

Tips for Drivers

Tour length: 146 miles (235 km).
Starting point: I-84 in Portland.
Stopping-off points: The most scenic places to enjoy a meal are the two historic lodges on the loop, one at Multnomah Falls in the gorge and the other at Timberline atop Mount Hood. At both, salmon, trout, and other fresh Pacific Northwest cuisine can be enjoyed in front of a blazing hearth.

⑥ Hood River
Winds and river currents create the ideal conditions that render this riverside town the wind-surfing capital of the world. Landlubbers enjoy the bounty of local fruit orchards.

⑨ **Parkdale** This pretty little town on the eastern slopes of Mount Hood is the terminus of the Mount Hood Railroad, which passes through apple and pear orchards to Hood River.

⑦ Historic Columbia River Highway
Blasted out of the steep cliffs and opened in 1915, this narrow road was designed to maximize the view, yet limit environmental damage as much as possible.

⑧ Hood River Valley
This beautiful and fertile valley offers blossoming fruit trees in season and magnificent views of majestic Mount Hood throughout the year.

⑩ Barlow Pass
Wheel tracks still rut this section of the Oregon Trail, which is so steep that wagons were often lowered down the hills with ropes.

For keys to symbols *see back flap*

The Astoria Column, with a scenic lookout of the port at its top

❷ Astoria

Road map 1 A3. 🗺 9,500.
ℹ 111 W Marine Dr, (800) 875-6807.
ⓦ oldoregon.com

Throughout the damp winter of 1805–1806, explorers Lewis and Clark *(see p41)* passed the time making moccasins, preserving fish, and recording in their journals accounts of bear attacks and the almost continual rain at a crude stockade near Astoria. This stockade at **Lewis and Clark National Historical Park – Fort Clatsop Unit** was rebuilt again after the first replica was destroyed by fire in 2005. In 1811, John Jacob Astor sent fur traders around Cape Horn to establish a trading post in this location at the mouth of the Columbia River, making Astoria the oldest American settlement west of the Rocky Mountains.

These days, the town is a major port for fishing fleets and commercial vessels; its Victorian homes climb a hillside above the river. One such home, the stately **Captain George Flavel House Museum**, retains the cupola from which the captain and his wife once observed river traffic. An even better view can be enjoyed from atop the 164-step spiral staircase of the **Astoria Column**, encircled with bas-relief friezes paying homage to the region's past – from the Native Americans to the arrival of the Great Northern Railway in 1892.

The town honors its seagoing past at the **Columbia River Maritime Museum**, where riverside galleries house fishing dories and Native American dugout canoes. The lightship *Columbia*, berthed in front, once guided ships across the treacherous mouth of the river – where more than 200 shipwrecks in the past century have earned for local waters the moniker "graveyard of the Pacific."

One of the town's most popular attractions is the historic 1913 **Astoria Riverfront Trolley**. The restored "Old 300" streetcar runs on original railroad tracks from East End Mooring Basin to West End Mooring Basin. This 3-mile (5-km) route provides great views, and covers docks, piers, shops, and restaurants along Astoria's historic waterfront. It is also possible to spot sea lions and seals lounging around on the docks. Despite their popularity with tourists, the sea lions pose concerns for town officials because of the noise they make and the fact that they steal a significant proportion of local fishermen's catch.

Locals and visitors alike gather at the lively **Astoria Sunday Market** held in downtown Astoria, which features up to 200 farmers, craftspeople, and artisans who sell locally made, grown, or gathered products. There is also live music and a food court.

Art walks take place every second Saturday in the evening in downtown Astoria. The venues, highlighted with colorful pinwheels, exhibit original works of art and culture, while businesses stay open late to provide food and entertainment.

🏛 **Lewis and Clark National Historical Park – Fort Clatsop Unit**
6 miles (10 km) southwest of Astoria, off Hwy 101. **Tel** (503) 861-2471. **Open** 9am–6pm daily (Labor Day–mid-Jun: to 5pm). **Closed** Dec 25. 🅿 ♿ 🛍

🏛 **Captain George Flavel House Museum**
441 8th St. **Tel** (503) 325-2203. **Open** May–Sep: 10am–5pm daily; Oct–Apr: 11am–4pm daily. **Closed** Jan 1, Thanksgiving, Dec 24 & 25. 🅿

🏛 **Astoria Column**
Atop Coxcomb Hill, off 16th St.
Tel (503) 325-2963. **Open** dawn–dusk daily. ⓦ astoriacolumn.org

🏛 **Columbia River Maritime Museum**
1792 Marine Dr. **Tel** (503) 325-2323. **Open** 9:30am–5pm daily. **Closed** Thanksgiving, Dec 25. 🅿 🛍 ⓦ crmm.org

🚋 **Astoria Riverfront Trolley**
480 Industry St. **Tel** (503) 861-5365. **Open** Memorial Day–Labor Day: noon–6pm daily, weather permitting; Labor Day–Memorial Day: check website for times. 🅿 ⓦ old300.org

🛒 **Astoria Sunday Market**
Commercial St & 12th St. **Tel** (503) 325-1010. **Open** May–Oct: Sun.
ⓦ astoriasundaymarket.com

Environs
Fort Stevens State Park, 10 miles (16 km) west of Astoria, dates back to the Civil War, when it guarded the Columbia River from Confederate incursions. The only time the fort saw action was on June 21, 1942, when a Japanese submarine fired 17 rounds toward the concrete bunkers that were still buried in the dunes.

The Astoria Riverfront Trolley, which runs along the Columbia River

🏕 **Fort Stevens State Park**
Off Hwy 101. **Tel** (503) 861-1671.
Open dawn–dusk daily. **Closed**
Dec 25. 🅿 🏕 🅦 visitftstevens.com

❸ Cannon Beach

Road map 1 A3. 🏔 1,600. 🛈 2nd &
Spruce Sts, (503) 436-2623.
🅦 cannonbeach.org

Despite its status as Oregon's
favorite beach town, Cannon
Beach retains a great deal of
quiet charm. The surrounding
forests grow almost up to
Hemlock Street, where buildings
clad with weathered cedar
shingles house art galleries.

Haystack Rock, one of the
tallest coastal monoliths in
the world, towers 235 ft (72 m)
above a long beach and tidal
pools teeming with life.

Ecola State Park, at the beach's
north end, carpets Tillamook
Head, an 1,100-ft (335-m) basalt
headland, with forests accessible
via Tillamook Head Trail. Viewpoints look across raging surf
to **Tillamook Rock Lighthouse**,
built in 1880 and soon known as
"Terrible Tillie," as waves, logs, and
rocks continually washed through
the structure. Decommissioned
in 1957, the lighthouse is now
a private mortuary. Tillamook
Rock, a wildlife refuge closed to
the public, is home to nesting
murres and cormorants.

🏕 **Ecola State Park**
2 miles (3 km) north of Cannon Beach,
off Hwy 101. **Tel** (503) 436-2844.
Open dawn–dusk daily. 🅿

❹ Tillamook

Road map 1 A3. 🏔 4,600.
🛈 3705 Hwy 101 N, (503) 842-7525.
🅦 gotillamook.com

Tillamook sits about 10 miles
(16 km) inland from the sea in
rich bottomland fed by five
rivers that empty into Tillamook
Bay. Green pastures, nurtured by
more than 70 inches (178 cm) of
rain a year, sustain 40,000 cows
that supply milk for the historic
**Tillamook County Creamery
Association**, commonly known
as "The Cheese Factory". Here,
visitors can view the facilities and

Packaging cheese at the Tillamook County
Creamery Association

sample its output of 78 million
lb (35 million kg) of cheese per
year, including smoked cheddar
and pepper jack.

During World War II, Tillamook
was the base for giant blimps
that patrolled the coast for
Japanese submarines. One of
the hangars – at 1,100 ft (335 m)
long and 15 stories tall the
largest wood structure in the
world – houses the **Tillamook
Air Museum**, which boasts a
fine collection of flying boats,
early helicopters, and some 30
other restored vintage aircraft.

**Tillamook County
Creamery Association**
4175 Hwy 101 N. **Tel** (503) 815-1300.
Open mid-Jun–Labor Day: 8am–8pm
daily; Labor Day–mid-Jun: 8am–6pm
daily. **Closed** Thanksgiving, Dec 25.
🏕 🅦 tillamook.com

🏛 **Tillamook Air Museum**
6030 Hangar Rd. **Tel** (503) 842-1130.
Open 9am–5pm daily. **Closed**
Thanksgiving, Dec 25. 🅿 ♿ 🖥 🏕
🅦 tillamookair.com

❺ Three Capes Scenic Route

Road map 1 A3. Oregon State Parks
Association: **Tel** (800) 551-6949.
🅦 oregonstateparks.org

Along this 35-mile (56-km)
loop that follows the marshy
shores of Tillamook Bay,
roadside markers recount
the fate of Bayocean, a resort
that thrived in the early 20th
century but was washed away
in winter storms. For most of
the drive, though, nature is
the main attraction.

The rocks below **Cape Meares
State Scenic Viewpoint** and
Cape Meares Lighthouse are
home to one of the largest
colonies of nesting seabirds in
North America. In **Cape Lookout
State Park**, trails pass through
old-growth forests to clifftop
viewpoints – good places to
spot migrating gray whales –
and to a sand spit between the
ocean and Netarts Bay. This is
also a popular camping area,
with campsites, cabins, and
yurts. In the **Cape Kiwanda
Natural Area**, waves crash into
massive sandstone cliffs and
offshore rock formations. The
beach along the cape draws
surfers as well as fishermen.
Pacific City, at the route's south
end, is home to a fleet of fishing
dories that daringly ply the surf
on their way out to sea.

The **Oregon State Parks
Association** provides detailed
information about the sights
along this stunning route.

Impressive sandstone cliffs at Cape Kiwanda Natural Area, along the Three Cape Scenic Route

Colorful kites at one of Lincoln City's many kite shops

❻ Lincoln City

Road map 1 A3. 🚇 8,000. 🛈 4039 NW Logan Rd, (541) 994-3070. 🆆 oregoncoast.org

In 1965, five individual communities united to form one town called Lincoln City. Situated along Highway 101, the long city boasts several natural attractions. Formerly called Devil's River, the D River flows only 120 ft (36 m) – from Devil's Lake to the Pacific Ocean – making it the world's shortest river. The 7.5-mile- (12-km-) long beach, littered with driftwood and agates, is popular with kite enthusiasts, who enjoy the strong winds off the sea.

To the north, the steep cliffs of **Cascade Head Preserve** rise out of the surf, then give way to mossy rainforests of Sitka spruce and hemlock and a maritime grassland prairie. Many rare plants and animals, including the Oregon silverspot butterfly, thrive in the preserve, which can be explored on steep but well-maintained trails.

🌲 **Cascade Head Preserve**
2 miles (3 km) north of Lincoln City, off Hwy 101. **Tel** (503) 230-1221. Lower trail: **Open** dawn–dusk daily. Upper trail: **Open** mid-Jul–Dec.

Environs
At Depoe Bay, a little fishing port 12 miles (19 km) south of Lincoln City, rough seas blast through narrow channels in the basalt rock, creating geyser-like plumes that shoot as high as

60 ft (18 m). A local amusement is watching the fishing fleet "shoot the hole," or navigate the narrow channel that cuts through sheer rock walls between the sea and the tiny inland harbor, which lays claim to being the smallest navigable harbor in the world.

More excitement may be in store at the Otter Crest State Scenic Viewpoint atop Cape Foul-weather, so named by Captain James Cook in 1778 because of the 100-mph (160-km/h) winds that regularly buffet it. This promontory provides an excellent view of the adjacent **Devil's Punchbowl State Natural Area**, where the foaming sea thunders into rocky hollows formed by the collapse of sea caves. Tidal pools on the rocky shore below are known as marine gardens because of the colorful sea urchins and starfish that inhabit them. The park is a popular whale-watching site.

Fish market sign in Newport

🔵 **Devil's Punchbowl State Natural Area**
15 miles (24 km) south of Lincoln City, off Hwy 101. **Tel** (800) 551-6949. **Open** dawn–dusk daily.

❼ Newport

Road map 1 A3. 🚇 10,000. 🛈 555 SW Coast Hwy, (800) 262-7844. 🆆 discovernewport.com

This salty old port on Yaquina Bay is home to the largest commercial fishing fleet on the Oregon coast and supports many oystering operations. The town is well accustomed to tourists, too. Shingled resort cottages in the Nye Beach neighborhood date from the 1880s, and in the late 1990s travelers came from around the world to visit Keiko, an orca whale that resided in the internationally renowned **Oregon Coast Aquarium** and gained stardom in the *Free Willy* films. Keiko left the aquarium in 1998. The place is still popular, however, with plenty to see and experience. Surf Perch, Pacific Cod, and flounders swim around pier pilings in the Sandy Shores exhibit, jellyfish float through the Coastal Waters exhibit, and Wolf Eels peek out of crevices along the Rocky Shores gallery. In Passages of the Deep, sharks and rays swim in an 800,000-gallon (3,028,329-liter) tank overhead, and alongside in glass viewing tunnels. Outdoors, tufted puffins and murres fly through North America's largest seabird aviary, and sea otters, sea lions, and seals frolic in saltwater pools.

Picturesque fishing boats moored in Newport's harbor

At the **Hatfield Marine Science Center**, headquarters of Oregon State University's marine research programs, thoughtful exhibits encourage visitors to explore oceanic science in many fascinating ways, from viewing plankton through a microscope to spotting patterns of sand buildup in time-lapse photography. An octopus that occupies the first large tank near the entrance is referred to as the "tentacled receptionist." It draws large crowds at feeding times, when the tank lid is open.

Yaquina Head Outstanding Natural Area, a narrow finger of lava that juts into the Pacific Ocean on the north end of town, makes it easy to watch marine animals in their natural habitats. Platforms at the base of the restored Yaquina Head Lighthouse are within close sight of rocks where seabirds nest. Pathways lead to the edge of tidal pools occupied by kelp crabs, sea urchins, sea anemones, sea stars, and octopi. The interpretive center looks at human and nonhuman inhabitants of the headland; shell debris attests to the presence of the former more than 4,000 years ago.

Newport's working waterfront stretches along the north side of Yaquina Bay. Here, the masts of the fishing schooners tower over shops and restaurants, and crab pots and pesky sea lions trying to steal bait are

The quiet and unspoiled shoreline near Yachats

as much of an attraction as underwater shows and wax-work replicas of sea animals.

📷 Oregon Coast Aquarium
2820 SE Ferry Slip Rd. **Tel** (541) 867-3474. **Open** Memorial Day–Labor Day: 9am–6pm daily; Labor Day–Memorial Day: 10am–5pm daily. **Closed** Dec 25. 🅿️ 🛗 📷 💻 🏛️
🌐 aquarium.org

📷 Hatfield Marine Science Center
2030 SE Marine Science Dr. **Tel** (541) 867-0100. **Open** Memorial Day–Labor Day: 10am–5pm daily; Labor Day–Memorial Day: 10am–4pm Thu–Mon. **Closed** Jan 1, Thanksgiving, Dec 25. 🅿️ by donation.
🌐 hmsc.oregonstate.edu

🏞️ Yaquina Head Outstanding Natural Area
3 miles (5 km) north of Newport, off Hwy 101. **Tel** (541) 574-3100. **Open** dawn–dusk daily. Interpretive center: 10am–4:30pm daily. Lighthouse: 10am–4pm daily (noon–4pm winter). 🅿️ 🛗

❽ Yachats

Road map 1 A3. 🚂 635. 🛈 241 Hwy 101, (541) 547-3530. 🌐 **yachats.org**

The town of Yachats (pronounced "ya-hots"), once home to the Alsea people who gave Yachats its name, is the sort of place a shore-lover dreams about: small, unspoiled, and surrounded by forested mountainsides and surf-pounded, rocky headlands. In the center of town, the Yachats River meets the sea in a little estuary shadowed by fir trees and laced with tidal pools. The rocky shoreline and a stunning sunset can be admired from the **Yachats Ocean Road State Natural Site**, a paved seaside loop on the south side of town.

🔲 Yachats Ocean Road State Natural Site
South of Yachats River, west of Hwy 100. **Tel** (800) 551-6949. **Open** dawn–dusk daily.

Shark-watching from the Oregon Coast Aquarium's suspended tunnel

Orcas

The largest members of the dolphin family, orcas are found throughout the world's oceans, especially in cold waters. They are also known as

Orcas swimming in the cold waters off the coast of Oregon

killer whales. Along the coast of the Pacific Northwest, transient orcas roam the ocean from California to Alaska in groups of up to 60 whales. Resident orcas, on the other hand, remain faithful to a given location; up to 300, organized into matrilinear pods, live off Vancouver Island in summer.

Heceta Head Lighthouse, near Cape Perpetua, in operation since 1894

❾ Cape Perpetua Scenic Area

Road map 1 A4. Interpretive center: 2400 Hwy 101. **Tel** (541) 547-3289. **Open** dawn–dusk daily. **Closed** Christmas, New Year's Day. 🌐 ♿

Part of the Siuslaw National Forest, Cape Perpetua is the highest – albeit often cloud-shrouded – viewpoint on the coast. A road ascends to the top at 800 ft (245 m), but those with time and stamina may prefer to make the climb on trails that wind through the old-growth rainforests from the interpretive center. An easy hike of about a mile (1.5 km) along the Giant Spruce Trail leads to a majestic, 500-year-old Sitka spruce.

From Cape Perpetua, Highway 101 descends into **Heceta Head State Park**, where trails offer spectacular ocean views. Birds nest on the rocks and sea lions and gray whales swim just off-shore. High above the surf rises Heceta Head Lighthouse, first lit in 1894 with a beacon that can be seen 21 miles (34 km) out to sea. Guided tours are likely to include imaginative accounts of hauntings by the wife of a light-keeper; despite this ghostly presence, the lightkeeper's house is a popular bed-and-breakfast.

A herd of Steller sea lions inhabits the **Sea Lion Caves**, the only rookery for wild sea lions found on the North American mainland. An elevator descends 208 ft (63.5 m) from the clifftop

to platforms near the floor of the 12-story cavern. Some 200 animals live in the cave during fall and winter; in spring and summer they breed on rock ledges just outside the entrance, where they also bear and nurse their young. Burly bulls weighing up to 2,000 lb (900 kg) boister-ously guard groups of 15 to 30 cows and the newborn pups.

🚗 Heceta Head State Park

Hwy 101, 19 miles (30.5 km) south of Yachats. **Tel** (541) 547-3696. **Open** dawn–dusk daily. Lighthouse: 🌐 ♿ Memorial Day–Labor Day: 11am–5pm daily; Labor Day–Memorial Day: call for times.

🦭 Sea Lion Caves

91560 Hwy 101 N, 11 miles (17.5 km) north of Florence. **Tel** (541) 547-3111. **Open** 9am–dusk daily. **Closed** Thanksgiving, Dec 25. 🌐 ♿
W sealioncaves.com

❿ Florence

Road map 1 A4. 🏙 8,200.
ℹ 290 Hwy 101, (541) 997-3128.
W florencechamber.com

It is easy to speed through Florence en route to the nearby sand dunes. The historic old town, though, tucked away along the banks of the Siuslaw River, warrants a stop. Many of its early 20th-century brick and wood buildings now house art galleries, and a sizable commercial fishing fleet docks alongside them. The fishing boats not only add a great deal of color to the surroundings but also provide the bounty that appears in the riverside fish markets and restaurants.

Fishing boats in the harbor at Florence, on the Siuslaw River

Environs

At nearby **Darlingtonia State Natural Site**, a short trail loops through a bog where Darlingtonia, also known as cobra lily, thrive. These rare, tall, carnivorous plants are reminiscent of the human-eaters of horror films. Their sweet smell traps insects, which fall to the bottom of the plant stem, where they are slowly digested.

🚗 Darlingtonia State Natural Site

5 miles (8 km) north of Florence, off Hwy 101. **Tel** (800) 551-6949. **Open** dawn–dusk daily. ♿

Dune buggy, Oregon Dunes National Recreation Area

⓫ Oregon Dunes National Recreation Area

Road map 1 A4. ℹ 855 Highway 101 South, Reedsport, (541) 750-7000. **Open** dawn–dusk daily. 🌐 **W** fs.fed.us

Massive sand dunes stretch south from Florence for 40 miles (64 km). The desert-like landscape has been created over thousands of years, as winds, tides, and ocean currents force sand as far as 2.5 miles (4 km) inland and sculpt it into towering formations that reach heights of as much as 300 ft (90 m). Not just sand but streams, lakes, shore pine forests, grasslands, and isolated beaches attract a wide variety of recre-ation enthusiasts to this area.

Boardwalks make it easy to enjoy stunning vistas from Oregon Dunes Day Use site, about 20 miles (32 km) south of Florence, whereas the 2.7-mile-(4.3-km-) John Dellenback Dunes Trail, 35 miles (56 km) south of Florence, leads to a beach over some of the area's largest dunes.

Sea stacks rising majestically from the ocean off Bandon, the lights of houses seen in the background

⑫ Bandon

Road map 1 A4. 🗺 2,900.
ℹ️ 300 2nd St, (541) 347-9616.
w bandon.com

The small town of Bandon, near the mouth of the Coquille River, is so weather-beaten, it is difficult to imagine that in the early 20th century it was a major port of call for cargo ships and passenger liners plying the route between Seattle and Los Angeles. These days, Bandon is famous for its cranberries, which are harvested in bogs north of the town.

Craggy rock formations rise from the sea just off Bandon's beach. These wind-sculpted shapes include Face Rock, allegedly an Indian maiden frozen into stone by an evil spirit. A wilder landscape of dunes and sea grass prevails at **Bullards Beach State Park**, which lies across the marshy, bird-filled Coquille Estuary from Bandon.

🏕 Bullards Beach State Park
2 miles (3 km) north of Bandon, off Hwy 101. **Tel** (541) 347-3501.
Open dawn–dusk daily.

Environs

In the early 1900s, lumber baron Louis J. Simpson built Shore Acres, an estate atop oceanside bluffs outside the town of Coos Bay, 25 miles (40 km) north of Bandon. It is now the site of **Shore Acres State Park**. Simpson enhanced this magnificent spot with formal gardens of azaleas, rhododendrons, and roses. An

enclosed observatory offers visitors a stunning view of the ocean, while interpretive panels educate them about the history of the site. Although the mansion is long gone, the gardens continue to thrive next to **Cape Arago State Park**, where seals and sea lions bask in the sun on offshore rocks.

Cape Blanco State Park, 27 miles (43 km) south of Bandon, is the westernmost point in the 48 contiguous states and one of the windiest spots on earth, with winter gusts exceeding 180 mph (290 km/h). The park's lighthouse is the oldest on the Oregon coast, having been first lit in 1870.

Highway 101 nears the California border in a stretch of dense forests, towering cliffs, and offshore rock formations. Some of the most spectacular scenery is within the boundaries of the **Samuel H. Boardman State**

Scenic Corridor, 4 miles (6.5 km) north of Brookings, a town whose claim to fame is supplying over 90 percent of the lily bulbs grown in North America.

🏕 Oregon State Parks
w oregonstateparks.org

🏕 Shore Acres State Park
Cape Arago Hwy, 13 miles (21 km) SW of Coos Bay. **Tel** (541) 888- 4902. **Open** 8am–dusk daily. 🅿️ ♿

🏕 Cape Arago State Park
End of Cape Arago Hwy, 15 miles (24 km) southwest of Coos Bay. **Tel** (800) 551-6949. **Open** dawn–dusk daily.

🏕 Cape Blanco State Park
9 miles (14.5 km) north of Port Orford, off Hwy 101. **Tel** (800) 551-6949. **Open** dawn–dusk daily. Lighthouse: **Open** Apr–Oct: 10am–3:30pm daily. 🅿️

🏕 Samuel H. Boardman State Scenic Corridor
Hwy 101, 4 miles (6.5 km) north of Brookings. **Tel** (800) 551-6949. **Open** dawn–dusk daily.

Driftwood on the beach near Bandon, looking toward the town

⓭ Wine Country of the North Willamette Valley

The rich, wet, temperate valley that surrounds the Willamette River as it flows north from Eugene to join the Columbia River has yielded a bounty of fruits and vegetables ever since Oregon Trail pioneers began farming the land in the mid-19th century. In the 1960s, the valley's soil was also found to be ideal for growing grapes, especially the pinot noir, pinot gris, and chardonnay varietals. Now, vineyards carpet the rolling hillsides, especially in Yamhill County. Though the wine country of North Willamette Valley is not as developed as that of Napa Valley, its output is arguably just as good. It is easy to conduct a taste test since dozens of wineries are conveniently located just off Highway 99 W between McMinnville and Newberg.

Farms dotting the valley slopes of Yamhill County

Typical of the valley, the lush vineyards at Domaine Serene

⑨ EIEIO & Company
The wines of many small producers whose wineries are not open to the public are available here for tasting and purchase.

⑧ Eyrie Vineyards
This pioneering winery, established in 1966, produced the Willamette Valley's first pinot noir and chardonnay and the US's first pinot gris.

⑦ Anne Amie Vineyards
The views of the Willamette Valley are one attraction of this hilltop winery; several fine white wines are another.

Yamhill

Carlton

McMinnville

Salem

0 kilometers 4
0 miles 2

③ Argyle Winery
This winery specializes in sparkling wines. The tasting room is in a picturesque Victorian farmhouse.

Tips for Drivers
Tour length: About 35 miles (56 km).
Starting point: On 99 W a few miles east of Newberg, which is 38 miles (58 km) west of Portland.
Stopping-off points: Dundee boasts many well-known restaurants, of which Tina's is arguably the star. Newberg, McMinnville, and Dayton also have good places to eat.

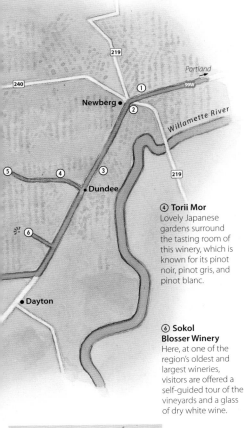

① Rex Hill Vineyards
Shady hillside gardens and an antiques-filled tasting room warmed by a fire are lovely spots to taste this winery's award-winning pinot noirs.

② Hoover-Minthorn House
An orphaned Herbert Hoover, who would become the 31st US president, came west from Iowa to live with his aunt and uncle in this handsome house in 1885, at the age of 11.

④ Torii Mor
Lovely Japanese gardens surround the tasting room of this winery, which is known for its pinot noir, pinot gris, and pinot blanc.

⑥ Sokol Blosser Winery
Here, at one of the region's oldest and largest wineries, visitors are offered a self-guided tour of the vineyards and a glass of dry white wine.

The Willamette River, meandering through the fertile North Willamette Valley

⑤ Maresh Red Hills Vineyard
Wines from Maresh vineyard grapes, custom-made by three Oregon wineries, are on offer here. The vineyard, Oregon's fifth-oldest, grows pinot noir and pinot gris, among other varietals.

Key
━━ Tour route
═══ Other road

For keys to symbols *see back flap*

Howard Hughes'"Spruce Goose" at the Evergreen Aviation & Space Museum

⓮ McMinnville

Road map 1 A3. 🚹 32,000.
🛈 417 NW Adams St, (503) 472-6196.
🌐 mcminnville.org

In this prosperous town surrounded by the Willamette Valley vineyards, the Downtown Historic District is graced by the old Oregon Hotel, McMinnville Bank, and many other late 19th- and early 20th-century buildings. The excellent reputation of ivy-clad Linfield College, chartered in 1858, has long put McMinnville on the map, but these days the university shares the honor with the "Spruce Goose." This wooden flying boat, built in the 1940s, is housed in the **Evergreen Aviation & Space Museum**, where its 320-ft (97.5-m) wingspan spreads above early passenger planes, World War II fighters, and other vintage civilian and military aircraft. There is also an indoor waterpark nearby.

🏛 Evergreen Aviation & Space Museum
460 NE Capt. Michael King Smith Way.
Tel (503) 434-4185. **Open** 9am–5pm daily. **Closed** major hols. 🅿️ ♿ 🅲
🌐 evergreenmuseum.org

⓯ Silverton

Road map 1 A3. 🚹 7,500.
🛈 426 S Water St, (503) 873-5615.
🌐 silvertonchamber.org

This pleasant old farming town in the foothills of the Cascade Mountains is the entryway to **Silver Falls State Park**, the largest state park in Oregon. The Trail of Ten Falls follows Silver Creek through a temperate rainforest

of Douglas firs, hemlocks, and cedars to the trail's cataracts; the largest, South Falls, plunges 177 ft (54 m) down a mossy cliff into a deep pool.

At the southern edge of Silverton is **The Oregon Garden**. Rising high above the groomed landscape is a magnificent stand of oaks that are over 100 years old. The **Gordon House**, set in a shady grove near the garden's entrance, is designed by renowned architect Frank Lloyd Wright.

The 1894 Deepwood Estate in Salem

🌳 Silver Falls State Park
Hwy 214, 10 miles (16 km) east of Salem. **Tel** (800) 551-6949.
Open dawn–dusk daily. 🅿️
🌐 oregonstateparks.org

🌳 The Oregon Garden
879 W Main St. **Tel** (503) 874-8100.
Open May–Sep: 10am–6pm daily; Oct–Apr: 10am–4pm daily. 🅿️ ♿ 🅲
📷 💻 🌐 oregongarden.org

⓰ Salem

Road map 1 A3. 🚹 154,500.
🛈 181 High St NE, (800) 874-7012.
🌐 travelsalem.com

Salem was a thriving trading post and lumber port on the Willamette River when it became the capital of the Oregon Territory in 1851.

At the edge of Bush's Pasture Park stands **Bush House Museum**, an 1878 home with ten marble fireplaces and a conservatory said to be the first greenhouse west of the Mississippi River, and the historic **Deepwood Estate**. The **Willamette Heritage Center** preserves some of the state's earliest structures: the 1841 home of Jason Lee, who helped found Salem; the 1847 home of state treasurer John Boon; and the Kay Woolen Mill, where waterwheels from the 1890s remain intact. The state's early history is also in evidence around the **Oregon State Capitol**. A gilded pioneer stands atop the rotunda of the building. Marble sculptures of a covered wagon and of Lewis and Clark (see p41) flank the entrance, and the murals inside depict Captain Robert Gray's discovery of the Columbia River in 1792.

On the Willamette University campus is **Waller Hall**, the oldest college building in Oregon, constructed in 1867; and the striking **Hallie Ford Museum of Art**, which houses an outstanding collection of 20th-century Native American basketry and paintings.

The Oregon State Capitol Building in Salem

🏛 Bush House Museum
600 Mission St SE. **Tel** (503) 363-4714.
Open 10am–5pm Tue–Fri, noon–5pm
Sat & Sun. **Closed** major hols. 🅿
📷 compulsory.

🏠 Deepwood Estate
1116 Mission St SE. **Tel** (503) 363-1825.
Open Grounds: dawn–dusk daily.
House: May–Sep: 9am–noon Wed–
Mon; Oct–Apr: 11am–3pm Wed,
Thu & Sat. **Closed** major hols. 🅿 📷
Ⓦ **historicdeepwoodestate.org**

🏛 Willamette Heritage Center
1313 Mill St SE. **Tel** (503) 585-7012.
Open 10am–5pm Mon–Sat. 🅿 📷
Ⓦ **willametteheritage.org**

🏛 Oregon State Capitol
900 Court St NE. **Tel** (503) 986-1388.
Open 8am–5:30pm Mon–Fri.

🏛 Waller Hall
900 State St. **Open** 8am–5pm Mon–Fri.

🏛 Hallie Ford Museum of Art
700 State St. **Tel** (503) 370-6855.
Open 10am–5pm Tue–Sat, 1–5pm
Sun. **Closed** major hols. 🅿 ♿ 📷

Bush House Museum, built in 1878,
a historic landmark in Salem

⓱ Eugene
Road map 1 A4. 🚇 160,000.
ℹ 754 Olive St, (541) 484-5307.
Ⓦ **eugenecascadescoast.org**

The University of Oregon
brings no small amount of
culture and animation to the
second-largest city in Oregon,
which straddles the banks of
the Willamette River at the
south end of the river valley.
The peak-roofed, glass-and-
timber **Hult Center for the
Performing Arts**, designed
by the New York firm Hardy
Holzman Pfeiffer Associates
and completed in 1982, is
considered to be one of the
best-designed performing arts
complexes in the world. The
**University of Oregon Museum
of Natural and Cultural History**
counts among its holdings the
world's oldest shoes – a pair of
sandals dating from 9500 BC.

Local artisans and farmers
sell their wares weekly at the
Saturday Market, a large collection of stalls on the downtown
Park Blocks; and the **5th Street
Public Market**, a collection
of shops and restaurants in
a converted feed mill, bustles with
locals and the more than 17,000
university students who make

Local arts and crafts at the Saturday Market
in Eugene

good use of the city's many
bicycle and rollerblading paths,
pedestrian malls, and parks.

🎭 Hult Center for the
Performing Arts
1 Eugene Center. **Tel** (541) 682-5000.
Ⓦ **hultcenter.org**

🏛 University of Oregon Museum
of Natural and Cultural History
1680 E 15th Ave. **Tel** (541) 346-3024.
Open 11am–5pm Wed–Sun.
Closed major hols. 📷
Ⓦ **natural-history.uoregon.edu**

🛒 Saturday Market
8th Ave & Oak St. **Tel** (541) 686-8885.
Open Apr–Nov: 10am–5pm Sat.
Ⓦ **eugenesaturdaymarket.org**

🛒 5th Street Public Market
High & 5th Sts. **Open** 10am–7pm
Mon–Sat, 11am–5pm Sun.
Ⓦ **5stmarket.com**

Salem City Center

① Bush House Museum
② Deepwood Estate
③ Willamette Heritage Center
④ Oregon State Capitol
⑤ Waller Hall
⑥ Hallie Ford Museum of Art

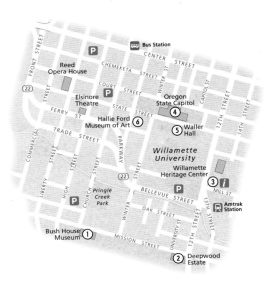

0 meters 400
0 yards 400

Swimming pool fed by hot springs at the Warm Springs Reservation resort

⑱ Madras and Warm Springs

Road map 1 B3. Madras:
ℹ 274 SW 4th St, (541) 475-2350.
🌐 **madraschamber.com**
Warm Springs: ℹ 1233 Veterans St,
(541) 553-1161. 🌐 **warmsprings.com**

Madras is a desert ranching town surrounded by rimrock and vast tracts of wilderness recreation lands. **Crooked River National Grassland** provides endless vistas as well as fishing and rafting opportunities on two US National Wild and Scenic Rivers – the Deschutes and the Crooked – that weave through the 175 sq miles (453 sq km) of juniper and sagebrush. **Cove Palisades State Park** surrounds Lake Billy Chinook, where deep waters reflecting the surrounding basalt cliffs are popular with boaters.

The Treaty of 1855 between the US government and the Wasco, Walla Walla, and Paiute tribes established lands for the tribes on the 1,000 sq miles (2,590 sq km) Warm Springs

Reservation, located on the High Desert plateaus and forested Cascade slopes of central Oregon. These Confederated Tribes preserve their heritage at the **Museum at Warm Springs** with a stunning collection of basketry and beadwork, haunting historic photographs, and videotapes of tribal ceremonies. The Tribes also manage a casino and a resort, where a large pool is heated by hot springs.

🌲 Crooked River National Grassland
10 miles (16 km) S of Madras, off Hwy 26. **Open** dawn–dusk daily.
ℹ 813 SW Hwy 97, Madras.
Tel (541) 475-9272. 🌐 **fs.usda.org**

🌲 Cove Palisades State Park
15 miles (24 km) SW of Madras, off Hwy 97. **Tel** (541) 546-3412.
Open dawn–dusk daily. 🅿
🌐 **oregonstateparks.org**

🏛 Museum at Warm Springs
2189 Hwy 26, Warm Springs.
Tel (541) 553-3331. **Open** 9am–5pm Tue–Sat. **Closed** Jan 1, Thanksgiving, Dec 25. 🅿 🖼
🌐 **museumatwarmsprings.org**

⑲ Sisters

Road map 1 B4. 🔼 2,000.
ℹ 291 E Main Ave, (541) 549-0251.
🌐 **sisterscountry.com**

Sisters is a ranching town that cashes in on its cowboy history with Old West-style storefronts and wood sidewalks. The setting, though, is authentic – the peaks of the Three Sisters, each exceeding 10,000 ft (3,000 m), tower majestically above the town and the surrounding pine forests, alpine meadows, and rushing streams. The downtown area has been renovated as part of a $6 million project.

Environs
The McKenzie Pass climbs from Sisters to a 1-mile (1.6-km) summit amid a massive lava flow. The **Dee Wright Observatory**, built from lava rock, provides panoramic views of more than a dozen Cascades peaks and buttes and of the sweeping lava fields, which can be examined at close range on the half-mile (0.8-km) Lava River Interpretive Trail.

The cold and clear waters of the Metolius River flow through fragrant pine forests on the flanks of Mount Jefferson. Near Camp Sherman, a tiny settlement of cabins 14 miles (22.5 km) west of Sisters, the river bubbles up from springs beneath Black Butte. The view from the scenic overlook above the headwaters usually includes fly-fishing enthusiasts casting their lines into one of the state's best trout streams.

🌲 Dee Wright Observatory
Hwy 242, 15 miles (24 km) west of Sisters. **Open** mid-Jun–Oct: dawn–dusk daily. **Closed** Oct–mid-Jun.

Galloping horses near Sisters, the towering peaks of the Three Sisters mountains visible in the distance

For hotels and restaurants see pp286–8 and pp296–8

Bend's High Desert Museum, showcasing life in central and eastern Oregon

⑳ Smith Rock State Park

Road map 1 B4. **Tel** (541) 548-7501. **Open** dawn–dusk daily. 🅿️
Ⓦ **oregonstateparks.org**

At Smith Rock, the Crooked River flows beneath towering rock faces of welded tuff – volcanic ash that was compressed under intense heat and pressure. These unusually shaped peaks and pinnacles – with compelling names like Morning Glory Wall and Pleasure Palace – are a lure for risk-taking rock climbers, who ascend the sometimes more than 550-ft (168-m) sheer faces on over 1,300 climbing routes. The less intrepid can enjoy the spectacle from roadside viewpoints or from one of the many hiking trails that follow the base of the cliffs.

㉑ Bend

Road map 1 B4. 🏙 82,000.
ℹ️ 750 NW Lava Rd, Suite 160,
(541) 382-8048. Ⓦ **visitbend.com**

Busy Bend, once a sleepy lumber town, is alluringly close to the ski slopes, lakes, streams, and the many other natural attractions of central Oregon. While unsightly development is quickly replacing juniper- and sage-covered grazing lands on the outskirts, the Old Mill District retains a good deal of small-town charm. Drake Park is a grassy downtown retreat on the bank of the Deschutes River, and **Pilot Butte State Scenic Viewpoint**, atop a volcanic cinder cone that rises 500 ft (150 m) from

the center of town, overlooks the High Desert and nine snowcapped Cascade peaks.

The **High Desert Museum** celebrates life in the rugged, arid High Desert terrain that covers much of central and eastern Oregon. Walk-through dioramas use dramatic lighting and sound effects in authentic re-creations of Native American dwellings, a wagon camp, a silver mine, and other scenes of desert settlement. Outdoors, a trail crossing the floor of a forest of ponderosa pine leads to replicas of a settler's cabin and a sawmill, and to natural habitats, including a trout stream, an otter pond, and an aviary filled with hawks and other raptors.

🏞 Pilot Butte State Scenic Viewpoint
East end of Greenwood Ave. **Tel** (800) 551-6949. **Open** 8am–8pm daily.
Ⓦ **oregonstateparks.org**

🏛 High Desert Museum
59800 S Hwy 97. **Tel** (541) 382-4754. **Open** May–Oct: 9am–5pm daily, Nov–Apr: 10am–4pm daily. **Closed** Jan 1, Jul 4, Thanksgiving, Dec 25. 🅿️ 📷 🎁
Ⓦ **highdesertmuseum.org**

㉒ Newberry National Volcanic Monument

Road map 1 B4. **Open** May–Oct: dawn–dusk daily. 🅿️ Ⓦ **fs.usda.gov**

The Newberry National Volcanic Monument encompasses eerie and bleak landscapes of black lava, as well as sparkling mountain lakes, waterfalls, hemlock forests, and

snow-capped peaks. Exhibits at the **Lava Lands Visitor Center** explain how Newberry Volcano has been built by thousands of eruptions that began about 400,000 years ago – the last eruption occurred about 1,300 years ago – and which, seismic activity suggests, may begin again. Other exhibits highlight central Oregon's cultural history. Well-marked roads and interpretive trails lead to major sites within the monument.

At Lava River Cave, a passage extends almost 1 mile (1.5 km) into a lava tube, a channel through which molten lava once flowed. At Lava Cast Forest, a paved loop trail transverses a forest of hollow molds formed by molten lava, which created casts around tree trunks. A road ascends the 18-mile- (29-km-) wide caldera, where Paulina and East Lakes sparkle amid pine forests. It then skirts a massive field of shiny black lava known as the Big Obsidian Flow as it climbs to the 7,987-ft (2,434-m) summit of Paulina Peak, the highest point within Newberry Monument.

In addition to magnificent scenery, the monument provides opportunities for hiking, fishing, boating, camping, and winter recreation.

Lava Lands Visitor Center
58201 Hwy 97. **Tel** (541) 383-5700. **Open** May–Jun & Sep: 9am–5pm Thu–Mon; Jul–Aug: 9am–5pm daily; Oct: 9am–5pm Sat & Sun. **Closed** Oct 13–Apr 30. Ⓦ **fs.usda.gov**

A rock outcrop at the Newberry National Volcanic Monument

㉓ Cascade Lakes Highway

This loop is often called Century Drive because the circuit is just under 100 miles (160 km) long. A stunning display of forest and mountain scenery unfolds in this relatively short distance. Most memorable are the many vistas of sparkling lakes backed by craggy Cascade peaks. Trails into the deep wilderness, idyllic picnic and camping spots, lakes and streams brimming with trout and salmon, and ski slopes and rustic resorts are likely to tempt even the most time-pressed traveler to linger on this scenic byway for as long as possible.

⑦ Mount Bachelor
Some of the best skiing and snowboarding in the Pacific Northwest is here, on Mount Bachelor's 88 runs. There are also numerous trails for cross-country skiing and snowshoeing.

⑤ Devil's Garden
Astronauts trained on foot and in moon buggies for their historic 1969 moonwalk on this enormous 45-sq-mile (117-sq-km) lava flow.

⑥ Sparks Lake
This large shallow trout lake, surrounded by mountains, lava formations, and meadow, was considered by photographer Ray Atkeson to be the most scenic place in Oregon.

④ Elk Lake
Conveniently located along the Cascade Lakes Highway, Elk Lake is a popular destination for sailing, windsurfing, and fishing. The store at the Elk Lake Resort rents canoes, motorboats, rowboats, and paddleboats.

③ Osprey Observation Point
Crane Prairie Reservoir hosts a large colony of osprey that plunge from the sky like meteorites to pluck fish out of the water.

⑧ Dutchman Flat
Quiet and seclusion are the rich rewards for hiking a short distance to this picturesque desert area.

Tips for Drivers

Tour length: 95 miles (153 km).
Starting points: Highway 372 or Highway 97 out of Bend.
When to go: June to mid-October.
Stopping-off points: Picnic spots abound, but since provisions are few, it's best to pack the hamper in Bend. Elk Lake and Cultus Lake have restaurants and grocery stores. Travelers in search of more sophisticated dining should stop at the lodges in Sunriver and at Mount Bachelor.

① High Desert Museum
This museum shows the desert in its full glory and explains its evolution, flora, and fauna. Visitors can see live animals in their natural habitats.

② Lava Butte
A paved road ascends to the top of this extinct volcanic cone, affording spectacular views of the Cascade Mountains.

Key

▬ Tour route
═ Other road

Striking view from Newberry National Volcanic Monument

For keys to symbols *see back flap*

㉔ Crater Lake National Park Tour

Oregon's only National Park surrounds a lake that, at 1,949 ft (594 m), is the deepest in the US and the ninth deepest in the world. Creation of Crater Lake began about 7,700 years ago when Mount Mazama erupted and then collapsed, forming the caldera in which the lake now sits. The crater rim rises an average of 1,000 ft (300 m) above the lake. On the drive that circles the lake, the many overlooks, 90 miles (144 km) of trails, and a beautiful lodge afford stunning views.

④ Merriam Point
This promontory is an excellent spot from which to admire the west side of the lake, with the cone-shaped Wizard Island and its surrounding black volcanic blocks.

③ The Watchman
This viewpoint, reached after a moderate climb, is named for its historic fire tower, and is the closest lookout to Wizard Island.

② Wizard Island
Wizard Island is a small volcanic island in the shape of a cone jutting 764 ft (233 m) above the surface of the lake. At the summit is a crater 300 ft (90 m) across.

```
0 kilometers          4
0 miles               3
```

Rim

Mazama Village

① Crater Lake Lodge
This rustic hotel perched on the caldera rim has welcomed guests since 1915. Extensive renovations have restored the structural integrity of the building, once at risk of collapsing under its own weight and that of the 15 ft (4.5 m) of snow that can accumulate in winter. Magnificent views can be enjoyed from here.

Tourists departing on a boat tour from Cleetwood Cove, on the north shore of the lake

Tips for Drivers

Tour length: 33 miles (53 km).
Starting point: Steel Information Center, on Rim Drive 4 miles (6.5 km) north of Route 62.
When to go: Rim Drive is open from the end of June to mid-October, weather permitting.
Stopping-off points: Meals are offered at Crater Lake Lodge and Annie Creek Restaurant near Mazama (Jun–mid-Oct); snacks are sold in Rim Village. Two-hour narrated boat trips (late Jun–mid-Sep: 10am–4pm daily) depart from Cleetwood Cove.

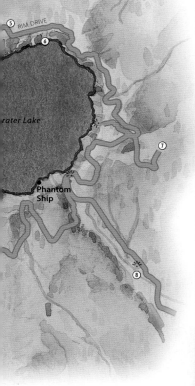

⑤ Rim Drive
On this 33-mile (53-km) circuit, spectacular vistas of the lake, the islands, and the surrounding mountains unfold at every turn.

⑥ Cleetwood Trail
This 1-mile (1.6-km) strenuous trail, which drops a steep 700 ft (210 m), provides the only access to the lake. In summer, a boat tour departs from the dock at the base of the trail.

⑦ Mount Scott
When weather allows, views from this peak – at 8,929 ft (2,722 m) the highest point in the park – extend as far as California's Mount Shasta, located 100 miles (160 km) to the south.

⑧ The Pinnacles
An eerie landscape of pumice spires, known as fossil fumaroles, rises from the caldera's eastern base. Many of the spires are hollow.

⑨ Castle Crest – Wildflower Trail
Spectacular wildflowers bloom in July and August alongside this easy-to-walk 0.4-mile (0.6-km) trail.

⑩ Sinnott Memorial Overlook
Breathtaking views reward the short descent to this point just below the caldera rim, where park rangers give geology talks.

Key
— Tour route
— Other road

For keys to symbols *see back flap*

A park ranger giving a tour in the Oregon Caves National Monument

㉕ Oregon Caves National Monument

Road map 1 A5. *i* Oregon Route 46, Cave Junction, (541) 592-2100. **Open** 9:30am–5pm daily. hourly Apr–Oct. **w** nps.gov

Visitors on the 70-minute guided tours of these vast underground caverns follow lighted trails past strange formations, cross underground rivers, squeeze through giant ribs of marble, and clamber up and down staircases into enormous chambers hung with stalactites. Discovered in 1874 by a hunter chasing his dog into a dark hole in the side of Elijah Mountain, the caves have been formed by the steady trickling of water over the past hundreds of thousands of years. Above ground, three trails cross a remnant old-growth coniferous forest and lead to an ancient and noble Douglas fir, famous for having the widest girth of any known tree in Oregon.

Jacksonville's Beekman House, built during the Gold Rush

㉖ Jacksonville

Road map 1 A4. 2,600. *i* 185 Oregon St, (541) 899-8118. **w** jacksonvilleoregon.org

In this Gold Rush boomtown, time has more or less stood still since the 1880s, when Rich Gulch Creek ceased to yield gold and the main railroad lines bypassed the town. Jacksonville is now the heart of the burgeoning southern Oregon wine region, where over 80 varietals are grown in diverse microclimates.

With more than 80 brick and wood-frame 19th-century buildings, Jacksonville has been designated a National Historic Landmark. A walking tour (a map is available from the information center in the old railroad depot) shows off the town's wealth of architecture and history. The **Beekman House** (c.1876) is a museum that offers a glimpse of how the town's prosperous burghers once lived, with original furnishings and actors dressed in costumes of the period. The beautiful hillside estate of 19th-century photographer Peter Britt is the setting of the annual **Britt Festivals**, the Pacific Northwest's premier outdoor performing arts summer festival. Internationally famous artists representing various music genres – including rock, country, jazz, folk, bluegrass, and pop – perform beneath a canopy of ponderosa pines *(see p35)*.

 Beekman House
352 E California St. **Tel** (541) 773-6536. **Open** by appointment.

 Britt Festivals
216 W Main St, Medford. **Tel** (541) 773-6077. **w** brittfest.org

㉗ Ashland

Road map 1 A5. 20,000. *i* 110 E Main St, (541) 482-3486. **w** ashlandchamber.com

At first glance, it may be difficult to believe that every year some 125,000 theatergoers descend on Ashland, an amiable town surrounded by farms and orchards. What draws them is the **Oregon Shakespeare Festival**, established in 1935, and now presenting, between February and October, an annual schedule of 11 plays by Shakespeare, in addition to other works by classic and contemporary playwrights. Theater buffs can also view props and costumes from past performances at the Festival Exhibit Center, and take backstage tours of the festival's three venues: the 1,200-seat, open-air Allen Elizabethan Theatre; the Angus Bowmer Theatre, which seats 600 people; and the modern Thomas Theater.

 Oregon Shakespeare Festival
15 S Pioneer St. **Tel** (541) 482-4331. **w** osfashland.org

Environs
Many commercial outfitters launch raft and jet boat trips from Grants Pass, 40 miles (64 km) north of Ashland on I-5. The Rogue River rushes 215 twisting miles (346 km) through Siskiyou National Forest and other wilderness before reaching the Pacific Ocean. Elk, mountain lions, and bears are often seen roaming the riverbanks, and bald eagles fly overhead.

A Renaissance stage set at the Oregon Shakespeare Festival

㉘ Steens Mountain Tour

Scenery does not get much more rugged and grand than it does here on this 9,700-ft (2,960-m) mountain. Steens Mountain is a fault-block, formed when land on two sides of a geological fault rose and fell to different levels. As a result, the west slope of this mountain rises gradually from sagebrush country through stands of aspen, juniper, and mountain mahogany, while the east face drops precipitously for more than a mile (1.5 km). Pronghorn, bighorn sheep, and wild horses roam craggy gorges and alpine tundra carpeted with wildflowers, and eagles and falcons soar overhead. The Steens Mountain National Back Country Byway traverses this remarkable landscape.

Tips for Drivers

Tour length: 58 miles (93.5km).
Starting point: North Loop Road in Frenchglen.
When to go: The entire Steens Loop Road is closed from November to June due to snow cover, though snow squalls and lightning storms can occur in any season.
Getting around: This dirt and gravel road is steep in parts. It is not suitable for vehicles with low clearance.
Stopping-off points: Many scenic overlooks, picnic spots, and some campgrounds are located on the route. Frenchglen has lodging and restaurants.

① Donner und Blitzen River
An army officer named this rushing torrent "Thunder and Lightning" while attempting to cross it during a thunderstorm in 1864.

③ Kiger Gorge
Massive glaciers bulldozed four immense gorges on the mountain; Kiger Gorge plunges half a mile (0.8 km).

② Lily Lake
Many Steens lakes have filled with sediment and plants and become alpine meadows. Lovely marsh-fringed Lily Lake is also slowly in the process of silting up.

⑤ Wildhorse Lake
Glaciers carved terraces out of the walls of the deep gorge that encircles this sparkling lake.

④ East Rim Viewpoint
This perch is a full mile (1.6 km) above the alkali flats of the Alvord Desert; sitting in the rain shadow of the mountain, this desolate desert receives a mere 6 inches (15 cm) of rain a year.

Key
Tour route

0 kilometers 8
0 miles 6

For keys to symbols *see back flap*

The seemingly endless desert landscape of the Jordan Valley

㉙ Jordan Valley

Road map 1 C4. 🚌 239.
W cityofjordanvalley.com

This scruffy desert ranching settlement is one of only a few towns in sparsely populated Malheur County, where just 28,000 people inhabit 10,000 sq miles (25,900 sq km). Jordan Valley makes two claims to fame. A legacy of the Basque sheepherders who settled the town in 1890 is the ball court, built in 1915, for playing pelota, a game that resembles American handball. A wind-swept, sagebrush-filled cemetery 17 miles (27 km) south of town on Highway 95 is the final resting place of Jean Baptiste Charbonneau, son of the Indian guide Sacagawea (see p41). Born in 1805, Jean was taken across the country with the Lewis and Clark party, which his mother helped guide. Years later, he died of a chill at a stagecoach stop near Jordan Valley in 1866.

㉚ Malheur National Wildlife Refuge

Road map 1 C4. **Tel** (541) 493-2612.
Refuge and museum: **Open** dawn–dusk daily. **Closed** major hols. Visitors' center: **Open** mid-Mar–mid-Oct: 8am–4pm daily; mid-Oct–mid-Mar: 8am–4pm Mon–Thu. **Closed** major hols. ♿ W fws.gov/malheur

One of the nation's largest wildlife refuges, Malheur spreads across 292 sq miles

(756 sq km) of the Blitzen Valley floor. More than 320 species of birds and 58 species of mammals inhabit the wetlands, meadows, and uplands, ensuring prime wildlife viewing for visitors. Sandhill cranes, tundra swans, snowy white egrets, white-faced ibis, pronghorn antelope, mule deer, and redband trout are among the most numerous of the refuge's denizens.

Spring and fall are the best times to view birds, which alight in the refuge on their annual migrations up and down the Pacific Flyway, a major north–south route for migrating North American waterfowl. A small museum houses specimens of birds commonly seen in the refuge. Starting at the center, the Central Patrol Road traverses the 40-mile (64-km) length of the refuge and provides access to the prime viewing spots. The P Ranch, at the south end, is the historic spread of Peter French, who settled the Blitzen Valley in the 1880s.

Environs
From the refuge, the 69-mile (111-km) **Diamond Loop National Back Country Byway** heads into sage-covered hills and red rimrock canyons. Along the route are Diamond Craters, a volcanic landscape formed between 17,000 and 25,000 years ago; the Round Barn, a distinctive 19th-century structure with a round stone corral surrounded by a circular paddock; and Diamond, a small,

poplar-shaded ranch town where the number of guests staying at the hotel determines whether the town's population exceeds the single digits.

🏞 **Diamond Loop National Back Country Byway**
ℹ 28910 Hwy 20 W, Hines.
Tel (541) 573-4400.

Resting mule deer in the Malheur National Wildlife Refuge

㉛ John Day Fossil Beds National Monument

Road map 1 B3. ℹ Hwy 19, 40 miles (64 km) west of John Day, (541) 987-2333. **Open** dawn–dusk daily; Thomas Condon Paleontology Center (Sheep Rock unit): **Open** 9am–5pm daily. **Closed** major hols between Thanksgiving & Presidents' Day.
W nps.gov

Prehistoric fossil beds litter the John Day Fossil Beds National Monument, where sedimentary rocks preserve the plants and animals that flourished in jungles and savannas for 40 million years, between the extinction of the dinosaurs and the beginning of

Formations at John Day Fossil Beds National Monument's Sheep Rock unit

The magnificent Painted Hills at John Day Fossil Beds National Monument

the most recent ice age. The monument comprises three units: Sheep Rock, Painted Hills, and Clarno. At all three, trails provide opportunities for close-up observation of the fossil beds. Painted Hills presents the most dramatic landscapes: volcanic rock formations are vivid hues of red, pink, bronze, tan, and black. Clarno contains some of the oldest formations, dating back 54 million years and including some of the finest fossil plant remains on earth. At Sheep Rock, where formations date from 16 million to 6 million years ago, the visitors' center displays many important finds from the beds.

Enteledont skull and forelimb fossils

The fossil beds are named in honor of John Day, a fur trader from Virginia who arrived in Oregon in 1812 and for whom the John Day River is named, though Day himself apparently never actually set foot near the beds.

㉜ Pendleton

Road map 1 C3. 🚹 17,300.
ℹ 501 S Main St, (541) 276-7411.
W **travelpendleton.com**

Pendleton is the largest town in eastern Oregon, and it has an outsized reputation for raucous cowboys and lawless cattle rustlers to match. Visitors may be disappointed to learn,

however, that these more colorful days belong to the past. **Pendleton Woolen Mills** (see p80), known for its warm clothing and blankets, particularly its "legendary" blankets whose designs are a tribute to Native American tribes, is now the big business in town. The mill wove its first Indian trade blanket in 1895. Native Americans used these blankets not only as standard clothing items but also in ceremonies and trade among each other, where the blankets were used as a measure of value and credit. Cowboy lore continues to come alive during the Pendleton Round-Up each September, when rodeo performers and some 50,000 spectators crowd into town. Previous rodeos are honored in the photographs and other memorabilia at the **Pendleton Round-Up and Happy Canyon Hall of Fame Museum**.

The **Pendleton Underground Tours** reveal much about the town's notoriety. The tours begin in an underground labyrinth of opium dens, gaming rooms, and Prohibition-era drinking establishments and include stops at the Cozy Room bordello and the cramped 19th-century living quarters of Chinese laborers.

Another chapter of local history is commemorated at the **Tamástslikt Cultural Institute**. Re-creations of historic structures and handsome exhibits of war bonnets and

other artifacts depict the horse culture, seasonal migrations, forced resettlements, and current success of the Cayuse, Umatilla, and Walla Walla tribes, who have lived on the Columbia River plateau for more than 10,000 years.

🏨 Pendleton Woolen Mills
1307 SE Court Pl. **Tel** (541) 276-6911. Salesroom: **Open** 8am–6pm Mon–Sat, 9am–5pm Sun. **Closed** Jan 1, Thanksgiving, Dec 25. 🕘 9am, 11am, 1:30pm, 3pm Mon–Fri. 📷
W **pendleton-usa.com**

🏛 Pendleton Round-Up and Happy Canyon Hall of Fame Museum
1205 SW Court Ave. **Tel** (541) 276-2553. **Open** 10am–4pm Sat. **Closed** major hols. W **pendletonroundup.com**

🎭 Pendleton Underground Tours
37 SW Emigrant Ave. **Tel** (541) 276-0730. **Open** 10am–4pm Mon & Wed–Sat. **Closed** major hols. 🅿️ 📷 W **pendletonunderground tours.org**

🏛 Tamástslikt Cultural Institute
47106 Wildhorse Blvd. **Tel** (541) 966-9748. **Open** 10am–5pm Mon–Sat. **Closed** Jan 1, Thanksgiving, Dec 25. 🅿️ 💻 📷 ♿ W **tamastslikt.org**

Environs
The town of La Grande, 52 miles (84 km) southeast of Pendleton, is best known as the jumping-off point for trips into the scenic wilds of the Blue and Wallowa Mountains and Hells Canyon (see pp116–19).

In downtown La Grande, charming turn-of-the-19th-century buildings now house shops and cafés.

A tule mat lodge at the Tamástslikt Cultural Institute

❸❸ Elkhorn Drive National Scenic Byway Tour

This drive through a mountain range takes in some of the finest scenery in eastern Oregon. To the west, the route climbs across the Elkhorn Range of the Blue Mountains, where dense pine forests interspersed with crystal-clear lakes give way to historic gold-mining towns. To the east, seen across Baker Valley, rise the snowcapped summits of the spectacular Wallowa mountain range.

⑥ Anthony Lakes
A string of mountain lakes sparkle amid forests of ponderosa pines. In winter, skiers and snowmobile enthusiasts glide across this hilly terrain on deep powder.

⑤ Granite
When pioneer gold-mining days came to a close, the town of Granite changed from a boomtown into a ghost town.

ELKHORN DRIVE NATIONAL SCENIC BYWAY

Blue Mountains

NORTH FORK JOHN DAY

Mount Ireland

Elkhorn Range

Key
- ▬ Tour route
- ═ Other road

④ **Sumpter**

③

John Day 26

• **McEwen**

Powder River

Phillips Reservoir

④ Sumpter Valley Dredge
This massive dredge once dug its way across the valley floor in search of gold. The hulking wood and steel beast is now the centerpiece of a unique heritage site.

0 kilometers
0 miles

**National Historic Oregon
Trail Interpretive Center**
Here, replicas of pioneer
scenes, accompanied by
the sounds of jangling
oxen, re-create life on
the Oregon Trail.

Vallowa Mountains

Hells Canyon

r City ①
②

② Baker City
Some rather grand
downtown blocks
and fine Victorian
residences are
reminders of the fame
and prosperity that
gold mining once
brought to this now
quiet ranching town.

③ Sumpter Valley Railway
A narrow-gauge steam train
once again chugs along a
historic route originally built
to haul lumber and gold.
Hawks and other wildlife
usually provide an escort.

㉞ Joseph

Road map 1 C3. 🚠 1,100. 🛈 201
E 2nd St, (541) 426-5546.

Joseph is named for Chief
Joseph, leader of the Nez Perce
people *(see p31)*. In 1877, he
led his tribe on a 1,800-mile
(2,880-km) flight to resist
resettlement from their lands
in the Wallowas; they were
apprehended near the Canadian
border and relocated to a
reservation in Washington State.

The brick storefronts, snowcapped Wallowa Mountains,
and outlying grasslands lend
Joseph a frontier-town air still.
These days, though, recreation
enthusiasts outnumber ranchers,
and artisans, particularly
sculptors, have established
galleries. Housed in the historic
former location of a
newspaper office,
hospital, and
bank built in
1888, the
**Wallowa
County
Museum**,
devoted to
Chief Joseph's
famous retreat, is
here. Chief Joseph Days, held in
July, feature a rodeo and carnival.
Other festivals include the
Annual Arts Festival and the
Wallowa Mountain Quilt Show,
both in June.

Bronze horse sculpture in Joseph

🏛 Wallowa County Museum
110 S Main St. **Tel** (541) 432-6095.
Open Memorial Day–3rd weekend
Sep: 10am–5pm daily. 🅿
w co.wallowa.or.us/museum

Restored historic corner building in
Joseph, Oregon

Motorboat moored on the blue waters
of Wallowa Lake

㉟ Wallowa Lake

Road map 1 C3.

The crystal-clear waters of this
long glacial lake sparkle at
the foot of the Wallowa
Mountains, which form a
10,000-ft- (3,050-m-) high,
40-mile- (64-km-) long wall
of granite. Though the lake
became a popular tourist
retreat in the early
20th century, the
forested shoreline
is remarkably
unspoiled. Much
of it falls within
the boundaries of
national forest lands
and **Wallowa Lake State Park**.
One of the few commercial
structures on the lake is
Wallowa Lake Lodge, a
beautifully restored log building
dating from the 1920s. It still
provides accommodation and
meals. The popular **Wallowa
Lake Tramway** whisks riders
up 3,700 ft (1,100 m) to the
summit of Mount Howard,
where spectacular views of the
lake below and the Wallowa
Mountains can be enjoyed.
Deep wilderness is only a
short hike or pack trip away
from the lake in the Eagle Cap
Wilderness, which climbs and
dips over mountainous terrain
to the west of the lake.

🏞 Wallowa Lake State Park
6 miles (10 km) S of Joseph off Hwy
82. **Tel** (541) 432-4185. **Open** dawn–
dusk daily. **w** oregonstateparks.org

🚠 Wallowa Lake Tramway
59919 Wallowa Lake Hwy, Joseph.
Tel (541) 432-5331.
Open mid-May–Sep. 🅿
w wallowalaketramway.com

❸ Hells Canyon National Recreation Area Tour

Some of the wildest terrain in North America clings to the sides of craggy, 9,400-ft (2,865-m) peaks at Hells Canyon and plunges to the famed basin far below, where the Snake River rushes through North America's deepest river-carved gorge. Visitors are awed by the massive canyon walls rising 7,993 ft (2,436 m) and delight in the dense upland pine forests and delicate flower-covered alpine meadows – 1,019 sq miles (2,641 sq km) in all. Much of the terrain is too rugged to cross, even on foot, making sections of the Snake River accessible only by boat. Many visitors settle for the stunning views from several lookouts, and not one is disappointed.

Hells Canyon National Recreation Area viewpoint

① Buckhorn Lookout
One of several spectacular overlooks in the Hells Canyon area, this remote spot offers superb views of the Wallowa-Whitman National Forest and the Imnaha River canyon.

② Nee-Me-Poo Trail
Hikers on this national trail follow in the footsteps of Chief Joseph and 700 Nez Perce Indians who, in 1877, embarked on an 1,800-mile (2,880-km) trek toward freedom in Canada (see p31).

⑥ Hells Canyon Reservoir
Formed by Oxbow Dam to the south and Hells Canyon Dam to the north, this 25-mile- (40-km-) long reservoir is part of a huge power-generating complex on the Snake River. A private road along the east shore provides boaters with access to the river.

Joseph

Big Sh

North R.

Baker

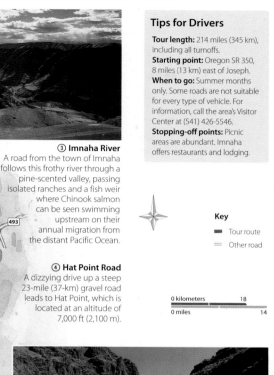

③ Imnaha River

A road from the town of Imnaha follows this frothy river through a pine-scented valley, passing isolated ranches and a fish weir where Chinook salmon can be seen swimming upstream on their annual migration from the distant Pacific Ocean.

④ Hat Point Road

A dizzying drive up a steep 23-mile (37-km) gravel road leads to Hat Point, which is located at an altitude of 7,000 ft (2,100 m).

Pittsburg Landing — 493

Snake River

240

Seven Devils Mountains

5

Hells Canyon Dam

454

Tips for Drivers

Tour length: 214 miles (345 km), including all turnoffs.
Starting point: Oregon SR 350, 8 miles (13 km) east of Joseph.
When to go: Summer months only. Some roads are not suitable for every type of vehicle. For information, call the area's Visitor Center at (541) 426-5546.
Stopping-off points: Picnic areas are abundant. Imnaha offers restaurants and lodging.

Key

▬ Tour route
═ Other road

0 kilometers   18
0 miles   14

⑤ Wild and Scenic River

A 31.5-mile (50.5-km) stretch of the Snake River, from Hells Canyon Dam to Upper Pittsburg Landing, is designated a Wild River. Experienced guides pilot rafters over the many stretches of rapids. Searing midsummer temperatures and inhospitable terrain, as well as rattlesnakes and an occasional patch of poison ivy, make an overland trek alongside the river more challenging.

A boat negotiating rapids on a trip on the Snake River

For keys to symbols *see back flap*

SEATTLE

Seattle at a Glance

Seattle's history, commerce, and quality of life are closely tied to its waterfront location on Puget Sound. The Klondike Gold Rush National Historical Park recalls the city's pivotal role as an embarkation point for the Gold Rush of 1897–8. The Seattle Aquarium explores Puget Sound's diverse natural habitat. Embracing both the past and the future, Seattle's architectural icons include a number of historic buildings, the once-futuristic Space Needle, and the provocative EMP Museum.

EMP Museum
This museum is dedicated to the history and exploration of music and science fiction (see pp150–51).

SEATTLE CENTER AND BELLTOWN
(See pp144–53)

ELLIOTT AVENUE

DENNY WA

BROAD STREET

2ND AVENU

Space Needle
Built for the 1962 World's Fair, the 605-ft (184-m) Space Needle is Seattle's official landmark. A 41-second elevator ride whisks visitors to the observation deck and a 360-degree view (see pp148–9).

Olympic Sculpture Park
Following a radical makeover, this former industrial area has now been converted into a well-designed green space that offers great views. Art installations and sculptures, such as *Eagle* by Alexander Calder, are displayed outdoors around the waterfront park by the Seattle Art Museum (see p148).

| 0 meters | 400 |
| 0 yards | 400 |

Seattle Aquarium
Offering a window into Pacific Northwest marine life, this popular aquarium has an underwater glass dome which surrounds visitors with sharks, salmon, octopus, and many other creatures (see pp142–3).

◄ Seattle and Mount Rainier at sunset

Benaroya Hall
Home of the Seattle Symphony, this $118 million complex occupies an entire city block. Its S. Mark Taper Foundation Auditorium is internationally acclaimed for its superior acoustics *(see p133)*.

Fairmont Olympic Hotel
This stately hotel is listed on the National Register of Historic Places *(see p132)*.

Seattle Art Museum
An acclaimed expansion has vastly increased exhibition space for this museum's 23,000 works of art, ranging from ancient Egyptian reliefs to contemporary American installations *(see pp132–3)*.

Smith Tower
Once the world's tallest office building outside of New York City, this 42-story tower boasts the last manually operated elevators of their kind on the West Coast *(see p128)*.

PIKE STREET

LACE
ET AND
ATERFRONT
(4–43)

MADISON STREET

2ND AVENUE

JAMES STREET

ALASKAN WAY VIADUCT

1ST AVENUE SOUTH

PIONEER SQUARE
AND DOWNTOWN
(See pp124–33)

Pike Place Market
Dating from 1907, one of the oldest farmer's markets in the country is a beloved Seattle landmark and a National Historic District *(see p138)*.

Klondike Gold Rush National Historical Park
This indoor park located in the Pioneer Square Historic District celebrates Seattle's role in North America's last great Gold Rush *(see p129)*.

PIONEER SQUARE AND DOWNTOWN

The birthplace of Seattle, Pioneer Square was the city's original downtown, established in 1852 when Arthur and David Denny arrived with a handful of fellow pioneers. Emerging from the ashes of the Great Fire of 1889, the rebuilt commercial area prospered as the 19th century drew to a close. By the time the much-touted Smith Tower opened in 1914, however, the city core had begun spreading north and Pioneer Square was less and less a prestigious business address. Today, the revitalized Pioneer Square – a National Historic District – is a thriving arts center, with First Thursday gallery walks and venues for author readings. A short walk leads to downtown – home to the city's modern skyscrapers, upscale shops, and luxury hotels, as well as green spaces such as Freeway Park. Lending cultural panache is the boldly designed Seattle Art Museum and the state-of-the-art Benaroya Hall.

Sights at a Glance

Buildings and Shops
1 Smith Tower
2 Pioneer Building
7 Columbia Center
8 Fairmont Olympic Hotel
10 Benaroya Hall
12 Central Library

Museums
9 Seattle Art Museum

Parks and Districts
3 Waterfall Garden Park
4 Occidental Square
5 Klondike Gold Rush National Historical Park
6 International District
11 Freeway Park

See also Street Finder maps 3 and 4

0 meters 400
0 yards 400

◀ The Pioneer Building, in the heart of Pioneer Square

For keys to symbols *see back flap*

Street-by-Street: Pioneer Square

Pioneer Square, Seattle's first downtown and later a decrepit skid row, is today a revitalized business neighborhood and National Historic District. The tall totem poles gracing the square are reminders of the Coast Salish Indian village that originally occupied this spot. The grand Victorian architecture, social service missions, and upscale shops that line the bustling streets and cobblestone plazas are further reminders of the area's checkered past and redevelopment since the 1960s. Many of the buildings standing today were constructed in the years between the Great Fire of 1889 and the Klondike Gold Rush of 1897–8, both pivotal events in Seattle's history. While the buildings look much as they did a century ago, their tenants have changed dramatically. Where saloons, brothels, and mining company headquarters once flourished, art galleries, boutiques, and antique shops now reside.

Locator Map
See Street Finder map 4

❹ Occidental Square
The Fallen Firefighters' Memorial in this square consists of four life-sized bronze statues designed and sculpted by Hai Ying Wu in 1998, as a tribute to Seattle's firefighters who have died in the line of duty.

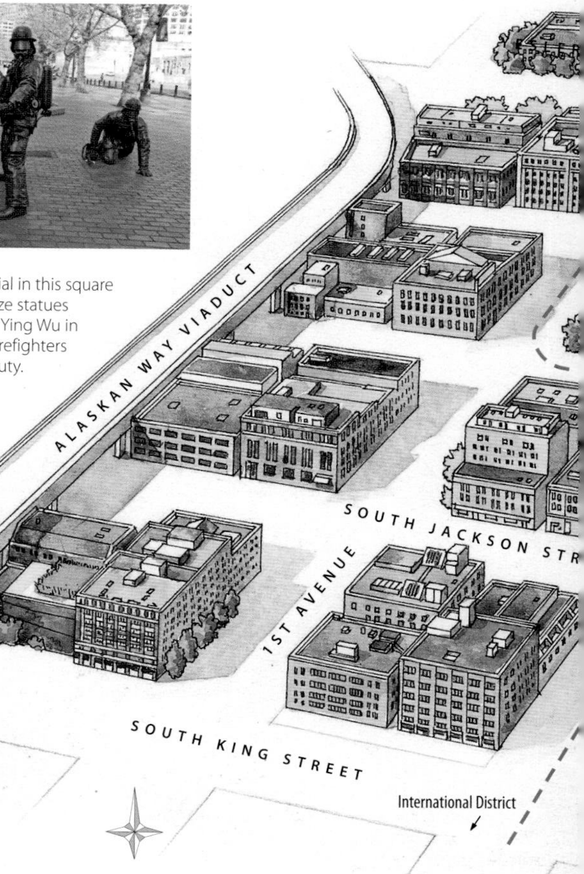

ALASKAN WAY VIADUCT

SOUTH JACKSON STR

1ST AVENUE

SOUTH KING STREET

International District

Key

— Suggested route

0 meters   100
0 yards   100

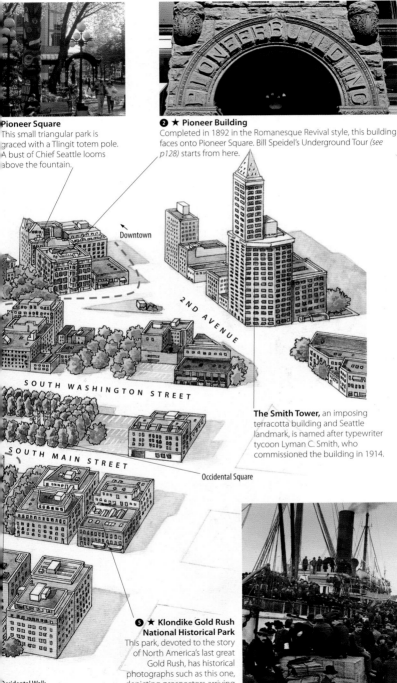

Pioneer Square
This small triangular park is graced with a Tlingit totem pole. A bust of Chief Seattle looms above the fountain.

❷ ★ Pioneer Building
Completed in 1892 in the Romanesque Revival style, this building faces onto Pioneer Square. Bill Speidel's Underground Tour *(see p128)* starts from here.

← Downtown

2ND AVENUE

SOUTH WASHINGTON STREET

SOUTH MAIN STREET

Occidental Square

The Smith Tower, an imposing terracotta building and Seattle landmark, is named after typewriter tycoon Lyman C. Smith, who commissioned the building in 1914.

❺ ★ Klondike Gold Rush National Historical Park
This park, devoted to the story of North America's last great Gold Rush, has historical photographs such as this one, depicting prospectors arriving in Seattle.

Occidental Walk

❶ Smith Tower

506 2nd Ave. **Map** 4 D3.
Tel (206) 622-4004. 🚌 39, 42, 136,
137. Observation deck: **Open** 10am–
dusk daily. **Closed** Easter, Thanksgiving, Dec 25. 🚹 to observation
deck. 🚻 except observation deck.
📷 for groups. 🌐 **smithtower.com**

When it opened in 1914, the
42-story Smith Tower was
heralded as the tallest office
building in the world outside
New York City and for nearly
a half century it reigned as the
tallest building west of Chicago.
    Commissioned by rifle and
typewriter tycoon Lyman
Cornelius Smith, Seattle's first
skyscraper is clad in white terracotta. While its height – 489 ft
(149 m) from the curbside to
the top of the tower finial – is
no longer its claim to fame, the
city's landmark does boast the
last manually operated elevator
of its kind on the West Coast.
For a fee, you can ride one
of the gleaming brass-cage
originals to the 35th-floor
Observatory. The carved wood
and porcelain-inlay ceiling and
the ornate blackwood furniture
adorning this banquet room
were gifts to Smith from the
last empress of China. The deck
here offers panoramic views
of Mount Rainier, the Olympic
and Cascade mountain ranges,
and Elliott Bay.
    The onyx and marble lobby,
which has been restored to its
former glamor, is presided over
by 22 carved chieftains.

Decorative brass elevator doors of the
1914 Smith Tower

❷ Pioneer Building

600 1st Ave. **Map** 4 D3. 🚌 15, 18,
21, 22. Underground Tour: **Tel** (206)
682-4646. 🚹 📷 call for hours
and reservations. 🌐 **pioneer-
building.com**

Completed in 1892, three years
after the Great Fire flattened
the core business district, the
Pioneer Building was voted the
"finest building west of Chicago"
by the American Institute of
Architects. It is one of more than
50 buildings designed by Elmer
Fisher (see p152) following the
devastating fire of 1889. Still
imposing without its tower,
destroyed in a 1949 earthquake,
the brick building houses offices
and Doc Maynard's Saloon,
starting point of Bill Speidel's

Underground Tour. This
90-minute walk offers a lively
look at Seattle's colorful past
and the original streets beneath
the modern city, including
the 1890s stores abandoned
in the 1900s when engineers
raised streets. Beware: the
subterranean portion is
musty and dusty.

❸ Waterfall Garden Park

219 2nd Ave S. **Map** 4 D3.
Tel (206) 624-6096. 🚌 15, 18, 21, 22,
56. **Open** 9am–3pm daily.

A peaceful, secluded oasis in the
middle of busy Pioneer Square,
this little park is the perfect
place to relax and enjoy a picnic.
The sounds of the man-made
waterfall cascading over huge
rocks soften any street noise.
There are several tables and
chairs set out around the
waterfall, some in the shade
and some catching the few
rays of sun that peer through
the Japanese maples.
    The park was designed by
Masao Kinoshita and built in
1977 by the Annie E. Casey
Foundation to honor the
workers of the United Parcel
Service (UPS). Jim Casey of
Seattle was one of the founders
of UPS, which was originally
formed as the American
Messenger Service in a
saloon at this site in 1907.

The Great Seattle Fire

On June 6, 1889, in a cabinet shop near Pioneer Square, a pot of flaming
glue overturned, igniting wood shavings. The tide, which the city's
water system depended on, was low at the time, and as numerous
hoses were connected to the hydrants, the water pressure dropped
and the water supply eventually gave out. The fire spread rapidly,
engulfing 60 city blocks before burning itself out. Miraculously, no
one died in the blaze, and
it came to be seen as a
blessing in disguise. Sturdy
brick and stone buildings
were erected where flimsy
wood structures once stood;
streets were widened
and raised; and the sewer
system was overhauled.
From the ashes of disaster
rose a city primed for
prominence as the 20th
century approached.

The aftermath of the Great Seattle Fire of 1889,
devastating to a city built of wood

The stately Smith Tower, once the tallest
building outside New York

For hotels and restaurants see p288 and pp298–300

❹ Occidental Square

Occidental Ave between S Main & S Jackson Sts. **Map** 4 D3. 🚌 15, 18, 21, 22, 56.

The brick-paved plaza known as Occidental Square offers relief from the busy traffic of Pioneer Square. The tree-lined pedestrian walk is flanked by upscale shops, galleries, and coffeehouses, many housed in attractive Victorian buildings.

Across South Main Street is Occidental Park, where the ambience changes considerably because of the local contingent of homeless people and panhandlers. Of special note here are four cedar totem poles carved by Northwest artist Duane Pasco and the Fallen Firefighters' Memorial, a moving tribute to the 34 Seattle firefighters who have died in the line of duty since the Seattle Fire Department was founded in 1889.

The striking cedar totem poles in Pioneer Square's Occidental Park

❺ Klondike Gold Rush National Historical Park

319 2nd Ave S. **Map** 4 D3. **Tel** (206) 220-4240. 🚌 15, 18, 21, 22, 56. **Open** 9am–5pm daily. **Closed** Jan 1, Thanksgiving, Dec 25. ♿ 🗾 **nps.gov**

In 1895, gold was discovered in a tributary of the Klondike River, in the middle of the Canadian Yukon wilderness. This discovery triggered a frenzied stampede,

Exhibit at the Klondike Gold Rush National Historical Park

as 100,000 gold-seekers from around the world rushed to the Klondike to find their fortunes.

The largest and closest US city to the gold fields, Seattle became the primary outfitting and embarkation point for the stampede north. Tens of thousands of miners passed through the city, purchasing $25 million worth of food, clothing, equipment, pack animals, and steamship tickets. While few Klondikers struck it rich during the Gold Rush of 1897–8, Seattle merchants made a fortune and established the city's reputation as the premier commercial center of the Pacific Northwest.

Established by Congress in 1976, Klondike Gold Rush National Historical Park comprises five units – three in Canada, one in Skagway, Alaska, and one in Seattle's Pioneer Square Historic District. Housed in the restored Hotel Cadillac building, the Seattle visitors' center celebrates the city's role in North America's last great Gold Rush. On display here are evocative black-and-white photographs and simulations of the "ton of provisions" that Canadian law required each prospector to bring with him, including 350 lb (160 kg) of flour and 150 lb (68 kg) of bacon. Personable park rangers staff the center, offering insights into this fascinating period in American history.

The park offers an expanded program in the summer. Activities include ranger-led walking tours of Pioneer Square, gold-panning demonstrations, and scheduled screenings of Gold Rush-themed films. (These films are shown at other times of the year by request.)

❻ International District

East of 6th Ave S, south of Yesler Way. **Map** 4 E4. 🚌 7, 14, 36. Wing Luke Museum of the Asian Pacific American Experience: 719 South King St. **Tel** (206) 623-5124. **Open** 10am–5pm Tue–Sun. **Closed** major hols. ♿ 🗾 🇼 **wingluke.org**

Located southeast of Pioneer Square, the International District was settled by Asian-Americans in the late 19th century. This bustling area still serves as the cultural hub for the city's Chinese, Japanese, Filipino, Vietnamese, Korean, and Laotian residents.

In addition to its fine ethnic restaurants, the area is home to **Uwajimaya** (600 5th Avenue South), the largest Asian market in the Pacific Northwest. The **Wing Luke Museum of the Asian Pacific American Experience**, a Smithsonian affiliate, is named after the first Asian Pacific American elected to office in the Pacific Northwest. It highlights the history, culture, and art of Asian Pacific Americans.

Items for sale at Uwajimaya, in Seattle's International District

The tall Columbia Center, dwarfing the Smith Tower

❼ Columbia Center

701 5th Ave. **Map** 4 D2. **Tel** (206) 386-5564. 🚌 16, 358. Sky View Observatory: **Open** Mar–Aug: 9am–10pm daily; Sep–Feb: 10am–8pm daily. **Closed** public hols. 🚻 ♿ 🖥 🆆 skyviewobservatory.com

The tallest building in Seattle, Columbia Center is the tallest building – according to the number of stories – west of the Mississippi River. Rising 1,049 ft (320 m) above sea level, the 1.5-million-sq-ft (139,500-sq-m), 76-story skyscraper was designed by Chester Lindsey Architects and completed in 1985 at a cost of $285 million. In 1998 it was sold for $404 million, and again in 2015 for $711 million, to a Hong Kong company.

A prestigious business address for more than 5,000 Seattle-area workers, the shimmering black tower also attracts visitors to its 73rd-floor observation deck, the Sky View Observatory, which offers spectacular vistas of the Cascade and Olympic mountain ranges, Mount Rainier, Lake Washington, and Puget Sound, as well as views of the city and its many suburbs.

The four-level retail atrium houses shops, food vendors, and, on the third floor, the *City Space* art gallery, which features the works of artists who have been commissioned for projects by the city.

◀ Iron Pergola on Pioneer Square

❽ Fairmont Olympic Hotel

411 University St. **Map** 4 D1. **Tel** (206) 621-1700. 🚌 17, 19, 24, 26, 28. ♿ 🅿 🖥 See Where to Stay *p288.* 🆆 fairmont.com

When it debuted in 1924, the Olympic Hotel was *the* place to see and be seen – not surprising since the bondholders who funded the $4 million construction were among the city's most socially prominent citizens. Designed by the New York firm of George B. Post and Sons, the Italian Renaissance-style building features high, arched Palladian windows, gleaming oak-paneled walls, and terrazzo floors laid by Italian workmen who were sent to Seattle for the task.

More than $800,000 was spent on furnishings, including hundreds of antique mirrors, Italian and Spanish oil jars, and bronze statuary. A glamorous venue for parties, weddings, and debutante balls, the Olympic reigned as the grande dame of Seattle hotels for half a century before losing its luster.

In 1979, the hotel was listed on the US National Register of Historic Places. A year later, the Four Seasons hotel chain assumed management of the building and gave the hotel a $62.5 million face-lift – the most costly hotel restoration in the US at that time – returning the landmark hotel to her original grandeur. Fairmont Hotels and Resorts assumed management in 2003.

The striking modern façade of the Seattle Art Museum

❾ Seattle Art Museum

1300 First Ave. **Map** 3 C2. **Tel** (206) 654-3100. 🚌 174. **Open** 10am–5pm Wed–Sun (to 9pm Thu). **Closed** major hols. 🚻 ♿ 🅿 🎧 🖥 🛍 🆆 seattleartmuseum.org

At the museum's south entrance is a giant *Hammering Man*. A tribute to workers, Jonathan Borofsky's 48-ft (15-m) animated steel sculpture "hammers" silently and continuously from 7am to 10pm daily, resting only on Labor Day.

The museum building is no less impressive. Designed by the Philadelphia firm Venturi Scott Brown and Associates, the original bold limestone and sandstone building was completed in 1991 at a cost of $62 million. An acclaimed expansion in 2007, designed by Brad Cloepfil, doubled the museum's public and exhibition space.

The opulent interior of the Fairmont Olympic Hotel

The museum's permanent collection includes 25,000 objects ranging from ancient Egyptian relief sculpture and wooden African statuary to Old Master paintings and contemporary American art.

Traveling exhibits are featured on the fourth floor, as are the permanent collections of African and European art. Northwest Coast Native American art figures prominently on the third floor. Highlights here include the 14-ft- (4-m-) tall red-cedar Native houseposts carved with bears and thunderbirds boasting 11-ft (3.5-m) wingspans, from the village of Gwa'yas-dams in British Columbia. The third floor also houses American art, ancient mediterranean and Islamic art, and modern and contemporary art, including works by contemporary Pacific Northwest artists.

Also in this museum family is the Asian Art Museum, in Volunteer Park *(see p157)*, housing extensive Asian art collections. The Seattle Art Museum's third venue is the Olympic Sculpture Park *(see p148)*, an outdoor "museum" on the north end of Seattle's waterfront.

Dale Chihuly's *Benaroya Hall Silver Chandelier,* one of a pair

🔟 Benaroya Hall

200 University St. **Map** 3 C1. **Tel** (206) 215-4800. 🚍 many. 🚗 check website for details. 🅿️ ♿ 💻 📷
🅆 seattlesymphony.org

Home of the Seattle Symphony and occupying an entire city block, the $118.1 million Benaroya Hall contains two performing halls, including the 2,500-seat S. Mark Taper Foundation Auditorium, acclaimed for its superior acoustics. The multi-level Grand Lobby, dramatic at night when lit, offers stunning views of Puget Sound and the city skyline.

Benaroya Hall, grand home of the Seattle Symphony

Even if time doesn't permit attending a symphony performance, visitors can gain an appreciation of this magnificent facility by taking one of the excellent tours offered, learning how this acoustical masterpiece was created atop a transit tunnel. Visitors can also admire Benaroya Hall's impressive private art collection, which includes *Echo*, Robert Rauschenberg's evocative 12-ft (3.5-m) mural, painted on metal, and Dale Chihuly's pair of chandelier sculptures – one silver-, one gold-colored – each with some 1,200 pieces of blown glass wired to a steel armature.

Within the hall's outdoor space along 2nd Avenue is the Garden of Remembrance, which honors more than 8,000 Washington citizens who have given their lives in the service of their country since 1941.

🔟 Freeway Park

Seneca St & 6th Ave. **Map** 4 D1. 🚍 2, 13. **Open** 6am–10pm daily. ♿
🅆 seattle.gov/parks

Tucked into the heart of Seattle's bustling commercial district, and adjoining the Washington State Convention and Trade Center, Freeway Park straddles the I-5, which runs through downtown. Inside the park, thundering waterfalls drown out the traffic roar, and shady footpaths invite leisurely strolling. Outdoor concerts are held here in summer.

🔟 Central Library

1000 Fourth Ave. **Map** 4 D2. **Tel** (206) 386-4636. 🚍 many. **Open** 10am–8pm Mon–Thu, 10am–6pm Fri & Sat, noon–6pm Sun. **Closed** public hols. 🅿️ ♿ 💻 📷 🅆 spl.org

This striking glass and steel structure, completed in 2004, was designed by the award-winning Dutch architect Rem Koolhaas as a replacement for the city's 1960 Central Library. The unusual shape of the building was once a source of controversy, but the Central Library is now regarded as one of Seattle's architectural highlights. The 11-floor library includes works of art worth a staggering $1 million and an innovative "Books Spiral," allowing visitors maximum access to the collection. In its first year, some 5,000 people visited the library every day to benefit from its 2 million items. Other facilities include Internet access, 340 computers for public use, and separate centers for children, teenagers, and adult readers.

Seattle's strikingly modern Central Library, designed by Rem Koolhaas

For hotels and restaurants see p288 and pp298–300

PIKE PLACE MARKET AND THE WATERFRONT

Situated above the shores of Elliott Bay, Seattle's Pike Place Market is both a venerable landmark and a veritable feast for the senses. Exuberant and engaging, this National Historic District is known as much for its colorful personalities as it is for its abundance of local produce. Pike Street Hillclimb, a system of stairs and elevators, connects the market to Seattle's bustling waterfront, with its briny scents, squawking seagulls, fish and chip joints, and fine seafood restaurants. Marine activity abounds, as this working waterfront is the departure point for ferries, cruise ships, and harbor tour boats. The Bell Street Pier Cruise Terminal (Pier 66) is home to restaurants, a pleasure craft marina, and a cruise ship terminal, while at Pier 59, the Seattle Aquarium showcases Pacific Northwest marine life. Nearby, The Seattle Great Wheel on Pier 57 offers fantastic views of the city.

Sights at a Glance

Attractions
6 *Seattle Aquarium pp142–3*
8 The Seattle Great Wheel

Shops, Markets, and Restaurants
1 Pike Place Market
2 Athenian Inn
3 Post Alley

4 Starbucks® Pike Place
9 Ye Olde Curiosity Shop

Ferry Terminal
10 Washington State Ferries Terminal

Parks
7 Waterfront Park

Piers
5 Pier 66

| 0 meters | | 300 |
| 0 yards | | 300 |

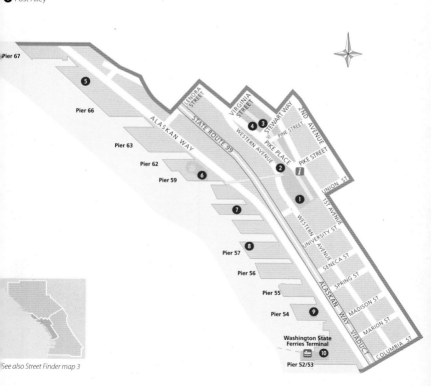

See also Street Finder map 3

◄ Bell Harbor Marina at Pier 66, with the skyscrapers of downtown in the background

For keys to symbols *see back flap*

Street-by-Street: Pike Place Market

Pike Place Market is said to be the soul of Seattle. Established in 1907, it is one of the oldest continuously operating farmer's markets in the US. Over the years, the market has mirrored national waves of immigration, with new arrivals from countries including Mexico, Laos, and the Philippines flocking here to set up small businesses. Bustling with some 100 farmers, 200 artists and craftspeople, engaging street performers, and 500 residents, the district contains art galleries, ethnic and specialty groceries, bistros, and an eclectic mix of shops.

❸ ★ Post Alley
This pedestrian walkway is lined with specialty shops, restaurants, and pubs. Its sister, Lower Post Alley, is home to similar businesses.

Key

— Suggested route

0 meters 40
0 yards 50

Waterfront

❹ Starbucks® Pike Place
This building, a former feed store, is the site of the first Starbucks® coffee shop, which moved here from its original Western Avenue location in 1976. The Starbucks® sign in the window sports the chain's original logo depicting a bare-breasted siren, based on a 16th-century Norse woodcut.

❷ Athenian Inn
This historic restaurant in Pike Place Market is as well-known for its appearance in the Tom Hanks movie *Sleepless in Seattle* as it is for its seafood and diner-style sandwiches, which can be enjoyed while sitting at a booth overlooking Elliott Bay.

Market sign and clock, c.1937, one of Seattle's oldest neon signs

SEATTLE CENTER & BELLTOWN

PIONEER SQUARE & DOWN-TOWN

PIKE PLACE MARKET & THE WATERFRONT

Locator Map
See Street Finder map 3

Newsstand
There are several newsstands in and around Pike Place Market, offering a wide range of US and international publications.

READ ALL ABOUT IT
93 PIKE ST.   624-0140
Around Back → Auto · Boating · Art ← If you don't see it.

Downtown

PIKE STREET

FIRST AVENUE

CAUTION!
LOW *flying* FISH

★ **Rachel**
Rachel, an enormous piggy bank, stands at the main entrance to Pike Place Market. Sculpted by Pacific Northwest artist Georgia Gerber, it collects funds for low-income families.

★ **Pike Place Fish**
Fish-flinging fishmongers are a long-standing tradition at this Pike Place Market store.

❶ Pike Place Market

Bounded by Pike & Virginia Sts, from
1st to Western Aves. **Map** 3 C1.
Tel (206) 682-7453. 🚌 15, 18.
Open 9am–6pm Mon–Sat,
11am–5pm Sun; may vary.
Closed Jan 1, Thanksgiving, Dec 25.
♿ 📷 Market Heritage Tour:
Call for details: (206) 322-2219.
Ⓦ **pikeplacemarket.org**

The heart of Pike Place Market
is the **Main Arcade** (1914) and
the adjacent **North Arcade**
(1922). Here, low metal-topped
counters display freshly picked
seasonal fruit, vegetables,
herbs, and flowers grown
by local farmers. Shoppers
at these low stalls get to "meet
the producer," as promised by
the market's signature green
sign. Each morning, the Market
Master, whose role at the
market dates back to 1911,
does roll call, assigning stalls
to farmers and craftspeople
based on seniority. This often
results in vendors selling their
wares from a different stall each
day. Originally, the North Arcade
consisted of two "rows." The Dry
Row, along the west wall, had
no access to running water.

A wide selection of fish on display at Pike Place Fish, in the Main Arcade

The Wet Row, with access to
running water, was also closest
to the exposed arcade entrance
and thus the damp weather.
Today, craftspeople sell from
the dry tables and farmers
from the wet tables, the run-off
still being channeled along
a trough. High stalls leased by
commercial greengrocers on a
permanent basis are also to be
found in the Main Arcade. Both
imported and locally grown
produce are on offer here.

Pike Place Fish, located in the
Main Arcade, is not Pike Place
Market's only seafood vendor.

It is, however, certainly the best
known. Situated beneath the
market's landmark clock, this
busy stall always draws a crowd
thanks to the loud, lively banter
and high-spirited antics of its
fishmongers, who are amazingly
adept at tossing fish over the
heads of cheering spectators
to co-workers behind the shop's
counter. The repartee is as fresh
as the seafood, which ranges
from wild king salmon and
Dungeness crab to rainbow
trout and live clams. Should
tourists care to buy, Pike Place
Fish will ship their seafood home.

To the south of the arcades
is the **Economy Market**,
a 1907 structure which was
incorporated into the market
in 1916, and where, among
other things, day-old goods
were sold at a discount.

The History of Pike Place Market

Hungry for fresh produce and fair prices, Seattleites mobbed Pike
Place Market when it opened on August 17, 1907, at Pike Street
and 1st Avenue, as an effort by the city council to eliminate "greedy
middlemen" and allow farmers to sell directly to the public. Sensing
opportunity, local Frank Goodwin used his Klondike gold to build
permanent arcades. At its height in the 1930s, hundreds of farmers
sold their produce at the market. But by World War II, it had fallen on
hard times: Japanese-Americans made up about 80 percent of the
sellers at the wet tables; their internment *(see p44)* had a disastrous
effect. In the years that followed, the decline continued as suburbs
and super-markets became entrenched in the American way of life.

By the late 1960s,
developers were
lobbying to tear
it down. Rallied
by architect
Victor Steinbrueck,
Seattleites rebelled,
voting in 1971 to
make the market a
historic district. Today,
over 80 farmers from
across the state sell
at the market and
its four neighbor-
hood markets in
downtown Seattle.

Local farmers selling their produce at Pike Place Market,
May 1912

One of many stands displaying artwork
at the market

across Pike Street are the **Corner Market** (1912) and **Sanitary Market** (1910) – two of the several buildings constructed during the market's first two decades as it prospered, and so named because horse-drawn carts were not allowed inside. Today all three market buildings house retail shops, restaurants, and cafés.

Pike Place Market will undergo a major expansion, termed Market Front, in 2017, which will add a public plaza and a path to the waterfront.

Pike Place Fish

Pike Place Market (Main Arcade). **Tel** 1 (800) 542-7732. **Open** 6:30am–8pm Mon–Sat, 7am–5pm Sun. **W** pikeplacefish.com

The entrance to the Athenian Inn in Pike Place Market

Athenian Inn

1517 Pike Pl (Main Arcade). **Map** 3 C1. **Tel** (206) 624-7166. 15, 18. **Open** 6:30am–8:30pm Mon–Thu, 6:30am–9:30pm Fri & Sat, 9am–4:30pm Sun. 1st floor only.

The Athenian Inn has been in operation nearly as long as the market itself. Opened by three brothers in 1909, it evolved from a bakery and luncheonette to a tavern and, later, a restaurant. It was, in 1933, one of the first restaurants in Seattle to get a liquor license. Neither flashy nor fancy, this diner serves old-time favorites like corned beef hash, with generous helpings of local color. However, the best reason to visit the Athenian Inn is not for the food but for the view of Elliott Bay. Nab one of the wooden booths at the back of the restaurant and you will see the Duwamish waterway, with its impressive container-ship loading facility; West Seattle;

Bainbridge Island; and ferries skimming across the bay.

If the inn seems oddly familiar, that may be because of its supporting role in the 1993 movie *Sleepless in Seattle*.

➌ Post Alley

Stewart to Virginia Sts between Pike Pl & 1st Ave. **Map** 3 B1. 15, 18.

Post Alley has a decidedly European ambience. Along this brick-paved passageway are two of the city's favorite haunts. **The Pink Door** (1919 Post Alley) is an Italian trattoria identified only by an unmarked pink door. Come summer, with the restaurant's terrace, with its impressive harbor view, is popular with locals – and tourists who happily stumble upon the elusive restaurant. Across the alley, **Kell's Irish Restaurant and Pub** (1916 Post Alley) pours Guinness and offers live Celtic music in cozy surroundings.

Above the shops of Post Alley are condominiums and apartments, many housing the market's some 500 residents, several of whom are low-income seniors.

➍ Starbucks® Pike Place

1912 Pike Pl. **Map** 3 B1. **Tel** (206) 448-8762. 15, 18. **Open** 6am–7:30pm Mon–Fri, 6:30am–7:30pm Sat & Sun. **W** starbucks.com

Seattle is said to be the most caffeinated city in the US, a distinction Seattleites don't refute. To see where the coffee craze started, visit Starbucks® Pike Place, the first shop in the omnipresent chain.

Opened in 1971, at 2000 Western Avenue, Starbucks® Coffee, Tea and Spices moved to its Pike Place location in 1976. Named after the first mate in Herman Melville's *Moby Dick*, the company's first logo – a voluptuous two-tailed mermaid encircled by the original name – still greets visitors at this small store.

In the early days, Starbucks® did not sell coffee by the cup; the focus was on whole-bean coffee. Occasionally, they offered tasting samples in porcelain cups, creating loyal customers by educating them on the finer points of quality coffee. In 1985, inspired by Italian coffeehouses, Starbucks® served its first caffè latte, made with espresso and steamed milk. Today, visitors to the flagship store can choose from a long list of coffee drinks, as can the millions of customers around the world. Indeed, more than 80 million customers visit Starbucks® each week.

The original Starbucks® sign, at its first location

In 2014, Starbucks® introduced the fascinating, one-of-its-kind **Starbucks Reserve® Roastery & Tasting Room** (1124 Pike St; 6:30am–11pm daily; http://roastery.starbucks.com). This 15,600-sq-ft (1,449-sq-m) expanse includes roasting facilities, coffee bars, shops, a restaurant, and a library, spread over two floors.

The interior of Starbucks® Pike Place

❺ Pier 66

Bell St Pier Cruise Terminal, Pier 66, Alaskan Way. **Map** 3 A1. 🚌 15, 18, 21, 22, 56, 99. 🅦 portseattle.org

One of the liveliest parts of the waterfront is the Port of Seattle's Pier 66, also known as Bell Street Pier Cruise Terminal. It is home to a thriving luxury cruise ship terminal, a pleasure craft marina, a conference center, and a handful of eateries.

There is a constant hub of activity, with Bell Street Pier Cruise Terminal and Smith Cove Terminal (at Pier 91, north of downtown) together greeting more than 200 cruise ships every year, most of which are bound for Alaska's stunning Inside Passage *(see pp278–9)*.

Pier 66 is also home to the Bell Harbor Marina, a small in-city marina for pleasure boats. For spectacular views of the moored boats here, visitors can gaze out from Bell Street Pier Cruise Terminal's rooftop plaza.

On and around the pier is a variety of restaurants, from take-out fish and chips to more comfortable and relaxed dining *(see pp298–300)*.

❻ Seattle Aquarium

See pp142–3.

❼ Waterfront Park

Pier 57–59, 1301 Alaskan Way. **Map** 3 B1. **Tel** (206) 684-4075. 🚌 15, 18, 21. Park: **Open** 6am–10pm daily. ♿ 🅦 seattle.gov/parks

The Waterfront Park comprises the area between Pier 57 and Pier 59. The park offers excellent views of the Seattle skyline and the waterfront, and visitors have even been known to spot a seal. At the north end of the park is *The Waterfront Fountain*, by James FitzGerald and Terry Copple. Made of casted and welded bronze, the sculpture

A lovely sunny day at Seattle's Waterfront Park

is composed of a number of cubical structures. At its south end is a large abstract statue of Christopher Columbus gazing out across the water. Other interesting sculptures, as well as coin-operated telescopes, picnic tables, and benches, are dotted around the park.

The Waterfront Streetcar, officially known as the George Benson Waterfront Streetcar Line, began in 1982 and was the first streetcar to run in Seattle since 1941. It used to be a great way to see Seattle's best attractions but was suspended in 2005, when the maintenance barn and one of the stations were demolished to make room for the Seattle Art Museum's Olympic Sculpture Park *(see p148)*. The track and other eight stations remain, but it is unclear whether it will ever be operational again. The route has been replaced by metro bus route 99. The buses have been made to look like streetcars.

❽ The Seattle Great Wheel

Pier 57, 1301 Alaskan Way. **Map** 3 B2. **Tel** (206) 623-8607. 🚌 15, 18, 21, 22, 56, 99. **Open** Jul–Sep: 10am–11pm Sun–Thu, 10am–midnight Fri & Sat; Sep–Jun: 11am–10pm Mon–Thu, 11am–midnight Fri, 10am–midnight Sat, 10am–10pm Sun. 🚻 ♿ 🅦 seattlegreatwheel.com

The Seattle Great Wheel, perched dramatically over Elliott Bay, offers spectacular views of the city skyline and the Olympic Mountains. Built in less than a year, it opened in 2012. Standing 175-ft (53-m) tall, The Seattle Great Wheel is the largest observation wheel on the West Coast. Visitors can get a ride lasting up to 20 minutes in 41 fully enclosed, climate-controlled gondolas, each of which can carry up to eight passengers. There is a special VIP gondola as well, with leather bucket seats, a stereo system, and a glass bottom floor, that can seat up to four people. Each ride is accompanied by a narration of Seattle's waterfront history.

The Ferris wheel is lit up each night with white lights. For certain events, such as Seattle Seahawks home football matches, and on holidays, a special light show is held on the wheel.

The Seattle Great Wheel, extending over Puget Sound on Seattle's waterfront

For hotels and restaurants see p288 and pp298–300

Sign for Ye Olde Curiosity Shop, a Seattle institution since 1899

❾ Ye Olde Curiosity Shop

Pier 54, 1001 Alaskan Way. **Map** 3 C2. **Tel** (206) 682-5844. 🚌 15, 18, 21, 22, 56, 57. **Open** 10am–6pm Sun–Thu, 10am–9pm Fri & Sat. **Closed** Jan 1, Thanksgiving, Dec 25. 🚻
🌐 yeoldecuriosityshop.com

The quintessential curio shop, this Seattle institution has been a fixture of the city's waterfront since 1899. Among the legendary curiosities are shrunken heads, a "freak pig" with two tails, two faces, three eyes, and eight legs, a walrus skull with three tusks, and three well-preserved mummies that were discovered in the Arizona desert a century ago, including the much-talked about "Sylvester." Oddities, both old and new, include The Lord's Prayer and oil paintings engraved on the heads of pins.

But there is much more to this tightly packed store than quirky curios and unusual souvenirs. From its first days of business, this waterfront shop has been a Native American trading post. Today, the arts and crafts of the region's Native Americans are sold through the store, which has also provided a number of private collections and prestigious museums, including the Smithsonian Institution in Washington, DC, with Native American art and artifacts.

Joseph Edward Standley of Ohio started this family-run shop in 1899 – reportedly earning only 25 cents in the first three days. Fortunately, Standley persevered, and in 1909 he sold his ethnological collection, which had garnered a gold medal at Seattle's World Fair that year, to New York's Museum of the American Indian for $5,000, establishing the shop with collectors. Nowadays, his well-stocked shop is run by Standley's great-grandson.

❿ Washington State Ferries Terminal

Pier 52, 801 Alaskan Way. **Map** 3 C2. 🚌 15, 18, 21, 22, 56. Ferry schedules: **Tel** (206) 464-6400 (recording). 🚻
🌐 wsdot.wa.gov/ferries

Both a highly efficient transit system and a top tourist attraction, Washington State ferries transport 23 million residents and travelers a year. Seattle's main terminal is Colman Dock, located on the waterfront at the foot of Columbia Street. The dock will be undergoing a long-term restoration and redevelopment project from 2017.

The original wharf was built in 1882 by Scottish engineer James Colman to accommodate steamships. Destroyed seven years later in the Great Seattle Fire *(see p128)*, it was immediately rebuilt to service Puget Sound's "mosquito fleet" of private ferries. It was also a bustling hub for ships bound for the northern gold fields during the gold rushes of the 1890s.

In 1908, Colman extended the dock, adding a domed waiting room and a clock tower. The elegant tower toppled four years later when the ocean liner *Alameda* rammed the pier. The tower's replacement met with similar misfortune when it was scorched in a 1914 pier fire.

Although not as architecturally interesting as its predecessors, the present terminal, which was built in 1964, does an admirable job accommodating the many passengers traveling to Bremerton and Bainbridge Island. The terminal also serves foot passengers traveling to Vashon Island.

A popular tourist activity is the 35-minute ferry ride to Winslow on Bainbridge Island, where galleries, shops, restaurants, and a waterfront park are all within walking distance of the ferry dock, making for a pleasant day trip.

Ivar's Acres of Clams

A waterfront landmark since 1938, the seafood restaurant Ivar's Acres of Clams on Pier 54 was founded by Seattle-born Ivar Haglund (1905–85), a radio and television personality and self-promoter. Eighteen years before opening his popular restaurant, Haglund established Seattle's first aquarium, also on Pier 54, scooping the "exhibits" out of Puget Sound himself. Wearing his trademark captain's hat, Haglund entertained visitors by singing songs he had written about his favorite sea critters. The aquarium's other attraction was a fish-and-chips counter across from the seal cage. It was the seed for Haglund's foray into the food-service business, an enterprise

Hungry visitors and seagulls – all are welcome at Ivar's

that grew to include three restaurants, nearly 30 fish bars throughout the Pacific Northwest, and Ivar's own brand of clam chowder. Known for his silly puns ("Keep Clam" remains the company motto) and frequent publicity stunts (he once hoisted a 16-ft/5-m salmon windsock to the flagpole atop Smith Tower), Haglund was – and remains – a colorful Seattle icon. Two months after his death in 1985, the city celebrated his 80th birthday with a boat parade in Elliott Bay. And each Independence Day, as Seattleites watch the lavish "Fourth of Jul-Ivar's" fireworks display over the bay, they remember with fondness the "firecracker" who started the tradition back in 1964.

❻ Seattle Aquarium

One of the top aquariums in the country, the Seattle Aquarium offers a fascinating window into Pacific Northwest marine life, showcasing more than 400 different species of fish, plants, and mammals indigenous to the area. Sea otters and seals cavort in pools, and feeding time is especially entertaining. Visitors can also learn about the aquarium's ecological and conservation work with the local environment, and even meet the wildlife in one of the interactive exhibits.

Encountering local sea creatures in the Life on the Edge exhibit

★ Window on Washington Waters
This 120,000-gallon (454,250-liter) tank is populated with brightly colored fish, anemones, and others. Three times a day, divers take to the water and talk back and forth with the audience.

Mezzanine Level

Main Entrance

Key

- Window on Washington Waters and Crashing Waves
- Life of a Drifter and Life on the Edge
- Pacific Coral Reef and Ocean Oddities
- Birds and Shores, Alcids and Salmon Ladder
- Marine Mammals
- Puget Sound Orcas and Underwater Marine Mammal Viewing
- Underwater Dome
- Puget Sound Fish
- Non-exhibition space

Aquarium Guide

The Seattle Aquarium is laid out on three levels. The ground floor houses the majority of the exhibits, while the lower level features an underwater dome that allows visitors to see some of the exhibits from underwater. Visitor facilities, including a café, are on the mezzanine level.

Caring for two of Seattle Aquarium's plentiful seal population

For hotels and restaurants see p288 and pp298–300

Birds and Shores
Learn how local seabirds make their homes in inhospitable conditions. Birds, including this tufted puffin and common murres, can be seen nesting, foraging, and more.

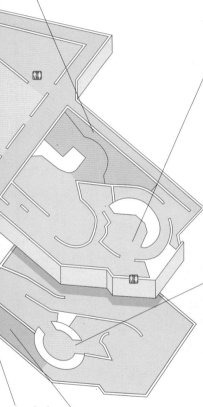

Lower Level

★ **Marine Mammals**
This popular attraction features the antics of the aquarium's sea otters, harbor seals, and fur seals. Visitors can also see these mammals in an underwater viewing area on the lower level.

★ **Underwater Dome**
Travel through a short tunnel to this stunning undersea dome, which offers a panoramic view from inside a 400,000-gallon (1,500,000-liter) tank housing rockfish, small sharks, salmon, lingcod, sturgeon, and many others.

Puget Sound Fish
Packed with bright, exotic fish such as this canary rockfish, Pacific spiny lumpsuckers, and midshipmen fish, Puget Sound Fish is a great chance for kids to snap some colorful photos.

SEATTLE CENTER AND BELLTOWN

Located north of downtown, Seattle Center is the proud legacy of the city's 1962 World's Fair. Best known to tourists as the home of the Space Needle, the center boasts numerous cultural venues and excellent museums, including the innovative EMP Museum, designed by architect Frank Gehry and funded by Microsoft billionaire Paul Allen (see p163). Just to the south of Seattle Center lies trendy Belltown, its hub stretching from Virginia to Vine Streets along 1st Avenue. Here, among the pricey condominiums, visitors will find high-end hair salons, upscale clothing boutiques, antique shops, home accessories stores, trendy restaurants, and a fashionable crowd.

Sights at a Glance

Museums and Theaters

1 Olympic Sculpture Park
2 Pacific Science Center and Boeing Imax Theater
6 EMP Museum pp150–51
8 The Children's Museum

Buildings

3 Space Needle
7 KeyArena
9 Austin A. Bell Building
10 Virginia Inn

Other Attractions

4 Chihuly Garden and Glass
5 Seattle Center Monorail

0 meters 500
0 yards 500

See also Street Finder maps 1, 2, and 3

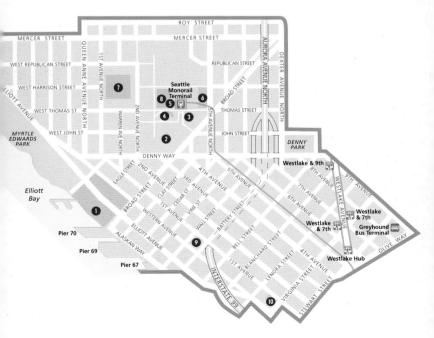

◀ Part of the innovative façade of the EMP Museum

For keys to symbols see back flap

Street-by-Street: Seattle Center

The Seattle Center grounds have long been a lively gathering spot for city residents and visitors. In the 1800s, this prized parcel of land was the setting for Indian potlatches. In 1962, it was transformed into a fairground for the World's Fair – Century 21 Exposition *(see p149)*. Today, the site is one of the most visited urban parks in the US. Strolling the pedestrian boulevards, you'll see several legacies of the World's Fair. Among the most notable and noticeable is the Space Needle, which now shares the spotlight with such innovative structures as the EMP Museum. Performing arts companies, sports teams, and a children's museum all call Seattle Center home.

International Fountain
A mainstay of the 1962 World's Fair, redesigned in 1995, this fountain features 274 water shooters and propels 9,000 gallons (34,000 liters) of water up to 120 ft (37 m).

Marion Oliver McCaw Hall is home to the Seattle Opera and Pacific NW Ballet.

MERCER STREET

Seattle Repertory Theatre
"The Rep" presents both contemporary and classic plays on its two stages: the Bagley Wright Theatre and the Leo K. Theatre.

1ST AVENUE NO

7 KeyArena
Now a sports and concert venue, the arena was built in 1962 for Seattle's second World's Fair.

Key

— Suggested route

| 0 meters | 50 |
| 0 yards | 50 |

❸ ★ Space Needle
The once futuristic Space Needle is a prominent feature of Seattle's skyline.

Locator Map
See Street Finder map 1

❹ Chihuly Garden and Glass
A gallery and garden that exhibits Dale Chihuly's stunning, colorful glassworks.

❷ Pacific Science Center
Interactive exhibits devoted to science, mathematics, and technology; two IMAX theaters; and a planetarium are housed in the center's six buildings.

BROAD STREET

DENNY WAY

WEST THOMAS STREET

❻ ★ EMP Museum
This exceptional museum situated at the base of the Space Needle was designed by the architect Frank Gehry.

Fisher Pavilion, facing the South Fountain Lawn, is a popular venue for trade shows and festivals.

❺ ★ Seattle Center Monorail
The Seattle Center Monorail travels directly through EMP Museum before it enters the Seattle Center Station. Each train has traveled over one million miles (1.6 million km) since being put into service in 1962.

❶ Olympic Sculpture Park

2901 Western Ave. **Map** 1 B5. **Tel** (206) 654-3100. 🚇 Seattle Center. 🚌 1, 2, 13, 15, 18, 99. **Open** dawn–dusk daily. PACCAR Pavilion: Mar 1–Oct 31: 10am–5pm Tue–Sun; Nov 1–Feb 28: 10am–4pm Sat & Sun. 🚫 🎫 ♿ **W** seattleartmuseum.org

Opened to the public in January 2007 as part of the Seattle Art Museum *(see pp132–3)*, the Olympic Sculpture Park sits on what used to be an industrial site, now transformed into a unique green space for public recreation and outdoor art. The innovative design for the park included environmental restoration schemes such as the creation of a salmon habitat and tree planting.

The park is made up of three areas linked by a 2,200-ft (670-m), Z-shaped path. Visitors can see over 20 modern sculptures scattered throughout a variety of typical Pacific Northwest landscapes such as *The Valley*, an evergreen forest similar to those found in the lowland coastal regions, *Schubert Sonata*, sculptor Mark di Suvero's towering steel wind vane, and *The Shore*, which features a beach and a naturally developing tidal garden.

The PACCAR Pavilion is the park headquarters. It houses a car park and a café where visitors can buy food for picnics. Guided tours of the park are also available starting from the Pavilion.

Perre's Ventaglio III, one of the pieces in the Olympic Sculpture Park

❷ Pacific Science Center and Boeing IMAX Theater

200 2nd Ave N. **Map** 1 B4. **Tel** (206) 443-2001. 🚇 Seattle Center. 🚌 19, 24, 33. **Open** 10am–6pm daily (to 5pm Mon–Fri in fall); IMAX open daily, call (206) 443-4629 for films and showtimes. **Closed** Thanksgiving, Dec 25. 🎫 additional charge for laser & IMAX shows and the planetarium. ♿ **W** pacificsciencecenter.org

The Pacific Science Center features four exhibit halls and two IMAX theaters surrounding five 110-ft (33.5-m) arches that rise over reflecting pools and fountains. While enjoyed by all ages, the science and math exhibits are especially appealing to kids.

Dinosaurs: A Journey Through Time takes visitors back to the Mesozoic Era to meet lifelike robotic dinosaurs. In Body Works visitors can pedal on the Calorie Bicycle to see how much energy they produce, and in Tech Zone they can challenge an industrial robot to games of tic-tac-toe. Also popular with youngsters and adults alike is the imaginative world of Professor Wellbody's Academy of Health & Wellness®. This innovative health exhibit uses games, activities, and other interactive experiences to highlight the importance of diet, exercise, sleep, lifestyle, and hygiene for personal well-being. Insect Village features huge robotic insects and a mini-zoo where brave visitors can touch a cockroach. The Tropical Butterfly House is filled with exotic free-flying butterflies. Outside, visitors can spin a 2-ton granite ball or ride the High Rail Bicycle perched 15 ft (4.5 m) above the ground on a 1-inch (2.5-cm) rail.

The Center also houses a planetarium, laser theater, the PACCAR IMAX Theater, and the futuristic Boeing IMAX Theater. The latter has laser projectors and a cutting-edge sound system, and shows documentaries on the natural world, space exploration, and a variety of children's films, 2D and 3D feature films, and animations.

The magnificent Space Needle, the pride of Seattle

❸ Space Needle

400 Broad St. **Map** 1 C4. **Tel** (206) 905-2100. 🚇 Seattle Center. 🚌 3, 4, 16. **Open** 10am–9:30pm Mon–Thu, 9:30am–10:30pm Fri–Sun (to 9:30pm Sun). ♿ 🚫 **W** spaceneedle.com

What started as a rough sketch on the back of a paper placemat has become Seattle's internationally recognized landmark and number one tourist attraction. Built for the 1962 World's Fair, the 605-ft (185-m) Space Needle was the brainchild of Edward Carlson, the fair's chairman, who was inspired by Germany's Stuttgart Tower. The final design by John Graham and Company architects of the first shopping mall in the US, was approved just 18 months before the fair's opening date; the Space Needle was built in 12 months, for a relatively inexpensive $4.5 million. At the time, it was the tallest building west of the Mississippi River.

Supported by three curved steel legs, the needle's glass-enclosed tophouse features an observation deck and, below it, a revolving restaurant – the second in the world – which is turned by a one-and-a-half-horsepower motor.

The underground foundation buried 30 ft (9 m) deep and stretching 120 ft (37 m) wide, took 467 cement trucks to fill – a mission accomplished in less than 12 hours. The tower is attached to the foundation with 72 30-ft- (9-m-) long bolts.

Solidly constructed, the Space Needle has weathered several earthquakes and has closed fewer than ten times in its history because of high winds. (While the structure itself can withstand winds up to 200 mph/ 322 km/h, its elevators can't.)

During the Seattle World's Fair, nearly 20,000 people a day rode the high-speed elevators to the top, enduring waits of up to 3 hours for the 43-second ride. Thankfully, the wait is much shorter today, and the view just as spectacular. Weather permitting, visitors can enjoy panoramic views of the Olympic and Cascade mountain ranges, Mount Rainier, Lake Union, Elliott Bay, and downtown Seattle.

In 1982, a "skyline level" was added 100 ft (30 m) above the ground. In 1999, on its 37th birthday, the Space Needle was proclaimed the city's official landmark by Seattle's Landmarks Preservation Board. And, in 2000, a $20 million revitalization included construction of a glass pavilion, which encircles the base of the tower.

❹ Chihuly Garden and Glass

305 Harrison St. **Map** 1 B4. **Tel** (206) 753-4940. 🚉 Seattle Center. **Open** 11am–6pm daily (to 7pm Fri & Sat; last entry 1 hr before closing). **Closed** Thanksgiving, Dec 25, for special events (check website). 🎥 🖥 **W** chihulygardenandglass.com

Chihuly Garden and Glass showcases the life and career of American glass sculpture artist Dale Chihuly (b. 1941). Designed by architect Owen Richards, it opened at the foot of the Space Needle in 2012. The highlight is the 40-ft- (12-m-) tall glasshouse, spread over 4,500 sq ft (418 sq m). Inside is one of Chihuly's largest suspended sculptures, a mesmerizing work about 100 ft (30 m) long, in shades of red, orange, and yellow. Several of his other artworks

and architectural installations, including intricate chandeliers, are displayed in the eight galleries, which bring to the fore the artist's expertise in the craft of glassblowing and his creative use of shapes and colors. The complex also includes a garden with sculptures surrounded by trees, plants, and flowers, and a theater that plays short videos on Chihuly's work.

❺ Seattle Center Monorail

Map 1 C4–3 C1. **Tel** (206) 905-2620. 🚉 Westlake Center, Seattle Center. **Open** 7:30am–9pm Mon–Thu, 7:30am–11pm Fri, 8:30am–11pm Sat, 8:30am–9pm Sun; departs every 10 mins (check website for details). 🎥 ♿ **W** seattlemonorail.com

Built for Seattle's second World's Fair in only 10 months, its foundations buried 25 ft (7.5 m) below street level, Seattle's Alweg monorail provided a link between the fairgrounds (now the Seattle Center) and downtown Seattle. At the time, it was described as a preview of the mass transit system of the future. Traveling between

Seattle Center Monorail, pulling into the Space Needle terminal

downtown and the foot of the Space Needle, the Monorail's trains carried as many as eight million passengers during the fair's six-month duration.

Today, this transit system is used by 2.5 million passengers per year, many of them locals who ride the Monorail to festivals, concerts, and sporting events at the Seattle Center. The fastest full-sized monorail system in the US, the Seattle Center Monorail covers the 1-mile (1.6-km) distance in 2 minutes, at a speed of up to 60 mph (97 km/h), zipping through the EMP Museum, which was built around and over the Monorail's tracks.

Seattle World's Fair

Officially known as the Century 21 Exposition, Seattle's second World's Fair was conceived as a way to commemorate the 50th anniversary of the Alaska-Yukon-Pacific Exposition held here in 1909. Billed as "America's Space Age World's Fair," the new exposition was dedicated to science and life in the 21st century. Ambitious plans and a desire to design a civic center that would be enjoyed by the community for generations to come pushed the original opening date back a few years, from 1959 to 1962.

Among the fair's most ambitious buildings and lasting legacies are the Space Needle, the Monorail, the US Science Pavilion (now the Pacific Science Center), and the Washington State Coliseum (now KeyArena). Designed to appear futuristic, in keeping with the Century 21 theme, the buildings now have a rather retro appeal, especially the Space Needle.

The fair drew 9,634,600 people. Today, more than five decades later, Seattleites and tourists continue to flock to the Seattle Center to enjoy a festival, cultural performance, or sporting event; visit a museum; or simply stroll the tree-lined, fountain-filled grounds.

Seattle's towering Space Needle under construction in 1961

❻ EMP Museum

Opened in 2000, Seattle's EMP Museum celebrates American popular music and culture, with rare memorabilia, interactive exhibits, and a live performance space – all housed in an exuberant structure that swoops and swirls at the base of the Space Needle. Designed by Frank Gehry, an architect with a penchant for atypical shapes and angles, innovative building materials, and bold colors, the building is said to resemble a smashed electric guitar. The museum was conceived by Microsoft co-founder Paul Allen *(see p163)*. EMP incorporates a science fiction gallery with exhibits on horror films, fantasy, and independent video games.

The Building
From the air, the seemingly random jumble of shapes and tortured metal designed by architect Frank Gehry takes form as the carcass of a smashed guitar.

Sound Lab
encourages experimentation with music.

Main Entrance

Level One

The Nirvana: Taking Punk to the Masses exhibit features an extensive collection of rare memorabilia from Seattle's iconic grunge band, including photographs, a guitar smashed by lead singer Kurt Cobain, and the band's first demo recording tape.

★ Sky Church
The "heart and soul" of EMP, this great hall is used as a performance space, which includes a large video screen.

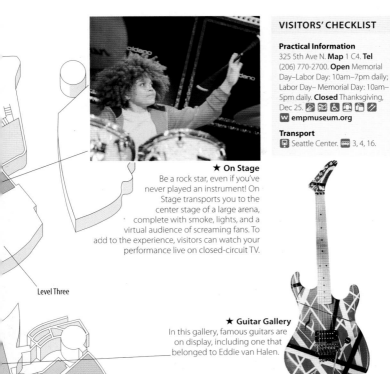

VISITORS' CHECKLIST

Practical Information
325 5th Ave N. **Map** 1 C4. **Tel**
(206) 770-2700. **Open** Memorial
Day–Labor Day: 10am–7pm daily;
Labor Day– Memorial Day: 10am–
5pm daily. **Closed** Thanksgiving,
Dec 25. 🅦 empmuseum.org

Transport
Seattle Center. 3, 4, 16.

★ On Stage
Be a rock star, even if you've
never played an instrument! On
Stage transports you to the
center stage of a large arena,
complete with smoke, lights, and a
virtual audience of screaming fans. To
add to the experience, visitors can watch your
performance live on closed-circuit TV.

Level Three

★ Guitar Gallery
In this gallery, famous guitars are
on display, including one that
belonged to Eddie van Halen.

Exhibitions, such as Infinite Worlds of
Science Fiction, Fantasy and Can't Look Away,
take visitors through the sci-fi universe, from
Bram Stoker's *Dracula* to *Back to the Future*.
The implications of new technology are
explored and fantastic worlds created.

Key

- Hendrix
- On Stage
- Sound Lab
- Demo Lab
- We Are 12: The Seattle Seahawks and the Road to Victory
- JBL Theatre
- Learning Labs
- Nirvana: Talking Punk to the Masses
- EMP store
- Infinite Worlds of Science Fiction, Fantasy and Can't Look Away exhibitions
- Sky Church
- Special exhibits gallery
- Guitar Gallery
- Roots and Branches
- Non-exhibition space

Level Two, Main Level

Museum Guide

*EMP has three levels. The main
galleries and exhibits are on
Levels Two and Three. The lower
level offers a theater for lectures,
films, and classes; the Learning
Labs; and a restaurant that
serves regional American cuisine.*

★ Roots and Branches
This sculpture offers a dynamic,
interactive, and historical journey
into the origins and evolution
of American popular music. An
audiovisual tour explores American
musical roots and influences.

❼ KeyArena

305 Harrison St. **Map** 1 B4. **Tel** (206) 684-7200. Event tickets: **Tel** (800) 745-3000. 🚇 Seattle Center. 🚌 1, 2, 13, 14, 15, 18. ♿ See Shopping in Seattle *p164*. 🌐 keyarena.com

In its first life, KeyArena was the Washington State Coliseum, offering Seattle World's Fair visitors a glimpse into the 21st century. Hailed as an architectural masterpiece in 1962 for its shape (a hyperbolic paraboloid) and lack of interior roof supports, this structure at the western end of the Seattle Center was designed by Paul Thiry (1904–93), main architect of Seattle's second World's Fair *(see p149)*, to last well into the 21st century as a sports and convention facility. Fairgoers fondly recall the coliseum's giant glass Bubbleator, which transported 150 passengers at one time high up into the World of Tomorrow exhibit.

After the fair, the futuristic building was converted into a sports arena. In 1964, it hosted the Beatles' first Seattle concert and, since then, has become one of the top big-ticket concert venues on the country's West Coast.

In 1995, architectural firm NBBJ led a $74 million renovation in which the interior was completely remodeled – the plastic, wood, steel, copper, and concrete from the gutted interior either recycled in the renovation or sold. Renamed, the 17,000-seat KeyArena is now home to Seattle's women's professional basketball team the Storm, and it is also a favored venue for a variety of entertainment acts.

Seattle's Children's Museum, popular for interactive exhibits

❽ The Children's Museum

305 Harrison St. **Map** 1 B4. **Tel** (206) 441-1768. 🚇 Seattle Center. 🚌 1, 2, 3, 4, 13, 14, 15, 16, 18. **Open** 10am–5pm Mon–Fri, 10am–6pm Sat & Sun. **Closed** Jan 1, Labor Day weekend, Thanksgiving, Dec 24, Dec 25. ♿ 📷 🌐 thechildrensmuseum.org

While most of Seattle Center is a delight for kids, the Children's Museum, founded in 1979 by parents and educators, is especially popular with youngsters. Located on the first level of the Seattle Center's Center House, the nonprofit interactive museum features eight permanent galleries, one temporary gallery, and three studio spaces.

Permanent exhibits include Global Village, where young visitors are introduced to the cultures and lifestyles of their contemporaries around the sworld. Children can visit a tailor shop in Ghana and taste sushi in Japan. In the Mountain Forest exhibit, kids learn about Washington's natural environment as they hike through a re-creation of a Pacific Northwest forest, complete with a bat-inhabited cave, a waterfall, and flowing lava. Interactive elements include sliding down a glacier.

Pulleys, pipes, mazes, and levers challenge hand-eye coordination in Cog City. Kids can experience the laws of physics firsthand by directing balls through a busy cityscape. The museum also has an interactive exhibit designed especially with toddlers in mind. Discovery Bay's aquarium contains kelp and a touch pool.

Three to four changing exhibitions throughout the year guarantee that there is always something new to see. The museum also features an artist-in-residence and a drop-in arts studio for kids – the first of its kind in the region.

Brick façade of the Austin A. Bell Building, with its Gothic features

❾ Austin A. Bell Building

2326 1st Ave. **Map** 1 C5. 🚌 15, 18, 21, 22, 56. **Closed** to the public.

The Austin A. Bell Building was designed by Elmer Fisher, Seattle's foremost commercial architect at the end of the 19th century and designer of more than 50 buildings in the years surrounding the Great Fire of 1889 *(see p128)*. While most were in Pioneer Square, including the still-standing Pioneer Building *(see p128)*, a few Fisher-designed structures graced the Belltown (then Denny Hill) area, chief among them this building.

The unique geometric roof of KeyArena at the Seattle Center

Combining Richardsonian, Gothic, and Italianate design elements, the handsome four-story brick structure was commissioned in 1888 by Austin Americus Bell, the wealthy son of Seattle pioneer William M. Bell, for whom Belltown is named. It was to be an apartment building and the young Bell's first major building project in the city. However, the 35-year-old entrepreneur did not live to see his building completed. Suffering from ill-health and depression, Bell took his own life in 1889. His wife saw the project through to completion, and had Bell's name etched into the top of the building's façade. Its interior was destroyed by fire in 1981, but the exterior survived relatively unscathed.

Listed on the National Register of Historic Places, the Austin A. Bell Building now houses pricey condominiums on its upper three floors and a coffee shop at street level.

workers, and the right through the Prohibition period (1920–33), when it served as a cardroom and lunch spot.

In the 1970s, the pub began to attract an arty clientele, who joined the old-timers at the long elegant bar. Over time the local community has changed as low-income housing was replaced by upmarket condominiums, and the clientele altered accordingly. The Virginia Inn has now become known as Seattle's

hottest art bar, with rotating exhibits by local artists adorning the walls. Each exhibition is displayed for two months at a time.

The pub is a good place to sample a local microbrew from one of the 16 beers on tap (or even try one from its good selection of Belgian beers). It also has an excellent wine list and specialty cocktails. The brick-and-tile Virginia Inn has something of a European feel to it – without the cigarette fumes.

A café-cum-laundry, one of Belltown's many eclectic businesses

Belltown History

With its broad avenues lined with hip clubs, chic restaurants, and eclectic shops, Belltown has been compared to Manhattan's Upper West Side. What Belltown conspicuously lacks is the one thing for which the rest of the city is famous: hills. This was not always the case. Originally home to a very steep slope, the area took on a new identity between 1905 and 1930, when Denny Hill was regraded and washed into Elliott Bay. In all, more than 50 city blocks were lowered by as much as 100 ft (30 m), turning Denny Hill into the Denny Regrade, a lackluster name for an unremarkable area of town inhabited by labor union halls, car lots, inexpensive apartments, and sailors' taverns. (Ironically, the intent of the regrade project was to encourage business development by making the area easier to navigate.)

Belltown coffee shop sign

For decades, the area's identity was its very lack thereof. This began to change in the 1970s, when artists, attracted by cheap rents and abundant studio space, started moving to the Regrade. It was also during the 1970s that a neighborhood association renamed the area Belltown, after William M. Bell, one of the area's pioneers. By the 1980s, as Seattleites and suburbanites began taking an interest in cosmopolitan urban living, condominiums began appearing on Belltown's periphery. Fueled by the software boom of the 1990s, the area experienced a huge building boom, attracting well-paid high-tech types to its amenity-rich towers. Although today Belltown bears little resemblance to its early days, a few original structures remain; among them, the Virginia Inn and the Austin A. Bell Building.

The European-style Virginia Inn, a favorite pub among Belltown locals

⓾ Virginia Inn

1937 1st Ave. **Map** 3 B1. **Tel** (206) 728-1937. ▨ 15, 18, 21, 22, 56. **Open** 11:30am–midnight Sun–Thu, 11:30am–2am Fri & Sat. ♿ ▨ ⓦ virginiainnseattle.com

Located on the southern boundary of Belltown, the Virginia Inn has been a popular watering hole since before the area came to be called Belltown. Established in 1903, it has operated continuously, first as a beer parlor for waterfront

FARTHER AFIELD

Seattle's outlying areas offer plenty of opportunities for exploration and recreation. Immediately to the south sit two spectacular professional sports stadiums – the pride and joy of the US Northwest's baseball and football fans. To the east, two of Seattle's prominent hills, First and Capitol, offer notable museums, grand cathedrals, and an eclectic assortment of shops and restaurants. For active outdoor pursuits, Green Lake, Discovery Park, and Alki Beach all feature paths for strolling, jogging, biking, rollerblading, or hiking. Those wanting to go the distance can opt for the Burke-Gilman Trail, stretching from Fremont to Kenmore. The city is also home to Woodland Park Zoo, one of the top zoos in the US, and the University of Washington, the heart of the University District. Other Seattle neighborhoods, such as Ballard, Fremont, and Madison Park, each with its own distinct character, are ideal destinations for a day trip.

Sights at a Glance

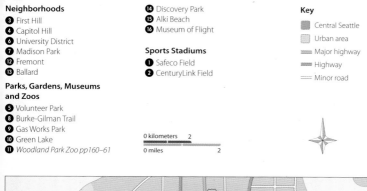

Neighborhoods
- ❸ First Hill
- ❹ Capitol Hill
- ❻ University District
- ❼ Madison Park
- ⓬ Fremont
- ⓭ Ballard

Parks, Gardens, Museums and Zoos
- ❺ Volunteer Park
- ❽ Burke-Gilman Trail
- ❾ Gas Works Park
- ❿ Green Lake
- ⓫ *Woodland Park Zoo pp160–61*

- ⓮ Discovery Park
- ⓯ Alki Beach
- ⓰ Museum of Flight

Sports Stadiums
- ❶ Safeco Field
- ❷ CenturyLink Field

Key
- ▪ Central Seattle
- ▫ Urban area
- ▬ Major highway
- ▬ Highway
- ═ Minor road

0 kilometers 2

0 miles 2

❶ Safeco Field

1250 1st Ave S. **Map** 4 D5.
Tel (206) 346-4000. 🚌 15, 18.
📅 Apr–Oct: 10:30am, 12:30pm,
2:30pm daily (except game days;
check the website for details); Nov–
Mar: 12:30pm & 2:30pm Tue–Sun. 🈯
♿ 🅆 seattle.mariners.mlb.com

Although Seattle is a rainy city,
Seattle baseball fans have not
endured the disappointment
of a rainout since the American
League's Seattle Mariners
christened Safeco Field on July
15, 1999. Its size is impressive,
seating over 47,000 fans, who
enter the stadium through the
curved entranceway, behind
the field's home plate.

The stadium's state-of-the-art
retractable roof can cover the
playing field with a simple push
of a button. This massive roof
contains enough steel to build a
skyscraper 55 stories tall. Utility
came with a hefty price tag,
however – an unprecedented
$516 million. Designed by
the Seattle firm NBBJ and
completed in 1999, Safeco
Field became the nation's most
expensive stadium ever built.

With its sweeping views of
the Seattle skyline, $1.3 million
in public art, and such amenities
as a children's playfield and
picnic patio, Safeco Field provides an excellent atmosphere
in which to watch a Major
League ball game. While many
games are sold out, tourists
may visit the stadium by taking
one of the regularly scheduled
tours or visiting the Mariners
Hall of Fame.

❷ CenturyLink Field

800 Occidental Ave S. **Map** 4 D4.
Tel (206) 381-7555. 🚌 15, 18.
📅 Jun–Aug: 12:30pm & 2:30pm
daily; Sep–May: 12:30pm & 2:30pm Fri
& Sat (except days of major events).
Events: **Tel** (206) 381-7582. 🈯 ♿
🅆 centurylinkfield.com

The designers of CenturyLink
Field, which opened in 2002,
were intent on factoring the city's
often inclement winter weather
into its design. So, despite the
harsh winds and rains associated
with winter in Seattle, the
stadium was left roofless. The
end result is a spacious, open-air
stadium with unobstructed views
of the Seattle skyline. With two
massive 760-ft (232-m) eaves,
nearly 70 percent of the 68,000
spectator seats are shielded
from falling rain. Some visiting
teams that are unfamiliar with
Pacific Northwest weather,
however, have found it to be
an inhospitable environment.
The stadium is home to the
NFL's Seattle Seahawks and the
MLS team, Seattle Sounders FC.

Just as the stadium design
by Minneapolis-based Ellerbe
Becket is unconventional, so,
too, is the mix of art scattered
within it, which draws visitors
from around the world. The
four Native American-inspired
steel disks by New Mexican
artist Bob Haozous are
especially striking. The disks,
each 24 ft (7 m) in diameter,
represent people's interaction
with and connection to the
earth and nature.

Entrance and rotunda of the Frye Art
Museum on First Hill

❸ First Hill

Bounded by E Pike St, E Yesler Way,
12th Ave E & I-5. **Map** 4 E1. 🚌 3, 4, 12.

Nicknamed Pill Hill for its several
hospitals and numerous doctors'
offices, First Hill lies just east of
downtown. A pedestrian-friendly
district (more than 40 percent of
its residents walk to work), First
Hill was Seattle's first neighborhood, home to the city's pioneer
families. It still boasts a number
of the original mansions from
Seattle's earliest days.

First Hill's most recognizable
landmark, **St. James Cathedral**,
(804 9th Avenue) is a parish
church and the cathedral of the
Catholic Archdiocese of Seattle.
Designed by the New York firm
Heins and LaFarge, the Italian
Renaissance structure dating
to 1907 features two tall spires,
which are illuminated at night.

One block southeast of
St. James Cathedral, the **Frye
Art Museum** showcases the
extensive art collection of
Seattle pioneers Charles
and Emma Frye, which
features 19th- and 20th-
century French, German,
and American paintings.
Temporary exhibitions are
held throughout the year.

🏛 **Frye Art Museum**
704 Terry Ave. **Tel** (206) 622-9250.
Open 11am–5pm Tue–Sun (to 7pm
Thu). **Closed** Jan 1, Jul 4, Thanksgiving,
Dec 25. 🎦 ♿ 🅓 📷
🅦 fryemuseum.org

The brick and steel façade of Safeco Field, home of the Seattle Mariners

For hotels and restaurants see p288 and pp298–300

❹ Capitol Hill

Bounded by Montlake Blvds E & NE, E
Pike & E Madison Sts, 23rd Ave E & I-5.
Map 2 F5. 🚌 7, 9, 10.

Northeast of downtown, lively
Capitol Hill is a colorful and
diverse urban neighborhood
where no one blinks at spiked
purple hair and multiple
body piercings.

The district's commercial
hub and major avenue is
Broadway (East Roy to East
Pike Streets). Referred to as the
"living room of Capitol Hill," it
offers shopping (from books
to home accessories to vintage
clothing), a number of ethnic
restaurants, and bronze footsteps embedded in the sidewalk
to teach passersby the tango
and fox trot.

While people-watching is a
major source of entertainment,
Capitol Hill also features a vintage
single-screen movie house:
the **SIFF Cinema Egyptian**
(805 East Pine Street, 206/324-
9996), which specializes in
independent and foreign
films and restored classics.

The hill is also home to
St. Mark's Episcopal Cathedral
(1245 10th Avenue East)
(1931), belonging to the
Diocese of Olympia. It is known
for its magnificent Flentrop
organ, installed in 1965 and
consisting of 3,944 pipes that
range in size from 1 inch
(2.5 cm) to 32 ft (9.7 m).

The internationally acclaimed
Cornish College of the Arts
(710 East Roy Street) features
a full roster of student exhibits
and performances.

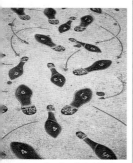

Dance Steps on Broadway, by Jack Mackie,
in Capitol Hill

Volunteer Park's Asian Art Museum, in an historic Art Deco building

❺ Volunteer Park

1247 15th Ave E. **Tel** (206) 684-4075.
🚌 7, 9, 10. **Open** 6am–11pm daily.
🌐 seattle.gov/parks

Located at the north end of
Capitol Hill, this elegant park
was designed in 1904–9 by
the Olmsted Brothers, the US's
famous landscape-architecture
firm. The park is named for the
Seattle men who enlisted to
fight in the Spanish-American
War of 1898.

The Olmsteds' design called
for an observation tower. The
city obliged by building a 75-ft
(23-m) brick water tower with
an observation deck open to
the public. A steep climb up the
107-step spiral staircase rewards
visitors with spectacular views
of the Space Needle, Puget
Sound, and the Olympic
mountain range.

A children's playground,
wading pool, tennis courts,
and bandstand make the park
a favorite outing for families.

Volunteer Park is the site
of the **Asian Art Museum**,
located in a 1933 Art Deco
building which formerly
housed the Seattle Art
Museum *(see pp132–3)*. The
Asian Art Museum's renowned
collection includes works
from Japan, Korea, China,
and Southeast Asia.

Highlights of the rotating
collection include wood and
lacquer furniture from imperial
China and 14th-century Chinese
sculpture. Other gems of
the collection are the Korean
ceramics and metalware, and
bronze figures of Buddha and
Bodhisattva that date back to
the country's Unified Shilla
dynasty (668–935 AD).

Across from the museum
is the **Volunteer Park Conservatory**, a botanical garden also
home to plants confiscated by
US Customs. The conservatory
consists of five houses, four of
which showcase bromeliads,
palms, ferns, and cacti, respectively. The seasonal display
house includes lilies, poinsettias,
azaleas, and a jade plant more
than 95 years old that blooms
November to January.

🏛 **Asian Art Museum**
1400 E Prospect St. **Tel** (206) 654-3100.
Open 10am–5pm Tue, Wed & Fri–Sun,
10am–9pm Thu. **Closed** Jan 1, Labor
Day, Thanksgiving, Dec 25. 🎟 by
donation; free 1st Thu of month. ♿
📷 🌐 seattleartmuseum.org

🌿 **Volunteer Park Conservatory**
1400 E Galer St. **Tel** (206) 684-4743.
Open 10am–4pm Tue–Sun.
📷 by donation. ♿ 📷
🌐 seattle.gov/parks

Summer flowers outside the Conservatory
at Volunteer Park

The University of Washington campus, with its mix of architectural styles

❻ University District

Bounded by NE 55th St, Portage Bay, Montlake Blvd NE & I-5. 🚌 7, 25, 43, 70, 71, 72, 73. ℹ️ UW Visitors Center: Ground floor, Odegaard Undergraduate Library, near 15th Ave NE and NE 41St, (206) 543-9198.

Eclectic and energetic thanks to the vibrant youth culture surrounding a major university campus, the University District makes for an interesting half- or full-day excursion. The hub of the district is the University of Washington (UW). The premier institution of higher learning in the Northwest US, this university is internationally known for its excellent research and graduate programs.

Located on the site of the 1909 World's Fair, the beautiful parklike campus is home to more than 43,000 students and 500 buildings in a mix of architectural styles. Just inside the main campus entrance is the **Burke Museum of Natural History and Culture**, featuring dinosaur fossils and a notable collection of Northwest Native American art. On the western edge of the campus sits the **Henry Art Gallery**, the first public art museum in the state of Washington. The museum has a special focus on photography and digital and projected media.

The university's main avenue is University Way Northeast, known to locals as "The Ave." Located just west of campus, it is lined with bookstores,

pubs, inexpensive restaurants, and shops. At the opposite end of the spectrum, University Village, located east of campus, offers an upscale shopping and dining experience.

A must-see, especially spring through autumn, is the **Washington Park Arboretum**, a garden and living plant museum, with 4,600 species, including 139 on the endangered list. The arboretum also features a Japanese garden with sculptures and wildlife, carp-filled ponds, and an authentic teahouse open for ceremonies once a month.

Neo-Gothic building, university campus

🏛 Burke Museum of Natural History and Culture

NE 45th St & 17th Ave NE. **Tel** (206) 543-5590. **Open** 10am–5pm daily, 10am–8pm 1st Thu of month. **Closed** Jan 1, Jul 4, Thanksgiving, Dec 25. 🎫 (free 1st Thu of month; separate adm to some exhibits). ♿ 📱 📷 🅿️ 🌐 burkemuseum.org

🏛 Henry Art Gallery

NE 41st St & 15th Ave NE. **Tel** (206) 543-2280. **Open** 11am–4pm Wed, Sat & Sun, 11am–9pm Thu & Fri. **Closed** Jan 1, Jul 4, Thanksgiving, Dec 25. 🎫 (by donation on Thu). ♿ 📷 for groups in advance. 📱 📷 🅿️ 🌐 henryart.org

🌳 Washington Park Arboretum

2300 Arboretum Dr E. **Tel** (206) 543-8800. 🚌 11, 43, 48. Visitors' center **Open** 9am–5pm. Grounds: **Open** dawn–dusk. 🎫 to Japanese Garden. ♿ 📷 🌐 washington.edu

❼ Madison Park

Bounded by E Madison St, Lake Washington Blvd & Lake Washington. 🚌 11. 🌐 seattle.gov/parks

Seattle's lakeside community of Madison Park is one of the city's most affluent. Its tree-shaded streets, lined with charming older homes, most built between 1910 and 1930, are ideal for leisurely strolling.

The area was established in the early 1860s, when Judge John J. McGilvra purchased a section of land, cutting a road through the forest from downtown Seattle to his property, which was later named Madison Street after former US president James Madison (1751–1836). In the 1880s, McGilvra divided his land into lots, decreeing that only "cottages" could be built on them. He also set aside an area for public use. This parcel of land is now known as Madison Park. By the end of the 19th century, this park had become the most popular beach in the city, complete with an ornate boathouse, piers, a bathhouse, a wooden promenade, a greenhouse, a playground, floating bandstands, and tennis courts. Reminiscent of a friendly village, the neighborhood's commercial area today offers a number of popular restaurants, upscale boutiques, and home accessories shops.

Children playing on Madison Park's sandy lakeside beach

❽ Burke-Gilman Trail

Numerous access points; main access point at Gas Works Park. 🚌 25, 43.

When the sun comes out in Seattle, cyclists, speed-walkers, joggers, rollerbladers, and lovers of the outdoors flock to the scenic Burke-Gilman Trail. Built on an old railway bed, this 27-mile (43-km) paved trail is used by more than one million people each year. It is both a popular recreation corridor and a pleasant, automobile-free commuter route for residents.

Although the Burke-Gilman Trail was extended west through Fremont *(see p162)* to 8th Avenue Northwest, it officially begins at Gas Works Park, at the north end of Lake Union. From there, it follows the shores of Lake Washington, beginning at the University of Washington and extending all the way to the city of Kenmore, where it connects with the Sammamish River Trail.

A warning to pedestrians: bicyclists comprise roughly 80 percent of all trail users, making attentiveness and keeping to the right-hand side a must.

❾ Gas Works Park

2101 N Northlake Way. **Tel** (206) 684-4075. 🚌 26. **Open** 6am–10pm daily.
Ⓦ seattle.gov/parks

Huge rusty pipes and pieces of decrepit machinery are not typically found in a park. But Gas Works Park on Lake Union is anything but typical. Established in 1906 as a gasification plant by the Seattle Gas Company for extracting gas from coal, Gas Works was once a primary source of power for Seattle. Shut down in 1956, the plant's machinery and towers stood dormant until 1975, when the site was renovated into an award-winning park under the direction of landscape architect Richard Haag. With its renovation, Gas Works became the first industrial site in the world to be converted into a public park. Today, Gas Works

Stunning view of the Seattle skyline from Gas Works Park

Park is a scenic knoll offering vast recreational opportunities and magnificent views of Lake Union and downtown Seattle. Besides serving as a model for urban renewal, the park is a haven for kite flying, kayaking, picnicking, and viewing the July 4 fireworks.

Boaters enjoying an outing on Seattle's Green Lake

❿ Green Lake

7201 E Green Lake Dr N. **Tel** (206) 684-4075. 🚌 16, 26. **Open** 24 hrs daily.
Ⓦ seattle.gov/parks

On any given day – and especially a sunny one – Green Lake hosts a spirited parade of people, from joggers, walkers, cyclists, and skaters to bird-watchers, dog walkers, and pram-pushing parents.

For wheeled sports, the 2.8-mile (4.5-km) asphalt path circling the lake is ideal. Joggers and walkers can use the adjacent 3.2-mile (5-km) trail, which runs closest to the lake and has a crushed granite surface.

Attracting more than a million outdoor enthusiasts a year, this park is populated by as many as 7,200 people a day on summer weekends. While kayaking, windsurfing, and paddleboating are popular pursuits during the warmer months, and boats can be rented at the lake, swimming may be restricted due to algae blooms and other problems caused by water stagnation.

Likened to New York's Central Park – albeit on a smaller scale – the lake and its surrounding park is a lively gathering spot for Seattle residents and a welcome recreational oasis in a high-density urban area. In addition to the lake, the park grounds include an indoor public pool, outdoor wading pool, tennis courts, soccer field, outdoor basketball court, baseball diamond, and pitch-and-putt golf course. The park is also home to many different species of wildlife, including ducks, turtles, squirrels, and eagles.

Jogger on the path that runs along Green Lake

⓫ Woodland Park Zoo

Purchased by the City of Seattle in 1899, Woodland Park Zoo is one of the oldest zoos on the West Coast and one of the region's major attractions. Of the nearly 300 animal species that reside at the botanical garden, most live in environments that closely resemble their native habitats. Unlike typical zoo models where animals are grouped by species, Woodland Park's wildlife residents are grouped in bioclimatic zones. Seven of the zoo's naturalistic exhibits have won top honors from the Association of Zoos and Aquariums. Among these is the Trail of Vines, which includes the first open-forested canopy for orangutans to be created at a zoo. The exhibit also features siamangs and tapirs.

★ Jaguar Cove
Visit the tropical world of the jaguar, the largest cat in the Western Hemisphere. This is one of the most naturalistic exhibits dedicated to jaguars in any zoo.

★ Tropical Rain Forest
The gorilla exhibit in the Tropical Rain Forest includes the endangered western lowland gorilla, a gentle giant that can eat as much as 70 lb (32 kg) of food each day.

Family Farm
A popular seasonal Contact Area is one of the features of the Family Farm, as is the year-round Bug World, exhibiting earth's smallest animals.

0 meters 100
0 yards 100

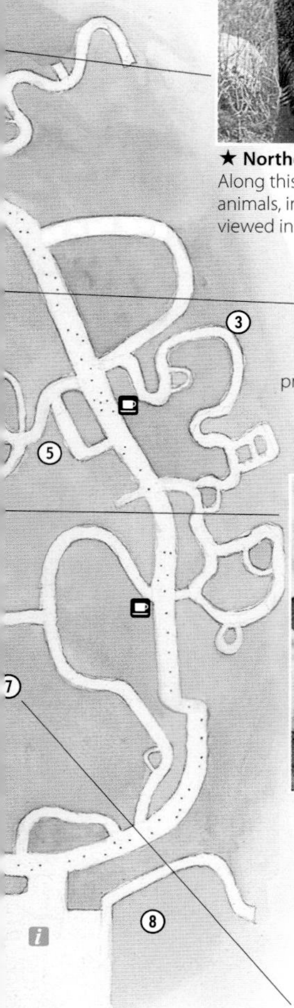

★ **Northern Trail**
Along this trail, indigenous North American animals, including grizzly bears, can be viewed in naturalistic exhibits.

③

Willawong Station
The bird-feeding experience offers an opportunity to feed free-flying birds, primarily small colorful Australian parrots, while learning about responsible care for birds in the wild and at home.

⑤

⑦

★ **Tropical Asia: Banyan Wilds**
At the heart of the zoo is Banyan Wilds, inhabited by Malayan tigers, sloth bears, Asian small-clawed otters, and tropical birds. Through activities and digital media, a conservation action center highlights the work being done by local communities and the zoo's field conservation partners to help save the forest and wildlife.

KEY

① Australasia
② Northern Trail
③ Tropical Asia: Trail of Vines
④ Willawong Station
⑤ Adaptations
⑥ Tropical Asia: Banyan Wilds
⑦ African Savanna
⑧ Woodland Park Rose Garden
⑨ Family Farm
⑩ Temperate Forest
⑪ Jaguar Cove
⑫ Tropical Rain Forest
⑬ Zoomazium
⑭ Humboldt Penguin Exhibit
⑮ Historic Carousel

ⓘ

⑧

★ **African Savanna**
Many species are found here, including zebras, hippos, and gazelles, which roam freely with the herd of imposing giraffes near a replica African village. There is a giraffe-feeding station where visitors may get up close to feed the long-necked creatures. This exhibit is open seasonally and requires an additional entry fee.

For keys to symbols *see back flap*

People Waiting for the Interurban, an aluminum sculpture in Fremont

⑫ Fremont

Bounded by N 50th St, Lake Washington Ship Canal, Stone Way Ave N & 8th Ave NW. 🚌 26, 28.

In the 1960s, when it was a community of students, artists, and bohemians attracted by low rents, Fremont declared itself an "artists' republic." By the late 1990s, the neighborhood's character began to shift, after a high-tech firm settled its Seattle office here. However, Fremont has managed to hold on to cherished traditions, such as the Summer Solstice Parade and an outdoor cinema series, and today, it is still one of Seattle's funkiest districts.

Public art is a fixture of Fremont. A 13.5-ft- (4-m-) tall statue of Lenin towers above pedestrians at Fremont Place, and a 15-ft- (4.5-m-) tall Volkswagen-eating troll lurks under the north end of the Aurora Bridge. On 34th Street, near the drawbridge, sculptor Richard Beyer's *People Waiting for the Interurban* is regularly clothed by locals.

The gigantic Fremont troll, waiting for unsuspecting cars

The dog's human face is modeled after an honorary mayor, with whom the artist had a dispute.

⑬ Ballard

Bounded by Salmon Bay, Shilshole Bay & Phinney Ridge. 🚌 15, 17, 18.

Settled by Scandinavian fishermen and loggers in 1853, Ballard was incorporated into Washington State in 1889 and annexed to Seattle in 1907. At the turn of the 19th century, Ballard was a mill town, producing an impressive three million wooden shingles a day. Many of the mill jobs were held by Scandinavian immigrants. Located north of the shingle mills, Ballard Avenue was the commercial center of this then-booming area. Its

The historic landmark bell tower in Ballard

buildings recall the area's industrial growth and strong Scandinavian heritage; many are open to the public. In 1976, King Carl XVI Gustav of Sweden read the proclamation establishing Ballard Avenue a Historic District.

The area's proud Scandinavian heritage is celebrated at the annual Norwegian Constitution Day Parade every May 17, at the excellent **Nordic Heritage Museum** (3014 Northwest 67th Street), and at the Bergen Place mural, located in Bergen Place Park. Ballard greets

the thousands of container ships, tugboats, fishing boats, and pleasure craft that make their way through the **Hiram M. Chittenden Locks** each year. Located at the west end of Ballard, the locks allow boats to travel between saltwater Puget Sound and freshwater Lake Union and Lake Washington. The best times to observe migrating salmon on the fish ladder are June through October. One of the city's major – and free – tourist attractions, the locks' grounds include botanical gardens.

🏛 **Hiram M. Chittenden Locks**
3015 NW 54th St. **Tel** (206) 783-7059. Grounds: **Open** 7am–9pm daily. Visitors' center: **Open** May–Sep: 10am–6pm daily; Oct–Apr: 10am–4pm Thu–Mon. ♿ 📷 Mar, Apr, Oct & Nov: 2pm Thu–Mon; May–Sep: 1pm 2pm, 3pm Mon–Fri, 11am, 1pm, 3pm Sat & Sun.

⑭ Discovery Park

3801 W Government Way. **Tel** (206) 386-4236. 🚌 24, 33. Park: **Open** 6am–11pm daily. Visitors' center: **Open** 8:30am–5pm Tue–Sun. **Closed** major hols. 🌐 seattle.gov/parks

Located on Magnolia Bluff, overlooking Puget Sound, Discovery Park is Seattle's largest park. It occupies most of the former Fort Lawton site, a defensive base for soldiers during World Wars I and II and the Korean War. Built at the turn of the 20th century, the still-occupied Officers' Quarters are listed on the National Register

The West Point Lighthouse, off the South Beach Trail, Discovery Park

A cyclist on Alki Beach, a stunning view of Seattle in the background

of Historic Places. A visitors' center at the east entrance offers trail maps and interactive exhibits for kids.

Home to over 250 species of birds and other wildlife, the park offers more than 7 miles (11 km) of hiking trails, including the 2.8-mile (4.5-km) Loop Trail, which circles the park and passes through forests, meadows, and dunes. For beach exploration, the park has two very different habitats: the rocky North Beach and the sandy South Beach.

Discovery Park is also home to the **Daybreak Star Cultural Center**. Operated by the United Indians of All Tribes Foundation, this cultural and educational center houses a collection of Native American art. The annual summer Pow Wow features some 500 dancers, 30 drum groups, arts and crafts, and a salmon bake.

Daybreak Star Cultural Center
Near north parking lot of Discovery Park. **Tel** (206) 285-4425. **Open** 10am–5pm Mon–Sat, noon–5pm Sun.

⓯ Alki Beach

1702 Alki Ave SW. **Tel** (206) 684-4075. 37, 56.

When the first European settlers landed on Alki Beach on a stormy November day in 1851, they were welcomed by Chief Seattle and his Duwamish tribe *(see p31)*. Today, this lively beach is the coolest place in town to be on a warm day. The beach offers spectacular views of Puget Sound, the Olympic Mountains, and the Seattle skyline.

⓰ Museum of Flight

9404 E Marginal Way S. **Tel** (206) 764-5720. **Open** 10am–5pm daily. **Closed** Thanksgiving, Dec 25.

w museumofflight.org

The West Coast's largest air and space museum, the Museum of Flight takes visitors on a fascinating journey from the earliest days of aviation to the Space Age. The museum features 39 historic airplanes, of which more than half are suspended from the ceiling of the six-story Great Gallery. Visitors can sit in the cockpit of an SR-71 Blackbird or F/A-18 Hornet, and board the first Air Force One, the US presidential jet.

The restored Red Barn, Boeing's original 1910 airplane factory and a National Historic Site, is part of the museum. Its exhibits include the world's first fighter plane.

The Personal Courage Wing, which opened in 2004, houses the Champlin Fighter collection containing 28 historical aircraft, mainly from World Wars I and II.

Especially popular are the museum's simulators, including the challenging space-docking simulators in which participants try to link up with the Hubble space telescope.

Aviatik D-1 in the Personal Courage Wing of the Museum of Flight

The Men Behind Microsoft

Seattle is home to two of the world's wealthiest men and most accomplished entrepreneurs. Bill Gates and Paul Allen met at a prestigious Seattle prep school. Sharing a fascination for computers, the boys soon landed jobs with a company that paid them in computer time instead of cash. There they pored over manuals and explored the computer system inside and out. In 1973, Gates left for

Bill Gates, co-founder of Seattle-based Microsoft

Harvard University but kept in touch with Allen, with whom he vowed to go into business one day. By 1975, Bill Gates was the US's most successful college dropout, having left Harvard to devote his energies to the company he founded with his friend. Microsoft went on to become the Goliath of the computer software industry. In 1985, its headquarters settled in Redmond, a suburb of Seattle. In 1986, the company began public trading. Today, Microsoft employs over 90,000 people in 135 countries.

Shopping in Seattle

Shopping aficionados will not be disappointed in Seattle. From 5th Avenue's ritzy boutiques to funky shops on Fremont's streets, you'll find plenty of irresistible buys. Without a car, you can shop until you drop downtown, at Pioneer Square, Pike Place Market, and Belltown, or hop on a bus and explore the shopping options farther afield.

Westlake Center shopping mall, in downtown Seattle

Shopping Districts

Seattle has several interesting shopping districts. Upscale clothing boutiques, antique shops, and home accessory stores make their home in trendy Belltown (see p145). Downtown (see p125), chic boutiques mingle with top retailers and multilevel malls. At Pike Place Market (see pp138–9) you'll find produce as well as antiques, art, crafts, jewelry, vintage apparel, and cookware. Pioneer Square (see p125) features bookstores, art galleries, antique shops, and a plethora of Oriental rug stores.

Department Stores and Shopping Centers

Seattle-based **Nordstrom** opened its opulent flagship department store in 1998. Known for its wide selection of shoes, the fashion specialty store pampers shoppers with excellent customer service and, at this location, a luxurious full-service day spa. **Macy's** department store downtown sells everything from linens and lingerie to love seats and luggage. Downtown Seattle also has several notable malls. The poshest is **Pacific Place**, a five-level complex featuring

dozens of upscale apparel, jewelry, and home accessory stores alongside well-known retailers such as Barneys New York and Barnes & Noble. Two blocks west, **Westlake Center** is home to top national and regional retailers and a sprawling food court. **City Centre**, located two blocks south of Pacific Place and Westlake Center, is a classy mall boasting an impressive collection of contemporary glass art.

Located just outside downtown Seattle, **University Village** is the area's most high-end open-air shopping center. Locally owned specialty shops share the pedestrian-friendly Village with national retailers such as Restoration Hardware and Pottery Barn.

Specialty Shops

You will find 150,000 titles at the **Elliott Bay Book Company**. **Made in Washington**, which sells everything from smoked salmon to handmade pottery, offers one-stop shopping for top-quality, locally made merchandise and food items. The **REI** (Recreational Equipment Inc.) flagship store sells all kinds of outdoor gear, and features an indoor climbing wall. **Sur La Table** offers the latest culinary utensils and kitchenware. **Ye Olde Curiosity Shop** (see p141) is a jam-packed

One of Seattle's many specialty shops, this one selling pottery

curiosity shop, known for both its kitschy souvenirs and fine Native American crafts.

What to Buy

Smoked salmon, and coffee beans from small local roasting companies, such as Tully's, Espresso Vivace, and Caffè Appassionato, are Seattle specialties. Handblown glass and pottery are popular souvenirs. More conventional items include Space Needle-inspired items, and bags with Pike Place Market motifs.

DIRECTORY

Department Stores And Shopping Centers

City Centre
1420 5th Ave. **Map** 3 C1.
Tel (206) 624-8800.

Macy's
1601 3rd Ave. **Map** 3 C1.
Tel (206) 506-6000.

Nordstrom
500 Pine St. **Map** 3 C1.
Tel (206) 628-2111.

Pacific Place
600 Pine St. **Map** 2 E5.
Tel (206) 405-2655.

University Village
2623 NE University Village.
Tel (206) 523-0622.

Westlake Center
400 Pine St. **Map** 3 C1.
Tel (206) 467-1600.

Specialty Shops

Elliott Bay Book Company
1521 10th Ave.
Tel (206) 624-6600.

Made in Washington
1530 Post Alley. **Map** 3 C1.
Tel (206) 467-0788.

REI
222 Yale Ave N. **Map** 2 E4.
Tel (206) 223-1944.

Sur La Table
84 Pine St. **Map** 3 C1.
Tel (206) 448-2244.

Ye Olde Curiosity Shop
Pier 54, 1001 Alaskan Way.
Map 3 C2. **Tel** (206) 682-5844.

Entertainment in Seattle

With Seattle's varied offerings, from baseball to ballet, and book readings to Broadway musicals, visitors won't be lacking for entertainment. The city is home to one of the top opera companies in the US, a critically acclaimed symphony orchestra, and a Tony Award-winning repertory theater company.

Window of the Crocodile Café, a Belltown favorite for live music

Information

The city's daily newspaper, the *Seattle Times*, offers complete entertainment listings for the week in its Friday "Ticket" supplement. For daily listings, visit the newspaper's website at www.seattletimes.com.

Buying Tickets

Tickets for sporting events and many performing arts events can be purchased through **Ticketmaster**.

Free Events

Free art and literary events abound in Pioneer Square: First Thursday Gallery Walks through museums, galleries, bars, and shops occur on the first Thursday evening of each month; and the Elliott Bay Book Company hosts author readings several times each week.

Film

Seattle has a thriving film scene, with the **Landmark Theatres** group and **Northwest Film Forum** screening art-house and independent films. One of the most respected and comprehensive film festivals in the US is the **Seattle International Film Festival (SIFF)**, which screens more than 300 new works during May and June.

Theater

Many of Seattle's performing arts venues are located at the Seattle Center, including the respected **Seattle Repertory Theatre**, which presents nine plays from September to May, and the **Intiman Theatre**, which stages classic and contemporary plays March through December. The popular **Seattle Children's Theatre**, the second-largest children's theater in the country, stages performances from September to June.

Dance

Internationally acclaimed, the **Pacific Northwest Ballet** performs at Marion Oliver McCaw Hall. Its *Nutcracker* is a must-see during the holiday season.

Music

The distinguished **Seattle Symphony** performs September through June at the stunning Benaroya Hall *(see p133)*. Marion Oliver McCaw Hall at Seattle Center is home to the acclaimed **Seattle Opera**, which attracts audiences from around the world with its productions of Wagner's *Ring Cycle* every four years. For live blues, jazz, rock, and folk music, there are

Young musicians performing in downtown Seattle

many venues to choose from in Pioneer Square, as well as in Belltown and Ballard.

Spectator Sports

Spectator sports are big in Seattle. Seattleites are justifiably proud of their two stadiums – Safeco Field *(see p156)*, home of the Seattle Mariners baseball team, and CenturyLink Field *(see p156)*, where the National Football League's Seattle Seahawks play. The city's professional women's basketball team, the Storm, plays at the Seattle Center's KeyArena *(see p152)*. For sporting events tickets, call **Ticketmaster**.

DIRECTORY

Ticket Outlets

Ticketmaster
Tel General: (800) 745-3000.
Arts: (800) 982-2787.
W ticketmaster.com

Film

Landmark Theatres
Tel (206) 633-0059.
W landmarktheatres.com

Northwest Film Forum
Tel (206) 329-2629.
W nwfilmforum.org

SIFF
Tel (206) 633-7151. W siff.net

Theater

Intiman Theatre
Tel (206) 441-7178.
W intiman.org

Seattle Children's Theatre
Tel (206) 441-3322. W sct.org

Seattle Repertory Theatre
Tel (206) 443-2222.
W seattlerep.org

Dance

Pacific Northwest Ballet
Tel (206) 441-2424. W pnb.org

Music

Seattle Opera
Tel (206) 389-7676.
W seattleopera.org

Seattle Symphony
Tel (206) 215-4747.
W seattlesymphony.org

Getting Around Seattle

Seattle may be a hilly city but its main tourist areas – Pioneer Square, downtown, Pike Place Market, the waterfront, Seattle Center, and Belltown – are relatively flat, close to each other, and easy to navigate on foot. The city's buses serve these areas and all "Farther Afield" sights and neighborhoods. A 2-minute ride on the Monorail connects downtown to the Seattle Center.

Street Layout

Interstate-5 runs north–south through the middle of Seattle. In the downtown area, avenues run north–south, and streets run east–west. With only a few exceptions, avenues are numbered and streets are named (for example, 3rd Avenue and Spring Street). Many of Seattle's streets and avenues run one-way. For a good selection of local street maps, as well as state and recreational maps, visit **Metsker Maps of Seattle**, in Pioneer Square.

Walking

Traffic sign to help pedestrians

Seattle is a great city for walking. Though it is quite hilly, the down-town area is compact enough to walk in its entirety, and locals are generally happy to offer directions. Keep in mind that jaywalking (crossing the street other than at designated crossings) is illegal in Seattle. Tourist offices provide free maps that will help visitors navigate the downtown area.

The Seattle Center Monorail, linking downtown to the Seattle Center

The metro bus running along Seattle's waterfront

Bicycling

Cyclists may wish to avoid Seattle's busy streets and head to one of the area's popular bike trails. The 27-mile (43-km) paved Burke-Gilman Trail *(see p159)* stretches from Fremont to Kenmore. Bike rental shops, such as the **Bicycle Center of Seattle**, are located near the trail. A 2.8-mile (4.5-km) path that encircles Green Lake *(see p159)* is ideal for shorter spins. **Gregg's Greenlake Cycle**, located beside the lake, rents touring, mountain, and hybrid bicycles.

Public Transit

Traveling by metro offers inexpensive transportation throughout the city. Buses are equipped with wheelchair lifts. Between 6am and 7pm, bus transportation is free in down-town Seattle. Bus schedules are available from the **Seattle Visitor Center and Concierge Services** at the Washington State Convention Center (at Seventh Avenue and Pike Street) and from the Metro Transit customer service office at Westlake Station, on the mezzanine level. The **Metro Transit Rider Information** phone line provides route and other information.

The 2.6-mile (4-km) **South Lake Union Streetcar** connects down-town Seattle with the South Lake Union neighborhood. It runs every 15 minutes from 6am until 9pm weekdays (to 11pm on Saturdays) and from 10am to 7pm on Sundays and holidays. Tickets can be purchased at the 11 streetcar stops, and metro transfers are also valid.

The 14-mile (23-km) **Sound Transit** light rail system connects downtown Seattle with Sea-Tac airport, a journey taking approximately 36 minutes. Trains operate from 5am to 1am Monday to Saturday, and 6am to midnight on Sunday. Tickets can be bought at the stations. There are stops at the International District/Pioneer Square, the stadiums and SODO, Beacon Hill, Mount Baker, Southeast Seattle, and Tukwila. Further extensions are underway.

A fare payment system that uses smart cards, ORCA (One Regional Card for All) was launched for light rail, streetcar, and buses in 2009 (www.orcacard.com).

Another convenient and inexpensive way to travel within the city is the **Seattle Center Monorail** *(see p149)*. Linking downtown Seattle to the Seattle Center *(see pp146–7)*, it operates Monday through Thursday from 7:30am to 9pm, Friday 7:30am to 11pm, Saturday 8:30am to 11pm, and Sunday 8:30am to 9pm. Check the website for the up-to-date hours of operation, as timings may vary by season. The Monorail departs every 10 minutes from the Seattle Center (across from the Space Needle) and from Westlake Center, at 5th Avenue and Pine Street. The 1-mile (1.5-km) trip takes 2 minutes.

Seattle taxi cab, a common sight on downtown streets

Taxis

Taxis can usually be flagged outside every major downtown hotel and attraction, as well on main streets and at taxi stands, found at bus stations and the airport. Taxis can also be ordered by telephone. Fares start at $2.60, and increase at a rate of approximately $2.70 per mile.

Ferries

Several of Seattle's outlying areas can be reached via the **Washington State Ferries** *(see p141)*, which offer scenic rides through the San Juan Islands and other destinations around Puget Sound. Sail from downtown Seattle's Pier 52 to nearby Bremerton and Bainbridge Island. **King County Water Taxi** takes visitors from Pier 50 to Bremerton and Vashon Island. Ferries leaving from Pier 52 carry automobiles and passengers, whereas those from Pier 50 are passenger-only. Several private companies offer ferry rides along similar routes as well as narrated tours of the Seattle waterfront.

Driving

The traffic in downtown Seattle can be daunting. Avoid driving during weekday rush hours, 7 to 9:30am and 3 to 7pm. Unless posted otherwise, the speed limit on arterial (city) streets is 30 mph (48 km/h). The speed

limit for non-arterial (residential) streets is 25 mph (40 km/h). A right-hand turn on a red light is permitted after coming to a full stop. Traffic circles (raised islands in intersections) are common in many neighborhoods. Drivers should yield to the motorist on the left, then proceed to the right.

Seat belts, safety seats for young children, and motorcycle helmets are mandatory. **American Automobile Association (AAA)** members can obtain free maps and tour books from the Seattle office.

A Seattle bus stop sign

Parking

Parking downtown is generally expensive. However, one of the best-kept secrets is the underground parking garage beneath Pacific Place *(see p164)*, where budget-savvy Seattleites usually park. On-street parking is available for cars in some areas of the city, but be aware that strict time limits apply and that these differ from street to street.

Towing

If your car is towed from a street within the city limits, call the **Seattle Police, Auto Records Department**. Staff here will tell you which impound yard your car has been taken to. Be prepared to provide the car's license plate number and the location from which the vehicle was towed. If you are renting a car, be sure to carry the vehicle license number with you. If the car was towed from a private lot, call the number posted on the sign.

A local seaplane, offering visitors a bird's-eye view of Seattle

DIRECTORY

Useful Numbers

American Automobile Association (AAA)
Tel (206) 448-5353. W aaa.com

Bicycle Center of Seattle
Tel (206) 523-8300.

Gregg's Greenlake Cycle
Tel (206) 523-1822.

King County Water Taxi
Tel (206) 477-3979.
W kingcounty.gov

Metro Transit Rider Information
Tel (206) 553-3000.

Metsker Maps of Seattle
Tel (206) 623-8747 or (800) 727-4430. W metskers.com

Seattle Visitor Center and Concierge Services
Tel (866) 732-2695 or (206) 461-5840. W visitseattle.org

Seattle Center Monorail
Tel (206) 905-2620.
W seattlemonorail.com

Seattle Police, Auto Records Department
Tel (206) 684-5444.

Sound Transit
Tel (206) 398-5000.
W soundtransit.org

South Lake Union Streetcar
Tel (206) 553-3000.
W seattlestreetcar.org

Washington State Ferries
Tel (206) 464-6400 for Seattle schedule. W wsdot.wa.gov

Taxis

Far West Taxi
Tel (206) 622-1717.
W farwesttaxi.net

Yellow Cab
Tel (206) 622-6500.

The Washington State Ferries service, linking Puget Sound communities

SEATTLE STREET FINDER

The key map below shows the area of Seattle covered by the *Street Finder* maps, which can be found on the following pages. Map references for sights, hotels, restaurants, shops, and entertainment venues given throughout the Seattle chapter of this guide refer to the grid on the maps. The first figure in the reference indicates which map to turn to (1 to 4), and the letter and number that follow refer to the grid reference on that map.

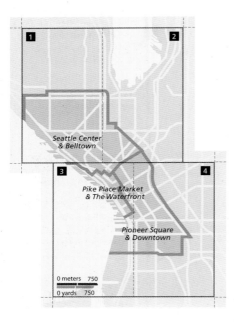

Seattle Center & Belltown

Pike Place Market & The Waterfront

Pioneer Square & Downtown

0 meters 750
0 yards 750

Key

▣	Major sight
▣	Minor sight
▣	Station building
🚉	Train station
🚌	Bus station – long-distance
🚋	Streetcar stop
🚈	Light Rail stop
🚝	Monorail station
ℹ	Information
✚	Hospital
✝	Church
⛴	Ferry boarding point
– –	Ferry route
══	Railroad line
	Pedestrian street
-----	Monorail/Light rail line
──	Streetcar line

Scale of maps 1–4

0 meters 300
0 yards 300

1st Avenue	**1 B5**	6th Avenue South	**4 E3**	Athenian Inn	**3 C1**	Broad Street	**1 B**
	& 3 C2	7th Avenue	**2 D5**	Aurora Avenue North	**1 C1**	Broadway Avenue	**4 E**
1st Avenue North	**1 B1**		**& 4 D2**	Austin A. Bell Building	**1 C5**		
1st Avenue South	**4 D4**	7th Avenue South	**4 E4**			**C**	
1st Avenue West	**1 A1**	8th Avenue	**2 D5**	**B**		Capitol Hill	**2 F**
2nd Avenue	**1 B5**		**& 4 E2**			Cedar Street	**1 C**
	& 4 D3	8th Avenue North	**2 D4**	Battery Street	**1 C5**	Central Library	**4 D**
2nd Avenue North	**1 B1**	8th Avenue South	**4 E4**	Bell Street	**1 C5**	CenturyLink Field	**4 D**
2nd Avenue West	**1 A1**	9th Avenue	**2 D5**	Bellevue Avenue		Cherry Street	**4 D**
3rd Avenue	**1 C5**		**& 4 E2**	East	**2 F3**	Chihuly Garden	
	& 4 D2	9th Avenue North	**2 D4**	Bellevue Place East	**2 F3**	and Glass	**1 B**
3rd Avenue North	**1 B3**	12th Avenue	**4 F1**	Belltown	**1 C5**	Children's Museum	**1 B**
3rd Avenue South	**4 D4**	12th Avenue South	**4 F5**		**& 3 B1**	Clay Street	**1 B**
3rd Avenue West	**1 A1**	13th Avenue	**4 F1**	Belmont Avenue		Coast Guard Museum	
4th Avenue	**1 C5**	13th Avenue South	**4 F5**	East	**2 F4**	Northwest	**3 C**
	& 3 C1	14th Avenue	**4 F1**	Benaroya Hall	**3 C1**	Colorado Avenue	
4th Avenue North	**1 C1**	14th Avenue South	**4 F5**	Bigelow Avenue		South	**3 C**
4th Avenue South	**4 D4**	15th Avenue South	**4 F5**	North	**1 C2**	Columbia Center	**4 D**
4th Avenue West	**1 A1**			Blaine Street	**1 B1**	Columbia Street	**4 D**
5th Avenue	**1 C5**	**A**		Blanchard Street	**1 C5**		
	& 4 D2			Boeing IMAX Theater	**1 C4**	**D**	
5th Avenue North	**1 C1**	Airport Way South	**4 E4**	Boren Avenue	**2 E5**		
5th Avenue South	**4 E3**	Alaskan Way	**1 B5**		**& 4 F2**	Denny Park	**2 D**
5th Avenue West	**1 A1**		**& 3 C5**	Boren Avenue		Denny Way	**1 B**
6th Avenue	**2 D5**	Alaskan Way Viaduct	**3 C2**	North	**2 E4**	Dexter Avenue North	**2 D**
	& 4 D2	Aloha Street	**1 B3**	Boylston Avenue	**4 E1**	Doctor Jose Rizal Park	**4**
6th Avenue North	**1 C2**			Boylston Avenue		Downtown	**4**
				East	**2 F4**		

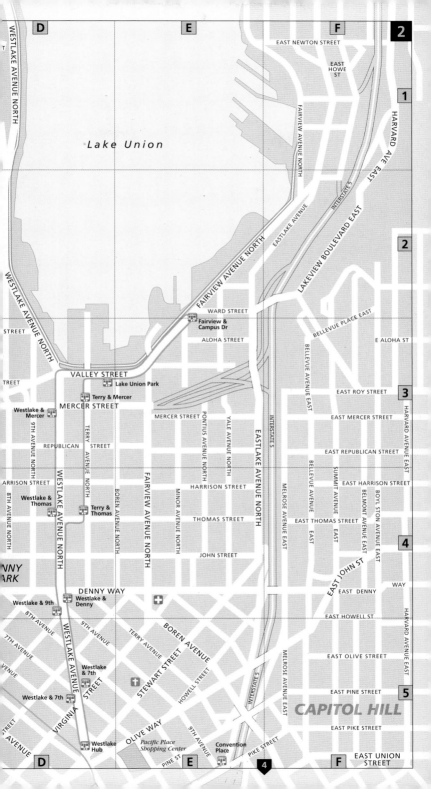

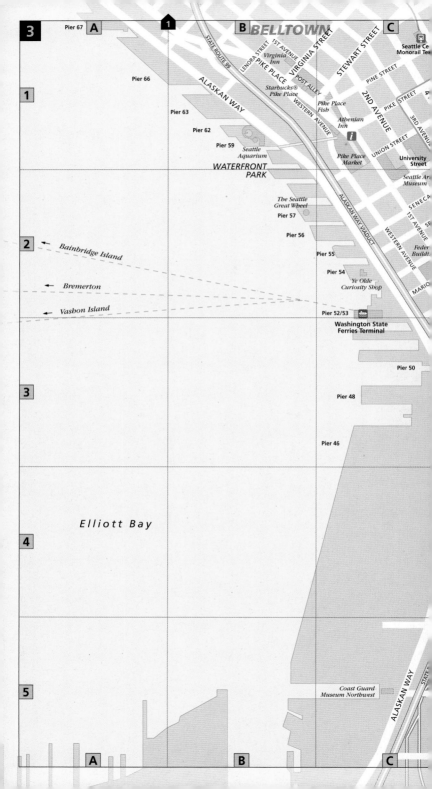

WASHINGTON

Named for the first president of the US, Washington was the 42nd state to enter the Union, in 1889. Washington is located in the far northwestern corner of the country, sharing a border with Canada. Within its 68,139 sq miles (176,466 sq km) of land lies an extraordinary geographical diversity; each of the state's three distinct regions has its own geology, personality, and climate.

The coastal region – bordered by the Pacific Ocean to the west, the Strait of Juan de Fuca to the north, Oregon to the south, and Puget Sound to the east – is dominated by the beautiful Olympic National Park and other great tracts of forest. Highlights include the charming Victorian seaport of Port Townsend, the spectacular views from the top of Hurricane Ridge, the expansive Crescent Lake, the towering moss-draped trees of the Hoh Rainforest, and miles of scenic coastline, which receive the highest amounts of rainfall in the state.

Western Washington contains the state's most populous areas, which lie in the corridor along Interstate-5, especially between Tacoma and Seattle. In the far northwest, scattered off the coast, are the San Juan Islands, enjoying on average 247 days of sunshine a year.

The Cascade mountain range, which runs between western and eastern Washington, provides wonderful opportunities for skiing, hiking, and numerous other outdoor activities. Mount Rainier, the highest peak in the range, is Washington's most-visited attraction.

The dry, sunny eastern region, stretching from the Cascades to the Idaho border, contrasts with the dense, damp greenness of western Washington. Both the fertile Yakima Valley, the fifth-largest producer of fruits and vegetables in the US, and the Walla Walla Valley are known for their many excellent wineries. Farther north, the magnificent Grand Coulee Dam harnesses the power of the mighty Columbia River to provide irrigation water for more than 800 square miles (2,072 square km) of farmland.

Sea kayaks at Snug Harbor in Mitchell Bay, on the west side of San Juan Island

◀ Beautiful fall foliage surrounding the Blue Lake, North Cascades National Park

Exploring Washington

Washington's many attractions are sprinkled liberally throughout the state, which consists of three distinct regions: coastal, western, and eastern. The Olympic Peninsula, in the coastal region, provides visitors with a choice of ocean, lake, forest, or mountain playgrounds. Western Washington's favorite islands, among them Bainbridge, Whidbey, and the San Juans, all offer charming towns, miles of terrain for cycling, and the opportunity to slip into "island time" for a day or two. A drive to the eastern region – at its best in late spring to mid-fall – leads to the western-themed Winthrop and the breathtaking peaks of North Cascades National Park.

Sailboats moored at Point Hudson marina, Port Townsend

Sights at a Glance

- **2** *Port Townsend pp180–81*
- **3** *San Juan Islands pp182–3*
- **4** Bellingham
- **5** La Conner
- **6** Whidbey Island
- **7** Bainbridge Island
- **8** Tillicum Village
- **9** Chateau Ste. Michelle
- **10** Snoqualmie Falls
- **11** Tacoma
- **12** Olympia
- **13** *Mount Rainier National Park pp188–9*
- **14** Crystal Mountain
- **15** Leavenworth
- **16** Lake Chelan
- **17** Stehekin
- **19** Winthrop
- **20** Grand Coulee Dam
- **21** Spokane
- **22** Yakima Valley
- **23** Walla Walla
- **25** Goldendale Observatory State Park
- **26** Maryhill
- **27** Mount St. Helens National Volcanic Monument
- **28** Fort Vancouver

Tours

- **1** *Olympic Peninsula pp178–9*
- **18** *North Cascades National Park pp192–3*
- **24** *Walla Walla Valley Wine Tour pp196–7*

The dramatic metal cone of Tacoma's Museum of Glass

Key

- Highway
- Major road
- Minor road
- Scenic route
- Main railroad
- International border
- State border
- ▲ Summit
- ✕ White Pass

Mount Rainier, as seen from Mount Rainier National Park

Getting Around

Bellingham, Seattle, Tacoma, and Olympia are all accessed by I-5, the state's main north–south interstate. I-90, the major east–west artery, leads from Seattle to Spokane. Five mountain passes and the Columbia Gorge link western and eastern Washington. US Highway 2 crosses Stevens Pass to Leavenworth. State Highway 20 (North Cascades Hwy), usually closed in winter, passes through Winthrop. Amtrak offers a rail service, and Greyhound, a bus service, to most of Washington's major cities. Washington State Ferries sail to destinations including around Puget Sound and the San Juan Islands.

For keys to symbols *see back flap*

❶ Olympic Peninsula Tour

The Olympic Peninsula, in the far northwestern corner of Washington, offers many opportunities for spectacular sightseeing. The centerpiece of the peninsula is Olympic National Park, a UNESCO biosphere reserve and World Heritage Site. Encompassing 1,442 sq miles (3,735 sq km), the park contains mountains with snowcapped peaks, as well as lakes, waterfalls, rivers, and rainforests. Opportunities for outdoor activities abound in the peninsula; among the most popular pursuits are deep-sea- and fly-fishing, kayaking, white-water rafting, mountain biking, and bird-watching.

⑤ Lake Crescent
Lake Crescent Lodge is an historic resort on the shores of Lake Crescent. The lake's crystal-clear fresh water, which reaches a depth of 625 ft (190 m), makes it a favorite location for divers.

⑥ Rialto Beach This long beach offers terrific views of the Pacific coast, with its tide pools, sea stacks, rocky islands, and the Hole in the Wall.

⑦ Forks This former logging town shot to fame in 2005 as the setting for Stephenie Meyer's bestselling vampire novels, the *Twilight* series.

⑧ Hoh Rainforest
Ancient trees tower to nearly 300 ft (91 m) in this old-growth forest, which receives 14 ft (4 m) of rainfall a year.

0 kilometers 20
0 miles 15

Key

▬▬ Tour route
═══ Other road

Cape Flattery

Neah Bay

112

Hoko

Hoko-Ozette Road

113

Lake Ozette

Beaver

⑥ 110 ⑦ *Forks*

LaPush

Bogachiel River

Pacific Ocean

Clearwater

101

Que

Out

⑨

⑨ Lake Quinault Snowcapped mountains encircle this lake and Lake Quinault Lodge.

④ **Hurricane Ridge**
The ridge's summit, at 5,230 ft (1,594 m), is covered with flowers in spring and offers panoramic views. Skiing and snowshoeing are popular winter activities here.

③ **Sequim**
Sitting in the rain shadow of the Olympic Mountains, Sequim features an elk-viewing site and the Olympic Game Farm, home to endangered wild animals.

Tips for Drivers

Tour length: 272 miles (438 km) including all detours off Hwy 101.
Starting point: Port Gamble on Hwy 104. Here, cross the Hood Canal Bridge to begin the tour.
Stopping-off points: As well as the numerous public campgrounds and lodges situated in or near Olympic National Park (see p289), a wide variety of restaurants and accommodations is to be found throughout this area.

① **Port Gamble**
Located on the Kitsap Peninsula, this former logging town has retained its original New England Victorian-style homes, country store, and church. The 1982 movie *An Officer and a Gentleman* was filmed here.

② **Port Townsend**
This seaport, a National Historic Landmark, is known for its Victorian architecture and vibrant arts community (see pp180–81). The town is also an excellent base from which to make kayaking, whale-watching, and cycling day trips.

⑩ **Mount Olympus**
With its West Peak rising 7,965 ft (2,428 m), this three-peaked, glacier-clad mountain is the highest in Washington's Olympic range.

➋ Port Townsend

Port Townsend was founded in 1851, almost 60 years after Captain Vancouver first saw its harbor and named it for his friend, the Marquis of Townshend. By the late 19th century, it was a bustling maritime community, with more ships in its port than in any other city in the US, with the exception of New York. Convinced that Port Townsend would be the end point for a transcontinental railroad, residents went on a building spree, erecting lavish mansions and grand buildings in anticipation of its becoming the "New York of the West." That dream never materialized, but most of the original structures from that era have survived. The city today enjoys a booming tourism business, thanks to its Victorian buildings. Port Townsend is one of only three seaports on the National Registry as a historic landmark.

Ann Starrett Mansion, with its unusual eight-sided domed tower

Exploring Port Townsend

Port Townsend is easily explored on foot. Water Street, the Downtown Historic District's main boulevard, is lined with brick-and-stone buildings housing art galleries, upscale shops, and restaurants. Many of the city's Victorian homes, churches, and inns are in the Uptown Historic District, between Clay and Lincoln Streets. The center of the uptown business district is Lawrence and Tyler Streets. Maps and information about tours are available at the visitors' center.

Jefferson County Courthouse tower

🏛 Jefferson County Courthouse

1820 Jefferson St. **Tel** (360) 385-9100. **Open** 9am–5pm Mon–Fri. **Closed** public hols. &

The jewel of Port Townsend's Victorian architecture, this neo-Romanesque building was designed in 1892 by Seattle architect Willis A. Ritchie, who ordered its bricks to be hauled west from St. Louis, rather than using the soft, local ones. The building's 124-ft- (38-m-) tall clock tower, its clockwork also dating to 1892, has long been a landmark for sailors.

🏛 Jefferson Museum of Art and History

540 Water St. **Tel** (360) 385-1003. **Open** 11am–4pm daily. **Closed** Jan 1, Thanksgiving, Dec 25. 🖼 & 🏛
W jchsmuseum.org

Occupying the old City Hall (1891), this building once housed the town's fire station, jail, court room, and city offices. Today it is home to the city council, as well as an excellent museum that showcases the county's heritage through artifacts, archives, and photographs. Highlights of the exhibits include a display on the area's Native peoples.

🏛 Ann Starrett Mansion

744 Clay St. **Tel** (800) 321-0644. **Open** to hotel guests only.
W starrettmansion.com

Built in 1889 by wealthy contractor George Starrett as a wedding gift for his bride, Ann, this grand Queen Anne-style mansion has received national recognition for its architecture,

frescoed ceilings, and three-tiered spiral staircase topped by a domed ceiling. A National Historic Landmark, it now serves as a hotel.

🏛 Rothschild House

Franklin & Taylor Sts. **Tel** (360) 379-8076 **Open** May–Sep: 11am–4pm daily. **Closed** Oct–Apr. 🖼

A departure from Port Townsend's more elaborate homes, this estate reflects the simplicity of the New England-style design that predated Victorian architecture. Built in 1868 for David C. H. Rothschild, it was donated by the sole remaining family member to the Washington State Parks and Recreation Commission in 1959.

Restored and listed on the National Register of Historic Places, the house contains original furnishings.

🏛 St. Paul's Episcopal Church

1020 Jefferson St. **Tel** (360) 385-0770. **Open** 9am–noon Mon–Thu. 🏛 8am & 10am Sun. & **W** stpaulspt.org

The oldest surviving church in Port Townsend – and the oldest Episcopal church in continuous use in Washington – the Gothic Revival-style St. Paul's was built in 1865. Originally located below

Union Wharf, jutting out from Port Townsend's waterfront

For hotels and restaurants see pp288–90 and pp300–2

he bluff, the church was placed
on logs and rolled to its present
location in 1883 with the help
of horses and a windlass.

🔔 Fire Bell Tower
Tyler & Jefferson Sts.
Located on the bluff overlooking
downtown, the 1890 fire bell
tower was once used to summon
the town's volunteer firefighters.
The number of rings indicated
which part of town the fire was
in. The tower is placed first on
Washington, DC's list of Ten Most
Endangered Historic Treasures.

🔔 Haller Fountain
Taylor & Washington Sts.
Donated to the city in 1906 by
Theodore Haller, the fountain's

The prominent 1889 Hastings Building, today housing
offices and upmarket shops

Water Street's N.D. Hill Building, used as a
hotel since 1889

centerpiece, a bronze maiden,
made her debut in the Mexican
exhibit at the 1893 World's Columbian Exposition in Chicago.

🌳 Fort Worden State Park
200 Battery Way. **Tel** (360) 344-4400.
W parks.state.wa.us
This former military base is
now a state park. Visitors
can explore the fort's bunkers,
attend arts and cultural events,
and tour the **Commanding
Officer's Quarters** (1904).
A museum refurbished
in late Victorian style, it
offers a glimpse into the
lives of the officers in
the early 20th century.
It is also possible to stay
in one of several historic
homes that were once
occupied by the officers.
The **Puget Sound Coast**

VISITORS' CHECKLIST

Practical Information
Road map 1 A2. 🕰 8,900.
ℹ️ 440 12th St, (360) 385-2722.
W enjoypt.com

Transport
🚌 from Keystone on
Whidbey Island.

Artillery Museum is devoted to
harbor-defense operations from
the late 19th century through
World War II.

🏠 Commanding
Officer's Quarters
Tel (360) 344-4452. **Open** May–Sep:
11am–4pm daily; Oct–Apr: 11am–
4pm Sat & Sun. 🐾 📷

🏛 Puget Sound Coast
Artillery Museum
Tel (360) 385-0373. **Open** 11am–4pm
daily. **Closed** major hols. 🐾 ♿
W coastartillery.org

Store window display on Port Townsend's
historic Water Street

Port Townsend

① Jefferson County Courthouse
② Jefferson Museum of Art
   and History
③ Ann Starrett Mansion
④ Rothschild House
⑤ St. Paul's Episcopal Church
⑥ Fire Bell Tower
⑦ Haller Fountain

❸ San Juan Islands

Scattered between the Washington mainland and Vancouver Island, the San Juan archipelago consists of over 450 islands, 172 of them named. Ferries sail from Anacortes to the four largest islands: Lopez, Shaw, Orcas, and San Juan. Lopez is affectionately called "Slopez" because of its laid-back nature. Gently rolling roads, numerous stopping points, and friendly drivers make it a popular destination for cycling. Horseshoe-shaped Orcas, the hilliest island in the chain, offers breathtaking views from atop 2,409-ft (734-m) Mount Constitution. The best destination for walk-on passengers, San Juan Island is home to Friday Harbor, the largest town in the archipelago. The nationally renowned Whale Museum is located here. The island is also one of the best locations in the world for shoreside whale-watching and sea kayaking. Primarily residential, Shaw Island has limited visitor facilities.

Sailboats in the Channel
Sailors love the many harbors and good winds in the San Juan Channel.

Victoria

Lime Kiln Point
State Park

San Ju
Islan

Seattle

★ **Roche Harbor**
A charming seaside village, Roche Harbor features a marina, Victorian gardens, a chapel, and the historic Hotel de Haro, built in 1886. There is also a spa, an outdoor swimming pool, and tennis and bocce ball courts.

Lime Kiln Point State Park
This state park, with its picturesque lighthouse, completed in 1919, is the only park in the US dedicated to whale-watching.

0 kilometers   2
0 mile   1

★ **Deer Harbor**
Sea kayakers flock to Deer Harbor and the other waters surrounding the islands of Orcas, Lopez, and San Juan.

VISITORS' CHECKLIST

Practical Information
Road map 1 A1.
📶 (888) 468-3701.
🅦 visitsanjuans.com
🅦 wsdot.wa.gov/ferries

Transport
🚌 Washington State Ferries from Anacortes or Sidney, BC, to the San Juan Islands. **Tel** (206) 464-6400. 🅦 takeaferry.com (book in advance).

★ **Lopez**
Despite its gently rolling hills, Lopez is the flattest of the San Juan Islands, making it a popular destination for recreational cyclists.

★ **Friday Harbor**
The largest town in the San Juans, Friday Harbor offers a number of restaurants, inns, galleries, and shops – all within easy walking distance of the ferry dock.

For keys to symbols *see back flap*

Key
🟦 Major road
🟦 Minor road
Ferry route

❹ Bellingham

Road map 1 A1. ✈ Bellingham Airport. 👥 81,000. 🛈 (800) 487-2032. 🌐 **bellingham.org**

Overlooking Bellingham Bay and many of the San Juan Islands, Bellingham has been inhabited by the Lummi Indians for thousands of years. The area – consisting of the four original towns of Whatcom, Sehome, Bellingham, and Fairhaven – was settled in 1853 and consolidated in 1904. The town's historic architecture includes Old Whatcom County Courthouse (1308 East Street), the first brick building north of San Francisco, built in 1858, and the majestic Old City Hall, built in 1892 in the Victorian Second Empire style. The latter is now the heart of the **Whatcom Museum**, a three-building campus that includes a children's museum. Highlights of the museum include exhibits on the Northwest Coast First Nations and on the birds of the Pacific Northwest.

South of downtown, the historic Fairhaven district is an artsy enclave of Victorian buildings housing galleries, restaurants, bookstores, and coffeehouses.

Just up the hill from downtown Bellingham sits the campus of **Western Washington University**, which has a famous collection of outdoor sculptures, including artworks by internationally recognized American artists Richard Serra, Mark di Suvero, and Richard Beyer.

Tower of Bellingham's former City Hall

Boats journeying along the Skagit River in La Conner

The town also attracts visitors to its craft breweries and art events.

🏛 **Whatcom Museum**
Old City Hall, 121 Prospect St. **Tel** (360) 778-8930. **Open** noon–5pm Thu–Sun; Lightcatcher Building: 250 Flora St. **Open** noon–5pm Wed–Sun (to 8pm Thu, from 10am Sat). Family Interactive Gallery: 250 Flora St. **Open** 10am–5pm Wed–Sun (from noon Sun). **Closed** major hols. 🅿 ♿ ▣ 📷 🌐 **whatcommuseum.org**

🏛 **Western Washington University**
516 High St. 🛈 S College Dr & College Way. **Tel** (360) 650-3000. Visitors' center: **Open** 7:15am–4:30pm Mon–Fri. **Closed** major hols. ♿ 🌐 **wwu.edu**

Environs
South of Bellingham, Chuckanut Drive (Highway 11) is a scenic 21-mile (34-km) loop with outlooks to Puget Sound and the San Juan Islands. Along the way are hiking and biking trails, restaurants, and oyster farms selling fresh oysters in season. Fifty-five miles (88.5 km) east of Bellingham is 10,778-ft-(3,285-m-) high Mount Baker, where the ski and snowboarding season runs from November through April.

❺ La Conner

Road map 1 A2. 👥 890. 🚍 🛈 (888) 642-9284. 🌐 **lovelaconner.com**

Long associated in the minds of Washingtonians with tulips, the town of La Conner draws thousands to the Skagit Valley Tulip Festival. And although the town's famous fields are abloom with spectacular color come springtime, there is more to La Conner than flowers. A magnet for artists since the 1940s, this tiny town is a thriving arts community. The highly respected **Museum of Northwest Art** showcases works by Mark Tobey, Guy Anderson, Morris Graves, and Kenneth Callahan (all of whom were inspired by the Skagit Valley's unique light), as well as Dale Chihuly and other prominent Pacific Northwest artists.

Listed on the National Register of Historic Places, La Conner was founded in the early 1860s. It was originally called Swinomish, after the area's first residents, the Swinomish Indians. In 1869, wealthy merchant John Conner renamed the town after his wife, Louisa Ann Siegfried, by combining her first two initials and her married name. Louisa Ann was the town's first non-Indian woman resident. For a glimpse into her life – and those of other early settlers – visit the **Skagit County Historical Museum**.

🏛 **Museum of Northwest Art**
121 S 1st St. **Tel** (360) 466-4446. **Open** noon–5pm Sun & Mon, 10am–5pm Tue–Sat. **Closed** major hols. 🅿 ♿ 📷 🌐 **museumofnwart.org**

🏛 **Skagit County Historical Museum**
501 S 4th St. **Tel** (360) 466-3365. **Open** 11am–5pm Tue–Sun. 🅿 ♿ 📷

Crab traps on a boat ready to set out from Bellingham Harbor

For hotels and restaurants see pp288–90 and pp300–2

❻ Whidbey Island

Road map 1 A2. ⛰ 60,000. ⛴
ℹ 905 NW Alexander St, Coupeville,
(360) 678-5434.

Whidbey Island boasts seven
state parks and two charming
seaside villages. **Coupeville**'s
Victorian homes, old barns,
and quaint waterfront recall
the town's beginnings. Nearby,
the extensive Ebey's Landing
National Historical Reserve
includes the historic army post,
Fort Casey State Park. At the
island's south end, the arts
community of **Langley** has
historic buildings, upscale
shops, art galleries, and bed-
and-breakfasts.

🏛 Fort Casey State Park
1280 Engle Rd. **Tel** (360) 678-4519.
Open 8am–dusk. **W** parks.wa.gov

❼ Bainbridge Island

Road map 1 A2. ⛰ 22,000. ⛴
ℹ 395 Winslow Way E, (206) 842-3700.
W bainbridgechamber.com

A 35-minute ferry ride from
Seattle, this island makes for a
pleasant outing. Near the ferry
terminal, a path leads through
Waterfront Park to downtown
Winslow's galleries, shops, and
cafés. The island's charming
inns make it a popular stop
for travelers to the Kitsap and
Olympic Peninsulas. **Bloedel
Reserve**, with its Japanese
garden, English landscape,
and bird refuge, is worth a visit.

🏛 Bloedel Reserve
7571 NE Dolphin Dr. **Tel** (206) 842-
7631. **Open** 10am–4pm Tue–Sun
(Jun–Aug: to 7pm). **Closed** Dec 25.
♿ &

Isolated coastline in one of Whidbey
Island's state parks

❽ Tillicum Village

Blake Island State Park.
Road map 1 A2. **Tel** (206) 623-1445.
Open Apr–Sep, two trips per day:
11:30am–3:30pm, 4:30–8:30pm
(schedule varies). 🚢 tours depart
from Pier 55, Seattle Central
Waterfront. ♿ 📖 📷 **W** argosy
cruises.com/tillicum-village

Tillicum Village, located in
Blake Island State Park, offers
visitors a fascinating cultural
and culinary experience. Guests
are taken on a 4-hour tour
of the village which starts with
a cruise from Pier 55 on Seattle's
Waterfront. Once at the village,
visitors can observe whole
Chinook salmon being prepared
and cooked around alder wood
fires, in the traditional style of
the Northwest Coast Indians.
A buffet-style meal is served,
followed by a performance
of the "Dance on the Wind"
stage show, a combination of
traditional songs, dances, and
stories about the Northwest
Coast Native culture. Also held
here are demonstrations of
the traditional carving

techniques and the creation
of local artwork.

Blake Island State Park is
named after Captain George
Blake, commander of the US
Coast Survey vessel in 1837.
The park is the ancestral camp-
ground of the Squamish and
Duwamish Indian tribes and
boasts unspoiled scenery.
The island is an excellent
example of Pacific Northwest
lowland forest and is home to
numerous native trees and
shrubs as well as deer, otter,
squirrels, mink, and many
varieties of bird. The island's
large number of walking trails
and a 5-mile (8-km) saltwater
beach make it an excellent
destination for hikers.

Tour group arriving at Tillicum in
Blake Island State Park

❾ Chateau Ste. Michelle

14111 NE 145th St, Woodinville.
Road map 1 B2. **Tel** (425) 488-1133.
Open 10am–5pm daily. **Closed** Jan 1,
Easter, Thanksgiving, Dec 25. ♿
🚗 10:30am–4:30pm daily.
🎵 Summer concerts.
W ste-michelle.com

Washington's founding winery,
Chateau Ste. Michelle is
located on a wooded estate
in Woodinville, 20 miles (32 km)
north of Seattle. This location
produces all Chateau Ste.
Michelle's acclaimed white
wines. (The red wines are made
in eastern Washington, where
grapes for both the white
and red wines are grown.)
Complimentary winery tours
and wine tastings are offered
daily. The winery's summer
concert series draws top blues,
jazz, classical, and contemporary
talents to its outdoor grass
amphitheater, where concert-
goers savor wine and picnics
while enjoying the music.

Chateau Ste. Michelle, founded in 1934, Washington's oldest winery

The magnificent cascades of Snoqualmie Falls

⑩ Snoqualmie Falls

Road map 1 B2.

The most famous waterfall in the state, Snoqualmie Falls is Washington's second-most-visited tourist attraction after Mount Rainier. This 268-ft (82-m) waterfall on the Snoqualmie River draws one and a half million visitors each year. Long regarded as a sacred site by the Snoqualmie Indians and other local Native American tribes, the cascade also fascinated the naturalist John Muir, who, in 1889, described it as the most interesting he had ever seen.

An observation deck 300 ft (91 m) above the river provides an excellent view of the thundering water. For a closer look, visitors can follow a steep half-mile (0.8 km) trail down to the river.

⑪ Tacoma

Road map 1 A2. 🚊 200,000. ✈ Seattle-Tacoma International Airport. 🛈 1516 Pacific Ave, (253) 627-2836. 🌐 traveltacoma.com

Washington's third-largest city, Tacoma was founded as a saw-mill town in the 1860s. With the arrival of the railroad in the late 1880s it prospered, becoming a major shipping port for commodities important to a growing nation: lumber, coal, and grain. Many of the Pacific Northwest's railroad, timber, and shipping barons settled in Tacoma's Stadium District. This historic area, with its stately turn-of-the-19th-century

mansions, is named for Stadium High School, which is also known as the "Castle." Designed in the 1890s to be a luxury hotel, the French chateau-style building was converted in the early 1900s into a high school.

The undisputed star of the city's revitalized waterfront is the striking **Museum of Glass**. Opened in July 2002, this landmark building was designed by top Canadian architect Arthur Erickson to showcase contemporary art, with a focus on glass. The 75,000-sq-ft (6,968-sq-m) museum includes a spacious glassblowing studio housed within a dramatic 90-ft (37-m) metal-encased cone.

The stunning Chihuly Bridge of Glass, a collaboration between Austin, Texas architect Arthur Andersson and world-renowned Tacoma glass artist Dale Chihuly, serves as a pedestrian walkway linking the museum to downtown Tacoma and the innovative **Washington State History Museum**. Tales of Washington's past are related using interactive exhibits, high-tech displays, and theatrical storytelling by characters in period costume.

The spectacular home of the **Tacoma Art Museum** was designed by architect Antoine Predock to be a dynamic cultural center and a showpiece for the city. The 50,000-sq-ft (4,645-sq-m), stainless-steel-wrapped museum boldly showcases the growing collection of works from the 18th century to the present day. These include a large assembly of Pacific Northwest art, European Impressionist pieces, Japanese woodblock prints, and American

The imposing Stadium High School, in Tacoma's Stadium District

graphic art. The museum also holds the world's largest retrospective permanent collection of glass art by Dale Chihuly. In 2014, a new wing, designed by Seattle's Olson Kundig Architects, was opened. This building doubled the museum's gallery space and houses the Haub Family Collection of Western American Art. In keeping with its vision of creating a place that "builds community through art," the museum's facilities also include the Bill and Melinda Gates Resource Center, providing access to a wide array of reference materials and state-of-the-art research equipment. As well, kids of all ages can make use of the in-house, interactive art-making studio, ArtWORKS.

Tacoma's most popular attraction is Point Defiance Park, ranked among the 20 largest urban parks in the US. Its grounds include Fort Nisqually, the first European settlement on Puget Sound and a major fur-trading establishment; several specialty gardens; a scenic drive

The modern exterior of the Tacoma Museum of Glass

Polar bear at Point Defiance Zoo and Aquarium, Tacoma

hiking and biking trails; beaches; a boat marina; and a picnic area. Fishing is permitted, and gear is available for rental.

Highlighting a Pacific Rim theme, the world-class **Point Defiance Zoo and Aquarium** is home to over 9,000 animals. A vantage point at the west end of the park offers terrific views of Mount Rainier, Puget Sound, and the Tacoma Narrows Bridge, one of the longest suspension bridges in the United States.

🏛 Museum of Glass
801 E Dock St. **Tel** (253) 284-4750 or (866) 468-7400. **Open** Memorial Day–Labor Day: 10am–5pm Mon–Sat, noon–5pm Sun; Labor Day– Memorial Day: 10am–5pm Wed–Sat, noon–5pm Sun. **Closed** Jan 1, Thanksgiving, Dec 25. 🅿 🚻 📷 💳 📶
w museumofglass.org

🏛 Washington State History Museum
1911 Pacific Ave. **Tel** (888) 238-4373. **Open** Jun–Aug: 10am–5pm Mon–Sat, noon–5pm Sun; Sep–May: 10am– 5pm Tue–Sat, noon–5pm Sun. **Closed** major hols. 🅿 🚻 💳 for groups. **w wshs.org**

🏛 Tacoma Art Museum
1701 Pacific Ave. **Tel** (253) 272-4258. **Open** Memorial Day–Labor Day: 10am–5pm Tue–Sat, noon–5pm Sun; Labor Day–Memorial Day: 10am–5pm Wed–Sat, noon–5pm Sun. **Closed** major hols. 🅿 (free 5–8pm 3rd Thu of month). 🚻 📷 💳 📶
w tacomaartmuseum.org

🐾 Point Defiance Zoo and Aquarium
5400 N Pearl St. **Tel** (253) 591-5337. **Open** 9:30am–4pm daily (Apr–May & Sep: to 5pm; Jun–Aug: to 6pm). Hours can vary; check in advance. **Closed** Jul: 3rd Fri; Nov–Feb: Tue & Wed, Thanksgiving, Dec 25. 🅿 🍴 🚻 📷 **w pdza.org**

Environs

Just 11 miles (17 km) from Tacoma, across the Narrows on the Kitsap Peninsula, is the charming fishing village of **Gig Harbor**, named by Captain Charles Wilkes, who, from 1838 to 1842, charted the area from his gig. The community's boutiques, galleries, and waterfront restaurants reflect the proud Scandinavian and Croatian heritage of many of its 6,500 inhabitants.

The bastion at Fort Nisqually historic site in Point Defiance Park

⑫ Olympia

Road map 1 A2. 🏙 43,000. 🛈 809 Legion Way SE, (360) 357-3362.
w visitolympia.com

Washington's state capital since 1853, Olympia was named for its magnificent view of the Olympic Mountains. Located 60 miles (97 km) south of Seattle at the southern tip of Puget Sound, the city is known first and foremost for its lovely **State Capitol Campus**, one of the most beautiful in the nation. It is dominated by the 28-story domed Legislative Building, and boasts stunning buildings, landscaped grounds (designed in 1928 by the Olmsted Brothers and known for their spectacular bulb and annual plantings), and numerous fountains and monuments. The **Legislative Building** (the Capitol) has a 287-ft (87-m) sandstone dome, one of the tallest masonry domes in the world.

The **State Archives** stores Washington's historical records and artifacts. Visitors can view such treasures as documents from the Canwell Committee, which blacklisted suspected Communists in the 1950s.

Located seven blocks south of the State Capitol Campus is the **State Capital Museum** that has exhibits dedicated to the history and culture of Washington.

Tree-lined streets, old homes, a picturesque waterfront, and a thriving cultural community all contribute to Olympia's charm. Tucked among the downtown historic buildings are restaurants, galleries, and shops. Within walking distance are attractions such as the **Olympia Farmers Market**, offering local produce, seafood, baked goods, and crafts.

Percival Landing (4th Avenue between Sylvester and Water Streets), a 1.5-mile (2.5-km) boardwalk, offers views of the Olympic Mountains, Capitol Dome, and Puget Sound.

State Capitol Campus
🛈 416 Sid Snyder Ave SW, (360) 902-8881. **Closed** Jan 1, Thanksgiving, day after Thanksgiving, Dec 25. Legislative Building: **Open** 7am–5:30pm Mon–Fri, 11am–4pm Sat & Sun. **Closed** Jan 1, Thanksgiving, Dec 25. 📷 hourly 10am–2pm. Temple of Justice: 8am–5pm Mon–Fri. ♿

🏛 State Capital Museum
211 21st Ave SW. **Tel** (360) 902-8880. **Closed** for renovation. 🅿 ♿

🏛 State Archives
1129 Washington St SE. **Tel** (360) 586-1492. **Open** 8:30am–4:30pm Mon–Fri. ♿

🛒 Olympia Farmers Market
700 N Capitol Way. **Tel** (360) 352-9096. **Open** Apr–Oct: 10am–3pm Thu–Sun; Nov–Dec: 10am–3pm Sat & Sun. ♿ **w olympiafarmers market.com**

The imposing Legislative Building on the State Capitol Campus, Olympia

⑬ Mount Rainier National Park

Established in 1899, Mount Rainier National Park encompasses 369 sq miles (956 sq km), of which 97 percent is designated Wilderness. Its centerpiece is Mount Rainier, an active volcano towering 14,410 ft (4,392 m) above sea level. Surrounded by old-growth forest and wildflower meadows, Mount Rainier was named in 1792 by Captain George Vancouver for fellow British naval officer Peter Rainier. Designated a National Historic Landmark District in 1997, the park, which features 1920s and 1930s National Park Service rustic architecture, attracts two million visitors a year. The summer draws hikers, mountain climbers, and campers; the winter lures snowshoers and cross-country skiers.

Mount Rainier Nisqually Glacier
Close to Paradise, the Nisqually Glacier is one of the most visible on Mount Rainier. It is currently retreating.

Mount Rainier Narada Falls
One of the more spectacular and easily accessible cascades along the Paradise River, Narada Falls is just a short, steep hike from the Nisqually road. The falls plummet 168 ft (51 m).

National Park Inn
This small and cozy inn, located in Longmire and open year-round, is a perfect spot from which to enjoy the stunning view of Mount Rainier.

For hotels and restaurants see pp288–90 and pp300–2

★ Emmons Glacier
Emmons Glacier, on Mount Rainier's eastern slope, is, at 4.3 sq miles (11.1 sq km), the largest glacier in the lower 48 states.

VISITORS' CHECKLIST

Practical Information
Hwy 706 near Ashford. **Tel** (360) 569-2211. *i* Jackson Visitor Center, Paradise. **Open** May–mid-Oct: 10am–5pm daily (Jun–Aug: to 7pm); mid-Oct–Apr: 10am–5pm Sat & Sun. Nisqually entrance: **Open** year-round. White River entrance: **Open** summer only.
W nps.gov/mora

★ Sunrise
Open only during the summer, Sunrise is, at 6,400 ft (1,950 m), the highest point to which you can drive in the park.

White River entrance

★ Paradise
Paradise, the park's most popular destination, is open year-round and has an excellent visitors' information center.

Grove of the Patriarchs Trail
Stevens Canyon entrance
Ohanapecosh
Yakima

Getting Around

From the southwest (Highway 706), enter the park via Nisqually gate. Open year-round, this is the only entrance in winter. Drive 6 miles (10 km) to Longmire, where facilities include an inn and museum, and the Wilderness Information Center, open from late May to October. The 12-mile (19-km) road between Paradise and Longmire is steep and winding; drive carefully. Carry chains when traveling by car during winter.

0 kilometers 4
0 miles 2

Key

▬▬ Minor road

═══ Dirt or four-wheel-drive road

– – Hiking trail

For keys to symbols *see back flap*

Downhill skiing on the sparkling snow-covered slopes of Washington's Crystal Mountain

⓮ Crystal Mountain

Road map 1 B2. **Tel** (360) 663-2265.
Open hours vary depending on
facility & season; call for details. 🏢 💻
🏠 W crystalmountainresort.com

Located near the northeast
corner of Mount Rainier National
Park and rising above the town
of the same name, Crystal
Mountain is Washington's largest
and only destination ski area.

Attracted by reports of local
gold finds in the late 1800s, the
first visitors to the area were
miners intent on making their
fortunes. However, by the end
of World War I, these claims
had not yielded the riches
envisioned, and investment
in this area, then known as
the Summit Mining District,
severely declined.

Its recreational attributes
were discovered in 1949, when
attempts to put a chairlift on
Mount Rainier failed, and a
group of avid Puget Sound
skiers began looking for another
spot to develop as a ski area.
Crystal Mountain opened for
business in 1962, receiving
national attention three
years later when it hosted the
National Alpine Championships,
an event that attracted skiing
legends such as Jimmie Heuga,
Billy Kidd, and Jean-Claude Killy.

The ski area, with over 50
named runs, encompasses
3.5 lift-serviced sq miles
(9 sq km) plus a large area of
backcountry terrain. Eleven
lifts, including two high-speed,

six-passenger chairs, transport
more than 19,000 skiers per
hour. There is also an extensive
network of trails for downhill
skiers. Lessons and equipment
hire cater to all ages.

During summer, mountain
biking, hiking, and scenic
gondola rides are Crystal
Mountain's main attractions.
On weekends, high-
speed lifts whisk
passengers to
the 6,872-ft
(2,095-m)
summit and
its panoramic
views of
the Olympic
and Cascade
Mountains, with Mount
Rainier dominating the western
horizon. Herds of elk and black-
tailed deer grazing the grassy
slopes are often spotted from
the lifts.

Snowboarding in the stunning backcountry
at Crystal Mountain

⓯ Leavenworth

Road map 1 B2. 🚶 2,000.
🛈 940 Highway 2, (509) 548-5807.
🏠 W leavenworth.org

Crossing over the Cascade
Mountains from the western
part of the state, first-time
visitors to Leavenworth never
fail to be surprised to encounter
an enchanting
Bavarian-style
village
seemingly
straight out of a
fairy tale. But this
small town was
not always so
charming. In
the early 1960s
it was a dying logging town,
with plenty of drive-through
traffic but no real business
to sustain it. Inspired by
Leavenworth's spectacular
mountain backdrop, a tourism
committee decided to develop
a Bavarian village theme to
revitalize the town. Buildings
were remodeled to echo
Bavarian architecture and,
today, every commercial
building in town, Starbucks®
and McDonald's included, looks
as though it belongs in the Alps.

Leavenworth now bustles
with festivals, art shows, and
summer theater productions,
attracting more than a million
visitors each year. Among
its most popular festivals are
Maifest, with its 16th-century
costumes, maypole dances,
Tyrolean Haflinger horses,

Shop sign in the Bavarian-themed village
of Leavenworth

nd jousting; the Leavenworth nternational Accordion elebration, in June, with ompetitions and concerts; ktoberfest, the traditional elebration of German eer, food, and music; and hristkindlmarkt, an open-air hristmas market. In addition to s many shops and restaurants eaturing Bavarian specialties, he **Leavenworth Nutcracker Museum** showcases 6,000 utcrackers from 38 countries, ome dating back 1,800 years.

Leavenworth Nutcracker Museum

35 Front St. **Tel** (509) 548-4573. **pen** May–Oct: 2–5pm daily; ov–Apr: 2–5pm Sat & Sun. for groups by appt. **nutcrackermuseum.com**

eavenworth's traditional horse-drawn 3-barrel beer wagon

Lake Chelan

oad map 1 B2. 3,500. 102 E ohnson Ave, (509) 682-3503. **lakechelan.com**

helan, a resort town on the outheast end of Lake Chelan, as been a popular summer acation destination for enerations of western Vashingtonians seeking the unny, dry weather on the east-rn side of the state. Basking in

Cyclists stopping for a refreshment at the Alley Cafe in Lake Chelan

the rain shadow of the Cascade Mountains, the town enjoys 300 days of sunshine each year.

Its namesake claims the distinction of being the third-deepest lake in the country, reaching 1,500 ft (457 m) at its deepest point. Fed by 27 glaciers and 59 streams, the lake, which is less than 2 miles (3 km) wide, stretches for 50.5 miles (81 km). In the summer, it buzzes with activity: water-skiing, boating, snorkeling, fishing, and windsurfing.

Strolling through the town, visitors can admire the vintage **Ruby Theatre** (135 East Woodin Avenue). Listed on the National Register of Historic Places, it is one of the oldest continuously running movie theaters in the Northwest US. The 15 murals painted on area buildings are another highlight of the town. Depicting the agricultural, recreational, cultural, and ecological history of the Lake Chelan Valley, all

Sign welcoming visitors to Lake Chelan

contain an image – obvious in some murals, obscure in others – of an apple, a crop that thrives in the area's soil, fertile thanks to the glaciers that melted here thousands of years ago.

Environs

Manson, 9 miles (14 km) along the north shore from downtown Chelan, is a charming town. Along with shops, restaurants, and recreational activities, the town boasts the Scenic Loop Trail, offering easy exploration of the nearby orchards and hilly countryside. Many businesses offer free route maps.

Stehekin

Road map 1 B2. 70. Golden West Visitor Center, by the Ferry Building, (360) 854-7365. **stehekinvalley.com**

At the northernmost tip of Lake Chelan, nestled at the base of the North Cascade Mountains, rustic Stehekin invites travelers to slow down and savor life without the distractions of televisions or telephones.

You won't find one single automated bank machine in this tiny community, but you will discover some of the most beautiful scenery in the state – accessible only by foot, horseback, plane, or boat.

Since the early 20th century, the Lady of the Lake boat service has ferried passengers from Chelan to Stehekin. This ride takes 4 hours; faster options include the *Lady Express* (just over 2 hours) and the high-speed *Lady Cat*, which zips to Stehekin in an hour.

Bird-watching, biking, hiking, horseback riding, fishing, and rafting the Stehekin River are all popular summer activities in the Stehekin Valley; cross-country skiing and snowshoeing are popular in winter.

Rainbow Falls, a 312-ft (95-m) waterfall near Stehekin Landing, is worth a visit (call 509/682-4494 for tour details).

ew of glacier-fed Lake Chelan, in its arid setting

⑱ North Cascades National Park Tour

The North Cascades National Park is a breathtakingly beautiful ecosystem of jagged snowcapped peaks, forested valleys, and cascading waterfalls. Its many wonders can be accessed from the scenic North Cascades Highway, which bisects the park. With more than 300 glaciers, the park is the most heavily glaciated region in the lower 48 states. It is home to a variety of animals, including bald eagles, beavers, gray wolves, and black and grizzly bears. The park and the adjacent Ross Lake and Lake Chelan National Recreation Areas attract over 400,000 visitors each year. The North Cascades Highway and the Lake Chelan National Recreation Area are linked by hiking trails to the quiet town of Stehekin on Lake Chelan, which is serviced by a ferry from Chelan *(see p191)*.

Mount Shuksan ④

Baker Lake

Skagit River

i ②

①

20

Marblemount

Mount Baker

Marble Creek •

CASCADE

North Ca
Nationa
(North

④ **Mount Shuksan** One of the state's highest mountains at 9,131 ft (2,783 m), and a dominant feature of the park, Mount Shuksan consists of a form of basalt known as Shuksan greenschist.

③ **Gorge Creek Falls** Plunging 242 ft (74 m) into Gorge Lake, the Gorge Creek Falls are visible from an overlook just off the North Cascades Highway. A fully accessible, paved trail leads to the overlook.

0 kilometers		15
0 miles		10

① **Skagit River**
The second-longest river in Washington, the Skagit is popular for steelhead and salmon fishing. The river has been dammed in three locations in the park, creating lakes and providing hydroelectric power for the state.

② **North Cascades Visitor Center**
Commanding an impressive view of the Picket Range, the visitor center, near Newhalem, offers interpretive displays, multimedia presentations, and daily ranger-guided programs in summer.

Key

━━ Tour route

═══ Other road

⊸⊸ Trail

**Ross Lake
National
Recreation Area**

Ruby Creek

**ascades
al Park
Unit)**

NORTH CASCADES HIGHWAY

Rainy Pass

⑦

MCALESTER TRAIL/RAINBOW CREEK TRAIL

Glory

**Lake Chelan
National
Recreation Area**

⑧
Stehekin

*Lake
Chelan*

he jagged peak of Glory Mountain's 7,228-ft-
2,203-m-) high summit

⑤ Diablo Lake
Diablo Lake owes its rich turquoise color to sediment from glacier-fed streams. Boat tours of Diablo Lake are offered Thursday to Monday in July and August; Saturday and Sunday in June and September.

⑥ Ross Lake Overlook
At this lookout, dramatic vistas of 24-mile- (40-km-) long Ross Lake, created by the damming of Skagit River, come into view.

Tips for Drivers
Tour length: 56 miles (90 km).
Starting point: State Route 20 (North Cascades Highway) at the entrance to Ross Lake National Recreation Area, approximately 5 miles (8 km) north of Marblemount.
When to go: Mid-Apr–mid-Oct, when all of Route 20 is open.
Stopping-off points: There are restaurants in Marblemount and Winthrop, but in the park itself there are only picnic facilities. It is a good idea to bring along your own provisions. You can stock up on groceries and buy hot soup and coffee at the Skagit General Store in Newhalem.

⑦ Washington Pass Overlook
This overlook, 5,477 ft (1,669 m) above ground level, offers heart-pounding views of the steep pass up Liberty Bell Mountain.

⑧ Rainbow Falls
Accessible on foot after a 20-mile (32-km) hike from Rainy Pass or a short hike from Stehekin, these spectacular falls are located on a creek leading into Lake Chelan.

Horseback riders enjoying the scenery along a Winthrop trail

⓴ Winthrop

Road map 1 B1. 📍 350.
ℹ️ 202 Hwy 20, (509) 996-2125.
🌐 winthropwashington.com

The Wild West lives on in Winthrop. In the spring or fall, more than one astonished traveler has witnessed a genuine cattle drive – right down the main street.

The town was founded in 1891 by Guy Waring, a Boston-bred businessman whose Winthrop enterprises included the Duck Brand Saloon. The saloon, now home to the Winthrop Town Hall, is still standing, as is Waring's pioneer log house, which sits on the grounds of the **Shafer Museum**, along with other relics from the past.

By the 1960s, Winthrop resembled any other small, non-descript town in the American West before its merchants, eager to revive the local economy, "renovated" the town to give it an Old West ambience. A popular overnight and vacation destination for tourists exploring the North Cascades, the Winthrop area offers a wealth of outdoor recreation possibilities.

🏛️ **Shafer Museum**
285 Castle Ave. **Tel** (509) 996-2712.
Open May–Sep: 10am–5pm daily. 🅿️ by donation. 🌐 shafermuseum.com

㉑ Spokane

Road map 1 C2. 📍 208,000.
✈️ Spokane International Airport.
ℹ️ 808 W Main Ave, 1-888-SPOKANE
🌐 visitspokane.com

Washington's largest inland city, Spokane is the commerce and culture center for the Inland Northwest. Founded in 1873 by real estate developer James Nettle·Glover, the city suffered a disastrous fire in 1889. It responded by rebuilding in brick and terracotta. Many handsome reminders of the building boom remain. Regional history is showcased at the **Northwest**

⓴ Grand Coulee Dam

Considered one of the modern engineering wonders of the world, Grand Coulee Dam is the world's second-largest concrete dam, the largest hydroelectric dam in North America, and the sixth-largest producer of electricity in the world. Spanning the mighty Columbia River – the seventh-largest river in the US – it generates more power than a million locomotives, supplying electricity to 11 western states. Construction of the dam began in 1933 and took over nine years. The dam was built primarily to supply irrigation water to eastern Washington, where inadequate rainfall threatened the livelihood of the region's farmers.

VISITORS' CHECKLIST

Practical Information
Road map 1 C2. **Tel** (509) 633-9265. **Open** daily. Jun & Jul: 8:30am–11pm; Aug: 8:30am–10:30pm; Sep: 8:30am–9:30pm; Oct–May: 9am–5pm. 🎟️

Irrigation Canal

Twelve irrigation pipes at the canal headworks pump water to lake and reservoir

The dam, nearly 1 mile (1.5 km) long, towers almost 550 ft (152 m) above bedrock.

The spillway doubles as a screen in summer for spectacular nightly laser shows.

Columbia River

The concrete poured to build the dam amounts to almost 12 million cubic yards (9 million cubic m), enough to build a 4-ft- (1-m-) wide sidewalk twice around the equator.

Inside the Dam

The power plants house the generators and turbines.

Trash-racks prevent debris from entering the generators.

Four gantry cranes are located on the dam to move heavy equipment.

Lake Roosevelt

A third power plant features three of the largest hydro generators in the world.

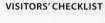

View of the Spokane River, the town in the background

Museum of Arts and Culture. Nearby **Campbell House** (1898) is an interactive museum.

The smallest city ever to host a world's fair (Expo '74), Spokane's fair site is now **Riverfront Park**, a large expanse in the heart of the city that offers views of the dramatic Spokane Falls. Other attractions are an IMAX theater and a 1909 carousel carved by Charles Looff, of Coney Island fame. The 37-mile (59-km) Centennial Trail starts at Riverside State Park and extends to the Washington-Idaho border.

🏛 **Northwest Museum of Arts and Culture**
2316 W 1st Ave. **Tel** (509) 456-3931.
Open 10am–5pm Wed–Sun.
Closed major hols. 🚻 ♿ 📷 🎁
W **northwestmuseum.org**

Environs
Just 6 miles (10 km) northwest of Spokane, **Riverside State Park** offers plenty of freshwater shoreline. The Bowl and Pitcher, with its suspension bridge and volcanic formations, is stunning.

🌲 **Riverside State Park**
9711 W Charles St, Nine Mile Falls.
Tel (509) 465-5064. **Open** dawn–dusk.

㉒ Yakima Valley
Road map 1 B2. 🛈 10 N 8th St, Yakima, (800) 221-0751. W **visityakima.com**

Boasting rich volcanic soil, an abundance of irrigation water, and 300 days of sunshine per year, the Yakima Valley is the 12th-largest producer of fruits and vegetables in the US, and home to more than 40 regional wineries.

For a taste of the valley's award-winning wines, drive 30 minutes south of Yakima

on I-82. Begin the wine tour at Exit 40 (Treveri Cellars), then continue on the Yakima Valley Highway. Columbia Crest and Preston Winery have some of the best tours.

The outstanding weather and beautiful landscape lend themselves to outdoor recreations. The two mountain passes, White Pass and Chinook Pass, offer great hiking, mountain biking, and skiing in the winter months; streams encourage fishing; and boating is available on lakes. The area is also rich in wildlife, including bald eagles.

Luscious grapes on the vine in the wine-growing area of Yakima Valley

㉓ Walla Walla
Road map 1 C3. 🛈 30,000.
🛈 26 E Main, (877) 998-4748.
W **wallawalla.org**

Located in the southeast corner of the state, Walla Walla is a charming and pretty town – and a green oasis in the midst of an arid landscape. The town features a large number of National Register buildings, lovely parks, and a wealth of public art. **Whitman College**, one of the nation's top-rated liberal arts colleges, is just three blocks from downtown. The attractive

campus is a delight to stroll, as is the surrounding neighborhood, with its tree-shaded streets lined with historic homes.

A popular destination for wine connoisseurs, the Walla Walla area offers more than 100 wineries (see pp196–7) – several in the heart of downtown Walla Walla. Among the town's other claims to fame are its delicious sweet onions and its annual Hot Air Balloon Stampede, a rally of some 45 pilots, held in October. Highlights of the stampede include the Friday "Night Glow" with its illuminated balloons, and a kids' day that offers tethered balloon rides.

For a historical perspective on the area, visit **Fort Walla Walla Museum**, a pioneer village consisting of 17 original and replica buildings, including a schoolhouse, jail, and train station, as well as the **Whitman Mission National Historic Site**. Here, visitors can discover the story of pioneer missionaries Marcus and Narcissa Whitman and their subsequent massacre by the Cayuse Indians. On weekends, the Living History Company honors the area's history through music and dance.

🏛 **Fort Walla Walla Museum**
755 Myra Rd. **Tel** (509) 525-7703.
Open Mar–Oct: 10am–5pm daily, Nov–Feb 10am–4pm daily. **Closed** Jan 1, Thanksgiving, Dec 25. 🚻 ♿ (call ahead). 📷 by appt. W **fwwm.org**

🏛 **Whitman Mission National Historic Site**
Hwy 12. **Tel** (509) 522-6360.
Open 8am–6pm daily (Oct–May: to 4:30pm). **Closed** Jan 1, Thanksgiving, Dec 25. 🚻 ♿ (except Monument Hill). W **nps.gov/whmi**

Balloons over Walla Walla during the annual Hot Air Balloon Stampede

㉔ Walla Walla Valley Wine Tour

Although grape-growing in the Walla Walla Valley dates back to the mid-1800s, it wasn't until 1977 that the valley's first winery was established. Seven years later, the region was recognized as an American Viticultural Area. Today, the Walla Walla area boasts more than 100 wineries. Lying at the same latitude as the great wine-producing regions of France, the valley enjoys long, sunny days and cool evenings, which together with ideal soil conditions create the perfect environment for growing grapes. The region has won national and international recognition for its wines and is especially known for its reds – in particular, cabernet sauvignon, merlot, and syrah.

② L'Ecole No 41
The cellars at this winery are located in a 1915 schoolho.. colorfully depicted on the wine bottle labels.

LOWER DRY CREEK ROAD

Yakima

12

Walla Walla River

① Woodward Canyon
This winery is known for its award-winning merlots, cabernets, and chardonnay

㉕ Goldendale Observatory State Park

1602 Observatory Dr, Goldendale. **Road map** 1 B3. **Tel** (509) 773-3141. Observatory: **Open** Apr–Sep: 1–11:30pm Wed–Sun; Oct–Mar: 1–9:30pm Fri–Sun. by donation. Discover Pass required (see p317). partial. Library. **W** parks.wa.gov

Perched atop a 2,100-ft (640-m) hill, the Goldendale Observatory, with its 20-ft- (6-m-) diameter dome, has more than a dozen telescopes with which to observe the countryside and night sky. The highlight is a 24.5-inch (62-cm) reflecting Cassegrain, one of the largest telescopes in the US available for public viewing. By day, visitors enjoy great views of

Mount Hood and the Klickitat Valley; by night, the sky can be observed well away from city lights. Programs on telescopes and sky-watching are offered.

㉖ Maryhill

Road map 1 B3.

A remote sagebrush bluff overlooking the Columbia River is where entrepreneur Sam Hill chose to build his palatial residence. In 1907, he purchased 7,000 acres, with the vision of creating a utopian colony for Quaker farmers. He called the community Maryhill, in honor of his daughter, Mary. Utopia never materialized, however. No one wanted to live in such a desolate place, and Hill was persuaded to turn his unfinished mansion into a museum.

The **Maryhill Museum of Art** houses the throne and gold coronation gown of his friend Queen Marie of Romania, 87 sculptures and drawings by Auguste Rodin, an impressive collection of Native American ar.. and many other treasures. The beautifully landscaped grounds include a lovely picnic area.

At the original Maryhill town site, 2.5 miles (4 km) east of the museum, is a replica Stonehenge built by Hill to honor locals killed in World War

Ⅲ Maryhill Museum of Art
35 Maryhill Museum Dr, Goldendale. **Tel** (509) 773-3733. **Open** mid-Mar–mid-Nov: 10am–5pm daily. **W** maryhillmuseum.org

㉗ Mount St. Helens National Volcanic Monument

Road map 1 A3. **Tel** (360) 449-7800. **W** fs.usda.gov/ mountsthelens

On the morning of May 18, 1980, Mount St. Helens literally exploded. Triggered by a powerful earthquake, the conical peak erupted, spewing a cubic mile (4.17 cubic km) of

Maryhill Museum of Art, overlooking the Columbia River Gorge

④ Three Rivers
In addition to its cellar and tasting room, this winery features three short holes of golf for its guests.

③ Isenhower Cellars
Guests here can chat with the winemakers while tasting a merlot or syrah.

⑥ Dunham Cellars
This winery is housed in a remodeled World War II-era airplane hangar. The surroundings may be stark, but the wines are worth the visit.

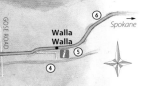

⑤ Seven Hills
The production facilities, tasting room, and restaurant of this winery are housed in the historic Whitehouse-Crawford building (1905).

Tips for Drivers

Tour length: 14 miles (22.5 km).
Starting point: US Highway 12 near Lowden, 116 miles (187 km) east of Yakima.
When to go: Thu–Sat, when tasting rooms are open. (Times vary depending on the season.)
Stopping-off points: Whitman Mission, 7 miles (11 km) west of Walla Walla, is a good picnic spot. Walla Walla offers many restaurants and a well-known deli, Olive Marketplace & Café, for provisions.

0 kilometers		3
0 miles		2

Key

— Tour route
--- Other road

Mount St. Helens and surrounding area after the 1980 explosion

rock into the air and causing the largest avalanche in recorded history. In the blink of an eye, the mountain lost 1,314 ft (400 m), and 234 sq miles (606 sq km) of forestland were destroyed. The eruption also claimed 57 human lives and those of millions of animals and fish.

Following the eruption, the US Congress created the monument in order to allow the environment to recover naturally and to encourage research, recreation, and education. NASA scientists have placed high-tech monitoring devices inside the volcanic crater to detect an impending eruption.

Roads and trails allow visitors to explore this fascinating region by car and on foot. On the mountain's west side,

Highway 504 leads to five visitor centers. The first is the **Mount St. Helens National Volcanic Monument Visitor Center** (tel 360/274-0962), at exit 49 from Interstate 5, featuring interpretive exhibits of the mountain's history. **The Hoffstadt Bluffs Visitor Center** (tel 360/274-5200), at milepost 27, gives visitors their first full view of Mount St. Helens and offers helicopter tours into the blast zone from May to September. The **Forest Learning Center** (tel 360/414-3439), at milepost 33, open in the summer only, teaches about reforestation efforts. **Johnston Ridge Visitor Center** (tel 360/274-2140), at milepost 52, offers a close-up view of the crater and lava dome.

㉘ Fort Vancouver

Road map 1 A3. **Tel** (360) 816-6230.
Open mid-Mar–Oct: 9am–5pm daily; Nov–mid-Mar: 9am–4pm daily. **Closed** Jan 1, Thanksgiving, Dec 24, 25 & 31. ⬛ partial. ⬛ nps.gov/fova

Between 1825 and 1849, this was an important trading outpost for British-based Hudson's Bay Company, the

The three-story bastion, dating from 1845, at Fort Vancouver

giant fur-trading organization (see p42). Located close to major tributaries and natural resources, it was the center of political and commercial activities in the Pacific Northwest during these years. During the 1830s and 1840s, the fort also provided essential supplies to settlers. A National Historic Site, Fort Vancouver features accurate reconstructions of nine of the original buildings, including the jail, fur store, and wash house, all on their original sites. Guided tours and re-enactments offer a window into the fort's past.

VANCOUVER

Vancouver at a Glance

Lively and livable, Vancouver is a young city with an eclectic sense of identity. The city's passion for the outdoors began with Stanley Park when it opened in 1888, and the love affair continues. The art and culture of coastal First Nations people is a source of pride, with totem poles and other artwork evident in the park and throughout the city. The cityscape reflects both old and new, from the historic buildings of Gastown to Science World's geodesic dome, built for the 1986 world exposition. As the gateway to the Pacific Rim, Vancouver has a large Asian population; its Chinatown is the second largest in North America, after that of San Francisco.

Vancouver Art Gallery
Emily Carr's works are featured in the gallery, which has a lovely flower garden on its north side *(see p215)*.

Vanier Park
Across English Bay from downtown, Vanier Park features a planetarium and two museums. Restored boats are docked in nearby Heritage Harbour *(see pp224–5)*.

SOUTH GRANVILLE AND YALETOWN
(See pp218–25)

Granville Island Public Market
Bustling and bright, this former industrial site is a must-visit for its fresh produce stalls, baked goods, and arts-and-crafts tables. Enjoy a snack or meal here, accompanied by live entertainment provided by the market's numerous buskers *(see p223)*.

Yaletown
Funky restaurants, brewpubs, and shops make Yaletown a great destination day or night *(see pp224–5)*.

◀ The city of Vancouver, its lights reflected in the harbor waters

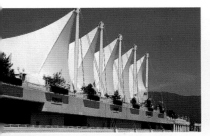

Canada Place
The Canada Place promenade offers a terrific view of Vancouver's port, busy with seaplanes, cruise ships, and harbor craft *(see p206)*.

Harbour Centre and Vancouver Lookout
Enjoy panoramic views of Vancouver and beyond from the Lookout observation deck, 553 ft (169 m) above the city *(see p207)*.

RFRONT, GASTOWN D CHINATOWN *(See pp202–9)*

Water Street
A distinctive triangular building stands opposite the eastern end of Water Street. The street is known for its red-brick paving and the steam clock, which instantly became one of the city's most beloved landmarks after its installation in 1977 *(see p207)*.

| 0 meters | | 800 |
| 0 yards | | 800 |

Science World
OMNIMAX shows inside the geodesic dome are just one of Science World's highlights *(see p217)*.

Chinatown
Straddling Pender Street, the classically proportioned Chinatown Millennium Gate was erected in 2002 as the gateway to historic Chinatown, with its 19th-century buildings and lively street market *(see p208)*.

Dr. Sun Yat-Sen Classical Chinese Garden
Built in the Classical style of Chinese gardens, this serene enclave in Chinatown was the first full-sized example of its kind built outside China *(see p209)*.

WATERFRONT, GASTOWN, AND CHINATOWN

Vancouver's waterfront, the city's birthplace, buzzes with activity, the five-sailed roof of Canada Place at its helm. The harbor view from here is memorable, as is that from the Vancouver Lookout atop the Harbour Centre tower. Clustered near the waterfront are shops, restaurants, and some of Vancouver's most interesting attractions. Nearby Gastown began as a haven for gold-seekers, loggers, and a host of ruffians. This changed when, in 1885, Canadian Pacific Railway (CPR) chose the town as its western terminus. After the Great Vancouver Fire of 1886, the newly renamed Vancouver – a CPR marketing decision – settled into respectability. Boutiques and restaurants now occupy the area's historic buildings, and Chinatown sprung up next door. Today, its bustling sidewalks and markets highlight an enduring presence.

Sights at a Glance

Museums and Galleries
7 Vancouver Police Museum
10 Chinese Cultural Centre Museum and Archives

Historic Buildings
1 Marine Building
3 Waterfront Station

Gardens and Viewpoints
2 Canada Place
4 Harbour Centre and Vancouver Lookout
9 Dr. Sun Yat-Sen Classical Chinese Garden

Historic Squares, Streets, and Districts
5 Water Street
6 Maple Tree Square
8 Chinatown

See also Street Finder maps 2, 3, and 4

0 meters 400
0 yards 400

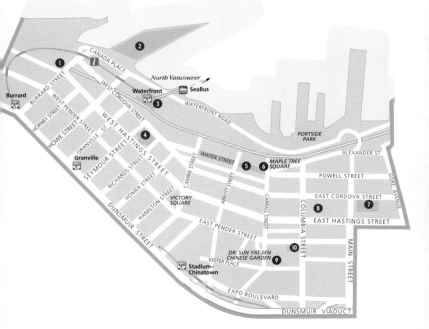

◀ Chinatown, full of bold and vibrant colors   **For keys to symbols** *see back flap*

Street-by-Street: Waterfront and Gastown

One of Vancouver's oldest areas, Gastown, which faces the waters of Burrard Inlet, is bounded by Columbia Street to the east and Burrard Street to the west. The district grew up around a saloon opened in 1867 by "Gassy Jack" Deighton, whose statue stands in Maple Tree Square. Gastown is a charming mix of cobblestone streets and restored 19th-century public buildings and storefronts. Chic boutiques and galleries line Water Street, and delightful restaurants and cafés fill the mews, courtyards, and passages. Visitors can watch the steam rise from the steam clock every 15 minutes, as well as be entertained by street performers.

② Canada Place
Canada Place is a waterside architectural marvel of white sails and glass that houses a hotel, two convention centers, a flight simulation ride, and a cruise ship terminal.

The SeaBus
This catamaran ferries passengers across Burrard Inlet between the central Waterfront Station and Lonsdale Quay in North Vancouver. The ride offers stunning views of the harbor.

Waterfront Station occupies the imposing 19th-century Canadian Pacific Railway building.

④ ★ Harbour Centre and Vancouver Lookout
Harbour Centre is a high-rise building best known for Vancouver Lookout, a viewing deck 553 ft (169 m) above the city. On a clear day it is possible to see as far as Vancouver Island.

Key
— Suggested route

For hotels and restaurants see p290 and pp302–3

Locator Map
See Street Finder map 3

⓪ ★ Water Street
Much of the historic charm of Gastown can be seen here. Water Street boasts brick streets and cobblestones, as well as shops and cafés.

"Gassy Jack" Statue
Gastown is named after "Gassy Jack" Deighton, an English sailor noted both for his endless chatter and for the saloon he opened here for the local sawmill workers in 1867.

The steam clock is said to be one of the world's only steam-powered clocks. It chimes every hour on the hour.

The Inuit Gallery displays original Inuit art such as sculpture and prints.

0 meters 100
0 yards 100

WATER STREET

CORDOVA STREET

CAMBIE STREET

ABBOTT STREET

CARRALL STREET

Shopping on West Cordova Street, with its wide range of small galleries and trendy boutiques, is a delightful experience.

Hotel Europe
Reminiscent of New York's Flatiron Building, this triangular structure at the corner of Powell and Alexander Streets was built in 1908–9 as a hotel. It now houses apartments.

❶ Marine Building

355 Burrard St. **Map** 3 A1.
🚇 Waterfront. 🚌 2, 22.
⛴ SeaBus: Waterfront.

Architects McCarter and Nairne described the Marine Building as "a great crag rising from the sea." Their design, built in 1929 in an extravagant Art Deco style near the waterfront, cost its Toronto developers $2.35 million before they went broke. The 25-story buff-brick tower, meant to house Vancouver's marine-related businesses, was sold in 1933 for a mere $900,000 to Ireland's Guinness family.

This now-beloved office building has seen $20 million worth of restoration and repair since the mid-1980s. Outside and in, it is the most impressive of all Vancouver's historic buildings. On the façade, terra-cotta marine fauna, including sea horses, frolic amid frothy waves. The main entrance, with its double revolving doors, features bronze grilles and brass bas-relief castings of starfish, crabs, and seashells. A 40-ft-(12 m) high terracotta arch includes depictions of a jutting ship's prow and Canada geese.

The lobby is a dramatic step back in time, with aqua-green and blue tiles and carved maritime-inspired friezes. The elevator, inlaid with 12 varieties of BC hardwood, whisks visitors up to the second floor, from where there is a bird's-eye view of the lobby.

Entrance to the Art Deco Marine Building, with its bronze grilles

Canada Place, resembling a sailing ship setting out to sea

❷ Canada Place

999 Canada Pl. **Map** 3 B1.
🚇 Waterfront. 🚌 3, 4, 6, 7, 8, 10, 50.
⛴ SeaBus: Waterfront.
Open daily. ♿

Built for Expo '86, Canada Place was the flagship pavilion of the Government of Canada. Today, Canada Place is home to a cruise ship terminal, the Vancouver Convention Centre, Vancouver's World Trade Centre, and an upscale hotel.

The structure's five white Teflon-coated fabric "sails," aside from being a pleasing sight on the waterfront, make possible a huge interior area free of support structures. On the west side of the complex, a cooling fountain, shady trees, and ample outdoor seating provide an oasis in the heart of the bustling city.

The three-block, open-air Canada Place Promenade juts into Vancouver Harbour and offers a panorama of busy sea and air traffic. More than 200 cruise ships a year dock alongside the promenade en route to Alaska or Seattle. Every year on July 1 (see p35), Canada Place hosts a spectacular celebratory fireworks display over the harbor; the promenade offers the best view in town.

Visitors can also soar over spectacular scenery in the FlyOver Canada flight simulation ride, a popular attraction at Canada Place.

❸ Waterfront Station

601 W Cordova St. **Map** 3 B2.
🚇 Waterfront. 🚌 3, 4, 6, 7, 8, 10, 50.
⛴ SeaBus: Waterfront. ♿ 🚻 📷

A busy transportation hub, Waterfront Station is the convergence point of the SeaBus, SkyTrain, and West Coast Express trains. Built by Canadian Pacific Railway, the current Waterfront Station is the third passenger train station built on the site (see p215). The first cross-Canada passenger train pulled into the original timber station on May 23, 1887. The second station here was a chateau-style structure built in 1898–9.

The grand columned entrance to Waterfront Station

WATERFRONT, GASTOWN, AND CHINATOWN

The present-day building was designed by the firm of Barott, Blackader and Webster and completed in 1914. It was restored in 1976–7 to make the most of its expansive waiting area, arches, and columns. Murals circling the upper walls portray romantic versions of Canadian landscapes. Shops and cafés now occupy the former waiting room.

Outside the station is *Wounded Soldier*, a sculpture by Charles Marega (1871–1939), Vancouver's premier artist of his day. Marega also carved the two stone lions that guard the Stanley Park entrance to Lions Gate Bridge.

Viewing platform at Harbour Centre's Vancouver Lookout

❸ Harbour Centre and Vancouver Lookout

555 W Hastings St. **Map** 3 A2.
Tel (604) 689-7304. 🚇 Waterfront.
🚌 3, 4, 6, 7, 8, 10, 50. 🚢 SeaBus:
Waterfront. **Open** 10am–6pm daily.
🅿 📶 📷 ⓦ **harbourcentre.com**
Vancouver Lookout: Harbour Centre.
Tel (604) 689-0421. **Open** Apr–Sep:
8:30am–10:30pm daily; Oct–Mar:
9am–9pm daily. 📶 ♿ 📷 📶
ⓦ **vancouverlookout.com**

Glass elevators glide 553 ft (169 m) up the tower of Harbour Centre to Vancouver Lookout, an enclosed observation deck with a superb 360-degree view of Vancouver and informative plaques to help visitors identify the sights below. These interpretive panels locate, among other sights, the distinctive retractable roof of BC Place Stadium,

Stanley Park, and Mount Baker in Washington.

When it opened on August 13, 1977, Harbour Centre was the tallest building in British Columbia. Among the guests at the opening was the first man on the moon, Neil Armstrong, who left his footprint in cement as an official memento of the opening. A ticket to the observation deck is valid all day, so return to watch the sun set over Vancouver Island. Also at the top of the tower is a revolving restaurant, providing fabulous views.

At street level, in Simon Fraser University's downtown campus, the small Teck Gallery showcases the work of Pacific Northwest artists. The two lower levels of Harbour Centre house a food fair, shops, and a well-stocked bookstore.

❹ Water Street

From Richards to Carrall Sts.
Map 3 B2. 🚇 Waterfront. 🚌 50.
🚢 SeaBus: Waterfront.

Water Street, with its distinctive red-brick paving, is Gastown's main thoroughfare and popular with tourists. Its turn-of-the-19th-century buildings house a mix of restaurants, nightclubs, boutiques, souvenir shops, rug merchants, offices, and First Nations art galleries. Water

Water Street's steam clock, drawing a crowd every hour

Street was not always so well-liked. Having slipped into decline after World War I, it wasn't until the 1960s that the area's potential was recognized and a wave of restoration begun. By 1971, Water Street was designated an historic area. Old-fashioned street lamps and mews enhance its historic flavor.

The world's first steam-operated clock stands 16 ft (5 m) tall at the corner of Water and Cambie Streets. Erected in 1977, it strikes its Westminster chimes on the hour and every 15 minutes emits a blast of steam. Other notable sights include The Landing, a seven-story heritage building; the 1899 Dominion Hotel; and the historically seedy Blood Alley.

The Great Vancouver Fire of 1886

On June 13, 1886, the lethal combination of a powerful westerly wind and sparks from a Canadian Pacific Railway brush fire near Drake and Homer Streets, in what is now Yaletown *(see pp224–5)*, burned through Vancouver's motley assortment of 1,000 wooden buildings. In 20 minutes, the city was devastated, barely two months after its incorporation. The raging fire – so hot it not only burned nearby St. James' Anglican Church but also melted its bell – killed at least 21 people; the exact number is unknown. Within 12 hours, rebuilding had begun. The Burns Block in Maple Tree Square *(see p208)* was built that same year and still exists.

City officials in front of a temporary city hall after the devastating fire of 1886

Statue of "Gassy Jack" Deighton in Gastown's Maple Tree Square

❻ Maple Tree Square

Water St at Carrall St. **Map** 3 B2.
🚌 50.

Search as you might, you will not find a maple tree in Gastown's Maple Tree Square. The famous tree, destroyed in the Great Vancouver Fire of 1886 *(see p207)*, marked a popular meeting spot for local residents.

Standing in the square is Okanagan artist Vern Simpson's 6-ft- (1.8-m-) tall hammered copper statue of John "Gassy Jack" Deighton, for whom Gastown is named. Commissioned in 1970, the statue recognizes this voluble, or "gassy," entrepreneur's place in Vancouver history.

In 1867, Deighton built, near Maple Tree Square, the first watering hole on Burrard Inlet. Deighton apparently persuaded local millworkers to build the Globe Saloon in just 24 hours. Deighton died on May 29, 1875, at age 44, and was buried in an unmarked grave in New Westminster, some 13 miles (20 km) from Gastown.

The restored Gaoler's Mews in the square marks the residence of Constable Jonathan Miller, the town of Granville's first policeman, in 1871. The two adjacent small log prisoner cells had doors but no locks.

❼ Vancouver Police Museum

240 E Cordova St. **Map** 3 C2.
Tel (604) 665-3346. 🚌 3, 4, 7, 8.
Open 9am–5pm Tue–Sat.
Closed major hols. 🖼 🎫 📷
🆆 vancouverpolicemuseum.ca

Opened in 1986 to mark the centennial of the Vancouver police force and housed in the former (1932–80) Coroner's Court Building, this museum includes the city's original morgue. Step into the autopsy laboratory to view the forensic table where actor Errol Flynn was declared dead on October 14, 1959. Scenes for the TV series *Da Vinci's Inquest* have been filmed here. A large mural depicts the colorful history of the police department, although it is not possible to see the entire mural as exhibits have been placed in front of some sections. Street weaponry, prohibited weapons, and antique firearms are on display in the Sins gallery, as well as three Thompson submachine guns. In the True Crime gallery, visitors can see real evidence from some of Vancouver's unsolved historical crimes. There is also an area where children can dress up in real police uniforms.

❽ Chinatown

E Hastings to Union Sts, from Carrall to Gore Sts. **Map** 3 C3. 🚇 Stadium–Chinatown. 🚌 3, 4, 7, 8, 19, 22.
📷 call (604) 632-3808.
🆆 vancouver-chinatown.com

Vancouver's Chinatown is older than the city itself. Pender

Chinatown's record-thin Sam Kee Building (1913)

Street, the main byway, is straddled near Taylor Street by Millennium Gate, a good spot from which to view architectur details of the area's restored buildings. The 1907 **Chinese Freemasons Building** (1 W Pender Street) was once home to Dr. Sun Yat-Sen. The 1913 **Sam Kee Building** (8 W Pender Street) is the resul of government expropriation of property in order to widen the street. In defiance, the owner built the world's thinnes commercial building on the 5-ft- (1.5-m-) wide plot that was left. The 1889 **Wing Sang Building** (51E Pender Street), the oldest in Chinatown, had an opium factory at its rear. It has now been transformed into a private exhibition space for the Rennie Collection.

Known for traditional shops, Chinese herbs, housewares, coffee shops, tearooms, and restaurants, Chinatown is large a daytime place.

The ornate Millennium Gate welcoming visitors to Chinatown

Classical pavilion at the Dr. Sun Yat-Sen Classical Chinese Garden

Dr. Sun Yat-Sen Classical Chinese Garden

8 Carrall St. **Map** 3 B3. **Tel** (604) 2-3207. 🚇 Stadium. 🚌 19, 22. **Open** May–mid-Jun & Sep: 10am– m daily; mid-Jun–Aug: 9:30am– m daily; Oct–Apr: 10am–4:30pm e–Sun. 🅿 ♿ 🛍 📷 📹 vancouverchinesegarden.com

odeled after private gardens eveloped in the city of Suzhou uring the Ming Dynasty, this the first complete Classical hinese garden created outside hina. A 52-member team of xperts from Suzhou spent an ntire year constructing the arden, building with materials ipped from China in more an 950 crates. No nails, screws, power tools were used in onstructing the buildings. At first, the garden, named honor of the founder of the epublic of China, seems a maze walls within walls. Designed appear larger than it really is, e garden is sprinkled with ndows and moon gates – ge circular openings in walls – at allow inviting glimpses of y courtyards wrapped around ll smaller courtyards, miniature vilions, intricate mosaic thways, bridges, and galleries. any of the plants and trees re symbolize human virtues: llow is a symbol of feminine ace; the plum and bamboo resent masculine strength.

🔟 Chinese Cultural Centre Museum and Archives

555 Columbia St. **Map** 3 C3. **Tel** (604) 658-8880. 🚇 Stadium, Main St– Science World. 🚌 3, 19, 22. **Open** 11am–5:30pm Tue–Sun. **Closed** Jan 1, Dec 25 & 26. 📷 (except to gallery). ♿ 🛍 📹 cccvan.com

The three-story Chinese Cultural Centre Museum and Archives building, styled after the architecture of the Ming Dynasty (1368–1644), is an impressive sight. At the edge of its curving tiled roof stand a pair of ornamental dragons, protecting the building from harm.

The museum and archives opened in 1998 as part of the Chinese Cultural Centre complex (50 East Pender Street). At the Pender Street entrance, the intricate red-and-green China Gate, which was originally displayed at the Expo '86 China Pavilion in Vancouver, is a distinguishing landmark for the complex. The museum and

archives are significant additions to Chinatown. On the first floor is the To-Yick Wong Gallery, with exhibits of both established and up-and-coming artists.

On the second floor, permanent exhibits of artifacts and photos, such as From Generation to Generation, portray the history of BC's Chinese population from the Gold Rush of 1858 to the present. The Chinese Canadian Military Museum is housed here also, recounting the lives of Chinese-Canadian veterans of World War II.

On the third floor, the S. K. Lee Academy hosts seminars and symposiums to promote cross-cultural understanding.

The Ming Dynasty-style Chinese Cultural Centre building

Vancouver's Chinese Community

Vancouver's Chinatown, home to over 35,000 people of Chinese descent, is the largest in North America after San Francisco's. The success of the community, which sprang up as a shantytown in the 1880s when over 18,000 Chinese immigrated to the city to build the cross-Canada railway *(see p215)*, did not come easily. Chinatown's growth was seen as a threat to non-Asian seasonal workers. In 1885, a closed-door immigration policy became law. Many Chinese still came, but women were largely excluded; the men who stayed often supported families they would not see for decades. Racial tensions culminated in two major riots in Vancouver, in 1887 and 1907. The Chinese Immigration Act of 1923 caused the local Chinese population to decline further. But by the 1940s, Vancouver's Chinatown was drawing tourists, prompting the government, in 1947, to grant Chinese Canadians citizenship and reopen immigration. Encouraged by this policy shift, Chinese immigrants ventured beyond Chinatown to settle in other areas of the city. Today, a second Chinatown is located in Richmond.

A Chinatown storefront with a variety of foodstuffs on display

DOWNTOWN VANCOUVER

Downtown Vancouver is a compact hub of activity, where shopping, business, and arts and culture all play a major role. In 1895, when Christ Church Cathedral opened at the corner of Burrard and Georgia Streets, its comforting lights could be seen from the harbor below. Today, the little church is almost buried by a cluster of office towers as the modern city grows around it. Nevertheless, quiet enclaves, such as the courtyard at Cathedral Place, can still be found amid the hustle of pedestrians. One of the city's most famous landmarks is in the center of downtown: the historic Fairmont Hotel Vancouver, which still hosts royalty and other celebrities from around the world. The Vancouver Art Gallery, with its important collection of paintings by Emily Carr and the Group of Seven, is located in a former courthouse overlooking Robson Square – a wonderful place to sit and watch the world pass by. Robson Street, which cuts through the heart of downtown, is known for its excellent shopping and numerous restaurants.

Sights at a Glance

Museums and Galleries
1. Vancouver Art Gallery
5. BC Sports Hall of Fame and Museum
12. Science World

Churches and Buildings
1. Christ Church Cathedral
2. Cathedral Place

3. Fairmont Hotel Vancouver
4. HSBC Building
8. Vogue Theatre
9. Vancouver Central Library
11. BC Place Stadium

Squares
6. Robson Square and Law Courts

Shopping Streets
7. Robson Street

See also Street Finder maps 2 and 3

A nurse sculpture on one of the corners of the Cathedral Place Building

For keys to symbols *see back flap*

Street-by-Street: Downtown

Vancouver's small downtown might have ended up an unlivable, daytime-only place crowded with office towers. That affliction has been avoided by preserving existing, often historic, apartment blocks, and by building new towers to accommodate inner-city dwellers. Although Vancouver is a relatively new city, it has taken care to preserve many of its historic buildings, which gives the downtown area a panache missing in many other North American city centers. A prime example is the Vancouver Art Gallery (see p215), housed in the former provincial courthouse, designed in 1906 by the preeminent Victoria architect Francis Rattenbury.

❶ Christ Church Cathedral
Stained-glass windows inside this cathedral, which was once a landmark for sailors, depict the lives of Vancouver heroes.

❸ Fairmont Hotel Vancouver
An historic building and Vancouver landmark, this building dates back to the 1920s. Much of the hotel's interior today has been restored to its former glory.

❷ Cathedral Place
This elegant building is indicative of Vancouver's efforts to preserve the past while building with an eye to the future.

BURRARD ST

HORNBY STREET

SMITHE S

NELSON STREET

Key

— Suggested route

❻ ★ Robson Square and Law Courts
This complex, with expanses of glass over the Great Hall, is quintessentially West Coast in style.

❺ ★ Vancouver Art Gallery
Work from British Columbia's major artists is shown at this gallery, alongside exhibits by acclaimed international artists.

For hotels and restaurants see p290 and pp302–3

❹ HSBC Building
A stunning, seven-story brushed-aluminum pendulum, created by BC artist Alan Storey, swings gracefully through the HSBC building's wonderful tree-filled atrium.

Locator Map
See Street Finder map 2

WATERFRONT, GASTOWN & CHINATOWN

DOWNTOWN

SOUTH GRANVILLE & YALETOWN

❾ ★ Vancouver Central Library
A coliseum is set in the heart of the city thanks to Moshe Safdie's innovative design.

GRANVILLE STREET

WEST GEORGIA STREET

...SON STREET

RICHARDS STREET

HOMER STREET

HAMILTON STREET

0 meters 100
0 yards 100

❼ Robson Street
Popular with the crowds, this busy street is a great place to shop and grab a bite to eat.

The stained-glass windows of Christ Church Cathedral

❶ Christ Church Cathedral

690 Burrard St. **Map** 2 F2. **Tel** (604) 682-3848. 🚇 Burrard. 🚌 2, 22. **Open** 10am–4pm Mon–Fri & Sun for services. **Closed** non-religious hols. ♿ ✝ 8am, 10:30am, 5:30pm & 8pm Sun. Concerts: 🆆 thecathedral.ca

Originally known as "the light on the hill," Christ Church Cathedral was once a beacon for mariners entering Vancouver's harbor. After undergoing several expansions since its consecration in 1895, the oldest surviving church in Vancouver now sits in the midst of the downtown business center. Modeled after a Gothic parish church by its designer, Winnipeg architect C. O. Wickenden, the interior features arched ceiling beams of Douglas fir. The sandstone cathedral remains to this day a quiet sanctuary.

In 1929, the church became a cathedral and, in 1930, the spacious chancel was added. The overhead lanterns were installed in 1937. Plans to build a bell tower were halted when a city bylaw restricting church bells was passed.

Thirty-nine impressive British- and Canadian-made stained-glass windows feature scenes from Old and New Testament stories. Several unique windows include images of Vancouver people and places. Three William Morris windows, on permanent loan from the Vancouver Museum, are set in the downstairs office vestibule. To see them, use the Burrard Street entrance.

After a major renovation in 2004, a new Kenneth Jones organ was installed in the cathedral. In 2016, the slate roof was replaced with a zinc roof and a bell tower made of stained glass was added.

❷ Cathedral Place

925 W Georgia St. **Map** 2 F2. **Tel** (604) 684-0925. 🚇 Burrard. 🚌 2, 22. **Open** 7am–6pm Mon–Fri, 9am–5pm Sat. **Closed** major hols. ♿ 📷 🆆 925westgeorgia.com

Cathedral Place is a high-rise makeover of the 1929 Art Deco Georgia Medical Dental Building that once stood on this site. The 23-story postmodern tower was designed by Paul Merrick Architects and constructed in 1990–91.

Cathedral Place preserves the stylistic ambience of its predecessor. Sculpted figures on the 11th-story parapet are copies of the three famous terracotta nurses dressed in World War I uniforms that graced the Medical Dental building and were demolished along with that building. Lions that adorned the third-story parapet are now at home at each of the entrances to Cathedral Place. Eight gargoyles on the 16th-story parapet echo those of the Fairmont Hotel Vancouver across the street. The exterior of Cathedral Place is a collection of 20,000 pieces of Kansas limestone, polished, cut to shape, numbered, and then hoisted by crane.

The Art Deco-inspired lobby is dominated by the glass-and-steel illuminated sculpture *Navigation Device: Origin Unknown*, by Robert Studer. Some 17,000 pieces of Spanish granite are set geometrically into the floor. Behind the lobby is an outdoor grassy courtyard offering benches and serenity.

Cathedral Place, as seen from the Vancouver Art Gallery

The copper-roofed Fairmont Hotel Vancouver, a city landmark

❸ Fairmont Hotel Vancouver

900 W Georgia St. **Map** 2 F2. **Tel** (604) 684-3131. 🚇 Burrard. 🚌 22. ♿ 🖥 ✏ 📷 See Where to Stay p290. 🆆 fairmont.com

The first Hotel Vancouver was built by the Canadian Pacific Railway (CPR) in 1887, two blocks east of where the current Vancouver icon stands. Construction of the current hotel, the fourth to bear the name, began in the late 1920s but came to a standstill after the stock market crash of 1929. When it was finally completed in 1939, the CPR closed the original hotel and entered into a joint-management contract for the new hotel with rival Canadian National Railway.

The building boasts a distinctive peaked green copper roof, a Vancouver landmark that has set the style for many downtown office towers. Ten craftsmen from ten countries worked for 12 months to carve the exterior stonework. Hermes, messenger of the gods in Greek mythology, is carved on the façade facing Georgia Street. Also visible are boats, trains, rams, winged goats, and griffins, noteworthy for their classic ugliness.

The hotel's lobby was restyled in 1996 by Fairmont Hotels, the current owners. The $12 million renovation restored the lobby according to the original architectural drawings. More than 8,000 sq ft (743 sq m) of marble were used

HSBC Building

5 W Georgia St. **Map** 2 F2.
Burrard. 2, 22. **Tel** (604) 683-
44. 885westgeorgia.
m Pendulum Gallery: **Open** 9am–
m Mon–Wed, 9am–9pm Thu & Fri,
m–5pm Sat. **Closed** major hols.

e skylit atrium is a striking
ntrance to the HSBC Building,
24-story tower which houses,
mong others, offices of the
ong Kong Bank of Canada.
stunning seven-story kinetic
endulum hangs from the
eiling. Swinging in a graceful
0-ft (6-m) arc 11,232 times
ich day, the hollow 3,527-lb
,600-kg) brushed-aluminum
ulpture by BC artist Alan
orey is enhanced by the
uilding's postmodern style.
The atrium's Pendulum
allery shows works of
anadian contemporary artists
nd international photographers.
ocal musicians sometimes
ay the baby grand piano
ext to the café.

e magnificent pendulum suspended
the HSBC Building

Vancouver Art Gallery

0 Hornby St. **Map** 2 F2.
el (604) 662-4719. Burrard.
5. **Open** 10am–5pm daily
9pm Tue).
vanartgallery.bc.ca

hat was once British
olumbia's imposing provincial
ourthouse now houses the
ancouver Art Gallery. The
uilding was created in 1906
y Francis Rattenbury, an

Logger's Culls (c.1935) by Emily Carr, Vancouver Art Gallery

architect known for his Gothic
design of Victoria's Parliament
building and Fairmont Empress
Hotel *(see p253)*. The interior
was modernized in 1983 by
Arthur Erickson, another noted
architect, who designed the
UBC Museum of Anthropology
(see pp234–5).

Among an impressive
assortment of Canadian
art, including works by the
Group of Seven, the gallery
houses the world's largest
collection of paintings by one
of Canada's best-loved artists,
Emily Carr. Born in Victoria in
1871, Carr studied local First
Nations cultures, capturing
their way of life and the scenery
of the western coastline in her
sketchbook. She often depicted
Haida artifacts such as totem
poles in her pictures. Her
palette is dominated by the
blues, greens, and grays of
the stormy West Coast.

❻ Robson Square and Law Courts

800 Hornby St. **Map** 2 F2–F3.
Tel (604) 660-8989. Vancouver
City Centre. 5. **Open** 9am–4pm
Mon–Fri. **Closed** major hols.
robsonsquare.ubc.ca

Designed by BC architect Arthur
Erickson, the four-level Robson
Square stretches several blocks.
On Robson Street's south side,
on the square's first level, trees
and a waterfall provide a shaded
background to Alan Chung
Hung's red steel sculpture,
Spring. Steps to the right of the
waterfall lead to a pool and
parkette offering a good view
north. From here, a walkway
leads to the law courts, built
from 1974 to 1979. Jack Harman's
statue *Themis Goddess of Justice*
overlooks the Great Hall. An
impressive but controversial (it
is prone to leaking) steel frame
rises four stories above the hall.

The Iron Road

In 1886, Prime Minister John A. Macdonald fulfilled his promise to
build the Canadian Pacific Railway (CPR) to unite the new Dominion
of Canada. The Iron Road linked eastern financial centers and the
emerging lumber town
of Vancouver. The first
cross-Canada passenger
train arrived in Vancouver
on May 23, 1887 *(see
p206)*. The Iron Road was
completed at last. Progress
came at the price of many
lives, including those of
over 600 Chinese laborers,
many of whom did the
most dangerous of jobs,
clearing and grading the
roadbed and securing rail
ties with gravel.

The first cross-Canada passenger train arriving
in Vancouver in 1887

Robson Street, Vancouver's stylish shopping strip

❼ Robson Street

Map 2 E1. 🚇 Vancouver City Centre.
🚌 5. 🌐 **robsonstreet.ca**

Once known as Robsonstrasse due to a multitude of German businesses, Robson Street, named after former BC premier John Robson (1889–92), today boasts restaurants from just about every continent. Local urban chic, international celebrities, and tourists alike flock here, making people-watching from outdoor cafés a popular pastime.

Shopping is the street's main attraction. Soaps, accessories, chocolates, lingerie, men's wear, and souvenirs are sold in stylish shops along Robson Street from Granville to Denman Streets. A women's lingerie (Victoria's Secret) megastore at the corner of Robson and Burrard Streets is located in the old **Vancouver Public Library** building, constructed in 1957. A sentimental favorite among locals, it is famous for being the city's first modernist glass-curtain building. Some traces of the original structure remain.

All stores on Robson Street are open seven days a week, with extended evening hours.

❽ Vogue Theatre

918 Granville St. **Map** 2 F3. **Tel** (604) 569-1144 (box office); (604) 688-1975 (general inquiries). 🚇 Vancouver City Centre. 🚌 5. **Open** Box office: 10am–6pm Mon–Sat, noon–4pm Sun.
🌐 **voguetheatre.com**

Designed in 1940 by Kaplan & Sprachman, the glamorous Art Deco Vogue Theatre was a defining architectural achievement for Vancouver at the time. With its symmetrical façades and 62-ft (19-m) neon sign topped by a silhouette of the Roman goddess Diana, the Vogue is a prominent landmark on busy Granville Street.

A National Historic Site of Canada, the Vogue has exceptional acoustics and hosts theater, live music, and movie events, including the Vancouver International Film Festival every fall.

The iconic Vogue Theatre, on Vancouver's former Theatre Row

❾ Vancouver Central Library

350 W Georgia St. **Map** 3 A3.
Tel (604) 331-3603. 🚇 Vancouver City Centre, Stadium. 🚌 5, 17.
Open 10am–9pm Mon–Thu, 10am–6pm Fri & Sat, 11am–6pm Sun.
Closed major hols. ♿ 🚻 special events. 🌐 **vpl.ca**

Imaginative and daring, the design of the Vancouver Central Library was inspired by a Roman coliseum. The wraparound, sand-colored, precast concrete colonnade occupies a full city block. The nine-story library building features a dramatic concourse, the ceiling soaring six stories overhead. The top two floors are occupied by the offices of the provincial government. Adjacent to the library is a 21-story federal government office tower.

Designed by Moshe Safdie & Associates (designers of the National Gallery of Canada in Ottawa) with DA Architects (designers of Canada Place, *see p206*) and opened in 1995, the building was decried by some as not fitting into the Vancouver cityscape. The negative opinions have been toppled by the unanimous support the dramatic building has subsequently received.

Engineered to high seismic standards, the building is also notable because it is not cooled by air conditioning but by an ecologically sound air circulation system.

More than 1.3 million items, including books, periodicals, DVDs, CDs, and audiocassettes are housed in the 350,000-sq-ft (32,500-sq-m) library space, which draws over 7,000 people daily. Items are transported through the building via vertical and horizontal conveyor belts.

On the impressive concourse there are several cafés, where visitors can pause for a drink or a light snack. During the warm months, the outdoor plaza is a popular meeting place.

The elliptical coliseum-style colonnade of the Vancouver Central Library

BC Sports Hall of Fame and Museum

ate A, BC Place Stadium. **Map** 3 A3.
l (604) 687-5520. Stadium.
17. **Open** 10am–5pm daily.
osed Dec 25.
bcsportshalloffame.com

anada's largest sports
useum, the BC Sports Hall
Fame and Museum is housed
20,000 sq ft (1,858 sq m)
space inside the BC Place
adium. Twenty galleries
howcase BC's sports history,
arting in the 1860s and
clude a Vancouver 2010
ames Gallery that celebrates
osting the Winter Olympics.
mong the artifacts on display
e medals, trophies, uniforms,
quipment, murals, and photos.
ever games test visitors'
nowledge. Interactive displays
rovide fascinating details of
e lives of famous athletes,
uch as Olympic medalists
rinter Harry Jerome and skier
ancy Greene. A series of
deos on the 1990s tells
e exciting stories
the Vancouver
anucks' skate to
e Stanley Cup
als, the BC Lions'
rey Cup victory,
nd Victoria's
ommonwealth
ames, all held
1994.

Children will
articularly enjoy
e Participation
allery, where they
an run against the clock,
ock climb, and see how fast
ey can pitch.

Percy Williams statue at BC Sports Hall of Fame

One of the most touching
splays is that honoring runner
erry Fox (1958–81), who lost
s leg to cancer. His run across
anada to raise money for
ancer research was halted only
y his death. The feat of local
heelchair athlete Rick Hansen
also highlighted. To raise
ublic awareness of the
otential of people with
sabilities, Hansen set out
1987 to wheel 24,855 miles
0,000 km) around the world.
vo years later, he had earned
e well-deserved title of Man
Motion.

The impressive retractable roof of BC Place Stadium

⑪ BC Place Stadium

777 Pacific Blvd. **Map** 3 A4.
Tel (604) 669-2300. Stadium.
15, 17. **Open** hours vary,
depending on events.
bcplacestadium.com

With its white-domed roof
standing out in the city's
skyline, BC Place Stadium
was, when it opened in 1983,
Canada's first covered stadium
and the largest air-supported
dome in the world. The
multipurpose stadium,
consisting of enough
cement to pour
a sidewalk from
Vancouver to Tacoma
(see p186), can be
converted in a
matter of hours
from a football
field seating 54,000
to a cozier concert
bowl seating
27,000. It has a
fully retractable
roof and is home to the CFL's
BC Lions and the MLS team,
the Vancouver Whitecaps FC.

⑫ Science World

1455 Quebec St. **Map** 3 C4. **Tel** (604)
443-7440. Main. 3, 8, 19. **Open**
10am– 6pm daily. **Closed** Dec 25.
scienceworld.ca

Overlooking the waters of False
Creek, the 155-ft- (47-m-) tall
steel geodesic dome built for
Expo '86 now houses Science
World, Vancouver's interactive
science museum. The dome
was designed by American
inventor Richard Buckminster
Fuller (1895–1983), who
patented the geodesic dome
in 1954. It remains one of the
city's most striking landmarks
to this day.

Science World hosts both
traveling and permanent
exhibitions. The latter include
hands-on activities such as
building structures with KEVA
wooden planks, testing agility,
and solving a variety of puzzles,
making this a museum popular
with children. In the Search: Sara
Stern Gallery, visitors can touch
fur, bones, and animal skins,
crawl into a beaver lodge or
look into a beehive. Kidspace,
aimed at children aged six and
under, has a huge kaleidoscope
kids can crawl into, and a flying
saucer. The Our World and
Eureka! exhibits are especially
educational, exploring themes
such as sustainability, motion,
and energy.

Science World is renowned for
its OMNIMAX Theatre, located
in the dome. A five-story screen
88 ft (27 m) in diameter shows
films on subjects ranging from
bears to Sir Ernest Shackleton's
epic 1914 Antarctic journey.

The futuristic geodesic dome defines Vancouver's Science World

SOUTH GRANVILLE AND YALETOWN

he neighborhoods of South Granville and aletown are separated by a drive across ranville Bridge or a nautical ride across alse Creek. On the south shore, South ranville offers a mix of grocers, cafés and estaurants, and upscale shops – clear signs hat people live as well as work here. The umerous commercial art galleries justify e local moniker "gallery row." Nearby anier Park and Kitsilano Beach are favorite ecreational areas. Since the early 1990s,

Yaletown, on the north shore of False Creek, has seen a dramatic transformation. Once an underused warehouse district, it is now a magnet for high-tech companies and downtown dwellers. High-rises and converted warehouses lend a flair both ultramodern and charmingly historic. Terrace cafés, designer outlets, and interior design stores draw visitors in the day; nightclubs and brew pubs attract revelers come evening.

ights at a Glance

useums, Galleries, and rt Schools
Emily Carr University of Art & Design

tudios and Markets
Kids Market
New-Small and Sterling Studio Glass
Granville Island Public Market

Waterways and Ferries
1 False Creek
7 Granville Island Market Ferries

Beaches, Parks, and Districts
5 Railspur Alley
8 Vanier Park
9 Sunset Beach
10 Yaletown

See also Street Finder maps 1, 2, and 3

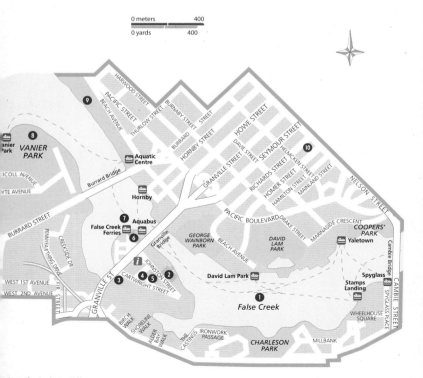

Pretty floating homes in Vancouver

For keys to symbols *see back flap*

Street-by-Street: Granville Island

Granville Island had its beginnings in 1916, as an industrial area situated on land dredged from False Creek. For decades, heavy industry belched out noxious fumes. By the 1950s, the area was nearly abandoned. In 1972, the Canadian government, backed by City Hall, took over the site, with a plan to make it a people place, and, in 1979, a public market opened. Today, stores – known for the originality of their wares, galleries, and studios – and restaurants are housed in brightly painted converted warehouses and tin sheds. Granville Island, which is not an island at all but a peninsula, is also home to music, dance, and theater.

Marina on False Creek, downtown buildings in the background

❻ ★ Granville Island Public Market
Enjoy a wonderful diversity of locally grown and imported fruits and vegetables in the colorful displays that make this market Vancouver's most popular attraction.

One of the many outdoor cafés and restaurants at Granville Island

❸ Kids Market
The Kids Market is a child's fantasyland, with more than 25 shopkeepers selling everything from games and toys to pint-sized clothing

❷ ★ Emily Carr University of Art & Design
Named in honor of one of BC's major artists *(see p215)*, this respected school is located in a former warehouse.

Locator Map
See Street Finder map 2

❹ New-Small and Sterling Studio Glass
Look through the windows of this glass-blowing studio and marvel as molten glass is transformed into beautiful works of art.

JOHNSTON STREET

CARTWRIGHT STREET

0 meters   80
0 yards   80

Key
— Suggested route

❺ Railspur Alley
A sign from one of the boutiques on Railspur Alley, a lively street lined with quirky local stores and businesses.

View of False Creek, looking northeast toward Yaletown from Granville Island

❶ False Creek

Map 3 B4.

As the name suggests, False Creek is not a creek at all but a saltwater inlet in the heart of the city, extending east from Burrard Bridge to Science World *(see p217)*. In the 1850s, Captain G. H. Richards sailed up this body of water, which originally covered what is now Chinatown eastward to Clark Drive, hoping to find the Fraser River. Disappointed, he named it False Creek.

The mudflats Richards saw originally served as the winter fishing grounds of the Squamish people. By the late 1800s, sawmills had set up on the south shore, followed by the railyards of Yaletown *(see pp224–5)* on the north shore.

Today, paved seawalls flank both the north and south shores, allowing walkers, bicyclists, and rollerbladers to admire the views of downtown and the mountains.

❷ Emily Carr University of Art & Design

1399 Johnston St. **Map** 2 E5.
Tel (604) 844-3800. 50.
False Creek Ferries, Aquabus.
Open 10am–6pm daily. **Closed** mid-Dec–Jan 1. ecuad.ca

The unpainted corrugated metal exterior of the famed Emily Carr University of Art & Design (ECUAD) is perfectly in keeping with the industrial ambience of Granville Island. Industrial design is a major focus within the school's three degree-granting Master's programs. Over 1,700 full-time students come from across Canada and 50 countries worldwide to attend ECUAD.

Established in 1925, the school moved into three abandoned industrial buildings on Granville Island in 1980. The original building, on the north side of Johnston Street, houses the **Charles H. Scott Gallery**, which hosts regional, national, and international exhibits of contemporary art. Student shows are held in the **Concourse and Media Galleries**.

The school's newest addition on the south side of Johnston Street is a 58,000-sq-ft- (5,400-sq-m-) structure built for $14 million.

Well-known alumni include painters Jack Shadbolt and Arnold Belkin, artist Stan Douglas, cartoonist Lynn Johnston, and author Douglas Coupland.

One of the galleries at Emily Carr University of Art & Design

❸ Kids Market

1496 Cartwright St. **Map** 2 D5.
Tel (604) 689-8447. 50.
False Creek Ferries, Aquabus.
Open 10am–6pm daily.
Closed Jan 1, Dec 25 & 26.
kidsmarket.ca

Children will be dazzled by the Kids Market: two floors filled with toys, games, gadgets, clothing, and jewelry. The more than 25 retailers here provide an eclectic shopping experience. Clownin' Around Magic is filled with puzzles and magic tricks, Knotty Toys features handmade wooden toys, Little Treasures "on the go" sells beachwear, while The Hairloft offers spa treatments and haircuts for girls. There is also the Adventure Zone, with a supervised play area, a picnic spot, and special events. Outside, Granville Island Waterpark is a joyful free-for-all of fountains, nozzles, and spray.

Pousse-café vessels at New-Small and Sterling Studio Glass

❹ New-Small and Sterling Studio Glass

1440 Old Bridge St. **Map** 2 D5.
Tel (604) 681-6730. 50.
False Creek Ferries, Aquabus.
Open 10am–6pm Mon–Sat, 11am–5pm Sun. **Closed** Jan & Feb: Mon; Jan 1, Dec 25 & 26.
hotstudioglass.com

Many of the best-known glassblowers in BC have worked for New-Small and Sterling Studio Glass since it opened here in 1982. Visitors can watch owner David New-Small and other artists create vases, bowls, and artwork using traditional techniques dating back hundreds of years.

The studio specializes in free-blown glass, made without molds using steel blowpipes and pontils. One of four furnaces keeps 150 lb (70 kg) of glass molten at 2,000°F (1,100°C) around the clock. The others are fired as needed to heat and shape works in progress. Complicated pieces require a team of glassblowers.

The adjacent shop is one of the best-known glass galleries in Western Canada.

➎ Railspur Alley

Railspur Alley. **Map** 2 D5. 🚌 50.
🚢 False Creek Ferries, Aquabus. ▨
🖼 🖼 🌐 **granvilleisland.com**

In the heart of this former industrial district, tucked away off Old Bridge Street on Granville Island, you can find Railspur Alley, a quiet, charming street that has been remodeled and is filled with boutique shops and artisan businesses. A highlight of Railspur Alley is the cluster of 12 artists' studios, where visitors can watch artists at work and browse the various items for sale.

Other shops include Alarte Silks Studio Gallery in the Alley Gallery, which has beautiful, hand-painted and wearable silk art, and Sadryna Design, which sells custom leather fashions with European flair. You can find belts and purses for sale as well as more theatrical stage costumes. Hartman Leather also sells hand-crafted leather bags and belts, using top-grain vegetable-tanned and latigo leathers.

Dalbergia Wood and Fine-Objects produces wooden furniture and sculptures with simple, clean lines. Fine art galleries Hilary Morris, Studio 13 Fine Art, and Peter Kiss Gallery round off the selection of art for sale.

The Artisan Sake Maker is Vancouver's only fresh, organic, premium sake producer, and offers tastings at its tasting counters between 11:30am and 6pm. Off the Tracks is a bistro that offers organic, fair-trade coffee and local wine. They also serve sandwiches, soups, salads, and desserts made by local chefs.

Abundant fresh produce at Granville Island Public Market

➏ Granville Island Public Market

1689 Johnston St. **Map** 2 D4.
Tel (604) 666-5784. 🚌 50.
🚢 False Creek Ferries, Aquabus.
Open 9am–7pm daily. **Closed** Jan: Mon, Jan 1, Dec 25 & 26. 🦽
🌐 **granvilleisland.com**

The Granville Island Public Market opened in 1979 in a former industrial building. Cleaned up and given new tin cladding, the public market building was the first renovated structure on the site to open for business. Food specialties at the market include high-quality fresh fruits and vegetables, meats, fresh pasta, cheese, breads and baked goods, chocolates, and herbs and spices. Flowers are also a big draw.

Throughout the market, vendors sell the wares of local artisans and craftspeople – candles, custom jewelry, and hats. Exhibitors are selected for their high standards of design and production.

A food fair on the market's west side offers a variety of ethnic cuisines. From the benches outside on the wharf, visitors take in one of the best views of the False Creek marina and docks, as well as a spectacular view of downtown and the North Shore mountains. Street performers – from musicians to stilt-walkers to magicians – entertain outside, adding to the market's eclectic, vibrant ambience.

➐ Granville Island Market Ferries

Map 2 D4. False Creek Ferries:
Tel (604) 684-7781.
🌐 **granvilleislandferries.bc.ca**
Aquabus: **Tel** (604) 689-5858.
🌐 **theaquabus.com** 🚌 50.
Open call for hrs. **Closed** Dec 25 & 26.
🚢 🦽 See Getting Around Vancouver p239.

A ride aboard one of the ferries that service Granville Island and the surrounding area is one of the best ways to see the sights of False Creek, such as Granville Island, the Maritime and Vancouver Museums, and the Aquatic Centre. These small boats offer a striking perspective of the city's downtown and west side.

Two ferry companies operate from Granville Island. **False Creek Ferries'** vessels depart daily from the wharf on the west side of the Granville Island Public Market. Routes cross False Creek to the south foot of Hornby Street and also go to Vanier Park (see pp224–5). Another route goes to Science World (see p217). The fleet includes four 20-passenger diesel ferries, plus six electric boats.

The **Aquabus** comprises 12 small vessels running three routes from the ferry dock north of Granville Island Public Market. The Hornby route takes passengers and bicyclists to the southern foot of Hornby Street. The Yaletown route drops passengers at the eastern foot of Davie Street. A third route encompasses Science World.

Both companies offer mini-cruises, including sunset cruises of False Creek, with frequent departures. The Aquabus evening cruise is aboard the Rainbow Hunter, a restored antique ferry.

An Aquabus vessel belonging to one of two False Creek ferry services

❽ Vanier Park

Vanier Park is a calming oasis on the city's west side. Although it is relatively small, it feels spacious. Boats sail by on English Bay, kites fly overhead, ferries dock and depart, and pedestrians and cyclists pass through on their way to Kitsilano Beach or Granville Island *(see pp220–21)*. Vanier Park was first inhabited by Coast Salish people. It is now the home of the Museum of Vancouver, the H. R. MacMillan Space Centre, City of Vancouver Archives, and the Vancouver Maritime Museum. In summer, the Bard on the Beach Shakespeare Festival is held here.

Gate to the Northwest Passage
This imposing giant red steel sculpture by Alan Chung Hung overlooks English Bay.

English Bay

Heritage Harbour

0 meters   150
0 yards   200

❾ Sunset Beach

Map 2 D3. 🚌 6. ⛴ False Creek Ferries, Aquabus.

The white sands of Sunset Beach, which marks the end of the English Bay seawall and the start of False Creek, make an ideal place to relax and do some serious suntanning or swimming. Summertime water temperatures rise to 65°F (18°C), and lifeguards are on duty from mid-May to Labor Day.

The western end of Sunset Beach provides a good view of the gray granite *Inukshuk*, which sits at the foot of neighboring English Bay Beach. This Inuit statue by Alvin Kanak, modeled on traditional markers used by the Inuit for navigation, is a symbol of friendship.

The **Vancouver Aquatic Centre**, at the beach's east end, has a 164-ft- (50-m-) long Olympic-size swimming pool, and diving pools, a sauna, a whirlpool, and a steam room. False Creek Ferries dock behind the center, with routes to Vanier Park, Granville Island, Yaletown, and Science World.

❿ Yaletown

Map 2 F3. 🚆 Stadium. 🚌 6. ⛴ False Creek Ferries, Aquabus.

Warehouses have been transformed into lofts, outdoor cafés have sprung up on old loading docks, and high-rise

Restaurant with outdoor seating on a street in Yaletown

buildings have filled in the horizon of Yaletown. The area was first settled by Canadian Pacific Railway (CPR) train crews and laborers after the CPR closed its construction

Museum of Vancouver

The curved white roof of the Museum of Vancouver resembles a Haida woven hat. *The Crab*, a stunning stainless-steel sculpture by George Norris, presides outside. Canada's largest civic museum boasts five re-creations of Vancouver's history, including an immigrant ship and a fur-trading post.

Vancouver Maritime Museum

The West Coast's rich maritime history is featured in this museum, from seagoing canoes to a 1928 police schooner.

H. R. MacMillan Space Centre

Space lore is presented in child-friendly hands-on displays and multimedia shows at the space center. The popular Cosmic Courtyard is an interactive gallery that focuses on space exploration.

amp in Yale, BC, on completion f the transcontinental railway o Vancouver in 1887. Yaletown emained the decaying heart f the city's industrial activity ntil the early 1990s, when a evelopment plan began its ransformation into a lively rban community.

A multitude of Yaletown ondominiums now house a outhful, sophisticated crowd. long with new residents came new look. Dirty and neglected ndustrial warehouses on Homer, Hamilton, and Mainland Streets vere given face-lifts. The result s a landscape of bistros, cafés, estaurants, nightclubs, studios, galleries, hair salons, interior design stores, and international nd local designer clothing outlets. On Beach Avenue, the **Roundhouse Community Arts and Recreation Centre**, in a former CPR switching building, includes a theater and gallery spaces and a host of community arts and athletics programs. It also houses the locomotive that pulled the first passenger train to Vancouver in 1887.

Joe Fortes, the Hero of English Bay

Vancouver's "Citizen of the Century" was a simple man named Seraphim "Joe" Fortes. Born in Barbados in 1865, he arrived in Vancouver in 1885 and was soon a regular at the English Bay Beach. He taught thousands of children to swim. As the city's first appointed lifeguard, he is credited with saving more than 100 lives. Joe's cottage was located right by the beach at the site of today's Alexandra Park. The Joe Fortes Memorial Drinking Fountain in the same park was designed by Charles Marega and installed in 1926, four years after Joe's death.

Joe Fortes in front of his cottage

FARTHER AFIELD

Beyond downtown Vancouver lie such memorable attractions as Stanley Park and the Museum of Anthropology. Other intriguing sights are located in outlying cities, easily reached by car or public transit. The North Shore, once home to the Coast Salish people, consists of two cities. Lions Gate Bridge spans the First Narrows to West Vancouver, featuring 17 miles (28 km) of scenic shoreline. The bridge also leads to North Vancouver and the physical wonders of Capilano Canyon and Grouse Mountain. At the mouth of the Fraser River is fast-growing Richmond. With its Chinese malls and markets, this city superbly reflects Greater Vancouver's multicultural character. The riverside community of Steveston is noted for its historic cannery.

Sights at a Glance

Museums and Galleries
- ❷ West Vancouver Museum
- ❾ *Museum of Anthropology pp234–5*

Areas of Natural Beauty
- ❶ Marine Drive
- ❸ Capilano Suspension Bridge Park
- ❹ Grouse Mountain
- ❼ *Stanley Park pp230–31*

Markets
- ❺ Lonsdale Quay Market

Neighborhoods and Cities
- ❻ West End
- ❿ Richmond
- ⓬ Steveston

Buildings
- ❽ University of British Columbia
- ⓫ Chinese Buddhist Temple

Key
- Central Vancouver
- Urban area
- Major highway
- Highway
- Minor road

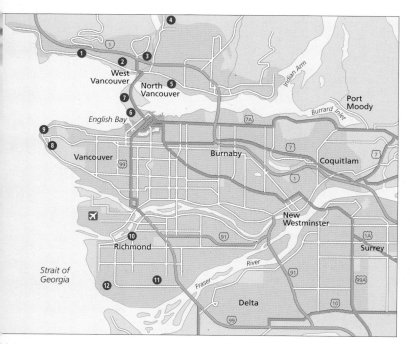

◀ Totem poles carved by the region's First Nations peoples in Stanley Park   **For keys to symbols** *see back flap*

Capilano Suspension Bridge, not for the fearful

❶ Marine Drive

🚌 250. **Tel** (604) 926-6614.
🌐 westvanchamber.com

Scenic Marine Drive winds through West Vancouver and makes for an ideal day trip. Park Royal Shopping Centre, with its 280 stores, is the area's major mall. The nearby seaside suburb of Ambleside boasts a par-three golf course on the Capilano Indian Reserve; a popular seawall walkway; and a park over-looking Burrard Inlet, which includes tennis courts, a paddling center, fitness circuit, skateboard park, and waterfowl pond. At the end of the Ambleside Sea Walk, Dundarave Pier offers a wonderful view of Vancouver and the Strait of Georgia. Both Ambleside and Dundarave are good places to shop and dine.

Atkinson Lighthouse, just off Marine Drive

From here westward, Marine Drive clings to the rocky shoreline, buffered by some of Canada's priciest real estate.

At Lighthouse Park, an easy walk through old-growth forest leads to the Atkinson lighthouse, built in 1912.

Horseshoe Bay welcomes visitors with a park, a marina, and a First Nations art gallery. Ice cream and fish and chips are Horseshoe Bay specialties.

❷ West Vancouver Museum

680 17th St, West Vancouver.
Tel (604) 925-7295. 🚌 251, 252.
Open 11am–5pm Tue–Sat.
Closed public hols. 🏛 by donation.
📷 ♿ partial. 🏛
🌐 westvancouvermuseum.ca

Small and inviting, the West Vancouver Museum is housed in the stately former home of Gertrude Lawson, daughter of John Lawson, the first permanent white settler in West Vancouver. The stones of the 1938 house were brought from New Zealand as ballast on a sailing ship; others came from the Capilano River. After Gertrude died in 1989, the District of West Vancouver acquired the property. The house was restored and then opened in 1995 as a museum.

The museum's exhibits relate to West Vancouver heritage and community interests, such as local sporting history and historic toys. West Vancouver communities are sometimes profiled and decorative arts are particularly well represented. The gift shop sells arts and crafts by local artists and books on West Vancouver history and architecture. Events include school programs as well as summer art and architecture programs for children.

❸ Capilano Suspension Bridge Park

3735 Capilano Rd, North Vancouver.
Tel (604) 985-7474. 🚌 232, 236.
⛴ SeaBus. **Open** Jan–Nov: 9am–5pm daily (extended hours mid-Mar–mid-Oct, check website); Dec: 11am–9pm. **Closed** Dec 25. 🎫 📷 May–Oct. ♿ partial. ♿ 📷 🌐 capbridge.com

The first Capilano Suspension Bridge, not much more than a hemp rope and cedar planks, was built in 1889 by Scotsman George Mackay and Squamish locals August and Willie Jack. Mackay was drawn by Capilano Canyon's wild beauty and built a cabin overlooking it. Access to the Capilano River below was almost impossible. It is said that Mackay built the bridge so that his son, who loved fishing, could reach the river.

The present bridge, dating to 1956 and the fourth to be constructed here, spans 450 ft (137 m). Secured by 13 tons of concrete, 230 ft (70 m) above the canyon floor, it is the longest such bridge in the world.

Visitors will be treated to spectacular views, old-growth woods, trout ponds and a 200-ft- (61-m-) high waterfall. Other highlights include the totem poles at the Kia'palano First Nations cultural area; Treetops Adventure, a walk through the mid-story of 250-year-old Douglas firs; and Cliffwalk, a series of high and narrow cantilevered walkways attached to a granite cliff face.

Costumed guides at the Capilano Suspension Bridge

View of Vancouver from Grouse Mountain

❹ Grouse Mountain

6400 Nancy Greene Way. **Tel** (604) 980-9311. 🚌 232, 236. 🚢 SeaBus. **Open** 9am–10pm daily. 🎿 ♿ 🅿
📷 **W grousemountain.com**

From the summit of Grouse Mountain, on a clear day visitors can see as far as Vancouver Island in the west and the Columbia Mountains in the east.

The 2-mile (3-km) Grouse Grind trail, leading to Peak Chalet at 3,700 ft (1,128 m), lives up to its name. A less energetic option is the Skyride gondola. The breathtaking Peak Chairlift ride (May–Oct) goes even further up to the peak of the mountain at 4,100 ft (1,250 m).

Popular activities include skiing, snowboarding, skating, snowshoeing, and sleigh rides in the winter; hiking, forest walks, helicopter tours, zip-ning, and tandem paragliding in the summer. Ski and snow-boarding schools, 26 ski runs, and equipment rentals are among the amenities here.

During the day, the World's Greatest Lumberjack Show sees two lumberjacks showcase their tree-climbing, axe-throwing, and log-rolling skills. At the Refuge for Endangered Wildlife, an enclosed natural habitat, that is home to orphaned grizzly bears and wolves, wildlife rangers give daily talks. The Theatre in the Sky video takes

viewers on a stunning aerial tour of British Columbia, while the Eye of the Wind is a 360-degree observation pod set at the top of a wind turbine, just meters from its rotating blades.

❺ Lonsdale Quay Market

123 Carrie Cates Ct, North Vancouver. **Tel** (604) 985-6261. 🚢 SeaBus. **Open** 9am–7pm daily. **Closed** Jan 1, Dec 25. ♿ 💻 📷 📷 🚫
W lonsdalequay.com

Opened in 1986, this striking concrete-and-glass building houses the Lonsdale Quay Market. The market has a floor devoted to food, as well as an array of cafés and restaurants that serve a variety of ethnic cuisines. On the second floor, visitors will find specialty shops that sell hand-crafted products, such as jewelry, pottery, and textiles; and Kid's Alley, a row of child-oriented shops. The complex also includes a hotel, a pub, and a brewery. In the summer, music festivals are held outside on the adjacent Plaza Deck, overlooking the city and port. Musical offerings include jazz, folk, African, and Celtic performances.

The Skyride gondola, Grouse Mountain

The fountain at Lonsdale Quay, Vancouver in the distance

Sailboat on English Bay, with West End high-rises in the background

❻ West End

🚌 5, 6. 🚇 Burrard.

Vancouver's West End is the most densely populated residential area in Canada, yet it maintains a relaxed and spacious ambience, in part because of its proximity to Stanley Park and English Bay. Offering everything from beaches to hip urban streetlife, it is one of the best neighborhoods in Vancouver for strolling and taking in the delights of the city.

The West End, as one of Vancouver's earliest neighborhoods, has preserved several important historic buildings, such as the exquisite 1893 **Roedde House**, home to Vancouver's first bookbinder and now a museum, and the ivy-clad Sylvia Hotel, built in 1911.

West End streets are generally busy with pedestrians at all hours of the day or night. Robson, Denman, and Davie Streets are the main West End thoroughfares, with Burrard Street as its eastern boundary. Among the many shops and restaurants on Robson Street (see p216) is the Robson Public Market. Denman Street reflects the beach culture of English Bay with its casual clothing boutiques and cafés. It is also popular with Vancouver's gay community. Although Davie Street is more residential, it too has many cafés and restaurants.

The West End also offers plenty of green space among the high-rise apartments and heritage homes.

🏛 **Roedde House**
1415 Barclay St. **Tel** (604) 684-7040. **Open** 1–4pm Tue–Fri & Sun. 📷
W roeddehouse.org

❼ Stanley Park

A magnificent park of tamed wilderness a short ride from downtown Vancouver, Stanley Park was originally home to Musqueam and Squamish peoples. In 1888, Lord Stanley, Governor General of Canada, opened the park to all. More than eight million visitors a year make this Vancouver's top attraction. Many walk the 5.5-mile (8.8-km) perimeter seawall with its lovely views of the harbor, English Bay, and the Coast Mountains. Bicycles can be rented near the Denman Street entrance to the park. In addition to the Vancouver Aquarium, Stanley Park boasts rose gardens, a lake, a lagoon, and a totem pole display, as well as beaches, a swimming pool, waterpark, a miniature railway, tennis courts, and a pitch-and-putt golf course.

Siwash Rock
A volcanic formation jutting from the inlet beside the seawall, the rock has inspired many First Nations legends. According to one, it is a young chief turned to enduring stone for his courage.

English Bay

PARK DRIVE

Third Beach

Ferguson Point

BRIDLE PATH

LAGOON DR

★ Second Beach
Second Beach is a hub of activity in the summer, with a swimming pool, children's playground, picnic areas, and traffic school.

Lost Lagoon is immortalized in the poetry of Pauline Johnson (1861–1913), the daughter of a Mohawk chief, who named it for its appearance of vanishing at low tide. It is now a permanent lake and wildlife sanctuary.

For hotels and restaurants see p290 and pp302–3

★ The Seawall
The Seawall winds around the rim of the park past *Girl in a Wetsuit*, a sculpture by Elek Imredy. This curious sculpture, which sits on an offshore rock, was introduced to the park in 1972.

VISITORS' CHECKLIST

Practical Information
2099 Beach Ave. **Tel** (604) 257-8400. **Open** 24 hrs daily (not all sights). 🚻 to some exhibits. 🚻
📷 🚫 🚮 🚟 **P** Horse-drawn carriage tours: (Mar–Oct), call (604) 681-5115. Stanley Park Shuttle: (Jun–Sep). Special events, call (604) 473-6204.
W vancouver.ca

Transport
🚇 Burrard. 🚌 19.

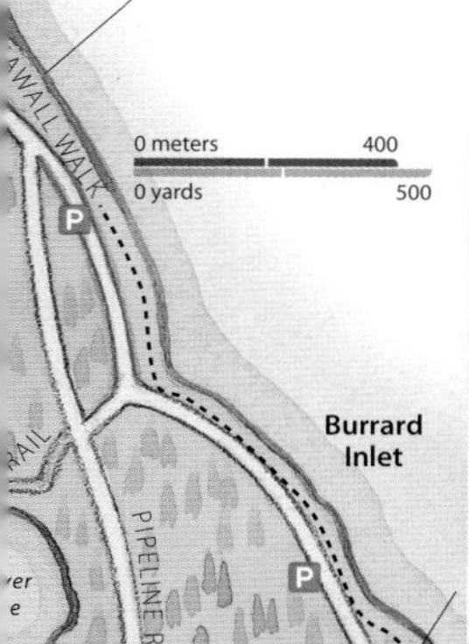

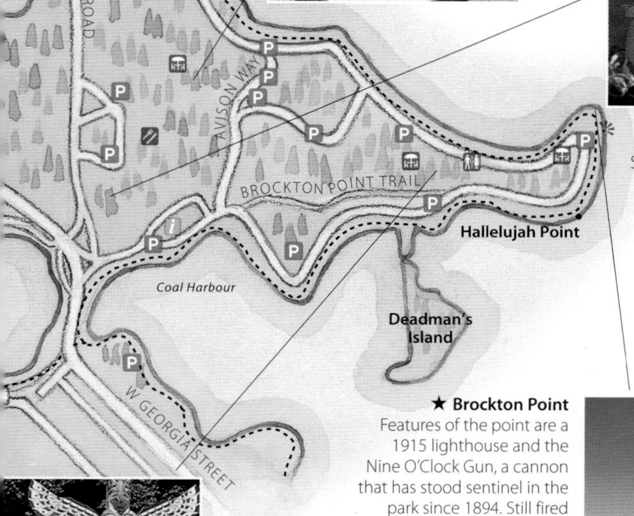

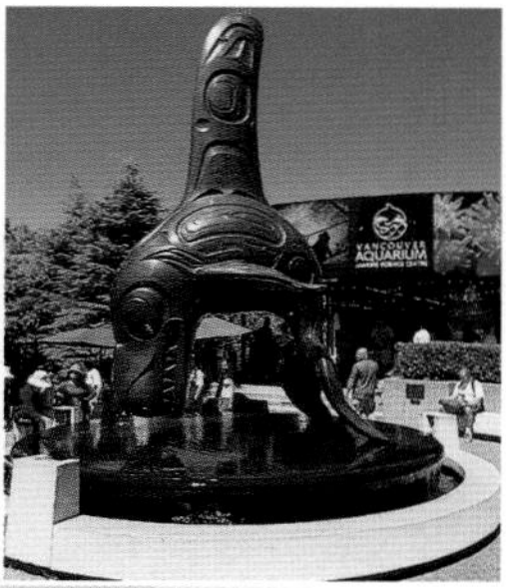

th Shore

0 meters 400
0 yards 500

Vancouver Aquarium Marine Science Centre
The surprisingly graceful white beluga whales are the stars of Canada's premier aquarium. Among the other 70,000 creatures to see here are sea otters, wolf eels, and penguins.

Burrard Inlet

Rose Garden
From May to September, the lovely formal Rose Garden, surrounded by a variety of perennial plantings, looks its very best.

BROCKTON POINT TRAIL

Hallelujah Point

Coal Harbour

Deadman's Island

★ Brockton Point
Features of the point are a 1915 lighthouse and the Nine O'Clock Gun, a cannon that has stood sentinel in the park since 1894. Still fired nightly, its boom once helped sailors synchronize their chronometers.

Totem Park
Situated beside Brockton Oval, where the city's first cricket match was played in the late 1800s, this area displays nine totem poles. Created by the Haida, Kwakiutl, and other indigenous peoples, each totem tells its own story.

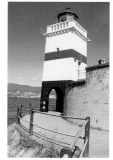

Key
···· Seawall walk

For key to symbols *see back flap*

Walter C. Koerner Library, University of British Columbia

❽ University of British Columbia

Tel (604) 822-2211. ▣ 4, 14, 99 B-Line. ⬛ ▢ ⓦ ubc.ca

The University of British Columbia (UBC), founded in 1915, is one of Canada's leading medical doctoral universities. A 30-minute drive from the heart of downtown Vancouver, the campus is an eclectic mix of architecture, the range of which can be seen by comparing the 1923 **Irving K. Barber Learning Centre** with the **Walter C. Koerner Library**, whose construction began in 1996. The former is a combination of imposing stone walls and medieval-style detail; the latter, designed with the help of Arthur Erickson, is a striking combination of concrete and glass.

Campus highlights include the **UBC Botanical Garden**, with over 8,000 species of rare or unusual plants, and the Greenheart TreeWalk, where visitors can walk on suspended canopy walkways amid the

treetops in the rainforest. The zinc-paneled **Chan Centre for the Performing Arts** *(see p237)* hosts classical and contemporary musicians, theater and opera productions, as well as film screenings. Works by leading Canadian and international contemporary artists are shown at the **Morris and Helen Belkin Art Gallery**. UBC's **Museum of Anthropology** *(see pp234–5)* is world-renowned. The **Pacific Museum of Earth** is a treasure chest of minerals and fossils, including an impressive collection of BC jade. The award-winning cedar-and-glass **First Nations Longhouse** resembles a traditional longhouse. The **Asian Centre** houses a photographic exhibit of Asian Canadians and one of North America's largest collections of rare Chinese books. The Japanese-style **Nitobe Memorial Garden**, part of the UBC Botanical Garden, is at the rear of the building.

Campus maps are available from kiosks at the bus loop, Student Union Building, and Chan Centre.

🔹 UBC Botanical Garden
6804 SW Marine Dr. **Tel** (604) 822-3928. **Open** 9:30am–5pm daily. ▨ ⬛ partial. ◪ Mar–Oct. ▦ ⓦ botanicalgarden.ubc.ca

▥ Morris and Helen Belkin Art Gallery
1825 Main Mall. **Tel** (604) 822-2759. **Open** 10am–5pm Tue–Fri, noon–5pm Sat & Sun. **Closed** major hols. ⬛ ⓦ belkin.ubc.ca

▦ Asian Centre
1871 West Mall. **Tel** (604) 822-2427. Library: **Open** 9am–5pm Mon–Fri.

❾ Museum of Anthropology

See pp234–5.

Richmond's public market

❿ Richmond

▨ 175,000. **Tel** (604) 271-8280 or (877) 247-0777. ▣ Canada Line SkyTrain. ⓦ tourismrichmond.com

Built on a group of islands, Richmond was originally an isolated farming community settled by Europeans in the 1880s. Before that, the Coast Salish used the islands as temporary dwelling grounds, for fishing and for collecting berries. Blueberry and cranberry are still important local crops, but Richmond today is predominantly a busy metropolis. Lulu Island, the largest island, is the site of the city proper.

Richmond is home to the second-largest North American Asian community. **Yaohan Centre**, one of several Asian malls, sells everything from traditional Chinese herbs to the latest high-tech gadgetry to Taekwon-do classes. Tea ceremonies, foot massages, and face readings are some of the less conventional offerings. The **Richmond Centre** combines mainstream shopping with Asian influences.

Richmond also offers international dining, art galleries, and live performances at the **Gateway Theatre**. Outdoor activities include year-round golfing, and visiting the **Richmond Nature Park**, which features trails through forests, bogs, and pond habitats. Walking and cycling the West Dyke Trail are also popular. The area is also rich in wildlife including seals and whales.

🔹 Richmond Nature Park
11851 Westminster Hwy. **Tel** (604) 718-6188. **Open** 7am–sunset daily. ⓦ richmondnatureparksociety.ca

The UBC's Irving K. Barber Learning Centre, its clock tower a campus landmark

restaurants lining the boardwalk along Steveston's waterfront

Chinese Buddhist Temple

60 Steveston Hwy, Richmond.
Tel (604) 274-2822. 402, 403, 407.
Open 9:30am–5:30pm daily. (by donation). **W** buddhisttemple.ca

The grace of Richmond's huge Chinese Buddhist Temple, completed in 1983 after much planning and fundraising by native Chinese immigrants, is immediately evident in the curved roof of golden porcelain tiles and the marble lions guarding the entrance. The temple's interior is richly adorned with sculptures of the Buddha, ornate murals, and sumptuous painting, woodwork, and embroidery. Visitors may encounter one of the daily ceremonies that take place and are welcome to observe the rituals. Outside, a majestic stone path lined with Tang Dynasty lanterns and brilliant marigolds leads to the statue of the Maitreya Buddha. The shade of twin gazebos and the restful sound of nearby fountains

offer a soothing respite from the bustling city. The bonsai garden in the courtyard is a delightful place to stroll.

⑫ Steveston

Tel (604) 271-8280. 401, 402, 410.
W steveston.bc.ca

The village of Steveston, in Richmond, offers visitors a peek into British Columbia's fishing and agricultural heritage. Steveston is proud of its past, which dates back to the turn of the 19th century. The charming **Steveston Museum** is housed in the last of the original 350 Northern Banks that once operated in Western Canada. The **London Heritage Farm** features a restored 1890s farmhouse.

Steveston's waterfront is home to Canada's largest commercial fishing fleet. Freighters and fishing boats share the mouth of the Fraser River as they head for the Strait of Georgia. On Fisherman's Wharf, shoppers can purchase

the catch of the day directly off the fishing boats. Restaurants overlooking the water serve up equally fresh fish and seafood dishes. Harbor cruises meander up the Fraser River. A block away, on Moncton Street, art shops and souvenir galleries mingle with local businesses. A short walk from the village center is **Garry Point Park**, whose rocky shores and sandy beaches offer vistas of Vancouver Island.

A highlight is the **Gulf of Georgia Cannery National Historic Site**. In the 1890s, 15 salmon canneries employed upwards of 10,000 men and women. Most of the complex, which includes an icehouse, a lead foundry, and an artifact collection featuring machinery from the early 1900s, sits on pilings built over the Fraser River. At its height, in 1897, the cannery produced over 2.5 million cans of salmon.

Steveston Museum
3811 Moncton St. **Tel** (604) 718-8439.
Open 9:30am–5pm Mon–Sat, noon–4pm Sun. **Closed** major hols. donation. 1st floor only. by appt.

London Heritage Farm
6511 Dyke Rd. **Tel** (604) 271-5220.
Farm: **Open** Feb–Jun & Sep–Dec: noon–5pm Sat & Sun; Jul–Aug: noon–5pm Wed–Sun. donation. by appt. **W** londonheritagefarm.ca

Gulf of Georgia Cannery National Historic Site
12138 4th Ave. **Tel** (604) 664-9009.
Open 10am–5pm daily. **W** gulfof georgiacannery.com

The intricately carved Chinese Buddhist temple and gate

The Mighty Fraser River

The majestic Fraser River travels from Mount Robson Provincial Park to the Strait of Georgia, near Vancouver. It broadens at Hope, transforming the Fraser Valley into lush farmlands. Once in the Vancouver area, it splits into two arms. One million migratory birds settle by the river near Steveston each winter, making this a great bird-watching area. The Fraser is also the largest salmon river in the world, with millions of sockeye flooding the river every summer.

The spectacular, winding Fraser Canyon

❾ Museum of Anthropology

Founded in 1947, this outstanding museum houses one of the world's finest collections of Northwest Coast First Nations peoples' art. Designed by Canadian architect Arthur Erickson in 1976, the museum is housed in a stunning building overlooking mountains and sea. The tall posts and huge windows of the Great Hall were inspired by the post-and-beam architecture of Haida houses and are a fitting home for a display of monumental totem poles, canoes, and feast dishes. Through the windows of the Great Hall, the visitor can see the magnificent outdoor sculpture complex, which includes two houses designed by contemporary Haida artist Bill Reid.

★ The Great Hall
The imposing glass and concrete structure of the Great Hall is the perfect setting for totem poles, canoes, and sculptures.

Carved Figures
These figures are on houseboards that were once displayed in the interior of a First Nations family house. Carved from cedar planks, the style is typical of Coast Salish sculpture.

Outdoor Haida Houses and Totem Poles

Set overlooking the water, these two Haida houses and collection of totem poles are faithful to the artistic tradition of the Haida of the Pacific Northwest, including the Nisga'a, Gitxsan, and Kwak-waka'wakw. Animals and mythic creatures representing various clans are carved in cedar on these poles and houses, made between 1959 and 1963 by Vancouver's renowned modern Haida artist Bill Reid and Namgis artist Doug Cranmer.

Carved red cedar totem poles

Museum Guide

The museum's collections are on one level. The Ramp leads to the Great Hall, which features the cultures of Northwest Coast First Nations peoples. The Multiversity Galleries contain artifacts from around the world, and a range of 16th- to 19th-century European ceramics is housed in the Koerner European Ceramics Gallery.

Ceramic Jug
This beautifully decorated jug was made in Central Europe in 1674 by members of the Anabaptist religious sect. The foliage motifs are in contrast to the freely sketched animals that run around the base.

★ The Raven and the First Men
(1980) Carved in laminated yellow cedar by Bill Reid, this modern interpretation of a Haida creation myth depicts the Raven, a wise and wily trickster, trying to coax mankind out into the world from a giant clamshell.

Wooden Frontlet
Decorated with abalone shell, this wooden frontlet was a chief's headdress worn only on important ceremonial occasions on the Northwest Coast.

Red Cedar Carved Doors
This detail comes from the set of stunning carved red cedar doors that guard the entrance to the shop. Created in 1976 by a group of First Nations artists from the 'Ksan cultural center near Hazelton, the doors show the history of the first people of the Skeena River region in British Columbia.

Key

- The Ramp
- The Great Hall
- The Rotunda
- Multiversity Galleries
- Koerner European Ceramics Gallery
- Michael M. Ames Theatre
- Temporary exhibition space
- Non-exhibition space

Shopping in Vancouver

The shops in Vancouver and surrounding areas showcase goods and fashions from every continent. Funky boutiques and vintage clothing stores abound in Gastown, as do shops specializing in First Nations art. Other shopping districts also offer myriad goods, from upscale furniture to kitchenware and specialty items.

Window display at a clothing store on Vancouver's Granville Island

Shopping Districts

Robson Street (see p216) is Vancouver's major shopping promenade. Specialty shops and boutiques line the streets of Gastown, Kitsilano, Kerrisdale, Yaletown, and Ambleside (see p228). South Granville is home to upscale clothing and furnishing stores. Granville Island (see pp220–21) offers an array of shops and galleries, as well as a huge food market. Visit Chinatown and the Punjabi market around Main Street and 49th Avenue for ethnic shopping. Richmond (see p232) is known for its Asian shopping malls.

Department Stores and Shopping Centers

Most of the city's shopping centers are anchored by major department stores. **The Bay** sells quality Canadian and international brand-name clothing, and its own clothing lines. **Holt Renfrew** features premier designer labels such as Alexander McQueen, Gucci, and Mulberry.

At the 140-store **Pacific Centre** and the 500-store **Metropolis at Metrotown**, BC's largest shopping mall, goods range from brand-name fashions to smoked BC salmon. The smaller **Sinclair Centre** features international fashions

in an Edwardian Baroque-style building that was formerly a post office. On the North Shore, Lonsdale Quay Market (see p229) offers a harbor view as well as a food market and boutiques, while **Park Royal Shopping Centre** (see p228) houses a multitude of shops under two roofs.

Specialty Shops

On the funkier side is **John Fluevog**, with its unique boot and shoe designs for both men and women. **Leone** houses sophisticated boutiques, with fashions from Dior, Prada, and Versace, among others. Internationally known **Roots** offers Canadian design in both casual and athletic wear, as well as quality leather goods.

The elegant selection at **Birks Jewellers** includes, along with fine jewelry, pens, watches, crystal, and classic gifts. The **Inuit Gallery**, one of several stores in Gastown specializing in First Nations art, carries high-quality Inuit prints and soapstone carvings, and Northwest Coast First Nations masks, bentwood boxes, prints, and jewelry.

Chocoholics will love **Rogers' Chocolates**, which first opened in 1885. There are two locations in Vancouver: one in Gastown and the other on Granville Island.

Sign for Lonsdale Quay Market

Store in Gastown selling western-style boots and other leather goods

What to Buy

Quality Canadian-made fashions, leatherwear, and handbags are good buys in Vancouver. First Nations and Inuit art – including carvings, prints, masks, and jewelry – is available at many stores and gallery shops. BC jade jewelry is also popular, as are Cowichan knit sweaters. Traditionally smoked wild sockeye salmon, often packaged in decorative cedar boxes, is another West Coast specialty.

Entertainment in Vancouver

Entertainment in Vancouver runs the gamut from world-class opera productions to amateur music concerts. Each year the city hosts folk music, jazz, theater, dance, comedy, literary, and film festivals, among others. Vancouver is one of Canada's top theater centers; homegrown talent mixes with performers from Europe and the US.

The Orpheum Theatre's spectacular gold-leaf interior, built in 1927

Information

The city's two dailies, the *Vancouver Sun* and *The Province*, publish events listings on Thursdays. The free weekly *Georgia Straight* also has extensive listings. *Where Vancouver*, available at downtown hotels and tourist kiosks, lists events and shows.

Buying Tickets

Tickets for most events can be purchased from **Ticketmaster** by phone or at one of its locations. Many venues also sell tickets directly. **Tickets Tonight**, in the main Visitor Centre *(see p239)*, sells full-price tickets for theater and sporting events, and half-price tickets for some performances on the day. Discount tickets must be bought in person; others can be bought online.

Free Events

The Vancouver Central Library *(see p216)* hosts a variety of lectures and author readings. Annual and community festivals are listed in *Georgia Straight*.

Theater

Classics by Shakespeare, Shaw, and others, along with modern US and Canadian plays, are features of the **Vancouver Playhouse**. The **Arts Club Theatre** owes its success to solid theatrical fare performed by BC's leading actors. A popular venue for musicals is the 1930 **Stanley Industrial Alliance Stage**, now restored to its sassy vaudeville style. The small **Firehall Arts Centre** showcases culturally diverse contemporary theater and dance.

Summer events include plays at the open-air Theatre under the Stars (tel 604/734-1917) in Stanley Park and the Bard on the Beach Shakespeare Festival (tel 604/739-0559) in Vanier Park.

Dance and Music

With its inspiring modern repertoire, **Ballet British Columbia** performs at the **Queen Elizabeth Theatre**, as does the **Vancouver Opera**, founded in 1958 and presenting four operas each year. The ornate 2,700-seat **Orpheum Theatre** hosts a variety of concerts, including classical, jazz, and pop. It is also home to the **Vancouver Symphony Orchestra**, whose series include classical and family concerts, often with internationally recognized guest musicians. The 1,200-seat **Chan Centre for the Performing Arts** *(see p232)* showcases musical recitals and opera ensembles. **Commodore Ballroom**, boasting a floating dance floor and table seating for 990, hosts an eclectic mix of local and international talent.

Performer in one of Vancouver Opera's many productions

DIRECTORY

Ticket Outlets

Ticketmaster
Tel (604) 280-4444.
W ticketmaster.ca

Tickets Tonight
Tel (604) 684-2787.
W ticketstonight.ca

Theater

Arts Club Theatre
Tel (604) 687-1644.

Firehall Arts Centre
Tel (604) 689-0926.

Stanley Industrial Alliance Stage
Tel (604) 687-1644.

Vancouver Playhouse
Tel (604) 873-3311.

Dance and Music

Ballet British Columbia
Tel (604) 732-5003.

Chan Centre for the Performing Arts
Tel (604) 822-9197.

Commodore Ballroom
Tel (604) 739-4550.

Orpheum Theatre
Tel (604) 665-3050.

Queen Elizabeth Theatre
Tel (604) 665-3050.

Vancouver Opera
Tel (604) 683-0222.

Vancouver Symphony Orchestra
Tel (604) 876-3434.

Sports Venues

BC Place Stadium
Tel (604) 669-2300.

Nat Bailey Stadium
Tel (604) 872-5232.

Rogers Arena
Tel (604) 899-7400.

Spectator Sports

Sporting events such as BC Lions CFL football and Vancouver Canucks NHL hockey games take place at **BC Place Stadium** and **Rogers Arena**. The Vancouver Canadians play baseball at **Nat Bailey Stadium** in Queen Elizabeth Park.

Getting Around Vancouver

Although somewhat sprawling, Vancouver is not so big as to be overwhelming. The Tourism Vancouver Visitor Centre, near Canada Place, provides information on sights, accommodation, and transit, as well as street maps. The various local tours on offer, such as the free tour of historic Gastown, are an excellent way of exploring the city.

City and Street Layout

The many bridges spanning Vancouver's bodies of water can confuse visitors, as can the occurrence of "west" in the names of several areas in the city. The residential West End shares the downtown peninsula with the business and commercial district and with Stanley Park. The West Side stretches from Ontario Street, on the south side of False Creek, to the University of British Columbia and encompasses several neighborhoods, including Kitsilano and Kerrsdale. The community of West Vancouver is adjacent to North Vancouver, on the North Shore.

Before heading anywhere, it is wise to consult a good street map. The mountains, which are to the north, are a useful landmark for orientation.

Most streets run north–south and east–west, though some run on the diagonal. Some downtown streets are one-way. Outside the downtown core, avenues, divided east–west by Ontario Street, are numbered; north–south streets are named.

Walking

Many of the city's attractions are within walking distance of the downtown core. Others are easily accessible by public transit. However, as the

The SeaBus heading from the North Shore to downtown Vancouver

neighborhoods are somewhat scattered, it is often best to drive or use public transit to get to a particular neighborhood and then walk around to soak up the atmosphere. Walking tours through various neighborhoods are available; for a tour of Gastown, contact **Walking Tours of Gastown.**

Taxis

Taxis are numerous in Vancouver and can be hailed on the street or ordered by telephone. Taxi fares start at $3.25 and increase at the rate of approximately $1.88 per half-mile (1 km).

Bicycling

Vancouver is a great city for cycling, with bikeways covering more than 249 miles (400 km). Bikeways can be found at False Creek, Stanley Park, the University of British Columbia, and elsewhere downtown. The free brochure "Cycling in Vancouver" includes a map of bike routes. It is available at bicycle shops and bookstores, or by calling the **City of Vancouver Bicycle Hot Line**, which also provides details on where to rent bicycles.

Traffic-calming circles and other measures, such as cyclist-friendly sensors at traffic lights, slow vehicle traffic on city street Bicycle helmets are mandatory.

Public Transit

The Greater Vancouver transportation authority, **TransLink**, operates an extensive public transit network. Transit maps are available for a minimal charge at major drugstores and supermarkets, and the main location of the **Tourism Vancouver Visitor Centre**.

The SeaBus, a 400-seat catamaran, crosses Vancouver Harbour from the downtown Waterfront Station to Lonsdale Quay in North Vancouver every 15 to 30 minutes until around midnight.

SkyTrain, a driverless above-ground light rail system, travels between Waterfront Station, Richmond, Coquitlam, and Surrey. Schedules vary, depending on the time of day and day of the week. Fares range from $2.75 to $5.50 and are based on a three-zone system. Tickets allow interchangeable travel on the SeaBus, SkyTrain, and buses, including TransLink trolleys. Children under the age of 4 ride free; those between the ages of 5 and 13, secondary-school students, and people over 65, pay a reduced fare. A transfer ticket is free and lasts for 90 minutes of travel in any direction. The reloadable Compass Card, usually available where transit maps are sold, provides a discount. A $9.75 day pass can be purchased at supermarkets and at SkyTrain vending machines in stations.

All trips after 6:30pm and on weekends and holidays are considered to be in one zone anywhere in the system.

The commuter rail service **West Coast Express** runs during peak periods on weekdays

The Stanley Park shuttle bus at Brockton Point, one of its many stops

etween Mission and Vancouver,
opping at several outlying
unicipalities. The West Coast
xpress, SkyTrain, SeaBus, and
any of the bus routes are
heelchair accessible.

erries

vo ferry companies operate
rries along False Creek: **False
reek Ferries** and **Aquabus**
ee p223). The ferries dock at
cience World, Yaletown, the
ancouver Aquatic Centre,
ranville Island, and Vanier Park.
dult single fares range from
.25 to $5.50. False Creek
rries' day pass ($15) allows
hlimited one-day travel. The
quabus all-day pass is also $15.

riving

espite some downtown
ongestion, traffic in Vancouver
sually flows reasonably
ell. Streets are generally
asy to navigate, although
reet signage is sometimes
onexistent. Some downtown
reets limit left-hand turns
n nonpeak hours. Right-hand
irns on a red light are allowed
ter coming to a full stop,
hless otherwise noted.
'eekday rush hours are from
to 9:30am and 3 to 6pm.
iday's crush of cars may
art even earlier and will
e especially busy on the
iday of a long weekend.
The city speed limit is 30 mph
0 km/h). Some intersections
re monitored by police cameras.
eat belts are mandatory, as are
elmets for motorcyclists.
The **British Columbia
utomobile Association**
CAA) offers assistance,
aps, and guidebooks
o members of the
anadian or American
utomobile Association.

arking

aid parking is
vailable in Vancouver's
umerous parking lots.
etered street parking
also available. Keep
variety of change on
and, including quarters

The SkyTrain, linking downtown with Vancouver suburbs

and $1 coins. Credit cards are
accepted for parking in many
places. It is also possible to pay
for metered parking with the
free PayByPhone smartphone
app. It may be less expensive
to park in a lot and pay the
day rate than to feed the meter
throughout the day. Infractions
ticketing is usually prompt and
always expensive. Check posted
street parking regulations; they
may limit parking during rush
hours or specify other parking
regulations, such as a maximum
of 2 hours' parking. Free street
parking is generally available
from 10pm to 6am. Again,
check the posted parking
regulations; they can vary. Some
shopping malls and attractions
offer free parking, although
these are usually situated
outside the downtown core.

Towing

If your car is towed from a city
street, contact **Busters Towing**.
Operating 24 hours day, its
main impound yard is located
near Science World on Industrial
Avenue. If towed from a private
lot, call the telephone number
on the sign posted nearby.

A False Creek Ferries boat waiting for passengers

VANCOUVER STREET FINDER

The key map below shows the area of Vancouver covered by the *Street Finder* maps, which can be found on the following pages. Map references for sights, hotels, restaurants, shops, and entertainment venues given throughout the Vancouver chapter of this guide refer to the grid on the maps. The first figure in the reference indicates which map to turn to (1 to 4); the letter and number that follow refer to the grid reference on that map.

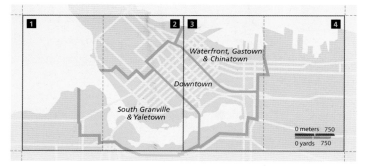

Key

- 🖼 Sight
- 🏛 Station building
- 🚆 Train Station
- 🚌 Bus station – long-distance
- 🚈 SkyTrain Station
- ℹ Information
- ✚ Hospital
- ✝ Church
- ⛴ Ferry boarding point
- – – Ferry route
- ▭▭ Railroad line
- — SkyTrain line

Scale of Maps 1–4

0 meters 250
0 yards 250

1

A **B** **C**

COMOX STRE
CHILCO STREET
BEACH AVENUE

1

*English
Bay
Beach*

*ALEXANDR
PARK*

BEACH AVENUE

2

English Bay

3

Vanier
Park

*VANIER
PARK*

*Vancouver
Maritime
Museum*

OGDEN AVENUE

*Museum of
Vancouver*

CHESTNUT STREET

McNICOLL AVENUE

WHYTE AVENUE

CREELMAN AVENUE

4

ARBUTUS STREET

LABURNUM STREET

WALNUT STREET

GREER AVE

*KITSILANO BEACH
PARK*

PENNY PARK

CORNWALL AVENUE

BALSAM STREET

YORK AVENUE

VINE STREET

YEW STREET

ARBUTUS STREET

MAPLE STREET

CYPRESS STREET

WEST 1ST AVENUE

BURRARD STREET

PINE STREET

WEST 2N

WEST 1ST AVENUE

WEST 2ND AVENUE

5

WEST 3RD AVENUE

KITSILANO

WEST 3RD AVENUE

YEW STREET

WEST 4TH AVENUE

WEST 4TH AVENUE

WEST 5TH AVENUE **A**

B

C WEST 5TH AVENUE

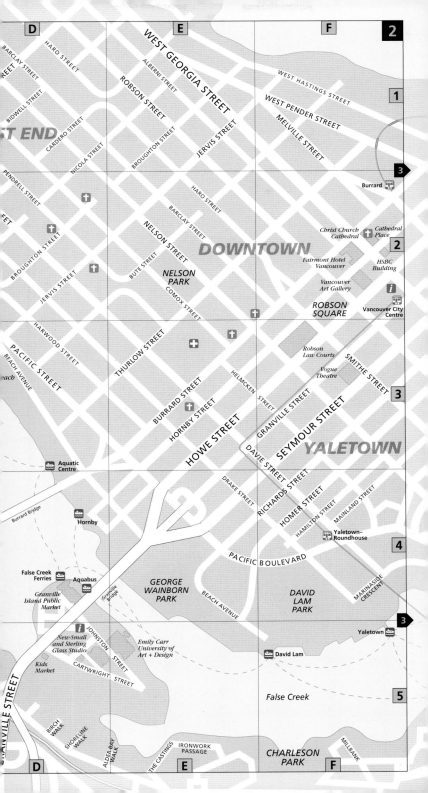

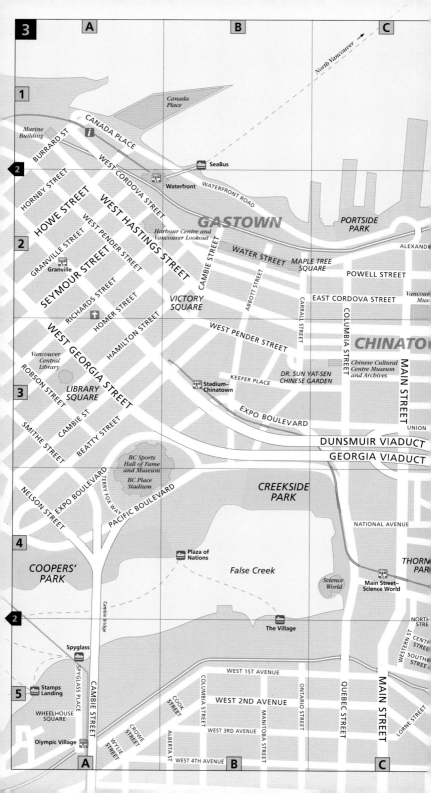

BRITISH COLUMBIA

British Columbia is one of Canada's most strikingly beautiful provinces. Tranquil islands grace its Pacific Ocean coastline while awe-inspiring mountain ranges on the mainland include the world-famous Rockies. Astounding natural vistas surround lively urban centers, from the large, modern cities of Vancouver and Victoria to small towns with a historic past.

Thousands of years before the first Europeans arrived, the 366,254-sq-mile (948,600-sq-km) area that is now British Columbia was home to First Nations tribes. Today, reconstructions of their cedar longhouses and semi-subterranean pit houses may be seen in museums.

Spanish and British ships explored the province's 16,800-mile (27,000-km) coastline from 1774 onward. In 1792, Captain George Vancouver – for whom the province's largest city was later named – was impressed, describing "innumerable pleasing landscapes." British Columbia joined the Confederation of Canada in 1871, and the Canadian Pacific Railway arrived in Vancouver in 1887, joining the new West Coast province to the already established eastern ones and bringing waves of new settlers. BC was built on logging, mining, and fishing, and while these industries have seen hard times over the years, they continue to support many communities today. Tourism, however, is now ranked second in the province's economy, after forestry.

British Columbia offers travelers an impressive array of breathtaking scenery and experiences. Vancouver Island's sandy beaches and rugged wilderness are a short drive or ferry ride from the urban pleasures of Victoria and of Vancouver, from which popular ski hills are only minutes away. Inland, the interior's many lakes provide glistening vistas and sunny playgrounds for water sports of all kinds. Nestled among the BC Rocky Mountains are historic mining towns, and provincial and national parks offering exciting winter skiing and summer hiking experiences. In the north, the Skeena River, the "river of mists," travels through ancient tribal lands, sprinkled with stunning First Nations totem poles. Prince Rupert is the port of call for the ferry to the remote, misty archipelago of Haida Gwaii, formerly known as the Queen Charlotte Islands.

The harbor in Masset on Graham Island, British Columbia

◀ Grizzly bear by the edge of a river near Prince Rupert, British Columbia

Exploring British Columbia

The exceptional beauty of British Columbia's coast, mountain ranges, forests, and lakes makes it a much-visited province. A wide variety of landscapes are to be found, from the northern Rockies with their bare peaks to the southern Okanagan Valley with its orchards and vineyards. To the west, Vancouver Island offers ancient rainforests and the impressive coastal scenery of the Pacific Rim National Park. Lying between the Pacific Ocean and the Coast Mountains, Vancouver is a stunningly attractive city, with good transportation links. The province's temperate climate means that BC has more species of plants and animals than anywhere else in the country. Millions of visitors come here every year, drawn by a range of outdoor activities.

Atlin
Simpson Peak 2173 m
Atlin Lake
Good Hope Lake
37
Meszah Peak 2164 m
Dease La
Glenora
Mount Ratz 3136 m
Mount Edziza 2787 m
Skeena Mou
Coast Mountains
Stikine
Mez Junc

CRUISE TO ALASKA
HAZELT
SMIT
㉚
㉘
Masset
Graham Island
PRINCE RUPERT
HAIDA GWAII
Skidegate
㉙
Moresby Island
Princes Royal Island
Bella Be
Queen Charlotte Sound
Port F

0 km 100
0 miles 100

Fountain at Butchart Gardens, Vancouver Island, British Columbia

For hotels and restaurants see pp290–91 and pp304–5

Key

- — Highway
- — Major road
- — Minor road
- — Main railroad
- — Minor railroad
- ▬ International border
- ▬ Provincial border
- ▲ Summit

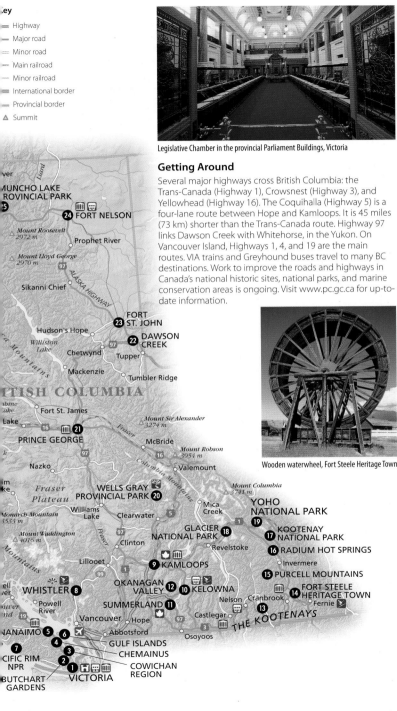

Legislative Chamber in the provincial Parliament Buildings, Victoria

Getting Around

Several major highways cross British Columbia: the Trans-Canada (Highway 1), Crowsnest (Highway 3), and Yellowhead (Highway 16). The Coquihalla (Highway 5) is a four-lane route between Hope and Kamloops. It is 45 miles (73 km) shorter than the Trans-Canada route. Highway 97 links Dawson Creek with Whitehorse, in the Yukon. On Vancouver Island, Highways 1, 4, and 19 are the main routes. VIA trains and Greyhound buses travel to many BC destinations. Work to improve the roads and highways in Canada's national historic sites, national parks, and marine conservation areas is ongoing. Visit www.pc.gc.ca for up-to-date information.

Wooden waterwheel, Fort Steele Heritage Town

MUNCHO LAKE PROVINCIAL PARK

24 FORT NELSON

Mount Roosevelt 2972 m
Prophet River

Mount Lloyd George 2970 m
97

ALASKA HIGHWAY

Sikanni Chief

23 FORT ST. JOHN

Hudson's Hope

Williston Lake
97
22 DAWSON CREEK

Chetwynd
Tupper

Mackenzie
Tumbler Ridge

BRITISH COLUMBIA

Fort St. James

Mount Sir Alexander 3274 m

16 21 PRINCE GEORGE

McBride

97
Nazko

Mount Robson 3954 m
16
Valemount

Fraser Plateau

WELLS GRAY PROVINCIAL PARK 20

Monarch Mountain 3533 m
Williams Lake
Clearwater

Mount Waddington 4016 m
97
Clinton

Mica Creek

Mount Columbia 3741 m

YOHO NATIONAL PARK
19

Lillooet

GLACIER NATIONAL PARK 18
Revelstoke

KOOTENAY NATIONAL PARK 17

16 RADIUM HOT SPRINGS

9 KAMLOOPS
Invermere

WHISTLER 8

15 PURCELL MOUNTAINS

Powell River

OKANAGAN VALLEY 12
10 KELOWNA
Nelson
Cranbrook
14 FORT STEELE HERITAGE TOWN
Fernie

NANAIMO 5
6
SUMMERLAND 11

Vancouver
Hope
Abbotsford
Castlegar
13
THE KOOTENAYS

7
4
3
GULF ISLANDS
97
Osoyoos

PACIFIC RIM NPR
2
CHEMAINUS

BUTCHART GARDENS
1
VICTORIA
COWICHAN REGION

❶ Victoria

A quiet city, Victoria has an old-fashioned atmosphere, one enhanced by the hanging flower baskets that decorate the streets. Established as a Hudson's Bay Company fur-trading post in 1843 by James Douglas, Victoria had its risqué moments during its Gold Rush years (1858–64), when thousands of prospectors drank in its saloons. Established as the capital of British Columbia in 1871, Victoria was soon outgrown by Vancouver. Today, this multicultural city is still BC's political center, as well as a popular attraction for visitors.

Historic buildings along Yates Street, typical of Victoria's Old Town

Parliament buildings illuminate the waters of the Inner Harbour

Exploring Victoria

Many of Victoria's attractions are downtown and in Old Town, which is bordered by Wharf, Humboldt, Douglas, and Fisgard Streets. Plaques on historic buildings, now housing funky shops and cafés, offer insight into this area that was, in the 1800s, Victoria's commercial center. Downtown stretches from Inner Harbour to Quadra, Belleville, and Herald Streets. Historic Fort Street is home to Fabulous Fort Street, lined with eateries, shops, and antique stores. The visitors' center provides details on walking tours, including ghostly walks and historical tours.

🌿 Inner Harbour
Foot of Government St.
Home to the Songhees, of the Coast Salish Nation, between 1850 and 1911, the Inner Harbour today is vibrant with boats, pedestrians strolling along the promenade, and street performers. Plaques along the walkway pay tribute to those who shaped the harbor's history. The promenade offers excellent views not only of the harbor but also of the Parliament Buildings and Empress Hotel, particularly in the reflecting sunlight of late afternoon.

Victoria's busy Inner Harbour at the foot of Government Street

For hotels and restaurants see pp290–91 and pp304–5

Sights at a Glance

Victoria Airport 25 km (15 miles)

FISGARD STREET
CENTENNIAL SQUARE
CORMORANT STREET
City Hall
PANDORA AVENUE
JOHNSON STREET
STREET
YATES STREET
VIEW STREET
⑦ St. Andrew's Cathedral
FORT STREET
Craigdarroch Castle
BROUGHTON STREET
Art Gallery of Greater Victoria, Government House
COURTNEY STREET
Victoria Bug Zoo
BURDETT AVE
NTOWN
FAIRFIELD ROAD
HUMBOLDT STREET
⑩ Helmcken House
ACADEMY CLOSE
SOUTHGATE STREET
al BC eum
⑮ Beacon Hill Park
DOUGLAS STREET
MES BAY

🏛 Bastion Square

Government St. **Open** daily. ♿

This beautifully restored square faces Victoria's picturesque harbor and contains some of the city's oldest 19th-century buildings. What were once luxury hotels and offices, built during the boom era of the late 1800s, now house boutiques and gift shops. Restoration began in 1963, when it was discovered that the Hudson's Bay Company's fur-trading post Fort Victoria (est.1843) once stood on this site. Today, this pedestrian square includes the 1863 MacDonald Block building, built in Italianate style, with elegant cast-iron columns and arched windows. In summer, the square bustles with visitors and workers alike, who come to lunch in one of the several courtyard cafés. From

Bustling Bastion Square, dating back to the late 1880s

May to September, the vibrant open-air Bastion Square Public Market (Thu–Sat) features local produce, handmade arts and crafts, and live entertainment.

Decorative banners lining Market Square, Victoria

🏛 Market Square

560 Johnson St. **Tel** (250) 386-2441.
Open 10am–5pm daily.
Closed Dec 25. ♿ partial.

Located two blocks north of Bastion Square on the corner of Johnson Street, Market Square boasts some of the finest Victorian saloon, hotel, and store façades in the city. Most of the buildings here date from the 1880s and 1890s, the boom period of the Klondike Gold Rush *(see p129)*. After decades of neglect, the area received a much-needed face-lift in 1975. Today, the square is a shoppers' paradise, with a variety of stores selling everything from books and jewelry to musical instruments and other arts and crafts. Concerts, festivals, and other events are held here throughout the year.

Chinatown

Bounded by Pandora Ave & Store, Government & Herald Sts.

Victoria's Chinatown, the oldest in Canada and once its largest, is now the country's smallest, yet its vegetable markets, curio shops, and restaurants provide hours' worth of exploration. The ornate **Gate of Harmonious Interest** (Fisgard and Government Streets) leads into the two-block-square area that was at one time home to Chinese railroad laborers and their families (see p215).

Fan Tan Alley, possibly the world's narrowest street, was once filled with opium dens and gambling houses. Today, visitors will find an eclectic mix of shops here. From the alley, enter though the backdoor of **Chinatown Trading Co**. (551 Fisgard Street) to see artifacts from the district's earlier days, including those from a 19th-century gambling house.

The sunken knot garden behind City Hall at Centennial Square

Centennial Square

Bounded by Fisgard, Douglas & Government Sts & Pandora Ave.

Created in 1963, Centennial Square is part of an effort to revitalize the city's downtown. Its centerpiece is a fountain with concrete "totems" adorned with mosaics by a local artist. Surrounding the public space are specialty shops, McPherson Playhouse – which opened in 1914 as the first Pantages Theatre and which has a beautiful Baroque interior – a knot garden, and City Hall.

The Second Empire-style south wing of City Hall – its red-brick façade and tin

The Second Empire-style City Hall, with its clock tower

mansard roof exemplifying this style – was built in 1878. In 1880, a fire station was added, and, in 1891, a northeast wing. The clock, installed in the tower in 1891, is still wound once a week. In 1963, the interior of City Hall was completely renovated and an International-style west wing was added.

The Bay Centre

1150 Douglas St. **Tel** (250) 952-5690. **Open** 10am–6pm Mon–Wed & Sat, 10am–9pm Thu & Fri, 11am–6pm Sun. **thebaycentre.ca**

The Bay Centre sits behind the façades of several historic buildings on Government Street. The 1892 Driard Hotel was saved from demolition by a public campaign, as were the fronts of the 1910 Times Building and the 19th-century Lettice and Sears Building. Behind these and other elegant façades, more than 90 shops on four floors sell everything from fashion to handmade chocolates. In the atrium hangs a clock, its several faces displaying the time in various ports of the former British Empire.

St. Andrew's Cathedral

740 View St. **Tel** (250) 388-5571. **Open** daily. 8am Tue–Fri, 12:10pm Mon–Fri; 5pm Sat; 8am, 9:30am, 11am & 5pm Sun. **standrewscathedral.com**

Built in 1892, this is the oldest Roman Catholic church in the area. The Victorian Gothic-style cathedral made of stone, slate, and brick features a 175-ft- (53-m-) tall spire and stained-glass windows. Works of local First Nations artists were introduced in the 1980s. The altar was designed by Charles Elliott, of the Coast Salish Nation; the candles on either side of the pulpit are decorated with First Nations designs.

St. Andrew's Cathedral, Victoria's oldest Roman Catholic church

Victoria Bug Zoo

631 Courtney St. **Tel** (250) 384-2847. **Open** 11am–5pm daily. **Closed** Jan 1, Dec 25. **victoriabugzoo.ca**

Located one block north of the iconic Fairmont Empress Hotel, this unusual mini-zoo occupies

The central atrium in Victoria's Bay Centre, with its suspended clock

only two rooms. Here, visitors can get up close and personal with some of the world's most exotic insects. The Victoria Bug Zoo exhibits more than 50 species of insects, arachnids, and myriapoda; it also boasts the largest ant farm in Canada, comprising a colony of leaf-cutter ants. Visitors can wander around the zoo independently or join a free tour during which the knowledgeable guides share a series of fascinating facts on their charges. It is also possible to hold one of the zoo's friendly tarantulas, a surefire way to get over a fear of spiders. Also on display are some glow-in-the-dark scorpions. The small gift shop stocks insect-collecting kits, edible bug snacks, and T-shirts.

The entranceway to the grand Fairmont Empress Hotel

🏨 Fairmont Empress Hotel

721 Government St. **Tel** (250) 384-8111. **Open** daily. ♿ See Where to Stay *p291*. 🌐 fairmont.com

Completed in 1908 to a Francis Rattenbury design and built on what were once mudflats and the site of the city's unofficial dump, the Empress is one of Victoria's best-loved sights. Overlooking the Inner Harbour, the hotel dominates the city sky-line with its ivy-clad Gothic splendor. You do not have to be a guest to experience the luxurious decor of the hotel's public bars and lounges, such as the Crystal Ballroom, with its Tiffany-glass dome. Afternoon tea, a popular Empress tradition, is served daily. In front of the hotel stands a statue of Captain James Cook *(see p40)*, who, though he explored much of BC's coast, never saw Victoria, ironically.

🏠 Helmcken House

10 Elliot Sq. **Tel** (250) 356-7226. **Open** May–Oct: noon–4pm daily; Nov–Apr: call for hours. 🚻 ♿ 📷 📞 🌐 royalbcmuseum.bc.ca/exhibits/tbird-park/html/early/earlhelm.htm

The home of Hudson's Bay Company employee Dr. John Sebastian Helmcken was built in 1852 and is one of the oldest surviving houses in British Columbia. The young doctor, who later helped negotiate BC's entry into the Dominion of Canada, built the house with his wife using Douglas firs felled in the surrounding forest. Built using the post-on-sill method popular in French Canada, it was one of the first residences outside the secure boundaries of Fort Victoria. A second section was added to the house in 1856, and a third in 1884. Together, the additions reflect the change in construction methods in the second half of the 19th century.

Woodburning stove at the historic Helmcken House

Sign for Helmcken House

The simple but elegant dwelling contains many of the original furnishings, including the piano, which visitors are permitted to play. Other highlights include Dr. Helmcken's medical kit and equipment.

From Fort to Capital

James Douglas fell in love with Camosack, the area known to many now as Victoria, when he sailed into its harbor in 1842. As chief factor of the Hudson's Bay Company (HBC), he was there to establish a fur-trading post and fort, in part an effort to thwart American expansion into the region. Douglas was welcomed by the Lekwammen, ancestors of the Esquimalt and Songhee Nations. In 1843, Fort Camosack (later Fort Victoria) was established. By the end of the decade, the First Nations of the area had signed treaties, selling much of their land to the HBC. Small farms quickly sprung up, and the harbor was soon a busy port and a stopping-off point for prospectors in the 1858 Gold Rush. Victoria incorporated in 1862, four years later becoming capital of the Colony of British Columbia, and the provincial capital once BC entered Confederation in 1871.

View of the growing community of Victoria, 1860

🏛 Thunderbird Park
Belleville & Douglas Sts.

This compact park, at the entrance to the Royal BC Museum *(see pp256–7)*, is home to an imposing collection of plain and painted giant totem poles. During the summer, First Nations artists carved these handsome totems in the Thunderbird Park Carving Studio. The poles show and preserve the legends of many different First Nations of the Northwest Coast. Also in the park, the Kwakwaka'wakw big house, built in 1952, is a replica of a 19th-century big house in Fort Rupert.

Giant totem poles, a signature feature of Thunderbird Park

🏛 Parliament Buildings
501 Belleville St. Tel (250) 387-3046.
Open 9am–5pm daily.
Closed Jan 1, Dec 25. 🦽 🛇

Facing the Inner Harbour, Victoria's many-domed Parliament Buildings are an impressive sight, particularly at night when the façades are illuminated by thousands of lights. This has been a tradition

The spectacular main dome of the Parliament Buildings

since 1956, though the buildings were first lit up as early as 1887, in celebration of Queen Victoria's diamond jubilee.

Designed by Francis Rattenbury in 1892, the buildings were completed in 1897, replacing the "Bird Cages," BC's first parliament buildings. (The carriage house on Superior Street behind the Parliament Buildings is the only remaining Bird Cage structure.) Rattenbury, a 25-year-old British architect who had arrived in British Columbia only the year before, won a national competition to design the buildings. He went on to design several of the province's landmarks, the Empress Hotel and Crystal Garden included.

The stone-and-marble buildings are home to the Provincial Legislature. The Legislative Chamber, where the assembly sits, is upstairs, off a small gallery that boasts lovely stained-glass windows by William Morris. Visitors can view assembly sessions from the third-floor public galleries. A magnificent dome caps the nearby Lower

and Upper Rotundas; the former, a perfect octagon, has a beautiful Italian mosaic floor.

British Columbia's history is depicted throughout the buildings. A statue of explorer Captain George Vancouver perches on top of the main dome. Inside, large murals painted during the Great Depression show scenes from BC history.

Emily Carr House, where the renowned artist lived as a child

🏛 Emily Carr House
207 Government St. **Tel** (250) 383-5843. **Open** May–Sep: 11am–4pm Tue–Sat. 🛇 🦽 🛇 🛇
🌐 **emilycarr.com**

Emily Carr, one of Canada's best-known artists *(see p215)*, was born in 1871 in this attractive 1864 clapboard house.

Rooms are furnished in late 19th-century period style, with some original family pieces. Carr taught her first art classes to local children in the dining room, while the sitting room was where she did her first sketches as an eight-year-old. Carr's drawing of her father is still on display. Reproductions of Emily Carr's artwork hang in the Morning Room; the People's Gallery exhibits works of contemporary Canadian artists. The English garden showcases plants popular during the Victorian era.

🌳 Beacon Hill Park
Douglas St & Dallas Rd. **Tel** (250) 361-0600. **Open** daily. 🦽
🌐 **beaconhillpark.ca**

In the late 19th century, this delightful park was being used for stabling horses. In 1888, John Blair, a Scottish landscape gardener, redesigned the park to include two lakes and initiated extensive tree

The Legislative Chamber at Victoria's Parliament Buildings

For hotels and restaurants see pp290–91 and pp304–5

A stately, centuries-old Garry oak tree in Beacon Hill Park

planting. Once a favorite haunt of artist Emily Carr *(see p215)*, this peaceful park, the oldest and largest in Victoria, is now renowned for its lofty old trees (including the rare Garry oaks); stretches of wild camas lilies, once highly valued by the area's First Nations; picturesque duck ponds; children's petting zoo; and a cricket pitch.

🏛 Art Gallery of Greater Victoria

1040 Moss St. **Tel** (250) 384-4171. **Open** 10am–5pm Mon–Sat (to 9pm Thu), noon–5pm Sun & most hols. **Closed** Sep 14–May 16: Mon, Thanksgiving, Dec 25. 🛒 ♿ 📷 **W** aggv.ca

This gallery's eclectic collection, the largest in BC, is housed in an impressive Victorian mansion east of the downtown area. Inside, fine wood moldings, original fireplaces, and tall ceilings provide a stately home for an array of exhibits, including a wide-ranging collection of Chinese and Japanese painting, ceramics, and pottery. The gallery also has the only authentic Shinto shrine in North America.

The collection of contemporary Canadian paintings includes those of famous local artist Emily Carr *(see p215)*. Executed between the 1900s and 1930s, Carr's paintings, with their haunting evocation of the stormy Northwest and the lives of First Nations peoples, are among the gallery's most popular exhibits. Carr's works, which include her writings, are

rotated so that all pieces in the extensive collection can eventually be viewed.

🏰 Craigdarroch Castle

1050 Joan Cres. **Tel** (250) 592-5323. **Open** mid-Jun–Sep: 9am–7pm daily; Oct–mid-Jun: 10am–4:30pm daily. **Closed** major hols. 🛒 📷 **W** thecastle.ca

Completed in 1890, Craigdarroch Castle was the pet project of respected coal miner and railroad baron Robert Dunsmuir, who built it to reflect his status as the wealthiest man in British Columbia. Although not a medieval, fortified castle, the design of this large house was inspired by stately homes in Scotland and mixes several architectural styles, including Gothic, Scottish Baronial, and Romanesque Revival.

When the castle was threatened with demolition in 1959, a group of local citizens successfully battled for its restoration. Today, the interior is a museum that offers an insight into the lifestyle of a wealthy entrepreneur.

The castle is noted for having one of the finest collections of Art Nouveau lead-glass windows in North America, and many of the rooms and hallways retain their patterned wood parquet floors and carved paneling in white oak, cedar, and mahogany. Every room is filled with opulent Victorian furnishings from the late 19th century and decorated in deep greens, pinks, and rusts. Several layers of the paint have been carefully removed from the drawing room ceiling to reveal the original stenciled and hand-painted decorations beneath.

A tower at Craigdarroch Castle in the French Gothic style

🏛 Government House

1401 Rockland Ave. **Tel** (250) 387-2080. **Open** daily (gardens only). Cary Castle Mews: May–Sep: Tue–Sat (check website for times). ♿ **W** ltgov.bc.ca

The present Government House building was completed in 1959 after fire destroyed the 1903 structure, designed by Francis Rattenbury and Samuel Maclure. The official residence of BC's lieutenant-governor, the house is normally closed to the public, but visitors can view the stunning public gardens with lawns, ponds, an English country garden, and a Victorian rose garden. Some 19th-century wooden buildings on the southeast side of the estate that form a part of the Cary Castle Mews are also open, including the Costume Museum, Interpretive Centre, and Tea House. Marvelous views of the grounds can be enjoyed from Pearke's Peak, a mount formed from the rocky outcrops that surround the property and which contain rock gardens.

Government House, restored in 1959 with blue and pink granite

The Royal BC Museum

The Royal BC Museum tells the story of British Columbia through its natural history, geology, and peoples. The museum is regarded as one of the best in Canada for the striking way it presents its exhibits. The Natural History Gallery on the second floor contains a series of imaginative dioramas re-creating the sights, sounds, and even smells of areas such as the Pacific seashore, the ocean, and the rainforest. An in-depth look at the region's history, including a reconstruction of an early 20th-century town, is presented on the third floor. Visitors can experience the streetlife of the time in a hotel and in a cinema showing silent films. The superb collection of First Nations art and cultural objects includes a ceremonial Big House.

Third Floor

19th-Century Chinatown
As part of an 1890 street scene, this Chinese herbalist's store displays a variety of herbs used in traditional Chinese medicine.

★ First Peoples Gallery
Made from spruce root in the late 19th century, the artwork on this Haida hat represents the raven.

First Nations Masks
These Kwakwaka'wakw masks are part of the ceremonial regalia of Chief Mungo Martin. They represent a mouse, a raccoon, a kingfisher, and a wren.

Key to Floorplan

- First Peoples Gallery
- Becoming BC
- Natural History Gallery
- Newcombe Conference Hall
- IMAX theatre
- Temorary exhibitions
- Non-exhibition space

Exterior of the Museum
The museum's complex opened in 1968. Previously the collections were displayed at several locations in the surrounding buildings. The grounds also house the BC archives.

For hotels and restaurants see pp290–91 and pp304–5

Becoming BC

A variety of streets, stores, and public buildings are re-created in this gallery. Here, the Grand Hotel stands on an early wood-cobbled street.

Second Floor

★ Natural History Gallery

A full-size woolly mammoth and dramatic glacial ice wall are exhibited in lifelike dioramas. Other exhibits re-create coastal forests since the last ice age, and predict future climate change scenarios.

★ Coast Seashore Diorama

This diorama features sound, lighting, live sea creatures in tidal pools, and taxidermy animals such as this northern sea lion.

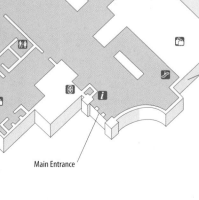

First Floor

Museum Guide

The main exhibits of the museum are housed on the second and third floors. The Natural History Gallery, on the second floor, reconstructs a range of environments in displays including a coastal rainforest to a river delta. The third floor has the First Peoples and Becoming BC galleries.

Main Entrance

❷ Butchart Gardens

800 Benvenuto Ave, Brentwood Bay, Vancouver Island. **Tel** (250) 652-4422. **Open** 9am daily; closing hrs vary by season. 🐾 ♿ 💷 📷 🎁 🛍
W butchartgardens.com

These beautiful botanical gardens were established in 1904 by Jennie Butchart, in the excavated quarry left behind by her husband's cement company. The site, home to thousands of rare plants, is arranged into distinct areas, including a formal Italian garden, a Japanese garden, and a lovely rose garden. There are also fountains, ponds, bronze statues, a boat tour, and a carousel. In summer, the gardens are illuminated and play host to a variety of musical entertainments in the evening. Fireworks displays are held on Saturday nights in July and August.

❸ Cowichan Region

Vancouver Island. 🛈 2896 Drinkwater Rd, Duncan, (250) 746-4636. 🚢 Sat.
W tourismcowichan.com

Cowichan region, on the south-central coast of Vancouver Island, consists of the Chemainus and Cowichan Valleys. Cowichan means "warm land" in the dialect of the Cowichan people. The main freshwater lake on the island, Lake Cowichan offers great opportunities for hiking, swimming, canoeing, cycling, whale-watching, and fishing.

Duncan, "City of Totems," has around 38 magnificent totem poles throughout the city. The **Duncan Farmer's Market**, held in Market Square every Saturday until 2pm, sells local fruits and vegetables, and a variety of homemade goods.

On the northern outskirts of the city lies the **BC Forest Discovery Centre**, with a replica logging camp and steam train rides. Nearby, the **Quw'utsun' Cultural and Conference Centre** shares the heritage of the Cowichan tribes through tours and events.

A short drive from Duncan is the **Raptors Birds of Prey Centre**, where visitors can learn about a variety of birds such as hawks, owls, falcons, and eagles.

🏛 **BC Forest Discovery Centre**
2892 Drinkwater Rd, Duncan. **Tel** (250) 715-1113. **Open** Apr & May: 10am–4pm Thu–Mon; Jun–Aug: 10am–4:30pm daily; Sep–mid-Oct: 10am–4pm daily. **Closed** mid-Oct–Mar. 🐾 ♿ 💷 🎁
W bcforestdiscoverycentre.com

🏛 **Quw'utsun' Cultural and Conference Centre**
200 Cowichan Way, Duncan. **Tel** (250) 746-8119. **Open** Jun–mid-Sep: 10am–4:30pm; mid-Sep–May: for groups of 25 only when pre-booked. ♿ 💷 🎁
W khowutzun.com/qcccc

❶ Pacific Rim National Park Reserve of Canada

Three distinct areas make up this reserve: Long Beach, the West Coast Trail, and the Broken Group Islands. Together they occupy an 80-mile (130-km) strip of Vancouver Island's west coast. The park is a world-famous area for whale-watching. Long Beach offers a range of hiking trails. The most challenging hike is the 46-mile (75-km) West Coast Trail, accessible from May to September. The Broken Group Islands can be reached by boat only.

The Broken Group Islands
This archipelago of some 100 islands and islets is popular with kayakers and scuba divers.

Schooner Trail is one of nine scenic and easy-to-follow trails through the coastal temperate rainforest.

The Wickaninnish Centre has viewing platforms for whale-watching.

Long Beach
The rugged, windswept sands of Long Beach are renowned for their wild beauty, with crashing Pacific rollers, unbeatable surfing opportunities, rock pools filled with marine life, and scattered driftwood.

Raptors Birds of Prey Centre

1877 Herd Rd, Duncan.
Tel (250) 746-0372. **Open** daily.
W the-raptors.com

Chemainus

Vancouver Island. 🚹 4,000.
ℹ 9796 Willow St, (250) 246-3944.
W chemainus.bc.ca

When the local sawmill closed in 1983, the picturesque town of Chemainus transformed itself into a major attraction with the painting of giant murals that depict the history of the region. Local and international artists continued the project and, today, over 40 murals appear on specially built panels throughout the town, depicting events in the region's past.

The Chemainus Theatre Festival, another main attraction in the town, stages world classics, musicals, and plays year-round.

Pleasure craft and fishing boats moored in Nanaimo Harbour

➎ Nanaimo

Road map 2 E4. 🚹 86,000.
ℹ 2450 Northfield Rd, (250) 751-1556. **W** tourismnanaimo.com

Originally the site of five Coast Salish villages, Nanaimo was established as a coal-mining town in the 1850s. Its Old City Quarter contains many 19th-century buildings, including the Nanaimo Court House (31 Front Street), designed in 1895 by Francis Rattenbury. Learn about the city's history at the **Nanaimo Museum**. One of the highlights is the replica coal mine, which gives visitors a chance to experience what it was like to work underground. Also part of the museum is the bastion located on the waterfront, North America's only freestanding Hudson Bay Bastion. This wooden structure, built in 1853, is the town's most recognizable landmark. When open, canon firings take place here at noon.

The opportunity to snorkel with sea lions also attracts visitors to Nanaimo throughout the year.

🏛 Nanaimo Museum

100 Museum Way. **Tel** (250) 753-1821. **Open** Victoria Day–Labor Day: 10am–5pm daily; Labor Day–Victoria Day: 10am–5pm Mon–Sat. Bastion: Pioneer Waterfront Plaza, 95 Front St. **Open** Victoria Day–Labor Day: daily. 📷 (donation for the bastion). ♿ 🎁 📷 by appt. **W** nanaimomuseum.ca

➏ Gulf Islands

Strait of Georgia. ℹ (250) 754-3500.
W gulfislandstourism.com

Their tranquility and natural beauty draw visitors to the Gulf Islands, where sightings of eagles and turkey vultures are common. Fishing charters and kayak tours provide views of otters, seals, and marine birds. The largest and most populated island, with about 10,000 residents, is **Saltspring**. In summer, visitors stroll around pretty Ganges Village. **Galiano** has many hiking trails; **Mayne**'s tiny century-old museum recounts this island's history as a stopping-off point for Gold Rush miners and rum-runners. **North** and **South Pender Islands** are linked by a wooden bridge. Relics of a 5,000-year-old First Nations settlement have been found here. **Saturna**, the smallest and most remote of the islands, hosts a lamb barbecue each Canada Day (see p35). Visitors to **Gabriola** can view Snuneymuxw First Nations petroglyphs.

West Coast Trail

Stunning scenery, including moss-draped rainforest, sea stacks, and sea arches, is typical of this trail.

VISITORS' CHECKLIST

Practical Information
Hwy 4. **Tel** (888) 773-8888.
Open daily. ♿ limited. 📷 Jun–Sep **W** pc.gc.ca/eng/pn-np/bc/pacificrim/index.aspx

Key

━━ Major road

━━ Minor road

╌ ╌ West Coast Trail

━━ National park boundary

━━ River

At the Nitinat Narrows, a short ferry ride transports hikers on the West Coast Trail across this pretty waterway.

kilometers 10

miles 10

Port Renfrew

For keys to symbols see back flap

❽ Whistler

Mild Pacific weather, reliable snow, and the greatest vertical rises of any ski resorts in North America make Whistler one of the most popular winter sports destinations in the world. Visitors flock to the two side-by-side mountains of Whistler and Blackcomb, linked by the Peak 2 Peak Gondola, where activities include dogsledding, snowshoeing, and snow-mobiling. In summer, hiking, mountain biking, canoeing, and horseback riding take place around the lakes and at nearby wilderness locations such as Garibaldi Provincial Park. Whistler also has four championship golf courses and is considered one of the top golf destinations in Canada. In 2010, Whistler co-hosted the Winter Olympic games with Vancouver.

One of a range of restaurant patios in Whistler Village

| 0 meters | 800 |
| 0 yards | 1000 |

Blackcomb Mountain

① Villa

The Rendezvous on Blackcomb Mountain
Snowboarders and skiers relax, refuel, and enjoy spectacular views at the Rendezvous restaurant and day lodge atop Blackcomb Mountain.

KEY

① **Blackcomb Mountain** is 7,494-ft-(2,284-m-) high and has more than 100 marked trails and seven alpine bowls, two of which are glaciers. Its longest run covers a 7-mile (11-km) stretch.

② **Whistler Mountain** is 7,160-ft-(2,182-m-) high and has more than 100 trails, and nine alpine bowls, one of which is a glacier. Its skiable terrain covers 7.4 sq miles (19 sq km).

★ **Fairmont Chateau Whistler**
The Fairmont Chateau Whistler *(see p291)* is as much a tourist attraction as it is a hotel, with its art-filled lobby, luxurious tapestries and chandeliers, and rooftop garden terrace.

Mountain biker in Whistler Bike Park

VISITORS' CHECKLIST

Practical Information
Road Map 2 B4. 🚠 10,000.
🛈 Tourism Whistler, 4230
Gateway Drive, Whistler, (604)
935-3357 or (888) 869-2777
(in Canada & US). 🎫 🎫 💻 📷
w whistler.com

Transport
🚌 🚆

Overlord Glacier

②

Whistler Mountain

Alta Lake

★ **Alta Lake**
Visitors come to this
1-mile- (1.6-km-) long
lake – surrounded by
forested mountains and
80 ft (24.5 m) at its
deepest point – to swim,
kayak, sailboard, and fish
for rainbow and Dolly
Varden trout. A hiking trail
encircles the lake.

★ **Whistler Village**
A tranquil pond proves a restful spot
amid the bustle of Whistler Village,
where hotels, restaurants, bars,
and shops line the cobblestoned,
pedestrianized streets.

For keys to symbols *see back flap*

⑨ Kamloops

Road map 2 B4. 👥 87,000. ℹ️ 1290
W Trans-Canada Hwy, (250) 372-8000.
🌐 tourismkamloops.com

Kamloops – which means
"where the rivers meet" in the
language of the Secwepemc,
or Shuswap, people – is situated
at the confluence of the North
and South Thompson Rivers.
Nestled amid mountains and
lakes, the city offers hiking,
biking, skiing, and golfing.

European settlement began
here in 1812, with fur traders
doing business with the Secwepemc. Remains of a 2,000-
year-old village and re-created
pit houses at the **Secwepemc
Museum and Heritage Park**
reflect the tribe's history.

US train robber Bill Miner
arrived in Kamloops in 1904,
on the run after committing
a robbery. Kamloops and
trains have been linked
ever since. It's possible
to take a trip along the
Kamloops Heritage
Railway, on the 1912
Steam Locomotive
No. 2141, one of the few
remaining steam engines,
when operational. If not,
a train ride can also
be taken at **British
Columbia Wildlife Park**,
home to threatened animals.

Okanagan Valley wine

🏛️ Secwepemc Museum and Heritage Park
200–355 Yellowhead Hwy. **Tel** (250)
828-9749. **Open** 8am–4pm daily.
Closed Sep–May: Sat & Sun. 🎫 🍴
♿ 📷 🌐 secwepemcmuseum.com

▨ British Columbia Wildlife Park
Hwy 1, 10.5 miles (17 km) E of
Kamloops. **Tel** (250) 573-3242.
Open 9:30am–5pm daily (to 9pm
Jul & Aug; to 4pm Nov–Apr). 🎫 ♿
📷 🖥️ 🌐 bczoo.org

Mission Hill Family Estate Winery in West Kelowna

⑩ Kelowna

Road map 2 B4. 👥 120,000.
ℹ️ 544 Harvey Ave, (250) 861-1515.
🌐 tourismkelowna.com

Kelowna lies on the eastern
shore of 84-mile- (135-km-)
long Okanagan Lake. The
Okanagan Valley's warm,
dry climate has long attracted
fruit growers, including
Father Charles Pandosy,
a French lay priest who
arrived in 1859. Pandosy
planted the area's
first fruit trees at the
Immaculate Conception
Mission, the first non-
Native settlement in the
region. Today, the
**Father Pandosy
Mission** is a heritage
site. Kelowna's peaches, apples,
and cherries are plentiful,
but its grapes make it the
center of the largest and oldest
wine-producing region in
the province. Many of the
Okanagan Valley's wineries
are within a 30-minute drive of
Kelowna. Wineries range from
intimate to expensive; tours
highlight grape-growing and
harvesting methods. Orchard
tours may include wagon rides
and visits to petting zoos.

Kelowna's lakefront parks
and sandy beaches add to
the enjoyment of fresh-fare
restaurants. Okanagan Lake,
and trails for hiking, biking,
and horseback riding,
offer recreational activities.
In winter, the powder snow
here makes **Big White Ski
Resort** (tel 250/765-3101)
a major draw for skiers.

🏛️ Father Pandosy Mission
3685 Benvoulin Rd. **Tel** (250) 860-836?
Open Grounds: dawn–dusk daily;
Buildings: Mar–Oct: 9am–5pm daily.
🎫 donation.

Ripe peaches from the orchards of
Summerland, Okanagan Valley

⑪ Summerland

Road map 2 B4. 👥 11,000.
ℹ️ 15600 Hwy 97, (250) 494-2686.
🌐 tourismsummerland.com

Summerland has been
synonymous with peaches sinc?
founder John Moore Robinson
arrived in 1902 and persuaded
farmers to turn to fruit growing.
Today, it is also home to some
world-renowned wineries.

The beautiful **Summerland
Ornamental Gardens** overlook?
Okanagan Lake and Trout Cree?
Canyon, with a viewpoint atop
Giant's Head Mountain.

Kettle Valley Railway, now a?
tourist attraction, operated her?
from 1915 to 1964. A 1924 Shay
steam engine pulls two 1950
coaches and two open-air cars
across the 240-ft- (73-m-) high
Trout Creek Bridge.

🌼 Summerland Ornamental Gardens
4200 Hwy 97 S. **Tel** (250) 494-6385.
Open 8am–sunset daily. 🎫 by
donation. ♿ 📷 🌐 **summerland
ornamentalgardens.org**

🚂 Kettle Valley Railway
18404 Bathville Rd. **Tel** (877) 494-
8424. **Open** mid-May–mid-Oct:
10:30am & 1:30pm (days vary). 🎫
♿ 📷 🌐 **kettlevalleyrail.org**

Vineyard in the Okanagan Valley sloping down to Okanagan Lake

For hotels and restaurants see pp290–91 and pp304–5

⑫ Okanagan Valley Tour

The Okanagan Valley is actually a series of valleys, linked by a string of lakes, that stretches for 155 miles (250 km) – from Osoyoos in the south to Sicamous in the north. The main towns here are connected by Highway 97, which passes through the desert landscape near Lake Osoyoos, and on to the lush green orchards and vineyards for which the valley is most noted. Mild winters and hot summers have made the Okanagan Valley one of Canada's favorite vacation destinations.

Tips for Drivers

Tour length: 110 miles (176 km).
Starting points: On Highway 97 from Vernon in the north, Osoyoos in the south.
When to go: Blossom and fruit festivals are held in spring and summer, when roadside stalls offer a cornucopia of fruit. Wine tours are available year-round.

④ Kelowna
The largest city in the Okanagan, Kelowna lies on the shores of Okanagan Lake between Penticton and Vernon, and is the center of the wine- and fruit-growing industries.

③ Summerland
This small but charming lakeside resort town boasts several 19th-century buildings and stunning views from the top of Giant's Head Mountain.

② Penticton
This sunny lakeside town is known for the long Okanagan Beach, windsurfing, and local winery tours, as well as for its Peach Festival, held every August.

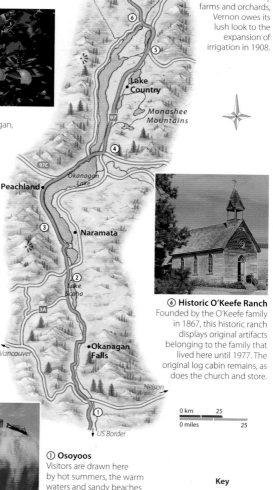

⑤ Vernon
Surrounded by farms and orchards, Vernon owes its lush look to the expansion of irrigation in 1908.

⑥ Historic O'Keefe Ranch
Founded by the O'Keefe family in 1867, this historic ranch displays original artifacts belonging to the family that lived here until 1977. The original log cabin remains, as does the church and store.

① Osoyoos
Visitors are drawn here by hot summers, the warm waters and sandy beaches of Lake Osoyoos, and the nearby pocket desert.

0 km   25
0 miles   25

Key

▬ Tour route
═ Other road

⑱ The Kootenays

The Kootenays, named for the local Ktunaxa (Kutenai) First Nations tribe, is one of British Columbia's prettiest regions. Alpine-style towns are tucked amid the Columbia and Rocky Mountains in this southeast corner of the province. The area's three districts – East Kootenay, Central Kootenay, and Kootenay-Boundary – are geographically isolated from major urban centers, resulting in a slow pace that has encouraged the development of a healthy community of artisans and writers. Snowcapped peaks and glacial lakes can be accessed within a series of parks, where the plentiful powdery snow makes for excellent skiing. Throughout the area, world-famous natural hot springs well up; they can be enjoyed at several resorts. Glacier-fed Kootenay Lake, 90 miles (145 km) long, is famed for its superb fishing opportunities.

Ainsworth Hot Springs
The temperature of these water which can be enjoyed in outdoo pools overlooking the mountair as well as in shallow natural poo in the nearby caves, average 95°F (35°C

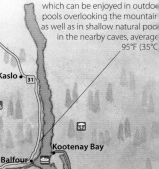

Kaslo 31

Kootenay Bay

Balfour 3A

Purce Mounta

Boswell

Kootenay Lake

3A

Salmo

6

3

Creston

Penticton

Castlegar
Located at the confluence of the Kootenay and Columbia Rivers, Castlegar features a reconstructed Doukhobor village.

★ Nelson
With its heritage buildings, and large community of artists, Nelson is a lovely town in which to stroll. It is also a good base for hiking, skiing, and other outdoor activities.

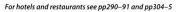

★ Fernie

This scenic town lies in one of the Kootenays' most popular areas for snow sports. In the 1880s, Fernie was reputedly cursed by an Indian chief when he was betrayed by its founder. In 1964, the curse was officially lifted by a peace-pipe-smoking ceremony.

VISITORS' CHECKLIST

Practical Information
Highway 3. **Road Map** 2 C4.
i 225 Hall St, Nelson, (250)
352-3433. *i* 2279 Cranbrook
St N, Cranbrook, (250) 426-5914.
i 102 Hwy 3, Fernie, (250)
423-6868. **Open** all three offices:
year-round: 9am–5pm Mon–Fri;
Victoria Day–Labor Day: 10am–
5pm Sat also.
W th.gov.bc.ca
W hellobc.com

Transport
⇲ Cranbrook & Castlegar. ⛴ BC
Ministry of Highways inland ferry
service Kootenay Bay-Balfour,
year-round, 6:30am–10:20pm
daily; 35 mins; (250) 229-4215.

mberley

● **Fort Steele**

Mount Fisher

Lake
cial
k

Moyie
Lake

The Kootenay Bay–Balfour ferry, offering magnificent views of surrounding mountains from its decks

★ Cranbrook
Panoramic views can be enjoyed just a short hike from this town, which lies between the Rocky and Purcell Mountains. This land, where the Ktunaxa once camped, has excellent cross-country ski and hiking trails.

For keys to symbols *see back flap*

:ey

≡ Major road

≡ Minor road

0 kilometers   25
0 miles   15

Exploring the Kootenays

Rushing rivers, deep lakes, and historic towns nestle among the sheer mountains of the Kootenays, a region at the southern end of the Canadian Rockies in the southeast corner of British Columbia. The Kootenays offer a wide range of outdoor activities, including heli-skiing, rock climbing, river rafting, and fly-fishing. Its horse ranches, ski lodges, and chartered houseboats offer visitors comfortable accommodation and opportunities for active and memorable vacations.

Nelson's pink-brick and marble City Hall, dating from 1902

Downhill skier on one of Fernie's spectacular ski runs

Fernie

Road map 2 C4. ⛰ 5,000. 🚌
ℹ 102 Hwy 3, (250) 423-6868.
🖥 tourismfernie.com

Fernie is an attractive, tree-lined town set amid the pointed peaks of Crowsnest Pass. The town owes its handsome appearance to a fire that razed it in 1908. All buildings constructed since are brick and stone. Among several historic buildings, the 1911 courthouse stands out as BC's only chateau-style courthouse.

Fernie boasts the best powder snow in the Rockies; the ski season runs from December to April. The Fernie Alpine Resort lifts can transport 12,300 skiers up the mountain every hour.

During the summer months, magnificent mountain scenery can be enjoyed from a variety of hiking and mountain biking trails in Mount Fernie Provincial Park. The Fernie Alpine Resort also offers scenic chairlift rides, a tree-top Aerial Park, zip lines, as well as lift accessed mountain biking. Guided fly-fishing and river rafting tours on the Elk River provide access to pristine wilderness.

Cranbrook

Road map 2 C4. ⛰ 19,000. ✈ 🚌
ℹ 2279 Cranbrook St N, (250) 426-5914. 🖥 cranbrookchamber.com

Cranbook, lying between the Purcell and Rocky Mountain ranges, is the largest town in southeast BC. A major transportation hub, it is within easy reach of spectacular scenery and boasts the highest density of grizzlies in the Rockies. These, along with the region's other wildlife, which includes elk, wolves, and cougars, may be spotted on the many trails in the area. Hikers should exercise caution (see pp312–13).

The Canadian Pacific Railway reached Cranbrook in 1898. The **Cranbrook History Centre** includes the magnificent Royal Alexandra Hall Café with its high decorative curved ceilings, and 17 restored luxury cars, including the 1929 Trans-Canada Limited.

🏛 **Cranbrook History Centre**
57 Van Horne St S. **Tel** (250) 489-3918.
Open mid-May–Aug: 10am–5pm daily; Sep–mid-May: 10am–5pm Tue–Sat. 🐾 ♿ partial. 📷 📸
🖥 trainsdeluxe.com

Nelson

Road map 2 C4. ⛰ 10,500. 🚌
ℹ 225 Hall St, (250) 352-3433.
🖥 discovernelson.com

One of the most attractive towns in southeastern British Columbia, Nelson overlooks Kootenay Lake. Established in the 1880s as a mining town, Nelson flourished with the arrival of the railroad in the 1890s, becoming a center for the transportation of ore and timber. Many of the town's public buildings and houses were constructed between 1895 and 1920. In 1979, a $3 million municipal renovatio program helped restore the historic façades of the downtown buildings.

The town has a thriving cultural scene, with bookstores, art galleries, cafés, and craft shops. Visitors can enjoy the short ride on Car 23, a 1906 streetcar that operated here from 1925 to 1949. Restored in 1992, it now travels along Nelson's delightful waterfront.

The opulent dining car on a restored train at the Cranbrook History Centre

Exploring Nelson

Nelson's downtown, though hilly, is easily walkable. Over 350 historic buildings, from elegant mansions to elaborate commercial structures, give the city its unique style. Many of these restored buildings are part of Nelson's historic downtown walking tour. The visitors' center provides maps and guides for the tour.

🏛 Bank of Montreal

298 Baker St. **Closed** bank & major hols. ♿

When it opened in 1900, after a year under construction, the Bank of Montreal was considered one of the finest commercial buildings in the BC Interior. Its Italian influences include rounded window arches and detailed brickwork.

🏛 Mara-Barnard Block

421–431 Baker St. ♿

This elaborate High Victorian building, with unusual bay windows on the second floor, housed the first branch of the Royal Bank of Canada to open in BC, in 1897.

🏛 K.W.C. Block

488–498 Baker St. ♿

Built by three merchants, Kirkpatrick, Wilson, and Clements, in 1901, the K.W.C. Block was the largest mercantile building in Nelson. The turret and window arches are noteworthy.

🏛 Houston Block

601–607 Baker St. ♿

Nelson's first mayor, John Houston, commissioned architect A. E. Hodgins to design the grand Houston Block, built in 1899, to house a bank.

🏛 Touchstones Nelson

502 Vernon St. **Tel** (250) 352-9813. **Open** 10am–5pm daily (to 8pm Thu, to 4pm Sun). 🎫 ♿

Spokane pink brick and Kaslo marble make for a picturesque mixture of textures and patterns on the 1902 Post Office and Customs House, now a museum of art and history.

🏛 Nelson Court House

320 Ward St. **Tel** (250) 354-6165. **Open** year-round: 8:30am–4:30pm Mon–Fri. **Closed** major hols. 🎫 ♿

F. M. Rattenbury, designer of Victoria's Parliament Buildings (see p254), designed this fine example of Beaux Arts chateau architecture. Dating from 1909, it features a high pitched roof, towers, conical caps, gables, and paired windows.

Castlegar

Road map 2 C4. 🏙 8,000. ✈ 🚌
ℹ️ 1995 6th Ave, (250) 365-6313.
🌐 castlegar.com

Located at the confluence of the Kootenay and Columbia Rivers, Castlegar is an angler's paradise. In the early 1900s, Doukhobors (Russian religious dissenters) fleeing persecution began arriving here. The **Doukhobor Discovery Centre** showcases the group's culture with displays of traditional clothes, and tools in a re-created village. Set in lovely grounds with river views and accessed via a 470-ft- (143-m-) long suspension bridge, **Zuckerberg Island Heritage Park** features a Lake Salish pit house and Russian Orthodox chapel.

Statue of Tolstoy, Doukhobor Village

🏛 Doukhobor Discovery Centre

112 Heritage Way. **Tel** (250) 365-5327.
Open May–Sep: 10am–5pm daily.
📷 ♿ 🌐 doukhobor-museum.org

🏛 Zuckerberg Island Heritage Park

901 7th Ave. **Tel** (250) 365-6440.
Open Park: year-round; Chapel: May–Sep, call for hours. 🅿️ by donation.
🎫 📷

Nelson City Center

① Bank of Montreal
② Mara-Barnard Block
③ K.W.C. Block
④ Houston Block
⑤ Touchstones Nelson
⑥ Nelson Court House

0 meters 200
0 yards 200

For keys to map symbols *see back flap*

19th-century barber's shop in Fort Steele Heritage Town

⓮ Fort Steele Heritage Town

Road map 2 C4. **Tel** (250) 426-7352.
Open May, Jun & Sep–mid-Oct:
9:30am–5pm daily; Jul & Aug:
9:30am–6pm daily; mid-Oct–Apr:
10am–4pm daily. 🅿 ♿ 🏪
W fortsteele.ca

Fort Steele is a re-creation of the mining supply town that was established at this site in 1864, when gold was discovered at Wild Horse Creek. Thousands of prospectors and entrepreneurs arrived by the Dewdney Trail, which linked the town of Hope to the gold fields. Originally called Galbraith's Ferry, the town was renamed

An historic dentist's sign in Fort Steele Heritage Town

after Samuel Steele, the North West Mounted Police superintendent who arrived in 1887 to restore peace between the warring Ktunaxa First Nations tribe and European settlers. The town enjoyed a brief boom with the discovery of lead and silver, but the mainline railroad was routed through Cranbrook instead, and by the early 1900s Fort Steele was a ghost town.

Today, there are more than 60 reconstructed or restored buildings, staffed by guides in period costume, including the general store, livery stable, and North West Mounted Police officers' quarters, where personal items such as family photographs, swords, and uniforms create the illusion of recent occupation. Demonstrations of traditional crafts such as ice-cream-making and quilting are also held here. "Living history" dramas and musical comedy shows staged in the Wild Horse Theater are inspired by the town's history, and tours at the nearby Wild Horse Creek Historic Site include a chance to pan for gold.

⓯ The Purcell Mountains

Road map 2 C4. 🄸 270 Kimberley Ave, Kimberley, (250) 427-0491.

The rugged and beautiful Purcell Mountains face the Rockies across the broad Columbia River Valley. The region is one of the most remote in the Rockies and attracts hikers and skiers from around the globe. A high range of granite spires, called the Bugaboos, also draws mountain climbers. In the north of the Purcell range, the Purcell Wilderness Conservancy – one of the range's few accessible areas – covers a vast 500,900 acres (202,709 ha).

From the nearby town of Invermere, it is possible to access the Earl Grey Pass Trail, which extends 35 miles (56 km).

The Purcell Mountains, noted for remote rivers and forests

It is named after Earl Grey, Canada's Governor General from 1904 to 1911, who chose the Purcell range as the place to build a vacation cabin for his family, in 1912. The trail he traveled followed an established route used by the Kinbasket Natives of the Ktunaxa First Nations tribe. Today, the trail is notoriously dangerous; bears, avalanches, and fallen trees are just some of the hazards hikers may encounter along the way. Hiking here requires skill and experience and therefore should not be attempted by novice hikers.

⓰ Radium Hot Springs

Road map 2 C4. 🄼 800.
Tel (250) 347-9331.
W radiumhotsprings.com

The town of Radium Hot Springs is famous for its mineral springs and is a good base for exploring nearby Kootenay National Park. In summer, flowerpots decorate motels along the highway through town, and the town has more visitors than residents. Many of the 1.2 million annual tourists come to bathe in the healing waters of the springs.

The nearby Columbia Valley Wetlands provide an important habitat for over 250 migratory waterfowl, such as Canada geese, great blue herons, and tundra swans. Fed by glacial waters, the Columbia River meanders through these extensive marshlands.

Fort Steele's Wasa Hotel, modeled on a popular 1904 East Kootenay resort

The dramatic peaks of the Rocky Mountains in Kootenay National Park

⓱ Kootenay National Park

Road map 2 C4. **ℹ** 7556 Main St E, Radium Hot Springs, (250) 347-9331. **Open** daily. Visitors' center: **Open** late May–mid-Oct: 9am–5pm daily (late closing during Jul & Aug). ♿ 🅿 ✉ **w** pc.gc.ca/kootenay

Kootenay National Park covers 543 sq miles (1,406 sq km) of the most diverse terrain in the Rockies. Much of this scenery can be seen from the Kootenay Parkway (Highway 93 South), which cuts through the park from north to south following the Vermilion and Kootenay Rivers. Most of the park's attractions can be seen from the many short trails that lead from the highway.

The road winds eastward through Sinclair Pass, where the high red walls of Sinclair Canyon, a limestone gorge, lead to the Sinclair Falls and the Redwall Fault. Here, rust-colored cliffs

The ocher-colored Paint Pot pools in Kootenay National Park

form a natural gateway across the highway. Farther north, the magical Paint Pots, ocher and red pools formed from iron-rich mineral springs, are reached by a short trail from the road.

⓲ Glacier National Park

Road map 2 C4. **ℹ** Rogers Pass, (250) 837-7500. **Open** daily. ♿ 🅿 ✉ **w** pc.gc.ca

Glacier National Park covers 520 sq miles (1,350 sq km) of wilderness in the Selkirk Range of the Columbia Mountains. The park was established in 1886, and its growth was linked to the expansion of the railroad, which was routed through Rogers Pass in 1885. Today, one of the park's most accessible trails follows an abandoned railroad line. Other trails here offer visitors spectacular views of the

park's many glaciers, including the Great Glacier, now known as the **Illecillewaet Glacier**.

Glacier National Park contains rainforests, glacial lakes, streams, and waterfalls. During winter, snow falls almost daily, totalling as much as 75 ft (23 m) per season. The threat of avalanches in the park is serious; skiers and climbers are always encouraged to obtain information about travel conditions before visiting.

The Rogers Pass line was eventually abandoned by the Canadian Pacific Railway because of the frequent avalanches, and a tunnel was built underneath it instead. The Trans-Canada Highway (Hwy 1) follows the route of the original rail line as it bisects the park en route to the lovely city of Revelstoke. From here, visitors may access the ancient forests and jagged peaks of **Mount Revelstoke National Park**.

Illecillewaet Glacier, one of 420 glaciers in Glacier National Park

Hot Springs Havens

The geology of the Canadian Rockies has created numerous hot springs, formed naturally by groundwater seeping downward, coming into contact with hot rock 2–2.5 miles (3–4 km) below the earth's crust, and rising back to the surface at a very high temperature. The region's many hot springs resorts offer hot pools in the 100°F (38°C) range, as well as larger warm pools for swimming. The waters are rich in sulfates, calcium, and hydrogen sulfide and are said to benefit arthritis and rheumatism sufferers.

Roadside sign welcoming visitors to Radium Hot Springs

⑲ Yoho National Park

Inspired by the beauty of the area's mountains, lakes, waterfalls, and distinctive rock formations, this park was named Yoho for the Cree word meaning "awe and wonder." Yoho National Park lies on the western side of the Rockies range in British Columbia, northwest of Kootenay National Park. The park is ideal for climbing, hiking, canoeing, and cross-country skiing. It is also home to the Burgess Shale fossil beds, an extraordinary find of perfectly preserved marine creatures from the Cambrian period, over 500 million years ago. Access to the beds is by guided hike, limited to 12 people each trip.

Wapta Icefield

Emerald Lake
Emerald Lake Lodge provides facilities at this secluded spot in the middle of the park. The lake, named for the intense color of its waters, is a popular place for canoeing and walking.

Natural Bridge
Found in the center of the park, over the waters of Kicking Horse River, Natural Bridge is a rock bridge formed by centuries of erosion, which have worn a channel through solid rock. The bridge is a short drive from Highway 1.

Vancouver, Glacier National Park

KEY

① **The Yoho Valley** is noted for its stunning scenery, which includes the Takakkaw Falls.

② **Burgess Shale** was declared a UN World Heritage Site in order to protect two fossil beds. Guided hikes here are by reservation only.

Hoodoo Creek
Erosion created these mushroom-like towers of rock. A very steep 1-mile (1.5-km) ascent should be tackled only by fit hikers.

VISITORS' CHECKLIST

Practical Information
Highway 1. **Road Map** 2 C4.
🛈 Park Info Centre, Field. **Tel** (250)
343-6783. **Open** daily, check
website for times. 🚻 🖉 🖵 🏛
🏔 ⓦ pc.gc.ca/yoho

Transport
🚌 to Field.

Takakkaw Falls
Takakkaw means "it is wonderful"
in the language of the local First
Nations people, and these, with a
drop of 833 ft (254 m), are among
the most impressive falls in Canada.
The falls can be accessed along the
Yoho Valley Road.

Calgary, Banff
National Park

Kicking Horse River
This wild river rushes through Yoho
alongside the original 1880s railroad.
Today the tracks carry freight and the
Rocky Mountaineer® tourist train *(see p324).*

ury Glacier

0 kilometers   3

0 miles   3

Key

▬ Highway

▬ Major road

— River

Lake O'Hara
Shadowed by the majestic peaks of Mounts Victoria and Lefroy,
Lake O'Hara is astonishingly beautiful. Visitors wishing to use
the area's excellent hiking trails must book in advance, as access
is limited in order to protect this fragile environment.

For keys to symbols *see back flap*

Helmcken Falls, crowned by a rainbow, in Wells Gray Provincial Park

⓴ Wells Gray Provincial Park

Road map 2 B4. 🛈 416 Eden Rd, Clearwater, (250) 674-2646. **Open** call for hours. 🅆 **wellsgray.ca**

Wells Gray Provincial Park, in the Cariboo Mountains, is not only one of the largest but also one of the most beautiful wildernesses in British Columbia, offering wonders comparable to the Rockies in eastern BC. The park, established in 1939, is distinguished by alpine meadows, thundering waterfalls, and glacier-topped peaks that rise as high as 8,450 ft (2,575 m). The Canadian National Railroad and Highway 5 follow the Thompson River along the park's western edge, and both routes provide stunning views.

From the Clearwater Valley Road, off Highway 5, there are several trails, from easy walks to arduous overnight hikes in remote country. A short trail leads to spectacular 450-ft (137-m) **Helmcken Falls**, the fourth-highest waterfall in Canada. Nearby Mushbowl Bridge provides the best view of the fast-moving Murtle River and the giant holes it has carved into the surrounding rock.

In late August and early September, Chinook salmon leap in futile attempts to continue upstream past the dramatic **Bailey's Chute**.

Four lakes located throughout the park provide excellent opportunities for canoeing and angling.

⓴ Prince George

Road map 2 B3. 🚹 72,000. 🛈 1300 First Ave, (250) 562-3700. 🅆 **tourismpg.com**

The traditional home of the Lheidli T'enneh and Carrier Sekani First Nations people, and the largest town in northern British Columbia, Prince George is a bustling supply-and-transportation center for the region. Two major highways pass through here: the Yellowhead (Highway 16) and Highway 97, which becomes the Alaska Highway at Dawson Creek. Established in 1807 as Fort George, a fur-trading post at the confluence of the Nechako and Fraser Rivers, the town is well placed for exploring the province.

Prince George has all the facilities of a larger city, including its own symphony orchestra, several art galleries, and a university specializing in First Nations, forestry, and environmental studies. **Exploration Place** lies on the site of the original fort, within the Fort George Park. It contains a small collection of artifacts from First Nations cultures, European pioneers, and early settlers of the region.

An important center for the lumber industry, the town of Prince George offers a range of free tours of local pulp mills, which take visitors through the process of wood production, from vast fields of young seedlings to hill-sized piles of planks and raw timber.

🏛 **Exploration Place**
333 Becott Pl. **Tel** (250) 562-1612.
Open 9am–5pm daily. **Closed** Jan 1, Dec 25 & 26. 🔊 🖥 🖼 ♿
🅆 **theexplorationplace.com**

Dinosaur models on display at Exploration Place

⓴ Dawson Creek

Road map 2 B3. 🚹 11,000. 🛈 900 Alaska Ave, (250) 782-9595. 🅆 **tourismdawsoncreek.com**

The formerly quiet town of Dawson Creek was transformed by the construction of the Alaska Highway, which began in 1942 and swelled the town's population from 600 to 10,000. Designated as historic Mile Zero on the road to Fairbanks, 1,486 miles (2,391 km) to the north, the city recognizes

Former grain elevator turned art gallery in Dawson Creek

this distinction with the **Mile Zero post** at 10th Street and 102nd Avenue. Located at the corner of Highway 97 and the Alaska Highway, the red-and-white 1931 **Northern Alberta Railway Station** is now a museum and information center. The site includes the Mile Zero stone cairn marking the official start of the Alaska Highway. Next to the railway station is a 1948 grain elevator annex that is now an art gallery. The conversion of elevator to gallery involved the removal of 10 tons of grain dust. Shows include the work of local artists as well as major traveling collections. On Saturday mornings from May to October, a farmers' market held across from the stone cairn sells local produce and crafts.

At **Walter Wright Pioneer Village**, restored buildings and farm machinery recreate the agricultural community of Dawson Creek before the highway was built.

🏛 **Walter Wright Pioneer Village**
1901 Alaska Hwy. **Tel** (250) 782-7144. **Open** mid-May–Aug: 9am–8pm daily. **Closed** Sep–mid-May.
donation. ♿ 🖥 **mile0park.ca**

㉓ Fort St. John

Road map 2 B2. 🌆 19,000.
ℹ 9324 96 St, (250) 785-3033.
🖥 **fortstjohn.ca**

The city of Fort St. John is located at Mile 47 of the Alaska Highway, among the rolling hills of the Peace River Valley. Fort St. John, originally one of six forts built in the area between 1794 and 1925, is the oldest non-Native settlement in British Columbia. At nearby Charlie Lake Cave, 10,000-year-old artifacts of the Paleo Indians have been found, making it the site of the earliest-known human activity in the province.

The area around Fort St. John is a unique ecosystem in which moose, deer, elk, and black bears abound. During the 1942 construction of the Alaska Highway, the town's population increased dramatically, from 800 to 6,000. When completed, the highway turned Fort St. John into a busy supply center catering to visitors to the area and supporting the agriculture industry in the surrounding countryside.

The town boomed in the 1950s, when oil was found here in what proved to be the largest oil field in BC. The city's pride in its industrial heritage is reflected in its **museum**, which has a 140-ft- (43-m-) high oil derrick at its entrance and exhibits telling the story of the local oil industry. Other activities include cross-country skiing at Beatton Provincial Park in the winter. Another popular seasonal activity is watching the northern lights, very visible here.

The Mile Zero post at Dawson Creek

㉔ Fort Nelson

Road map 2 B2. 🌆 3,900.
ℹ 5319 50th Ave S, (250) 774-2956.
🖥 **tourismnorthernrockies.ca**

Despite the growth of the oil, gas, and lumber industries in the 1960s and 1970s, Fort Nelson retains the atmosphere of a northern frontier town. Before the building of the Alaska Highway in the 1940s, Fort Nelson was an important stop en route to Yukon and Alaska, and until the 1950s it was without telephones, running water, or electricity.

The steaming waters of the Liard River Hot Springs, near Fort Nelson

Fur trading was the main activity until the energy boom; even today trappers continue to hunt beaver, wolf, and lynx, for both their fur and their meat.

This town at Mile 300 of the Alaska Highway has an air and bus service, a hospital, and good visitor facilities such as motels, restaurants, and gas stations. Local people are known for their friendliness, and during the busy summer months they run a program of free talks for visitors, describing life in the North.

The small **Fort Nelson Heritage Museum** displays photographs and artifacts that tell the story of the building of the Alaska Highway, and features a frontier-town general store and blacksmith's forge. The trapper's log cabin behind the museum is also worth visiting.

The region has over a dozen parks, including **Liard River Provincial Park**; its hot springs are open year-round. The area is a world-class cross-country skiing destination.

Farmland alongside the Peace River near Fort St. John

The green waters of Muncho Lake framed by mountains in Muncho Lake Provincial Park

㉕ Muncho Lake Provincial Park

Road map 2 A1. **Tel** (250) 776-7000.
Open May–Oct: daily. 🏕 to campsites.
🌐 env.gov.bc.ca/bcparks/explore/
parkpgs/muncho_lk/

One of three provincial parks that were established after the building of the Alaska Highway in 1942, Muncho Lake occupies the most scenic section of the road. The park encompasses the bare peaks of the northern Rockies, whose stark limestone slopes incorporate the faults, alluvial fans, and fantastic rock formations that are a testament to thousands of years of glacial erosion. Flash floods are common here.

The highway skirts the eastern shoreline of the 7.5-mile- (12-km-) long Muncho Lake before crossing the Liard River, where the Mackenzie Mountains begin. In early summer, passing motorists are likely to see moose grazing in wildflower meadows. The park's bogs are popular with botanists eager to see the rare yellow Lady's Slipper orchid. The roadside also attracts great numbers of goats, sheep, and caribou, which are drawn by deposits of sodium, known as mineral licks.

Visitors may stay in the park at one of its many campgrounds (May–Sep) or lodges in order to explore its 341 sq miles (883 sq km) of wilderness. The deep waters of Muncho Lake offer a good supply of trout for anglers. Narrated boat tours of the lake are offered by Double G Service (tel 250/776-3411).

㉖ The Hazeltons

Road map 2 A3. 🏔 7,000. ℹ 3026 Bowser St, New Hazelton, (250) 842-6571. 🌐 newhazelton.ca

In the 1860s, pioneer communities were established at the confluence of the Skeena and Bulkley Rivers, 180 miles (290 km) east of Prince Rupert. Today, three villages at this location – Old, New, and South Hazelton – are known collectively as the Hazeltons. The towns, named for the hazel bushes covering the region's river-carved terraces, lie near the cliffs of Mount Rocher Déboulé, which tower over the area at 3,300 ft (1,005 m).

All the Hazeltons are charming, particularly Old Hazelton (officially known as Hazelton Village), where the old-fashioned storefronts offer a reminder of the days when the town was a bustling river terminus. The Old Hazelton walking tour shows off remnants of a Victorian steam engine from early forestry days, Skeena River paddlewheelers, the century-old St. Peter's Anglican Church, and the **Hazelton Pioneer Museum and Archives** in the library, which portrays the early days of the initial settlement.

The highlight of the area is the **'Ksan Historical Village**, a replica of a Northwest Coast-style Gitxsan village. Gitxsan First Nations people have lived in the area for thousands of years, particularly along the beautiful Skeena River valley. Their way of life was threatened by white settlers who arrived in the 1850s at Prince Rupert to work their way upriver to mine or farm, but the tribe has been recovering its traditions since the 1950s.

Noted for their skill in creating carved and painted masks, totems, and canoes, Gitxsan elders are now schooling new

'Ksan totem poles at the 'Ksan Historical Village

generations in these skills at the 'Ksan village. Within the village complex are seven traditional longhouses, containing a carving school, totems, and a museum.

A 70-mile (113-km) self-guided driving tour winds through several First Nations villages, where one can see dozens of totem poles. Indeed, the Hazeltons are known as the "totem pole capital of the world." The area also abounds with recreational opportunities, including hiking and fishing.

🏛 Hazelton Pioneer Museum and Archives
4255 Government St, Hazelton.
Tel (250) 842-5961.

🏛 'Ksan Historical Village
High Level Rd, Hazelton.
ℹ️ New Hazelton, (250) 842-5544.
Open Apr–Sep: 9am–5pm daily;
Oct–Mar: 9:30am–4:30pm Mon–Fri.
🅿️ ♿ 🎁 📷 🏠 🆆 **ksan.org**

A main street in Smithers, against a backdrop of steep mountains

㉗ Smithers

Road map 2 A3. 🔢 6,000.
ℹ️ 1027 Aldous St, (250) 847-5072.
🆆 **tourismsmithers.com**

The picturesque town of Smithers, located in the center of the fertile Bulkley Valley, is surrounded by the panoramic scenery of local mountain ranges over which the snow-crested 8,599-ft (2,621-m) Hudson Bay Mountain presides. Smithers is a year-round outdoor center where Babine Lake is recommended for its plentiful rainbow trout and char,

and rafters on the challenging Bulkley River twist past pine-lined shores through a beautiful canyon. A bicycle ride or hike along the forested 8-mile (13-km) Perimeter Trail may offer sightings of moose, deer, and grouse, while grizzly and black bears, mountain goats, and caribou live higher on the slopes. In winter, downhill, cross-country, and telemark skiing are predominant. Hudson Bay Mountain resort (tel 250/847-2058) features 37 runs and 1,750 ft (533 m) of vertical thrills. Snowmobiling and dogsledding are also popular.

Smithers' main street has an alpine theme, evident in the brick sidewalks, alpine-style storefronts, and *Alpenhorn Man*, a 7-ft (2-m) wooden statue of a man playing an alpenhorn. Colorful murals decorate the street, enhancing its shops and boutiques.

㉘ Prince Rupert

Road map 2 A3. 🔢 13,000.
ℹ️ 100 1st Ave W, (250) 624-5637.
🆆 **visitprincerupert.com**

Prince Rupert is the largest urban center on BC's northern coast. Located on Kaien Island, at the mouth of the Skeena River, the city is encircled by forests and mountains, and overlooks the fjord-studded coastline. The harbor, busy with cruise ships, ferries, and fishing boats, is the main access point for the rugged Haida Gwaii archipelago and Alaska. Like many of BC's major towns, Prince Rupert's development

A gift shop and gallery in Cow Bay, Prince Rupert

is linked to the growth of the railroad. Housed in the 1914 Grand Trunk Railway Station, the **Kwinitsa Station Railway Museum** tells the story of businessman Charles Hay's big plans for the town, which were largely unfulfilled: he went down with the *Titanic* in 1912.

Tsimshian First Nations people were the area's first occupants; in the mid-19th century, the harbor was lined with their cedar houses and totems. The excellent **Museum of Northern British Columbia** focuses on Tsimshian history; tours showcase the culture over the past 10,000 years. In summer, a First Nations-led walking tour of nearby Laxspa'aws (Pike Island) provides information on five significant archaeological and village sites 1,800 years old.

🏛 Museum of Northern British Columbia
100 1st Ave W. **Tel** (250) 624-3207.
Open Jun–Sep: 9am–5pm daily;
Oct–May: 9am–5pm Tue–Sat.
Closed Dec 25 & 26. 🅿️ ♿ 🎁 📷
🆆 **museumofnorthernbc.com**

One of the many renovated buildings by Prince Rupert's harbor

❷ Haida Gwaii (Queen Charlotte Islands)

Haida Gwaii, formerly known as the Queen Charlotte Islands, is an archipelago of about 150 islands, many with unique ecosystems. For thousands of years they have been home to the Haida Nation, a people renowned for their carvings and sculptures made of silver, gold, cedar, and argillite (a black, slate-like stone found only on these islands). The remote Gwaii Haanas National Marine Conservation Area Reserve and Haida Heritage Site protects ancient Haida villages nestled amid lush cedar and hemlock rainforest, home to distinctive species such as dusky shrews, ermine, and pine martens. Bald eagles nest along the coast, and in spring hundreds of migrating humpback whales and, sometimes, gray whales can be seen. Haida Gwaii offers some of the West Coast's finest fishing, kayaking, hiking, boating, and whale-watching.

Masset

The oldest fishing community in Haida Gwaii, Masset is popular with both anglers and tourists. Its Delkatla Wildlife Sanctuary, an intertidal wetland and bird-watcher's paradise, is refuge to more than 140 recorded species, including large flocks of migrating shorebirds. In the nearby Haida village of Old Massett, traditional jewelers, carvers, and weavers work in home studios.

Queen Charlotte

This quaint fishing village, also known simply as Charlotte, is a good base from which to explore the islands and take an ecotour. Its tiny downtown offers cafés, hotels, and shops that sell a variety of goods including wood carvings, Haida carvings, pottery, paintings, glasswork, and handmade clothing.

Key

▬ Paved road

▬ Dirt or four-wheel-drive road

- - Hiking trail

For hotels and restaurants see pp290–91 and pp304–5

LANGARA ISLAND

Jalun River

Naden River

Virago Sound

O'
M.

Sewall

Masset Inlet

Port
Cleme

GRAHAM ISLAND

Rennell Sound

MORESBY ISLAND

M
Mc

★ **Naikoon Provincial Park**
Naikoon Provincial Park has breathtaking views of
Hecate Strait and Dixon Entrance. On clear days, Alaska
is visible from the north end. Tow Hill, at the park's north
end, is an ancient volcano with a massive basalt cliff.
The Pesuta shipwreck, located on East Beach, can be
accessed by a 3-mile (5-km) hiking trail.

★ **Haida Heritage Centre**
Haida Heritage Centre
celebrates Haida culture,
past and present.
Highlights here include
argillite and wood
carvings, totems dating
to 1878, and Loos Taas,
a 49-ft- (150-m-) long
canoe carved by Haida
artist Bill Reid.

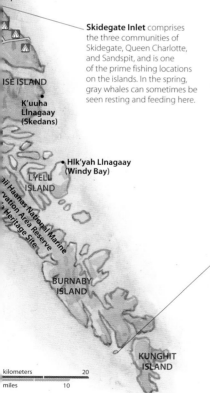

Skidegate Inlet comprises
the three communities of
Skidegate, Queen Charlotte,
and Sandspit, and is one
of the prime fishing locations
on the islands. In the spring,
gray whales can sometimes be
seen resting and feeding here.

★ **SGang Gwaay (Ninstints)**
A UNESCO World Heritage Site since 1981,
this Haida village on Anthony Island has
more totems standing on their original sites
than any other Haida village. Accessible
by boat only.

For keys to symbols *see back flap*

⓴ Cruise to Alaska

Continuing a tradition that began in 1880, cruise ships ply the Inside Passage, a protected waterway that runs along the BC coast to the inlets of Alaska. The waters are calmer than those of the open Pacific Ocean, so that whales and porpoises are often sighted. The popular cruises, many of which are combined with shore excursions, attract over one million passengers a year.

The sails of Vancouver's Canada Place, starting point for cruises

⑤ **Prince William Sound**
More than 20 active tidewater glaciers are to be found at the sound, with its 3,000 miles (4,830 km) of coastline. A horned puffin colony lives here year-round and up to 5,000 bald eagles summer here.

⑥ **Kenai Fjords National Park**
In the Seward region, the glacier-carved fjords of Kenai are home to whales, sea lions, and tufted puffins.

⑦ **Anchorage**
Fabulous views of the Chugach Mountains can be enjoyed from Anchorage, situated on a broad peninsula in Cook Inlet. The Alaska Native Heritage Center here displays historic tableaux illustrating the daily lives of the region's First Nations tribes.

Key

-- Cruise route

▬ Major road

0 kilometers 200
0 miles 150

④ Skagway
The historic Klondike train, which steams through the cliff-hugging White Pass, starts in Skagway. The boardwalk and false-fronted buildings of this city evoke the 19th century.

Tips for Drivers
Starting point: Canada Place and Ballantyne Pier cruise ship terminals, Vancouver.
Cruise length: to Sitka, 736 miles (1,184 km); to Skagway, 956 miles (1,538 km); to Seward, 1,443 miles (2,322 km).
Highlights: views of glaciers, mountains, and wildlife, as well as historic and scenic ports of call.

③ Juneau
Alaska's capital is also its most beautiful city. Juneau is the gateway to the impressive 12-mile- (19-km-) long Mendenhall Glacier, which flows from the Juneau Ice field.

② Sitka
Sitka is one of Alaska's most beautiful seaside towns, with its colorful houses and impressive spruce forests.

① Ketchikan
19th-century buildings and boardwalks, Tlingit clan houses, a totem collection, and an eagle population make this town unforgettable.

For keys to symbols *see back flap*

TRAVELERS' NEEDS

WHERE TO STAY

The Pacific Northwest offers accommodation to suit every taste – from historic and boutique city hotels with desirable in-house restaurants, to simple, modern budget hotels and cozy bed-and-breakfasts perched on the beach or in wine country. In addition to this range of options, rustic inns and lodges, usually located outside towns and cities and near scenic areas, give easy access to unforgettable outdoor experiences. For those who prefer to camp, the numerous state, provincial, and national parks throughout the region offer a choice of campsites, including smaller sites for rough camping. In order to help you select a place to stay, the listings on pages 286–91 recommend a variety of accommodations, in all price ranges, each representing the best of its kind.

Finding Accommodation

For accommodation in Oregon, **Travel Oregon** offers a handy online reservation service as well as a free publication called *Where to Stay in Oregon*. **Washington State Tourism** provides lodging and camp-ground listings in its free booklet *Experience Washington*, which can be ordered by phone or downloaded from the Internet. **Tourism BC**'s *British Columbia Approved Accommodation* guide, available at no charge at tourist information centers, rates more than 800 BC government-inspected accommodations and campgrounds. Local bed-and-breakfast and inn agencies also offer accommodation listings; check with the local visitors' center for details.

How to Book

Reservations are recommended whatever the season, as festivals, conferences, and other events *(see pp34–7)* are held year-round throughout the Pacific Northwest. Campgrounds are especially popular during the summer, as are ski resorts in the winter. Most major hotels have toll-free reservation numbers and accept Internet bookings. Rooms can also be booked through online booking agencies, such as **Kayak**, **Booking**, **Priceline**, and **Expedia**.

If you have special requirements, such as a quiet room away from ice machines and elevators, make them known when you book your room. Reservations usually require a credit card number or a deposit the equivalent of one night's stay. Generally, refunds are made for cancellations if enough notice has been given; however, administration charges may apply. Notify the hotel if you expect to arrive later than 5pm or you may lose your reservations.

Prices

With so many accommodation options, prices vary tremendously and depend on the season and availability. During peak tourist months (May to September) and public holidays, prices are higher in the city and at seaside or lakeside accommodations. The best deals at these locations are to be found in the off-season, October to April. Ski resorts are on an opposite schedule, which means that mountain accommodations in mid-summer are readily available and prices quite affordable.

It is best to stay in cities on weekends, when hotels have almost no business clientele, and to opt for bed-and-breakfasts outside cities or popular weekend destinations during the week, when prices often drop considerably. Always inquire about package deals – many hotels offer discounts on tours and entrance to attractions, restaurant and store coupons, as well as free airport and city shuttle services.

Increasingly, hotels offer discounts on room rates when bookings are made over the Internet. Reserving a room with an Internet booking agency *(see How to Book)* can also result in savings, especially on last-minute deals. Also, many hotels offer discounts to members of auto clubs, and often to students and seniors, so it is always a good idea to inquire about these discounts when calling to reserve a room. Watch for hidden costs such as parking fees and single-occupancy surcharges.

Oregon's hotel tax varies from county to county. Hotel tax in Seattle is 15.6 percent but varies throughout the rest of Washington. In British Columbia prices are subject to a 5 percent federal Goods and Services Tax (GST); an 8 percent provincial

Modern art and clean lines abound at the boutique Hotel Lucia *(see p286)*, Portland

◀ A lodge and restaurant at the Emerald Lake, Yoho National Park, British Columbia

otel tax on rooms in properties with four or more units; and, in certain municipalities, an additional tax of up to 2 percent.

Hotels

Hotels in the Pacific Northwest's major destinations are counted among the world's best. Luxury chains, such as the Four Seasons, Fairmont, Kimpton, and Westin, as well as numerous independents, are generally located downtown. They usually offer stylish decor, an upscale restaurant, a spa, and valet parking. Reservations are recommended, especially if you plan to visit during a holiday or a popular festival or event *(see pp34–7)*.

If you are looking for personalized guest services and luxurious amenities, consider one of the many boutique hotels – small, exclusive, independently owned hotels – usually situated in city centers and resort destinations. All the major hotel chains, including Best Western, Holiday Inn, and Marriott, can be found in the larger cities and often in smaller towns near popular destinations. These chains provide rooms that are not only affordable but also standardized: no matter where the hotel is located, they offer clean, reliable accommodations as well as facilities that typically include a hotel restaurant, swimming pool, and fitness center.

Bed-and-Breakfasts and Inns

The Pacific Northwest prides itself on its many welcoming and charming bed-and-breakfasts. Guest rooms are typically located in a large house in which the host also resides. Accommodations range from rooms in historic Victorian homes with beautiful gardens, situated in residential city neighborhoods, to rooms in rustic log homes near the mountains, and everything in between.

As the name suggests, guests are served breakfast, often buffet-style. Some bed-and-

The heritage Gatsby Mansion Inn *(see p291)* in Victoria, BC, now a bed-and-breakfast

breakfasts also serve lunch and dinner; inquire when booking. Most bed-and-breakfasts prohibit smoking, and some also have restrictions on children and pets.

The **Oregon** and the **Washington Bed and Breakfast Guilds** provide extensive information and listings detailing bed-and-breakfasts in these two states. For visitors to British Columbia, the **British Columbia Bed and Breakfast Innkeepers Guild** publishes a guide to accommodations that are approved by the agency. Like bed-and-breakfasts, inns come in all shapes and sizes, from small and rustic to large and luxurious.

Visitors to British Columbia may choose to stay at one of the province's numerous guest ranches, which include working cattle ranches. These properties offer a variety of activities, such as horseback riding and fishing, as well as the opportunity to participate in real ranch work. Visitors can choose from basic cabins, ski lodges, and luxury ranches featuring fireplaces, room service, air conditioning, hot tubs, and spa facilities. Contact the **BC Guest Ranchers' Association** for information.

Traveling on a Budget

Hostels can be ideal for travelers on a budget. **Hostelling International** (HI) operates in locations throughout the Pacific Northwest. HI memberships are available at a nominal fee (free for youths 17 years and younger) and entitle members to discounts on rooms,

restaurant meals, car rentals, bus travel, airport shuttles, and more. Ask about other benefits at HI's regional offices.

A variety of accommodations are available, though many are dormitory-style with shared bathrooms. Some hostels also have communal kitchens. Calling ahead to reserve a space is advisable. Several hostels are centrally located within the metropolitan Seattle and Portland areas. There are also hostels, both HI and those unaffiliated to HI, throughout Oregon and Washington. In British Columbia, hostels are to be found in Vancouver, Whistler, Vancouver Island, and at major destinations in the BC Interior. Hostel-style accommodation is also available at the YMCA and YWCA in Vancouver and, in summer, at several universities and colleges, including the University of British Columbia. For an online directory of hostels, visit **www.hostels.com**.

Motels offer much to travelers who are looking for simplicity and cleanliness. Most are located near busy highways and are a comfortable and inexpensive option as long as transportation into the city is not an issue. Motels generally offer fewer amenities than hotels, although cable TV, private bathrooms, air conditioning, and ice and soda machines are standard. Reservations are usually not necessary. Online agencies such as **Oregon Coast Motels**, Booking, and Kayak are good sources to find motels.

Campgrounds

Throughout the Pacific Northwest, park facilities are basic – running water, flush or pit toilets, and a tenting area – although some sites have showers and running water. Privately owned tent, trailer, and recreational vehicle (RV) parks offer both simple sites with outhouses and full-service campgrounds with flush toilets, showers, electricity, and even playgrounds and games rooms.

In Oregon and Washington, some campgrounds accept reservations, whereas others are first come, first served. Campsites may be reserved up to a year in advance for certain weekends and holidays, such as July 4. Reservations for Oregon and Washington campsites can be made by contacting **Oregon State Parks** or **Washington State Parks**, or online at **Reserve America**. Campgrounds at British Columbia's provincial and national parks fill up quickly. Check the **BC Parks** website to determine which parks take reservations, and reserve with **Discover Camping** by phone or online.

Travelers with Disabilities

Hotels and motels in both the US and Canada are required by law to be wheelchair accessible, with the exception of some in older buildings. The reality, however, is that this is not always the case. The vast majority of large private

Geiser Grand Hotel *(see p287)*, a landmark of Baker City, Oregon

and chain hotels are equipped with the necessary facilities, including visual notification of the fire alarm and of incoming phone calls. Many also have suites designated specifically for people with disabilities. However, many of the older buildings and bed-and-breakfasts in the Pacific Northwest have narrow hallways that can obstruct wheelchairs and that are without ramps. As always, it is best to check in advance. In the US, the Society for Accessible Travel and Hospitality *(see p319)* provides travel tips and information about wheelchair access.

Many BC properties participate in the Access Canada program, which seeks to make traveling easier for seniors and people with disabilities. Look for the Access Canada logo, which uses a numbered system from 1 to 4: 1 indicates accommodation suitable for active seniors and people with minor disabilities; 2, for seniors and people with moderate disabilities; 3, for people with advanced agility, hearing, mobility, and vision disabilities and independent wheelchair users; and 4, for those with severe disabilities.

Traveling with Children

Children are welcome in most hotels in the Pacific Northwest. Many hotels and motels offer family packages, services such as babysitting, and family rooms. Call ahead to inquire about special rates and services for families and special accommodations for young children, such as cots, for which there is often a nominal fee of $10 to $15. It is advisable to inquire about a bed-and-breakfast's policy on accommodating children before booking a room.

Business Travelers

Larger hotels often maintain full-service business centers, which provide secretarial and courier services as well as Internet facilities. They may also have conference rooms that can be reserved in advance. If you plan to stay at an older property and wish to do business from there, make sure it has the facilities you require.

Where to Stay in Portland

Most of the major hotel chains are represented in downtown Portland, providing good bases for visitors who want to feel the pulse of the city and visit its museums and cultural attractions. Downtown hotels are also in close proximity to some of Portland's most vibrant neighborhoods, such as the Pearl District. Most of the city's bed-and-breakfasts are located a bit farther afield.

Where to Stay in Seattle

Seattle's downtown is relatively small and many sights can be easily reached on foot, making the area an ideal base for

The luxurious Fairmont Chateau Whistler *(see p291)*, BC

travelers. Accommodations in or near Pike Place Market are convenient for all the major shops and many rooms have stunning views of Elliott Bay and Puget Sound. Most of the major hotels are clustered together and are within walking distance of many of the city's best bars and restaurants. Pioneer Square and Belltown, two neighborhoods flanking downtown, on the south and north respectively, offer more affordable accommodations. Still central, though just outside the downtown area, Capitol Hill and Queen Anne Hill offer comfortable accommodations in neighborhood surroundings.

Where to Stay in Vancouver

The majority of Vancouver's hotel options are clustered in the city's downtown shopping and business districts, although there are also several big-name chain hotels located near the airport. Bed-and-breakfasts are generally also located downtown, but visitors who prefer a quieter atmosphere will find homely bed-and-breakfasts in residential neighborhoods such as Kitsilano or Shaughnessy.

Plush furnishings complement the views at the Edgewater Hotel *(see p288)*, Seattle

Recommended Hotels

The lodging options featured in this guide have been selected across a wide price range for their excellent facilities, good location, and value. From rustic, family-owned inns and relaxing coastal resorts to stylishly modern boutique hotels, accommodations run the gamut across all price levels and environments. Luxury options abound, offering the Pacific Northwest's very best in service and amenities. Style-conscious, trendy types feel most at home in the region's numerous hip boutique hotels. For a more intimate experience, consider a cozy, atmospheric inn or bed-and-breakfast. There are budget options across most categories that can help to keep vacation costs down. If traveling with a family, consider the region's world-class resorts, several of which include skiing and activity packages.

For the best of the best, look out for listings in this guide labeled as DK Choice. These establishments have been highlighted in recognition of an exceptional feature – be it a stunning location, notable history, or inviting atmosphere. The majority of these are exceptionally popular, so be sure to book in advance.

DIRECTORY

Finding Accommodation

Tourism BC
Tel (800) 435-5622.
W hellobc.com

Travel Oregon
Tel (800) 547-7842.
W traveloregon.com

Washington State Tourism
W experiencewa.com

How to Book

Booking
W booking.com

Expedia
W expedia.com

Kayak
W kayak.com

Priceline
W priceline.com

Bed-and-Breakfasts and Inns

BC Guest Ranchers' Association
Tel (877) 278-2922.
W bcguestranches.com

British Columbia Bed and Breakfast Innkeepers Guild
W bcsbestbnbs.com

Oregon Bed and Breakfast Guild
Tel (800) 944-6196.
W obbg.org

Washington Bed and Breakfast Guild
Tel (800) 647-2918.
W wbbg.com

Traveling on a Budget

Hostelling International Canada
Tel (604) 684-7101.
W hihostels.ca

Hostelling International USA
W hiusa.org

Hostels.com
W hostels.com

Oregon Coast Motels
W oregoncoastmotels.net

Campgrounds

BC Parks
W env.gov.bc.ca

Discover Camping
W discovercamping.ca

Oregon State Parks
Tel (800) 452-5687.
W oregonstateparks.org

Reserve America
W reserveamerica.com

Washington State Parks
Tel (888) 226-7688.
W parks.wa.gov

Where to Stay

Portland

Old Town and the Pearl District

The Mark Spencer Hotel $$
Boutique   **Map** 1 B5
409 SW 11th Ave, 97205
Tel *(503) 224-3293*
W markspencer.com
Most rooms in this eco-friendly, stylish hotel are equipped with kitchenettes. Complimentary afternoon tea, evening wine reception, and packages for art events all enhance the stay.

Downtown

McMenamins Crystal Hotel $
Boutique   **Map** 1 B5
303 SW 12th Ave, 97205
Tel *(503) 972-2670*
W mcmenamins.com
This music-themed hotel was decorated in honor of the neighboring Crystal Ballroom. The establishment also has a funky café and a soaking pool.

The Benson $$
Historic   **Map** 1 C4
309 SW Broadway, 97205
Tel *(503) 228-2000*
W coasthotels.com
A stately hotel built in 1912, The Benson is filled with marble and polished Russian walnut details. Classically furnished rooms.

Heathman Hotel $$
Luxury   **Map** 1 C4
1001 SW Broadway, 97205
Tel *(503) 241-4100*
W heathmanhotel.com
This charming 1927 institution is a magnet for visiting musicians and writers. Old World charm, city views, and works by local artists.

Hotel Lucia $$
Boutique   **Map** 1 C4
400 SW Broadway, 97205
Tel *(503) 225-1717*
W hotellucia.com
A stylish establishment, Hotel Lucia houses acclaimed artwork. It offers a pillow menu, luxurious beds, and pampering bath products.

Hotel Monaco $$
Boutique   **Map** 1 C5
506 SW Washington St, 97204
Tel *(503) 222-0001*
W monaco-portland.com
This 1912 architectural gem boasts a large contemporary art collection and plush, colorful decor inspired by Anglo-Chinois style.

Hotel Vintage Plaza $$
Luxury   **Map** 1 C4
422 SW Broadway, 97205
Tel *(503) 228-1212*
W vintageplaza.com
The rooms here are named after Oregon wineries; suites have floor-to-wall windows with city views. Complimentary wine reception nightly.

Sentinel $$
Historic   **Map** 1 B5
614 SW 11th Ave, 97205
Tel *(503) 224-3400*
W sentinelhotel.com
A 1909 hotel that features historic murals. Some of the elegantly furnished rooms offer fireplaces and balconies.

Farther Afield

DK Choice

Ace Hotel $$
Boutique   **Map** 2 D5
1022 SW Stark St, 97205
Tel *(503) 228-2277*
W acehotel.com/portland
In a city full of trendy options, this is one of the funkiest hotels. After a complete overhaul, the former Clyde Hotel has a mix of original 1912 details and stylishly modern, eco-friendly features. Each guestroom is one of a kind. Guests enjoy free bicycle rentals. Pet friendly.

Inn at Northrup Station $$
Inn/B&B   **Road Map** 1 A3
2025 NW Northrup St, 97209
Tel *(503) 224-0543*
W northrupstation.com
Built in the 1970s and later transformed by architect Steve Routon, this offbeat, psychedelically colored destination has suites with full kitchens. There is also a rooftop deck.

Price Guide

Prices are based on one night's stay in high season for a standard double room, inclusive of service charges and taxes.

$	up to $150
$$	$150 to 275
$$$	over $275

Lion and the Rose Victorian Bed & Breakfast $
Historic   **Road Map** 1 A
1810 NE 15th Ave, 97212
Tel *(503) 287-9245*
W lionrose.com
Located in the leafy, historic Irvington area, this majestic 1906 Queen Anne-style mansion has rooms with private baths.

McMenamins Kennedy School $$
Inn/B&B   **Map** 2 F
5736 NE 33rd Ave, 97211
Tel *(503) 249-3983*
W mcmenamins.com
Once an elementary school, now a B&B, this place features a movie theater and whimsically decorated rooms, furnished with chalkboard

Oregon

ASHLAND: Ashland Springs Hotel $
Historic   **Road Map** 1 A
212 E Main St, 97520
Tel *(541) 488-1700*
W ashlandspringshotel.com
This nine-story landmark dates back to 1925. It has a gorgeous lobby and the rooms have fine French fabrics.

ASTORIA: Hotel Elliott $
Boutique   **Road Map** 1 A.
357 12th St, 97103
Tel *(503) 325-2222, (888) 434-7374*
W hotelelliott.com
Many of the original 1924 details have been retained at this centrally located hotel. The luxurious rooms feature 440-count cotton sheets.

Funky decor at Ace Hotel, Portland

BAKER CITY: Geiser Grand Hotel
Luxury $$
Road Map 1 C3
1996 Main St, 97814
Tel *(541) 523-1889*
W geisergrand.com
This restored 1889 landmark features mahogany mill-work and a huge stained-glass skylight above the highly rated restaurant's dining room.

BEND: Seventh Mountain Resort
Resort $$
Road Map 1 B4
18575 SW Century Dr, 97702
Tel *(541) 382-8711*
W seventhmountain.com
Simple bedroom units as well as fully equipped suites are available here. A good base for skiers, rafters, and anglers.

CANNON BEACH: Stephanie Inn
Inn/B&B $$$
Road Map 1 A3
2740 S Pacific St, 97110
Tel *(503) 436-2221*
W stephanieinn.com
The rooms at this romantic beachfront inn have fireplaces and whirlpool tubs. No children under 12.

CRATER LAKE NATIONAL PARK: Crater Lake Lodge
Inn/B&B $$
Road Map 1 B4
565 Rim Village Dr, 97604
Tel *(800) 774-2728*
W craterlakelodges.com
Set on the rim of Crater Lake, this grand 1915 lodge has stunning views. The elegant rooms have a rustic charm. Open late May to Oct.

EUGENE: Excelsior Inn
Inn/B&B $$
Road Map 1 A4
754 E 13th Ave, 97401
Tel *(541) 342-6963*
W excelsiorinn.com
The rooms at the Excelsior have hardwood floors, arched windows, and marble baths.

GLENEDEN BEACH: Salishan Spa & Golf Resort
Resort $$
Road Map 1 A3
7760 N Hwy 101, 97388
Tel *(541) 764-2371*
W salishan.com
This sprawling complex is nestled in a wooded area near Siletz Bay. Golf course and trails for hiking.

HOOD RIVER: Hood River Hotel $
Historic
Road Map 1 B3
102 Oak St, 97031
Tel *(541) 386-1900*
W hoodriverhotel.com
Enjoy gorgeous views of the Columbia River from this charming 1913 hotel. The cozy lobby is a lovely place to relax in.

Impressive lobby at Sunriver Resort, Sunriver

IMNAHA: Imnaha River Inn $
Inn/B&B
Road Map 1 C3
73946 Rimrock Rd, 97842
Tel *(541) 577-6002*
W imnahariverinn.com
This charming inn offers easy access to hiking, hunting, fishing, biking, and rafting areas. Rustic rooms; shared bathrooms.

JACKSONVILLE: Country House Inns $
Inn/B&B
Road Map 1 A4
830 N 5th St, 97530
Tel *(800) 367-1942*
W countryhouseinns.com
The cottages, rooms, and suites are set in homes dating to the 1860s. Wine-tasting packages are also offered.

LINCOLN CITY: The Coho Oceanfront Lodge $$
Inn/B&B
Road Map 1 A3
1635 NW Harbor Ave, 97367
Tel *(541) 994-3684*
W thecoholodge.com
Take in the breathtaking views of the ocean at this aesthetically pleasing lodge, which also offers spa services, an indoor heated pool, and concierge service.

MCMINNVILLE: McMenamins Hotel Oregon $
Inn/B&B
Road Map 1 A3
310 NE Evans St, 97128
Tel *(503) 472-8427*
W mcmenamins.com
This hotel has a variety of comfortable rooms, some with private baths. The rooftop bar offers stunning views.

MCMINNVILLE: Youngberg Hill Vineyards and Inn $$$
Inn/B&B
Road Map 1 A3
10660 SW Youngberg Hill Rd, 97128
Tel *(503) 472-2727*
W youngberghill.com
Set on a hill, this craftsman-style inn overlooks rolling vineyards. The luxurious rooms feature gas fireplaces and Jacuzzis.

DK Choice

MOUNT HOOD: Timberline Lodge
Inn/B&B $$
Road Map 1 B3
27500 E Timberline Rd, 97028
Tel *(800) 547-1406*
W timberlinelodge.com
This historic lodge, famous from the exterior shots in the film *The Shining*, was built in the 1930s. The lobby's huge stone fireplace is an attraction in itself. The skiing packages and award-winning dining also lure visitors.

NEWPORT: Sylvia Beach Hotel $$
Boutique
Road Map 1 A3
267 NW Cliff St, 97365
Tel *(888) 795-8422*
W sylviabeachhotel.com
A delightfully quirky hotel housed in an old Craftsman-style building. It has ocean-facing rooms.

SALEM: Grand Hotel $
Luxury
Road Map 1 A3
201 Liberty St, 97301
Tel *(503) 540-7800*
W grandhotelsalem.com
This hotel has comfortable rooms and spacious suites, along with a restaurant, wine bar, and gym.

STEAMBOAT: Steamboat Inn $$$
Inn/B&B
Road Map 1 A4
42705 N Umpqua Hwy, 97447
Tel *(541) 498-2230*
W thesteamboatinn.com
A complex of suites, cabins, and cottages are set on a remote stretch of river. Ideal for fly-fishing.

SUNRIVER: Sunriver Resort $$
Resort
Road Map 1 A4
17600 Center Dr, 97707
Tel *(800) 801-8765*
W sunriver-resort.com
This resort has lodge suites and private condos. Golf courses, restaurants, biking trails, and pools.

TROUTDALE: McMenamins Edgefield $
Inn/B&B
Road Map 1 B3
2126 SW Halsey St, 97060
Tel *(503) 669-8610*
W mcmenamins.com
This 1911 property includes a winery, brewery, distillery, theater, pool, and more.

WALLOWA LAKE: Wallowa Lake Lodge $$
Inn/B&B
Road Map 1 C3
60060 Wallowa Lake Hwy, 97846
Tel *(541) 432-9821*
W wallowalake.com
Built in 1923, this lodge has rooms with lake views; cabins feature fireplaces and kitchens. Look out for black tail deer on the lawns.

For more information on types of hotels *see pp283–5*

WARM SPRINGS: Kah-Nee-Tah Resort and Casino $
Resort   **Road Map** 1 B3
6823 Hwy 8, 97761
Tel *(800)-554-4786*
Ⓦ kahneetah.com
This modern lodge on a desert-based Indian reservation, overlooks the Warm Springs River. Spa and casino.

Seattle

Pioneer Square and Downtown

Fairmont Olympic Hotel $$
Luxury   **Map** 4 D1
411 University St, 98101
Tel *(206) 621-1700*
Ⓦ fairmont.com/seattle
This hotel is modeled on an Italian Renaissance palazzo, with marble and plush carpets.

Grand Hyatt Seattle $$
Luxury   **Map** 4 D1
721 Pine St, 98101
Tel *(206) 774-1234*
Ⓦ grandseattle.hyatt.com
A sleek and stylish hotel designed to appeal to high-tech professionals. Ultramodern amenities.

Mayflower Park Hotel $$
Boutique   **Map** 3 C1
405 Olive Way, 98101
Tel *(206) 623-8700*
Ⓦ mayflowerpark.com
This well-located 1927 property is one of the city's last independently owned classic hotels.

Palladian Hotel $$
Boutique   **Map** 1 B4
2000 2nd Ave, 98121
Tel *(206) 448-1111*
Ⓦ palladianhotel.com
A short walk from Pike Place Market, this hip hotel has a seafood restaurant, cocktail bar, and complimentary afternoon wine hour.

Striking colors and contemporary art at the 1920s Hotel Max, Seattle

Pike Place Market and the Waterfront

Alexis Hotel $$
Boutique   **Map** 3 C2
1007 1st Ave, 98104
Tel *(206) 624-4844*
Ⓦ alexishotel.com
The rooms and public spaces at Alexis Hotel showcase works by local artists. Luxurious decor and celebrated service.

DK Choice

The Edgewater Hotel $$
Luxury   **Map** 3 C2
2411 Alaskan Way, 98121
Tel *(206) 728-7000*
Ⓦ edgewaterhotel.com
Get stunning views of Puget Sound and the Olympic Mountains from the eco-friendly rooms of this waterfront hotel. The interior feels like a plush lodge: all rooms feature knotty-pine furniture, river-rock fireplaces, and impressive bath amenities. Top-notch restaurant. Pet friendly.

Inn at the Market $$
Luxury   **Map** 3 C1
86 Pine St, 98101
Tel *(206) 443-3600*
Ⓦ innatthemarket.com
Set in a landscaped courtyard, the floor-to-ceiling windows here offer spectacular views of Elliott Bay.

Seattle Center and Belltown

Hotel Five $
Boutique   **Map** 2 D2
2200 5th Ave, 98121
Tel *(206) 441-9785*
Ⓦ hotelfiveseattle.com
These eco-friendly lodgings feature hardwood floors and urban industrial art. Free bike rentals. Dog friendly.

Inn at Queen Anne $
Inn/B&B   **Map** 1 B5
505 1st Ave N, 98109
Tel *(206) 282-7357*
Ⓦ innatqueenanne.com
A converted 1928 apartment building, this inn comprises simply decorated rooms with kitchens.

MarQueen Hotel $
Boutique   **Map** 1 B3
600 Queen Anne Ave N, 98109
Tel *(206) 282-7407*
Ⓦ marqueen.com
The hotel's quaint, tasteful rooms have kitchens, hardwood floors, and upscale toiletries. The on-site cocktail bar, The Tin Lizzie Lounge, is popular.

Ace Hotel $$
Boutique   **Map** 1 C5
2423 1st Ave, 98121
Tel *(206) 448-4721*
Ⓦ acehotel.com
The arty rooms at Ace Hotel have high ceilings and low platform beds with army-surplus blankets.

Hotel Max $$
Boutique   **Map** 2 E5
620 Stewart St, 98101
Tel *(866) 986-8087*
Ⓦ hotelmaxseattle.com
A 1920s-era relic that is known for contemporary Northwest art and Miller's Guild restaurant, with its entirely wood-fired menu.

Farther Afield

Ballard Hotel $$
Boutique   **Road Map** 1 A2
5216 Ballard Ave NW, 98107
Tel *(206) 789-5012*
Ⓦ hotelballardseattle.com
Ballard's first boutique hotel has luxurious rooms and a superb restaurant. Guests have access to the Olympic Athletic Club.

Sorrento Hotel $$$
Boutique   **Map** 4 D1
900 Madison St, 98104
Tel *(206) 622-6400*
Ⓦ hotelsorrento.com
Rooms at this elegant hotel have marble bathrooms and great views. Exceptional service.

Washington

BELLINGHAM: Chrysalis Inn & Spa $$
Inn/B&B   **Road Map** 1 A1
804 10th St, 98225
Tel *(888) 808-0005*
Ⓦ thechrysalisinn.com
This hotel has a warm decor, a full-service spa and a romantic Mediterranean-style wine bar.

CHELAN: Campbell's Resort $$
Resort   **Road Map** 1 B2
104 W Woodin Ave, 98816
Tel *(509) 682-2561*
Ⓦ campbellsresort.com
A prime beachfront location, this resort features a spa, outdoor heated pool, and bar.

DEER HARBOR: Inn on Orcas Island $$
Inn/B&B   **Road Map** 1 A1
114 Channel Rd, 98243
Tel *(360) 376-5227*
Ⓦ theinnonorcasisland.com
In a marsh-side setting close to Deer Harbor, the rooms in this New England-style structure have water views. No children or pets.

Country-cottage charm at the Inn at Abeja, Walla Walla

FORKS: Kalaloch Lodge $
Inn/B&B **Road Map** 1 A2
157151 Hwy. 101, 98331
Tel *(866) 297-7367*
W thekalalochlodge.com
The lodge and cabins are set
on a bluff overlooking the Pacific
Ocean. The restaurant serves
regional specialties and seafood.

FRIDAY HARBOR: Friday
Harbor House $$
Boutique **Road Map** 1 A1
130 West St, 98250
Tel *(360) 378-8455*
W fridayharborhouse.com
Rooms at this romantic getaway
offer water views, fireplaces, and
whirlpool baths.

LEAVENWORTH:
Haus Rohrbach Pension $$
Inn/B&B **Road Map** 1 B2
12882 Ranger Rd, 98826
Tel *(509) 548-7024*
W hausrohrbach.com
Most rooms at this Alpine-style
lodging have private baths and
balconies offering valley views.

MT. RAINIER NATIONAL PARK:
National Park Inn $$
Inn/B&B **Road Map** 1 B2
Mount Rainier National Park, 98304
Tel *(360) 569-2275*
W mtrainierguestservices.com
Charming rooms, afternoon tea,
and a communal fireplace are a
few highlights at this rustic retreat.

MT. RAINIER NATIONAL PARK:
Paradise Inn $$
Inn/B&B **Road Map** 1 B2
Mount Rainier National Park, 98304
Tel *(360) 569-2270*
W mtrainierguestservices.com
This lodge has exposed beams and
decorative woodwork dating to
its 1916 origins. Open May to Oct.

NAHCOTTA: Moby Dick Hotel $
Historic **Road Map** 1 A2
25814 Sandridge Rd, 98637
Tel *(360) 665-4543*
W mobydickhotel.com
A delightful 1930s hotel set on an
oyster farm. The lobby has a fine
collection of books.

OLYMPIA: DoubleTree by
Hilton Hotel Olympia $$
Inn/B&B **Road Map** 1 A2
415 Capitol Way, 98501
Tel *(360) 570-0555*
W doubletree3.hilton.com
The suites come with refrigerators
and flat-screen TVs. Complimen-
tary continental breakfast.

QUINAULT: Lake
Quinault Lodge $$
Inn/B&B **Road Map** 1 A2
345 S Shore Rd, 98575
Tel *(360) 288-2900*
W olympicnationalparks.com
This grand 1926 lodge sits by the
rainforest above the shore of
Lake Quinault. Old-style comfort.

ROCHE HARBOR: Roche
Harbor Resort $$
Luxury **Road Map** 1 A1
248 Reuben Memorial Dr, 98250
Tel *(360) 378-2155*
W rocheharbor.com
A charming complex with an
1886 hotel, deluxe suites, as well
as historic cottages.

SEAVIEW: Shelburne Inn $$
Inn/B&B **Road Map** 1 A2
4415 Pacific Way, 98644
Tel *(360) 642-2442*
W theshelburneinn.com
Rooms at this 1896 inn are
decorated with antiques;
most have private decks.

SNOQUALMIE: Salish Lodge $$$
Inn/B&B **Road Map** 1 B2
6501 Railroad Ave, 98065
Tel *(425) 888-2556*
W salishlodge.com
Set above the Snoqualmie Falls,
this lodge has whirlpool tubs
and fireplaces. There are two
restaurants on-site.

SPOKANE: The Davenport
Hotel $$
Historic **Road Map** 1 C2
10 S Post St, 99201
Tel *(509) 455-8888*
W thedavenporthotel.com
This hotel, dating back to 1914,
has a stunningly ornate lobby and
ballroom. Elegant guest rooms.

STEHEKIN: North Cascades
Lodge at Stehekin $$
Resort **Road Map** 1 B2
1 Stehekin Landing, 98816
Tel *(509) 682-4494*
W lodgeatstehekin.com
Hidden in the North Cascades,
this lodge is accessible by ferry,
float plane, or hiking trail.
Comfortable rooms.

STEVENSON: Skamania Lodge $$
Inn/B&B **Road Map** 1 B3
1131 SW Skamania Lodge Way, 98648
Tel *(509) 427-7700*
W skamania.com
This place is popular with windsurfers, hikers, and mountain
bikers. A golf course, spa, and
fine-dining restaurant are just
some of the luxuries on offer.

TACOMA: Hotel Murano $$
Boutique **Road Map** 1 A2
1320 Broadway Plaza, 98402
Tel *(253) 238-8000*
W hotelmuranotacoma.com
This hip downtown spot
showcases sculptures and
art in public spaces. Modern
rooms, an upscale restaurant,
and spa services.

TACOMA:
Silver Cloud Inn $$
Inn/B&B **Road Map** 1 A2
2317 N Ruston Way, 98402
Tel *(253) 272-1300*
W silvercloud.com
The stylish rooms here have
microwaves and refrigerators,
as well as spectacular bay views.

WALLA WALLA: Marcus
Whitman Hotel $
Historic **Road Map** 1 C3
6 W Rose St, 99362
Tel *(866) 826-9422*
W marcuswhitmanhotel.com
This 1928 high-rise provides
good accommodations and
fine dining. The hotel has six
wine-tasting rooms.

DK Choice

WALLA WALLA: Inn
at Abeja $$$
Luxury **Road Map** 1 C3
2014 Mill Creek Rd, 99362
Tel *(509) 522-1234*
W abeja.net
This early 20th-century
farmstead is home to both a
winery and a sophisticated Inn.
Original cottages, the old
carriage house, and a barn all
house immaculate suites with
fine furnishings. Guests are
encouraged to explore the
surrounding acres of gardens,
creeks, and vineyards.

For more information on types of hotels *see pp283–5*

WOODINVILLE: Willows Lodge $$$
Luxury **Road Map** 1 B2
14580 NE 145 St, 98072
Tel *(425) 424-3900*
W willowslodge.com
This riverside resort in western
Washington's wine country has
award-winning restaurants.

YAKIMA: Birchfield Manor $$
Inn/B&B **Road Map** 1 B2
2018 Birchfield Rd, 98901
Tel *(509) 452-1960*
W birchfieldmanor.com
A farmhouse with elegant rooms
that are furnished with antiques.
The restaurant serves gourmet
New American fare.

Vancouver

Waterfront, Gastown, and Chinatown

Skwachàys Lodge $
Boutique **Map** 3 B3
31 W Pender, V6B 1R3
Tel *(604) 687-3589*
W skwachays.com
Aboriginal art is displayed throughout this Victorian building. Each
room is individually decorated
along a specific Aboriginal theme.

Pan Pacific Vancouver $$
Luxury **Map** 3 A1
999 Canada Pl, V6C 3B5
Tel *(604) 662-8111*
W panpacific.com
Pan Pacific Vancouver has
beautifully appointed rooms with
marble bathrooms. Lovely views.

Downtown

Fairmont Hotel Vancouver $$
Luxury **Map** 2 F2
900 W Georgia St, V6C 2W6
Tel *(604) 684-3131*
W fairmont.com
This landmark railroad hotel is
famous for its copper roof. Indoor
pool and spa services are available.

Sutton Place Hotel $$
Luxury **Map** 2 F2
845 Burrard St, V6Z 2K6
Tel *(604) 682-5511*
W suttonplace.com
A lavishly appointed property with
plush rooms. Spa, health center,
and a popular restaurant on-site.

Rosewood Hotel Georgia $$$
Luxury **Map** 2 F2
801 W Georgia St, V6C 1P7
Tel *(604) 682-5566*
W rosewoodhotels.com
Celebrities frequently opt for this
1920s Georgian Revival structure.
Elegant rooms and spa.

Mid-level views of downtown from Rosewood Hotel Georgia, Vancouver

South Granville and Yaletown

**Howard Johnson Vancouver
Hotel** $
Boutique **Map** 2 F3
1176 Granville St, V6Z 1L8
Tel *(604) 688-8701*
W hojovancouver.com
A popular and affordable choice
with a central location. There is free
Wi-Fi and a good hotel-restaurant.

Granville Island Hotel $$
Boutique **Map** 2 E5
1253 Johnston St, V6H 3R9
Tel *(604) 683-7373*
W granvilleislandhotel.com
The rooms here are stylish and
spacious, some with wooden
beams and Persian rugs. Enjoy
beautiful views of the water from
the popular in-house restaurant.

DK Choice

Opus Hotel $$
Boutique **Map** 2 F4
322 Davie St, V6B 5Z6
Tel *(604) 642-6787*
W opushotel.com
A hip hotel exuding opulence
and sophistication. The dramatically structured guest rooms,
defined by vibrant design
schemes, have spa bathrooms
and striking artwork by local
artists. Trendy on-site bar and
restaurant are popular with the
city's jet set.

Farther Afield

O Canada House $
Inn/B&B **Map** 2 E2
1114 Barclay St, V6E 1H1
Tel *(604) 688-0555*
W ocanadahouse.com
This restored 1897 house has a
wrap-around porch and a garden.
Try the gourmet breakfast and
various home-baked treats.

Sylvia Hotel $$
Boutique **Map** 1 C1
1154 Gilford St, V6G 2P6
Tel *(604) 681-9321*
W sylviahotel.com
A landmark 1912 brick and
terracotta building near English
Bay. The rooms with kitchens are
perfect for families. The hotel bar
is favored for its old-world charm.

British Columbia

**CLEARWATER:
Helmcken Falls Lodge** $$
Inn/B&B **Road Map** 2 B4
6664 Clearwater Valley Rd, V0E 1N1
Tel *(250) 674-3657*
W helmckenfalls.com
The lodge offers accommodations
at the Wells Gray Provincial Park
entrance. Outdoor activities.

**CRANBROOK:
Kootenay Country Inn** $
Inn/B&B **Road Map** 2 C4
1111 Cranbrook St, V1C 3S4
Tel *(250) 426-2296*
W kootenaycountryinn.com
A pet-friendly motel, the many
facilities here include a sauna
and laundry.

FERNIE: Griz Inn $
Inn/B&B **Road Map** 2 C4
5369 Ski Hill Rd, V0B 1M6
Tel *(800) 661-0118*
W grizinn.com
A ski-in, ski-out location close to
hiking options. This inn has an out-
door hot tub. Perfect for families.

**FORT ST. JOHN: Quality Inn
Northern Grand** $$
Inn/B&B **Road Map** 2 B2
9830 100th Ave, V1J 1Y5
Tel *(250) 787-0521*
W qualityinnnortherngrand.com
Set in the heart of Fort St. John,
this is a popular option with com-
fortable, well-equipped rooms.

GOLDEN: Palliser Lodge **$$**
Resort **Road Map** 2 C4
1420 Palliser Lodge Trail, V0A 1H0
Tel *(250) 344-8650*
W palliserlodgeresort.com
There are studios and condo suites with fireplaces, hot tubs, and fully equipped kitchens at this lodge.

HARRISON HOT SPRINGS:
Harrison Hot Springs
Resort & Spa **$**
Resort **Road Map** 2 B4
100 Esplanade Ave, V0M 1K0
Tel *(604) 796-2244*
W harrisonresort.com
A massive mineral springs pool complex, with outdoor pools. Spa, steam room, and sauna.

KAMLOOPS: Plaza Hotel **$**
Boutique **Road Map** 2 B4
405 Victoria St, V2C 2A9
Tel *(250) 377-8075*
W plazaheritagehotel.com
This heritage-style hotel dates from the 1920s and has individually decorated rooms.

KELOWNA: Manteo Resort **$**
Resort **Road Map** 2 B4
3762 Lakeshore Rd, V1W 3L4
Tel *(250) 860-1031*
W manteo.com
A lakefront resort that has pools, tennis courts, and a movie theater. Rent boats from the marina.

KOOTENAY NATIONAL PARK:
Kootenay Park Lodge **$$**
Inn/B&B **Road Map** 2 C4
Vermilion Crossing, Hwy 93, T1L 1B3
Tel *(403) 762-9196*
W kootenayparklodge.com
These simple log cabins were built by the Canadian Pacific Railway in 1923. Close to good hiking trails. Open early May–Sep.

NANAIMO: Buccaneer Inn **$**
Inn/B&B **Road Map** 2 B4
1577 Stewart Ave, V9S 4E3
Tel *(250) 753-1246*
W buccaneerinn.com
Buccaneer Inn has spacious rooms, lots of amenities, as well as manicured grounds with a BBQ area.

NELSON: Dancing Bear Inn **$**
Inn/B&B **Road Map** 2 C4
171 Baker St, V1L 4H1
Tel *(877) 352-7573*
W dancingbearinn.com
A backpacker lodge in a beautifully restored building. Comfortable dorms and double rooms.

PARKSVILLE: Tigh-Na-Mara **$$**
Resort **Road Map** 2 B4
1155 Resort Dr, V9P 2E5
Tel *(250) 248-2072*
W tigh-na-mara.com
This is British Columbia's largest spa resort, with log cottages, ocean-view condos, and studios.

PENTICTON: Naramata
Heritage Inn & Spa **$$$**
Historic **Road Map** 2 B4
3625 1st St, Naramata., V0H 1N0
Tel *(250) 496-6808*
W naramatainn.com
This elegant 1908 lakeside hotel has rooms with modern touches, such as heated bathroom floors.

PRINCE GEORGE: Esther's Inn **$**
Inn/B&B **Road Map** 2 B3
1151 Commercial Cres, V2M 6W6
Tel *(250) 562-4131*
W esthersinn.com
Esther's Inn has an indoor tropical garden courtyards, hot tubs, and an indoor pool with a water slide.

RADIUM HOT SPRINGS:
Bighorn Meadows Resort **$**
Resort **Road Map** 2 C4
8100 Golf Course Rd, V0A 1M0
Tel *(250) 347-2323*
W bighornmeadows.com
This resort has hotel rooms, condos, and villas – some with a BBQ grill. Gorgeous views and lots of activities, including golfing and skiing.

SMITHERS: Hudson Bay Lodge **$**
Inn/B&B **Road Map** 2 A3
3251 E Hwy 16, V0J 2N0
Tel *(250) 847-4581*
W hudsonbaylodge.com
Set at the base of Hudson Bay, this pleasant lodge has well-appointed rooms.

SOOKE:
Sooke Harbour House **$$$**
Inn/B&B **Road Map** 2 B5
1528 Whiffen Spit Rd, V0S 1N0
Tel *(250) 642-3421*
W sookeharbourhouse.com
A country-style inn by the sea, Sooke Harbour House has a fine-dining restaurant and spa.

TOFINO: Wickaninnish Inn **$$$**
Luxury **Road Map** 2 A4
500 Osprey Lane, Chesterman Beach, V0R 2Z0
Tel *(250) 725-3100*
W wickinn.com
Enjoy wonderful panoramic views of nearby islands from this oceanfront property. Spacious rooms.

VICTORIA: Gatsby Mansion Inn **$**
Inn/B&B **Road Map** 2 B5
309 Belleville St, V8V 1X2
Tel *(250) 388-9191*
W huntingdonmanor.com
Stained-glass windows, crystal chandeliers, fireplaces, and frescoed ceilings add to the charm of this elegant place.

> ### DK Choice
>
> **VICTORIA: Fairmont**
> **Empress** **$$$**
> Luxury **Road Map** 2 B5
> *721 Government St, V8W 1W5*
> **Tel** *(250) 384-8111*
> W fairmont.com
> This "grand duchess" of the Fairmont group is famed for its afternoon tea. Guest rooms are sumptuously appointed in period furnishings; many have city views. Superlative spa.

WHISTLER: Riverside RV Resort **$**
Resort **Road Map** 2 B4
8018 Mons Rd, V0N 1B8
Tel *(604) 905-5533*
W whistlercamping.com
This cluster of cabins and yurts is a good alternative to nearby hotels. The log cabins each have a kitchen.

WHISTLER: Fairmont
Chateau Whistler **$$$**
Luxury **Road Map** 2 B4
4599 Chateau Blvd, V0N 1B4
Tel *(604) 938-8000*
W fairmont.com
The opulent lobby at this stunning hotel has a gold-leaf-domed ceiling. The rooms and suites are luxurious. Famous golf course.

YOHO NATIONAL PARK:
Cathedral Mountain Lodge **$$$**
Luxury **Road Map** 2 C4
Yoho Valley Rd, V0A 1G0
Tel *(866) 619-6442*
W cathedralmountain.com
Surrounded by mountains, these beautiful log cabins come with fireplaces and private decks.

Evening view of the Fairmont Empress from Victoria's waterfront, BC

For more information on types of hotels *see pp283–5*

WHERE TO EAT AND DRINK

The Pacific Northwest is known for its large number of coffee bars as well as the vast range of fresh local seafood it has to offer, from wild salmon to oysters, clams, and crab. Portland, Seattle, and Vancouver have all experienced a culinary revolution – small neighborhood, chef-owned restaurants have popped up on seemingly every block, showcasing a broad array of cuisines and adding depth to the choices. Visitors can often find a terrific French bistro neighbored by an affordable Thai noodle house and a mid-range Mediterranean seafood restaurant. Farm-fresh, local flavors mark the ingenious creations of the region's finest restaurants, while numerous less expensive eateries boast down-to-earth fare with the same freshness.

Pacific Northwest Cuisine

Increasingly, Pacific Northwest restaurants offer menus that highlight local produce, of which there is a wide variety. Oregon's climate is particularly conducive to growing wild mushrooms. Washington is perhaps best known for its apples, though it also grows many types of berries. In British Columbia, tree fruits, including apples, pears, peaches, cherries, and plums, often feature in its cuisine. Pacific Northwest grapes and wineries are celebrated as some of the best in the world, so it is no surprise that there are many wine bars throughout the region. Seafood is very much the focus of Pacific Northwest cuisine. On just about every menu and in just about every type of restaurant, salmon, halibut, crab, mussels, clams, and oysters are on offer, whether in the form of cakes, chowder, or fish and chips. Smoked salmon, which has its origins in Native customs, is ubiquitous. Oysters are gaining in popularity, and, with so many varieties to choose from, making a meal of several types of oysters on the half-shell while sipping a local beer at one of the many oyster bars is a popular pastime of locals and visitors alike.

Eating healthily in the region's restaurants is easy. Low-fat dishes are staples on most menus, as are vegetarian options, ranging from salads and wraps to Mongolian grills and Buddhist banquets. Native cuisine, using local ingredients such as seaweed, fern shoots, wild berries, oolichan (a small silvery fish), and caribou, can also be enjoyed, and is sometimes combined with traditional Native song and dance performances in an authentic setting.

Alcohol and Smoking

Smoking is banned in all indoor public places in British Columbia. Washington has banned smoking statewide in all public places and in places of employment. In Oregon it has similarly been banned in workplaces, bars, and restaurants.

Alcohol is available only in licensed establishments. Dining in taverns or certain parts of restaurants may be restricted. Diners who plan to order alcohol in any establishment should always bring a valid form of picture identification, such as a driver's license or passport, as waiting staff are required by law to check the age of patrons who order alcohol. The legal drinking age in Washington and Oregon is 21; in British Columbia, 19.

Hours

Coffee shops and cafés serving full breakfasts open at 6 or 7am. With one on just about every downtown street corner, coffee shops are the best bet for a toasted bagel or pastry and a cup of coffee. Breakfast, which generally consists of some combination of pancakes, toast, eggs, omelets, sausages, and bacon, is typically served until 11am. On Sundays, brunch is served between 8am and 2pm at many restaurants that are not open for breakfast during the week.

Lunch hours are usually between 11:30am and 3pm. In the cities, many of the more upscale restaurants offer lunches that mirror the dinner menu in every aspect but price, making the midday meal a smart choice for travelers who want to dine at the best restaurants while on a budget.

Dinner hours generally run from 5pm to 9 or 10pm, later in busier areas and on weekends. Some exclusive restaurants open for dinner only. Almost all restaurants are open on Fridays

View over the vines at Old Vines Restaurant, Kelowna, BC *(see p304)*

and Saturdays, but it is not uncommon to encounter closures on Sundays and Mondays. Check in advance with each establishment for specific times.

Reservations

Reservations are needed for the better or more popular restaurants and some will only accept reservations for parties of six or more. However, most restaurants do not require reservations. If booking more than a day in advance, confirm the booking on the day of your reservation.

Prices

Dinner entrées in Oregon and Washington usually cost between $9 and $16 at casual restaurants; between $17 and $40 at fine-dining establishments. Taxes on foods and alcoholic beverages in Oregon and Washington vary from county to county; in the Seattle area, it is 9.5 percent. In BC, dinner entrées range from CAN $12 to $24 at casual spots, from CAN $25 to $40 at the more exclusive restaurants. Restaurant meals are not subject to the 8 percent tax. Lunch costs from CAN $7 to $20, breakfast CAN $5 to $12. Alcoholic drinks are subject to a tax of 10 percent.

Paying and Tipping

Nearly all restaurants accept major credit cards. Traveler's checks in US or Canadian currency are normally accepted

Meat-lovers' mecca, Metropolitan Grill steakhouse, Seattle *(see p300)*

Hastings House hosts genteel dining on Saltspring Island, BC *(see p305)*

with appropriate identification. Personal checks are usually not welcome.

At any sit-down restaurant with a waitperson, it is customary to tip 15 to 20 percent of the price of the meal. As a general rule, tipping 15 percent is about average; a 20 percent tip is generally given when service has been exceptionally good. When paying for the meal with a credit card, the tip amount can be added on the credit card slip. In addition, many restaurants charge a mandatory 18 percent gratuity for groups of more than six.

Dress Codes

The Pacific Northwest is, in general, a casual place. At most city restaurants, business-casual is appropriate: khakis and button-down shirts for men; a sweater or blouse and pants or skirt for women. Outside the cities, dress is often more casual, and most restaurants do not have dress codes. Usually, the more exclusive the restaurant, the more formal it is.

Children

Well-behaved children are welcome at most restaurants and many establishments cater especially to families with children. High chairs and booster seats are often available, as is a special kids' menu or portions.

Recommended Restaurants

Culinarily-speaking, among North American regions the Pacific Northwest is widely considered to be one of the strongest and most diverse. The restaurants

featured in this guide have been selected for their value, good food, atmosphere, and location. From authentic, no-frills snack shacks to creative New American gastronomy, these restaurants run across all price levels and cuisine types.

Alongside the ubiquitous oyster bars and seafood shanties, many of the Pacific Northwest's top-rated restaurants focus on fresh, local, seasonal ingredients in all elements of their cooking. International inspiration and innovative cooking techniques combine to create a distinctive regional cuisine. Attentive diners will note a heavy emphasis on regional wines and local craft beers, many of which garner national acclaim. Ethnic restaurants – French, Italian, Greek, and Indian to mention a few – are thriving and have given rise to a fusion cuisine unique to the West Coast. Lovers of Asian cuisines (particularly Japanese, Chinese, and Thai) are also well-served; due to the region's proximity, it has become a haven for expats from the Asian continent. There is usually at least one Thai and Japanese restaurant in every neighborhood. Sushi bars here are good as well, since the fish is so varied and fresh.

For the best of the best, look out for restaurants labeled as DK Choice. These establishments have been highlighted in recognition of an exceptional feature, such as a celebrity chef, exquisite food, or an inviting atmosphere. The majority of these are exceptionally popular among local residents and visitors, so be sure to inquire regarding reservations or you may be facing a lengthy wait for a table.

Where to Eat and Drink

Portland

Old Town and the Pearl District

Pearl Bakery　　　　　　　$
Bakery　　　　　　　　**Map** 1 C4
102 NW 9th Ave, 97209
Tel *(503) 827-0910*
A perfect stop for breakfast or lunch on the go, this small artisanal bakery serves superb breads. It uses organic Batdorf and Bronson coffee and locally sourced ingredients.

Clyde Common　　　　　　$$
New American　　　　　**Map** 1 B4
1014 SW Stark St, 97205
Tel *(503) 228-3333*
Visit this popular tavern for its innovative cocktails and small plates. Try the tagliarini with clams, chanterelles, and crab butter, or the scallops and spicy cantaloupe. Save room for the buttermilk blackberry ice cream.

Grüner　　　　　　　　$$
German　　　　　　　**Map** 1 B4
527 SW 12th Ave, 97205
Tel *(503) 241-7163*
Ultramodern furnishings adorn the dining room here, while the menu retains a distinctly alpine influence. The extensive European wine list features many German labels.

Little Bird Bistro　　　　$$
French　　　　　　　**Map** 1 C4
219 SW 6th Ave, 97204
Tel *(503) 688-5952*
The casual sister restaurant to the legendary Le Pigeon, Little Bird is a lovely lunch or dinner spot serving expert renditions of Parisian bistro fare such as crêpes, cassoulet, and Gruyère soufflé.

Maurice　　　　　　　$$
Nordic-French　　　　**Map** 1 C4
921 SW Oak St, 97205
Tel *(503) 224-9921*
Experience the perfect blend of Scandinavian and French flavors at this charming café, with an extensive vermouth menu. The desserts are prepared by one of the city's renowned pastry chefs. Don't miss the black pepper cheesecake.

Seres　　　　　　　　$$
Chinese　　　　　　　**Map** 1 B2
1105 NW Lovejoy St, 97209
Tel *(971) 222-7327*
Savor artfully prepared dishes from different provinces, including peppery Szechuan fare, in a quiet, stylish dining room. Fruity cocktails, myriad kinds of tea, and a great selection of white wines.

Downtown

Grassa　　　　　　　　$
Italian　　　　　　　**Map** 1 B4
1205 SW Washington St, 97205
Tel *(503) 241-1133*
Industrial decor and impeccable pasta dishes at great prices make Grassa a top pick. It offers seasonal salads, antipasti, and cocktails made with locally sourced inputs.

Departure　　　　　　$$$
Asian　　　　　　　　**Map** 1 C5
525 SW Morrison St, 97204
Tel *(503) 802-5370*
Enjoy the beautiful view from this restaurant that gives a modern twist to Northwestern seafood and Asian classics. Tuna and black truffle sashimi and Dungeness crab fried rice are highlights.

Higgins Restaurant　　　$$$
New American　　　　**Map** 3 B1
1239 SW Broadway, 97205
Tel *(503) 222-9070*
Inspired by classic Parisian bistros, this light-filled, multilevel space offers a menu featuring inventive preparations of locally sourced produce, meats, and fish. The wine list has a strong Northwest focus.

Jake's Famous Crawfish　$$$
Seafood　　　　　　**Map** 1 B4
401 SW 12th Ave, 97205
Tel *(503) 226-1419*
Opened in 1892, this fish house boasts dozens of varieties of fresh fish, that can be steamed, stuffed, seared, sautéed, or simply grilled. The polished paneling and old artwork on the walls create a lovely atmosphere.

Traditional Chinese styling and Szechuan flavors at Seres, Portland

Farther Afield

Apizza Scholls　　　　　$
Pizzeria　　　　**Road Map** 1 A3
4741 SE Hawthorne Blvd, 97215
Tel *(503) 233-1286*
This wildly popular spot is devoted to classic New York-style pies made from slow-fermented dough and cooked at nearly 900 degrees. Service can be brusque, and the place closes early if the dough runs out.

Genies Café　　　　　　$
New American　　**Road Map** 1 A3
1101 SE Division St, 97202
Tel *(503) 445-9777*
This breakfast and lunch spot serves seasonal, sustainable cuisine. Specials may include a morel scramble or sausage frittata with fiddleheads. Several versions of eggs Benedict and classic sandwiches available.

Hopworks Urban Brewery　$
New American　　**Road Map** 1 A3
2944 SE Powell Blvd, 97202
Tel *(503) 232-4677*
This friendly establishment, located in a converted tractor showroom, is committed to being as carbon-neutral as possible. Mainly organic, local ingredients are used in both their beers and food. Fantastic root beer. Don't miss the pretzels, black bean corn cakes, and craft-beer hummus.

Lardo　　　　　　　　$
New American　　**Road Map** 1 A3
1212 SE Hawthorne Bvd, 97214
Tel *(503) 234-7786*
This food cart turned bricks-and-mortar restaurant serves sophisticated interpretations of classic burgers and sub sandwiches. The dirty fries with fried herbs and pork belly are a must-try. Craft beers and cocktails.

Podnah's Pit Barbecue　　$
Barbecue　　　　**Road Map** 1 A3
1625 NE Killingsworth St, 97211
Tel *(503) 281-3700*
Come here for slow-smoked, Texas-style barbecue beloved by many. The dining room is decidedly no-frills, but the moist, tender meats from the oak-fired

smoker keep the place packed. Small selection of wines and microbrews on offer.

Screen Door $
Southern **Road Map** 1 A3
2337 E Burnside St, 97214
Tel *(503) 542-0880*
This bright, roomy restaurant serves an authentic survey of Southern cuisine made with ingredients from Oregon farms. Standouts include buttermilk fried chicken, pecan-crusted trout and milk chocolate cream pie.

La Sirenita $
Mexican **Road Map** 1 A3
2817 NE Alberta St, 97211
Tel *(503) 335-8283*
This good-value eatery serves fast food such as tacos and burgers to a wide following. Has almost everything on the menu, including hefty, meaty burritos. Also try their authentic *menudo* (tripe) and *birria* (lamb) soups.

Tasty n Sons $
New American **Road Map** 1 A3
3808 N Williams Ave, 97212
Tel *(503) 621-1400*
Tasty does hearty American fare, such as chicken and dumplings, barbecue ribs, and shrimp and grits. It sports communal tables, with folks lining up around the block for its weekend brunch.

Wong's King Seafood Restaurant $
Chinese **Road Map** 1 A3
8733 SE Division St, 97266
Tel *(503) 788-8883*
Authentic, handmade dim sums plus an extensive list of Chinese standards are available here. A no-frills dining hall atmosphere, but gets really hectic on weekends. Two other locations in Greater Portland area.

Bamboo Sushi $$
Sushi **Road Map** 1 A3
310 SE 28th Ave, 97214
Tel *(503) 232-5255*
Dine in or enjoy a takeaway of sustainable seafood sushi at reasonable rates. Signature house rolls, such as ring of fire with fried oysters and jalapeno marmalade, should not be missed.

Davenport $$
New American **Road Map** 1 A3
2215 E Burnside St, 97232
Tel *(503) 236-8747*
Juxtaposing a casual setting with a refined menu, Davenport is known for its varied wine list and the use of seasonal Northwestern ingredients. The halibut in tomato broth is excellent.

A rustic setting to enjoy spicy Thai cuisine at Pok Pok, Portland

Nostrana $$
Italian **Road Map** 1 A3
1401 SE Morrison St, 97214
Tel *(503) 234-2427*
The rustic decor at Nostrana complements the comfort food on the menu. Known for its wood-fired pizzas, it also serves excellent salads and pastas. Book ahead.

Olympia Provisions $$
New American **Road Map** 1 A3
107 SE Washington, 97214
Tel *(503) 954-3663*
Pick up home-made salamis and local cheese boards from Portland's favorite charcuterie shopping spot, that also serves refined European-style cuisine. The French saucisson with white beans and salsa verde is worth trying.

DK Choice

Pok Pok $$
Thai **Road Map** 1 A3
3226 SE Division St, 97202
Tel *(503) 232-1387*
One of the region's most renowned restaurants, Pok Pok churns out delicious northern Thai specialties. The varied drinks list includes drinking vinegars and inventive cocktails. Fiery salads and spicy-sour curries provide flavors and textures rarely enjoyed in the US. The bedrock of a culinary empire that has extended successfully to NYC.

Woodsman Tavern $$
New American **Road Map** 1 A3
4537 SE Division St, 97206
Tel *(971) 373-8264*
Part old-school tavern, part big-city restaurant, Woodsman pays homage to Oregon's heritage. The local landscape adorns the walls; local bounty, the menu. Sophisticated all-American entrées such as dry-aged rib-eye and whole grilled trout. An impressive raw bar.

Ava Gene's $$$
Italian **Road Map** 1 A3
3377 SE Division St, 97202
Tel *(971) 229-0571*
This polished Roman trattoria is in SE Division's up-and-coming restaurant row. It specializes in rustic pastas, with beautifully presented vegetable sides. A well-curated, reasonably priced list of Italian wines.

Castagna $$$
New American **Road Map** 1 A3
1752 SE Hawthorne Bvd, 97214
Tel *(503) 231-7373*
The stunning, artful presentations of contemporary Northwest cuisine feature flora, fauna, wild mushrooms, game, and more. Choose between the four-course fixed menu or the ten-course tasting menu. Reservations are a must.

Langbaan $$$
Thai **Road Map** 1 A3
6 SE 28th Ave, 97214
Tel *(971) 344-2564*
This modern, family-friendly place serves flavorful Thai fare. The dishes are always well-presented, be it scallops in rice cups floating on a sea of coconut milk or hand-spun egg nets with a filling of pork and peanuts.

DK Choice

Paley's Place $$$
New American **Road Map** 1 A3
1204 NW 21st Ave, 97209
Tel *(503) 243-2403*
A shrine of Northwest cuisine, Paley's Place is an intimate spot located inside a charming Victorian house in a historic neighborhood. It is owned and run by one of the city's star chefs. The menu focuses on local, seasonal, and sustainable ingredients. Do not miss the house-made charcuterie and local cheeses.

For more information on types of restaurants *see p293*

Le Pigeon $$$
New American   Map 2 F4
738 E Burnside St, 97214
Tel *(503) 546-8796*
The adventurous French-inspired food at Le Pigeon has won national acclaim. The intimate dining room has communal tables as well as a chef's counter. The menu changes regularly, however some dishes remain such as beef cheeks bourguignon. A wide selection of wines on offer.

Oregon

ASHLAND: Peerless Restaurant $$
New American   **Road Map** 1 A5
265 4th St, 97520
Tel *(541) 488-6067* **Closed** *Sun & Mon*
Savor tasty, creative Northwest cuisine with a focus on sustainability, served in a handsomely restored hotel. Fresh local meats, produce, and artisanal cheese from local dairies. Award-winning wine list.

ASHLAND: Smithfields Restaurant and Bar $$
Steakhouse   **Road Map** 1 A5
36 S 2nd St, 97520
Tel *(541) 488-9948*
The award-winning chef/owner turns out a nose-to-tail menu at this local favorite. While there are excellent vegetarian options, the steak and charcuterie are the specialties. Don't miss the bacon beignets.

ASTORIA: Wet Dog Café $
American   **Road Map** 1 A3
144 11th St, 97103
Tel *(503) 325-6975*
Housed in a huge old warehouse on the Columbia River waterfront, this café offers typical pub fare and craft brews by Astoria

Chandeliers below a ceiling of stained glass at Palm Court, Baker City, Oregon

Brewing Company, located in the same space. Sit outside on the deck in summer.

ASTORIA: Columbian Café $$
New American   **Road Map** 1 A3
1114 Marine Dr, 97103
Tel *(503) 325-2233* **Closed** *Mon & Tue*
A local institution, this hole-in-the-wall diner features a small but funky environs, with an eclectic clientele. Popular for its specialty crêpes and hearty breakfasts. Fresh, local seafood, as well as plenty of vegetarian options.

BAKER CITY: Paizano's Pizza $
Italian   **Road Map** 1 C3
2940 10th St, 97814
Tel *(541) 524-1000*
This beloved eatery is known for inexpensive, tasty pizzas and great toasted subs. The menu also includes large salads, home-made desserts, and several gluten-free choices. Friendly service.

BAKER CITY: Palm Court $$$
New American   **Road Map** 1 C3
1996 Main St, 97814
Tel *(541) 523-1889*
The ambience in the historic Geiser Grand Hotel's restaurant is stately, with crystal chandeliers, crisp linens, wood trim, and a stained-glass skylight. Specialties on the menu include the must-try mesquite-smoked prime rib.

BEND: Deschutes Brewery and Public House $
American   **Road Map** 1 B4
1044 NW Bond St, 97701
Tel *(541) 382-9242*
This award-winning brewery is one of the region's top beer producers. The standard pub fare, including specialty sandwiches, freshly ground burgers, and home-made sausages, holds up to the craft beers.

BEND: Zydeco Kitchen & Cocktails $$$
Southern   **Road Map** 1 B4
919 Bond St, 97701
Tel *(541) 312-2899*
Zydeco serves American favorites with a Southern twist, using mostly organic ingredients. The menu features a range of Cajun-inspired staples, including barbecued ribs, corn fritters, and jambalaya. Festive atmosphere, top-notch service.

CANNON BEACH: Mo's Cannon Beach $$
Seafood   **Road Map** 1 A3
195 Warren Way, 97145
Tel *(503) 436-1111*
An Oregon coast classic, Mo's servies basic seafood such as

The pleasant terrace at Deschutes Brewery and Public House, Bend

rich clam chowder and fish and chips in excellent family-friendly environs. Stunning location, with views of waves lapping the shore and Haystack Rock in the distance.

CANNON BEACH: The Irish Table $$$
Irish   **Road Map** 1 A3
1235 S Hemlock St., 97145
Tel *(503) 436-0708* **Closed** *Wed & Thu*
This homey, welcoming spot dishes up authentic Irish dishes, made with local produce and seafood. Selections from local wineries prove popular, as do the single malt Scotches, Irish whiskeys, and imported beers.

CARLTON: Cuvée $$
French   **Road Map** 1 A3
214 W Main St, 97111
Tel *(503) 852-6555* **Closed** *Mon & Tue*
This refined restaurant, in a charming small town, offers traditional French country fare to accompany the wines of the local vineyards. The menu is strong on seafood, with excellent bouillabaisse and coquilles St. Jacques, but also includes such delicacies as escargot.

DK Choice

DAYTON: Joel Palmer House $$$
New American **Road Map** 1 A3
600 Ferry St, 97114
Tel *(503) 864-2995* **Closed** *Sun & Mon*
A top wine-country destination, Joel Palmer House is set in a historic antebellum mansion. The internationally inspired tasting menus place a focus on wild, local mushrooms and truffles, and whatever else is in season. Knowledgeable servers help choose from the varied wine list that features Oregon pinot noir, pinot gris, and chardonnay.

DUNDEE: Tina's $$$
New American   **Road Map** 1 A3
760 Hwy 99 W, 97115
Tel *(503) 538-8880*
Renowned as a pioneer in wine-country fine dining, Tina's offers a French-Northwest menu focusing on seasonal, regional ingredients, which are sourced from local farmers. The terrific wine list reads like an Oregon winemakers' Hall of Fame.

EUGENE: Taqueria Mi Tierra $
Mexican   **Road Map** 1 A4
68 Blair St, 97402
Tel *(541) 743-0779*
This family-run, hole-in-the-wall taqueria churns out authentic Mexican flavors. On the menu are combo plates for under $10, served with a variety of fresh salsas. Tacos are also popular; choose from a range of fillings including chicken, goat, pork, and shrimp.

EUGENE: Beppe & Gianni's Trattoria $$
Italian   **Road Map** 1 A4
1646 E 19th Ave, 97403
Tel *(541) 683-6661*
This restaurant is known for a variety of expertly executed pastas alongside meat and fish dishes, with fine fresh produce incorporated throughout. Magnificent Italian wine list.

EUGENE: Oregon Electric Station $$
New American   **Road Map** 1 A4
27 E 5th Ave, 97401
Tel *(541) 485-4444*
Housed in the beautiful 1912 train depot, this charming place serves top-notch steak, fish, and pasta dishes complemented by more than 250 wines. Sit in one of many lounges, aboard antique train cars, or on a patio.

GLENEDEN BEACH: The Dining Room at Salishan $$$
New American   **Road Map** 1 A3
7760 N Hwy 101, 97388
Tel *(800) 452-2300*
Located in the exclusive Salishan Spa & Golf Resort, this place enjoys a long-established reputation as one of the region's best restaurants. Expertly prepared regional delicacies along with a wine list featuring an unrivaled collection of Oregon labels.

GOVERNMENT CAMP: Huckleberry Inn $$
American   **Road Map** 1 B3
88611 E Government Camp Loop, 97028
Tel *(503) 272-3325*
A rustic inn set in a mountainside village near Mt. Hood. There is

Warm interior at Celilo, Hood River, Oregon

24-hour dining in the family-style restaurant, plus an adjoining steakhouse open on weekends during ski season. Burgers, sandwiches, and breakfast favorites dominate the menu.

HOOD RIVER: Full Sail Brewing Company $
American   **Road Map** 1 B3
506 Columbia St, 97031
Tel *(541) 386-2247*
This popular brewery's pub and tasting room is an ideal spot to take in the Columbia River breeze while sampling a range of award-winning craft brews. Delicious small plates, sandwiches, and salads to accompany the beer.

HOOD RIVER: Celilo $$
New American   **Road Map** 1 B3
16 Oak St, 97031
Tel *(541) 386-5710*
Celilo is driven by a devotion to using fresh and local ingredients, and the kitchen turns out seasonal, delicious dishes, including superb home-made pastas. The decor resembles a timbered lodge.

HOOD RIVER: Mount Hood Railroad Dinner Train $$$
American   **Road Map** 1 B3
110 Railroad Ave, 97031
Tel *(541) 386-3556* **Closed** *Nov–Mar; Apr–Oct: Mon–Fri*
Hop aboard a 4-hour rail excursion on Saturday night or Sunday afternoon and enjoy gorgeous mountain views. Prime rib, eggs Benedict and other classic dishes served in restored dining cars with roomy booths and large windows.

JOSEPH: Embers Brewhouse $
American   **Road Map** 1 C3
204 N Main St, 97846
Tel *(541) 432-2739*
This casual brewery offers more than a dozen regional craft brews, along with appetizers,

sandwiches, burgers, pizzas, and calzones. Large deck offers views of the beautiful Wallowa Valley.

JOSEPH: Outlaw Restaurant and Saloon $
American   **Road Map** 1 C3
108 N Main St, 97846
Tel *(541) 432-4321* **Closed** *Sun*
This relaxed, family-friendly option serves American standards such as steaks, pastas, burgers, and seafood dishes. Kids appreciate the in-house ice-cream bar. Lots of space for outside dining, making for a great summer spot.

LINCOLN CITY: Blackfish Café $
New American   **Road Map** 1 A3
2733 NW Hwy 101, 97367
Tel *(541) 996-1007* **Closed** *Mon & Tue*
The award-winning chef at Blackfish has ties with local fishermen, growers, and foragers to obtain the freshest ingredients possible. Seafood dominates the ever-changing and reasonably priced menu.

MCMINNVILLE: Nick's Italian Café $
New American   **Road Map** 1 A3
521 NE 3rd St, 97128
Tel *(503) 434-4471*
This wine-country landmark in a former soda fountain is popular for its hearty, multi-course, fixed-menu dinners. It also has a good wine list featuring local labels.

NEWPORT: April's at Nye Beach $$$
Italian   **Road Map** 1 A3
749 NW 3rd St, 97365
Tel *(541) 265-6855*
This cozy café offers scenic ocean views, and fine, creatively conceived Northwest cuisine with Italian accents, accompanied by a well-chosen, affordable wine list. Excellent desserts.

For more information on types of restaurants *see p293*

OTIS: Otis Café $
American **Road Map** 1 A3
1259 Salmon River Hwy, 97368
Tel *(541) 994-2813*
This little roadside café is an obligatory stop for those headed to the coast on the Salmon River Highway. Renowned for its huge, delicious breakfasts, cinnamon rolls, and marionberry pie.

PACIFIC CITY: Pelican Pub and Brewery $$
American **Road Map** 1 A3
33180 Cape Kiwanda Dr, 97135
Tel *(503) 965-7007*
Located at the foot of Cape Kiwanda's sandstone bluffs, this award-winning craft brewery has a sophisticated pub menu served all day in a relaxed atmosphere.

SALEM: La Capitale Brasserie $$
French **Road Map** 1 A3
508 State St, 97301
Tel *(503) 585-1975* **Closed** *Sun*
Housed in a historic downtown building, this restaurant focuses on local, seasonal ingredients, craft beers, and fine wines. Savor creative preparations of classic French dishes, and do not miss the home-made charcuterie.

Seattle

Pioneer Square and Downtown

Salumi $
Italian **Map** 4 D3
309 3rd Ave S, 98104
Tel *(206) 621-8772*
This tiny Pioneer Square lunch spot is famous for its authentic, intensely flavorful, Italian cured meat products. There is also a small menu of sandwiches, soups, and pastas.

Pike Place Market and the Waterfront

Athenian Inn $
American **Map** 3 C1
1517 Pike Pl, 98101
Tel *(206) 624-7166*
An old-time spot in Pike Place Market offering friendly service along with an extensive, seafood-heavy menu of American fare and microbrews. Renowned for its appearance in the movie *Sleepless in Seattle (see p139).*

Tango Restaurant & Lounge $
Spanish **Map** 3 C1
1100 Pike St, 98101
Tel *(206) 583-0382*
The favorites at this tapas bar, located in a 1908 brick building, are

The busy dining room at Matt's in the Market, Seattle

shrimp ceviche, paella, and chocolate diablo cake. Latin-inspired cocktails go great with the upbeat atmosphere. Attentive service.

Damn the Weather $$
New American **Map** 4 D4
116 1st Ave S, 98104
Tel *(206) 946-1283*
Expect the unexpected at this fashionable gastropub that serves great cocktails and inventive small plates of chicken fat fries, duck pot pie, beef heart tartare, and octopus risotto.

Le Pichet $$
French **Map** 3 C1
1933 1st Ave, 98101
Tel *(206) 256-1499*
This crowded bistro brings a little piece of Paris to Seattle, complete with a zinc bar. Highlights include escargots, lamb and garlic sausage, and roasted chicken. Head here in the morning for coffee and pastries and at lunch for charcuterie.

The Pink Door $$
Italian **Map** 3 B1
1919 Post Alley, 98101
Tel *(206) 443-3241*
A lively trattoria serving hearty fare. A commitment to organic and sustainable products extends to the excellent wine list. Burlesque and cabaret performances are featured throughout the week.

Ivar's Acres of Clams $$$
Seafood **Map** 3 C2
1001 Alaskan Way, 98104
Tel *(206) 624-6852*
This venerable local institution offers terrific crab, clam, oyster, and salmon dishes, as well as the classic fish and chips they have been serving since 1938.

Matt's in the Market $$$
New American **Map** 3 C1
94 Pike St, suite 32, 98101
Tel *(206) 467-7909*
Tucked into the Corner Market Building, this gourmet restaurant has a convivial atmosphere and a seasonal, ever-changing, menu. Wines and local ales on offer.

Place Pigalle $$$
French **Map** 3 C1
81 Pike St, 98101
Tel *(206) 624-1756*
A quiet little nook, in a former fisherman's tavern, Place Pigalle is perfect for a romantic evening. Serves up scrumptious cuisine, with award-winning seafood dishes. Gorgeous views.

Seattle Center and Belltown

FareStart $
American **Map** 2 D5
700 Virginia St, 98101
Tel *(206) 267-7601*
FareStart provides culinary training for the homeless and other disadvantaged individuals. Open for lunch on weekdays, with a dinner service featuring local chefs on Thursday nights.

Kedai Makan $
Malaysian **Map** 2 F4
1802 Bellevue Ave, 98122
Tel *(206) 267-7601* **Closed** *Tue*
Crowds throng to Kedai Makan for authentic Malaysian street food and a creative cocktail list. The menu features hand-cut noodles

with prawns, chicken, and sprouts and an innovative take on *nasi goreng* (Malaysian fried rice).

Pagliacci Pizzeria $
Pizzeria **Map** 1 B3
550 Queen Anne Ave N, 98109
Tel *(206) 285-1232*
This popular local pizzeria chain offers traditional New York-style pies with thin crusts and tangy sauce. The many toppings include spicy pepperoni made by the local stalwart, Salumi.

Dahlia Lounge $$
New American **Map** 2 D5
2001 4th Ave, 98121
Tel *(206) 682-4142*
The sophisticated menu at Dahlia Lounge highlights the best of Pacific Northwest cuisine. The daily changing menu may include offerings such as rotisserie Peking duck or grilled Yakutat king salmon. Knowledgeable staff.

Palace Kitchen $$
New American **Map** 2 D5
2030 5th Ave, 98121
Tel *(206) 448-2001*
This stylish spot under the Monorail serves excellent dishes such as local mussels with chorizo, artisanal cheeses, and burgers.

Shiro's $$
Sushi **Map** 1 C5
2401 2nd Ave, 98121
Tel *(206) 443-9844*
A pleasant, intimate space where sushi master Shiro Kashiba serves a repertoire of familiar cuts and special rolls, plus other seafood specialties including monkfish liver pâté, broiled black cod, and sea urchin tempura.

Taylor Shellfish $$
Seafood **Map** 2 F4
1521 Melrose Ave, 98101
Tel *(206) 501-4321*
Savor farm-to-table shellfish such as Geoduck clams and Washington oysters, before moving on to oyster stew and shrimp dumplings. The wine list is impressive.

Farther Afield

Beth's Café $
American **Road Map** 1 A2
7311 Aurora Ave N, 98103
Tel *(206) 782-5588*
Legendary dive for more than half a century, Beth's serves massive breakfasts and other greasy-spoon classics to both the early-morning and the late-night crowd. Their signature omelets come in 6- and 12-egg versions.

Café Flora $
Vegetarian **Road Map** 1 A2
2901 E Madison St, 98112
Tel *(206) 325-9100*
This airy Madison Valley haunt celebrates the possibilities of vegetarian cooking by utilizing the seasonal bounty of the region. Signatures include inventive pizzas and coconut-breaded tofu with sweet chili sauce. Eclectic, well-chosen wine list.

Elemental Pizza $
Pizzeria **Road Map** 1 A2
2630 NE University Village St, 98105
Tel *(206) 524-4930*
This popular University Village eatery is renowned for its award-winning, wood-fired pizzas – with offbeat toppings such as ghost pepper salami – and local craft brews. Friendly staffers maintain an upbeat vibe. Fun desserts include ice-cream sandwiches, so make sure you leave room.

House of Hong $
Chinese **Road Map** 1 A2
409 8th Ave S, 98104
Tel *(206) 622-7997*
A top-rated dim sum restaurant during the day, with carts speeding through the vast dining room carrying a plethora of Cantonese treats. At night, the menu changes to Hunan and Szechuan dishes.

Elliott's Oyster House $$
Seafood **Road Map** 1 A2
1201 Alaskan Way, 98101
Tel *(206) 623-4340*
This busy seafood house is located in the heart of the downtown waterfront. Focal point of the teak- and copper-accented interior is the 21-ft- (7-m-) long oyster bar housing as many as 20 different varieties.

The Walrus and the Carpenter, one of Seattle's most popular establishments

Gastropod $$
New American **Road Map** 1 A2
3201 1st Ave S, 98134
Tel *(206) 403-1228*
A tiny restaurant and pub serving its own craft ales alongside an inventive menu. Try the jalapeño, sour cream, and tequila ice cream; and the *okonomiyaki* (Japanese pancake balls). Ask about beer pairings – they know their stuff.

Mamnoon $$
Lebanese/Syrian **Road Map** 1 A2
1508 Melrose Ave, 98122
Tel *(206) 906-9606*
Sample a fusion of Middle Eastern flavors from Lebanon, Syria, and Iran, including charred eggplant and lamb ragu meze, and garlicky grilled *shish taouk* (chicken kebab). Finish with a chocolate *labneh* (strained yogurt) ice-cream sandwich.

Manolin $$
Seafood **Road Map** 1 A2
3621 Stone Way N, 98103
Tel *(206) 294-3331*
Specializing in wood-fired meat and seafood, Manolin also has a wooden bar that serves rum-based cocktails. The inventive menu features dishes such as black cod and mole, and rockfish ceviche with fried sweet potato shreds.

RockCreek $$
Seafood **Road Map** 1 A2
4300 N Fremont Ave, 98103
Tel *(206) 557-7532*
A relaxed atmosphere awaits diners here. The seafood menu lets the catch of the day speak for itself. Fast and friendly service.

Sitka & Spruce $$
New American **Road Map** 1 A2
1531 Melrose Ave, 98122
Tel *(206) 324-0662*
This award-winning restaurant offers inviting small plates featuring a dizzying kaleidoscope of local, seasonal ingredients. The special Mexican menu on Monday nights is good value.

> ### DK Choice
>
> **The Walrus and the Carpenter** $$
> Seafood **Road Map** 1 A2
> *4743 Ballard Ave NW, 98107*
> **Tel** *(206) 395-9227*
> Nationally renowned, this rustic oyster bar is set in the hip Ballard neighborhood. The seasonal small-plates menu includes local clams and mussels, house-smoked fish, and specialty meats. It also offers a wide selection of wine, craft cocktails, and beer.

For more information on types of restaurants *see p293*

Canlis $$$
New American   **Road Map** 1 A2
2576 Aurora Ave N, 98109
Tel *(206) 283-3313*
Part of the vanguard of Seattle
fine dining since 1950, this special-
occasion favorite has terrific Lake
Union views, fabulous seafood
and steaks, and an extensive wine
list. There's also live music. Casual
clothing not allowed.

Crush $$$
New American   **Road Map** 1 A2
2319 E Madison St, 98112
Tel *(206) 302-7874*
Set in a remodeled Tudor house,
Crush serves modern Northwest
cuisine devoted to seasonal,
sustainable ingredients. The ever-
changing menu may feature
seared scallops with persimmon
or black cod with Syrah sauce.

The Herbfarm $$$
New American   **Road Map** 1 A2
14590 NE 145th St, 98072
Tel *(206) 485-5300*
Experience extravagant dining in
a charming, comfortable setting.
Nine-course dinners utilize the
on-site farm's produce, and are
expertly paired with wines from
the 26,000-bottle cellar.

Metropolitan Grill $$$
Steakhouse   **Road Map** 1 A2
820 2nd Ave, 98104
Tel *(206) 624-3287*
This luxurious steakhouse
provides a sophisticated setting
for enjoying top-notch steaks and
chops. The wine list specializes in
big West Coast reds.

Washington

**ASHFORD: Alexander's
Country Inn** $$
New American   **Road Map** 1 B2
37515 State Rd 706 E, 98304
Tel *(800) 654-7615*   **Closed** *Winter:
Mon–Thu*
A classic 1912 inn serving award-
winning fare just a mile from
Mt. Rainier National Park. Fresh
steelhead trout from the on-
site pond headlines a menu of
seafood, steaks, and pasta.

BELLINGHAM: The Oyster Bar $$$
Seafood   **Road Map** 1 A1
2578 Chuckanut Dr, 98232
Tel *(360) 766-6185*
This venerable institution dates
back to the 1920s. The stellar
seafood is accompanied by jaw-
dropping views of the San Juan
Islands. Menu highlights include
crab cakes, steamed mussels, and
a variety of local oysters.

New American cuisine served in a charming old-world setting at The Herbfarm, Seattle

CHELAN: Lakeview Drive-In $
American   **Road Map** 1 B2
323 W Manson Hwy, 98816
Tel *(509) 682-5322*
Since 1957 this place has been
a local institution thanks to an
old-school drive-in atmosphere,
friendly service, and affordable
food. Big beef burgers prove
popular, as do French fries served
with home-made seasoning and
tartare sauce.

CHELAN: Local Myth Pizza $
Pizzeria   **Road Map** 1 B2
122 S Emerson St, 98816
Tel *(509) 682-2914*   **Closed** *Sun &
Mon*
This funky little pizzeria is always
busy in the summer, when locals
and tourists pack the surrounding
resort community. Go for the thin-
crust pies with gourmet toppings
such as prosciutto and walnuts.

COLVILLE: Lovitt Restaurant $$
New American   **Road Map** 1 C1
149 US-395, 98862
Tel *(509) 684-5444*
Set in a restored farmhouse,
this delightful restaurant uses
locally produced, seasonal
ingredients in its dishes. Also
known for its list of local wines.

**EASTSOUND: Rose's
Bakery & Café** $
American   **Road Map** 1 A1
382 Prune Alley, 98245
Tel *(360) 376-5805*   **Closed** *Sun*
This popular lunch spot serves
salads, sandwiches, and thin-crust
pizzas made with local, organic
ingredients. House favorites
include pasta with fire-roasted
vegetables and Mediterranean
lamb meatloaf sandwiches.

ELLENSBURG: Valley Café $
New American   **Road Map** 1 B2
105 W 3rd Ave, 98926
Tel *(509) 925-3050*
The decor at this Art Deco bistro
in the heart of Washington's

cowboy country, is that of a
1930s diner. The menu highlights
local meats and produce. Terrific
wine list full of regional wines.

**FRIDAY HARBOR:
Duck Soup Inn** $$
New American   **Road Map** 1 A1
50 Duck Soup Ln, 98250
Tel *(360) 378-4878*   **Closed** *Mon*
Elegant, cozy restaurant situated
by a pond in the woods of San
Juan Island. Innovative, globally
influenced dishes are made with
locally sourced meats, seafood,
herbs, and flowers.

**FRIDAY HARBOR: The Place
Bar & Grill** $$
Asian   **Road Map** 1 A1
1 Spring St, 98250
Tel *(360) 378-8707*
Small, sophisticated waterfront
spot offering exquisite Asian-
inflected meals. Menu highlights
include a Pacific Rim shrimp
noodle bowl and New Zealand
lamb chops with Indonesian
ginger-soy marinade.

**LEAVENWORTH:
Andreas Keller** $
German   **Road Map** 1 B2
829 Front St, 98826
Tel *(509) 548-6000*
Casually traditional Bavarian-style
eatery serving hearty schnitzel,
Weinkraut, and other German
classics. Live accordion music
adds to the fun, kid-friendly
atmosphere. Impressive beer
list featuring Bavarian brews.

**LEAVENWORTH:
Café Mozart** $$
German   **Road Map** 1 B2
829 Front St, 98826
Tel *(509) 548-0600*
The elegant Café Mozart offers
refined Middle European fare
such as schnitzels, roast duck,
and *Sauerbraten*. Germany and
Washington are well represented
on the varied wine list.

Friendly service at The Depot Restaurant, Seaview, Washington

LOPEZ ISLAND: Bay Café $$
New American   **Road Map** 1 A1
9 Old Post Rd, 98261
Tel *(509) 468-3700* **Closed** *Mon & Tue*
A magnet for epicures, Bay Café affords magnificent views of the waterfront. Flavor combinations are unusual, with dishes often drawing on far-flung, global influences.

MAZAMA: Freestone Inn $$
New American   **Road Map** 1 B1
31 Early Winters Dr, 98833
Tel *(509) 996-3906*
The mountain views and the stone hearth are as memorable as the creative fare at this luxury lakeside inn. Typical dishes include pan-fried local goat's cheese and herb-crusted chicken with three-mushroom sauce.

OLYMPIA: McMenamins Spar Café $
American   **Road Map** 1 A2
114 4th Ave E, 98501
Tel *(360) 357-6444*
Ales are brewed on the premises of this homey 1935 café with an old-time, blue-collar feel. Try the Olympic oyster stew.

PORT TOWNSEND: Khu Larb Thai $
Thai   **Road Map** 1 A2
225 Adams St, 98368
Tel *(360) 385-5023* **Closed** *Tue*
In the heart of historic downtown resides what was the first Thai restaurant on the Olympic peninsula. The menu is strong on seafood and vegetarian dishes.

PORT TOWNSEND: Silverwater Café $
New American   **Road Map** 1 A2
237 Taylor St, 98368
Tel *(360) 385-6448*
Airy, mellow spot offers creative Northwest cuisine with occasional Mediterranean and Asian accents. Outstanding soups and seafood dishes, made with local produce.

SEAVIEW: The Depot Restaurant $$$
New American   **Road Map** 1 A2
1208 38th Pl & L St, 98644
Tel *(360) 642-7880*
This fine-dining restaurant is housed in a former railroad depot dating from 1905. Small plates and dinner entrées include wild broiled oysters in garlic butter, rack of lamb with Middle Eastern spices, and pork shoulder in Southern Comfort barbecue sauce.

SPOKANE: Steam Plant Grill $
American   **Road Map** 1 C2
159 S Lincoln St, 99201
Tel *(509) 777-3900*
This stylish grill, set in an old steam and electric plant, is popular for power lunches, with a bustling bar for after work hours. Sandwiches, pastas, and creative meat and fish preparations.

SPOKANE: Wild Sage American Bistro $$
New American   **Road Map** 1 C2
916 W 2nd Ave, 99201
Tel *(509) 456-7575*
All three dining areas at this elegant bistro offer quality seasonal fare. Top choices include white cheddar fondue with local mushrooms, Brandt Farm steak, and coconut cream layer cake. Good wine list.

TACOMA: Pacific Grill $$
American   **Road Map** 1 A2
1502 Pacific Ave, 98402
Tel *(253) 627-3535*
Pacific Grill uses the freshest regional meat and fish to prepare classic steak and seafood dishes. The brick dining room is spacious and service is attentive.

VANCOUVER: Beaches Restaurant & Bar $$
American   **Road Map** 1 A1
1919 SE Columbia River Dr, 98661
Tel *(360) 699-1592*
Enjoy stunning sunset views at this family-friendly, beach-themed spot on the north shore of the Columbia River. Varied

menu from steaks and wood-fired pizzas to an extravagant seafood boil.

VANCOUVER: Hudson's $$
New American   **Road Map** 1 A1
7805 NE Greenwood Dr, 98662
Tel *(360) 816-6100*
Housed in a faux-rustic, upscale lodge, Hudson's offers regional comfort food, with an emphasis on osso bucco, venison, prime rib, and beef tenderloin. The wine list is devoted to West Coast wineries.

WALLA WALLA: Brasserie Four $
French   **Road Map** 1 C3
4 E Main St, 99632
Tel *(509) 529-2011* **Closed** *Sun & Mon*
Brasserie Four's diverse menu features creative pizzas and salads with French-inspired fare, such as quiches and steamed mussels. Sunday brunch is a favorite.

WALLA WALLA: Olive Marketplace & Café $
American   **Road Map** 1 C3
21 E Main St, 99362
Tel *(509) 525-0200*
Olive is popular for healthy, hearty breakfasts and lunches. The gourmet grocery area has everything from vinegars and jams to cheeses and sauces.

DK Choice

WALLA WALLA: Whitehouse-Crawford $$$
New American **Road Map** 1 C3
55 W Cherry St, 99362
Tel *(509) 525-2222* **Closed** *Tue*
Housed in a converted 1904 sawmill, this elegant restaurant has helped transform the region's culinary culture. The kitchen follows the seasons with a menu that draws heavily on local farmers and artisans – the six-course tasting menu is a favorite. The sweet onion rings and the burger are both highly recommended. Impressive wine list shines a spotlight on local producers.

The brick dining room at the Pacific Grill, Tacoma

For more information on types of restaurants *see p293*

WINTHROP:
Arrowleaf Bistro $$
New American   **Road Map** 1 B1
253 Riverside Ave, Winthrop 98862
Tel *(509) 996-3919*   **Closed** *Mon &*
Tue
Savor local cuisine with a French twist at this intimate bistro. Fresh, organic ingredients are used for the constantly changing menu. Pretty riverside views. Outside dining in the summer.

YAKIMA: Miner's Drive-In $
American   **Road Map** 1 B2
2415 S 1st St, 98903
Tel *(509) 457-8194*
Flourishing since 1949, this independent establishment offers excellent burgers, fries, and shakes. Old-fashioned drive-in service.

YAKIMA: Birchfield Manor
Restaurant $$$
New American   **Road Map** 1 B2
2018 Birchfield Rd, 98901
Tel *(509) 452-1960*   **Closed** *Sun–Wed*
Experience acclaimed dining at this stately 1910 farmhouse. King salmon in puff pastry with Yakima Valley chardonnay sauce is the specialty. For a romantic evening, ask to be seated in the cellar.

Vancouver

Waterfront, Gastown, and Chinatown

Bestie $
German   **Map** 4 E3
105 E Pender St, BC V6A
Tel *(604) 620-1175*
Seemingly out of place in Chinatown, this stylish restaurant dishes up home-made sausages and pretzels, gourmet sauerkraut, currywurst, and seasonal vegetable sides. Local wine and beer list is also available.

Bao Bei $$
Chinese   **Map** 4 D3
163 Keefer St, V6A 1X3
Tel *(604) 688-0876*
The menu at this film-noir style brasserie features modern versions of Chinese dishes such as steamed pork belly buns, lamb shao bing, and sticky rice cake with mushrooms and bamboo shoots.

Steamworks Brewing
Company $$
North American   **Map** 3 B2
375 Water St, V6B 5C6
Tel *(604) 689-2739*
Pub fare such as beer soup, grilled seafood, filling salads, and sandwiches make this a popular spot. Beers are brewed in-house using underground steam lines.

Chambar $$$
Belgian   **Road Map** 3 A3
568 Beatty St, V6B 2L3
Tel *(604) 879-7119*
This fine dining restaurant is perfect for a romantic evening. Exquisite dishes such as *duo de porc et Saint-Jacques* and mussels Congolaise are on the menu.

Miku $$$
Japanese   **Map** 3 A1
200 Granville St, BC V6C
Tel *(604) 568-3900*
Renowned for its innovative *aburi*-style (flame-torched) sushi, Miku's multi-course *omakase* menus are ideal for special occasions. Great waterfront location.

Water Street Café $$$
North American   **Map** 3 B2
300 Water St, V6B 1B6
Tel *(604) 689-2832*
High ceilings, dark wood, and white tablecloths form the decor at this upscale dining room. The varied Italian-inspired menu utilizes regional ingredients. Don't miss the gnocchi or the salmon risotto.

Downtown

Diva at the Met $$$
International   **Map** 3 A2
645 Howe St, V6C 2Y9
Tel *(604) 602-7788*
This multi-tiered dining room in the stylish Metropolitan Hotel has local ingredients in dishes such as the signature smoked black cod. Bar menu has lighter fare.

Hawksworth $$$
Regional   **Map** 2 F2
801 W Georgia St, V6C 1P7
Tel *(604) 673-7000*
Housed in Rosewood Hotel Georgia, Hawksworth boasts an elegant dining hall and beautifully presented plates of organic, seasonal fare. The grilled sturgeon with squid in risotto is delicious.

Yew Seafood & Bar $$$
North American   **Map** 2 F2
791 W Georgia St, V6C 2T4
Tel *(604) 692-4939*
Varied raw bar and British Columbia specialties such as steelhead and Dungeness crab are available here. Wonderful desserts, too. Housed in the Four Seasons Hotel. Knowledgeable, friendly staff.

South Granville and Yaletown

Stepho's $
Greek   **Map** 2 E3
1124 Davie St, V6E 1N1
Tel *(604) 683-2555*
Stepho's serves generous portions of tasty traditional Greek fare such as *souvlaki* and roast lamb. Inviting decor, with terracotta floors, white stucco walls, and lots of colorful flowering plants.

Urban Thai Bistro $
Thai   **Map** 2 F4
1119 Hamilton St, V6B 5P6
Tel *(604) 408-7788*
Urban Thai combines Asian spices with Western ingredients, resulting in interesting dishes such as ostrich in *panang* curry. Traditional offerings include chicken satay.

Bridges $$
Regional   **Map** 2 D4
1696 Duranleau St, Granville Island,
V6H 3S4
Tel *(604) 687-4400*
Bridges offers three dining options: a fine-dining room; a casual bistro; and a nice lounge serving local craft brews.

Dining room with a lovely waterfront setting at Miku, Vancouver

Bustling outdoor seating area at Bridges, Vancouver

Edible Canada $$
Regional   Map 2 D5
1551 Johnston St, V6H 3R9
Tel *(604) 682-6681*
Sit on the patio of this bistro for a view of the Granville Island Public Market, while enjoying duck poutine, bison short ribs, Dungeness crab risotto, and wild mushroom bennies are other highlights on the menu.

Homer Street Café and Bar $$
Café   Map 2 F4
898 Homer St, V6B 2W5
Tel *(604) 428-4299*
This stylish café is renowned for its rotisserie chicken. Elaborate sides include roasted peewee potatoes in pan drippings and brussel sprouts with *padano* cheese. In the evening, this place transforms into a lively cocktail bar.

Blue Water Café $$$
Seafood   Map 2 F4
1095 Hamilton St, V6B 5T4
Tel *(604) 688-8078*
The menu here lays emphasis on locally harvested, wild seafood. An inviting raw bar houses one of the city's largest selections of oysters.

C Restaurant $$$
Seafood   Map 2 D4
1600 Howe St, V6Z 2L9
Tel *(604) 681-1164*
This restaurant is one of the city's most upscale venues for seafood, enhanced by wonderful views of False Creek through floor-to-ceiling windows. Choose from the lengthy à la carte menu or the chef's tasting menu.

Farther Afield

Aphrodite's Organic Café and Pie Shop $
Café   Road Map 2 B4
3598 W 4th Ave, V6R 1N8
Tel *(604) 733-8308*
This casual café offers a widely popular brunch, as well as sandwiches, quiches, and pies. The strawberry rhubarb with ice cream is not to be missed.

Naam $
Vegetarian   Road Map 2 B4
2724 W 4th Ave, Kitsilano, V6K 1R1
Tel *(604) 738-7151*
The city's oldest vegetarian restaurant is open 24 hours daily. Large servings, friendly service, and creative meatless dishes.

Forage $$
Regional   Map 2 B4
1300 Robson St, V6E 1C5
Tel *(604) 661-1400*
A farm-to-table bistro that serves inspired dishes such as bison tortellini and foraged mushrooms with goat's cheese. Local craft beer and wine are on tap.

Kirin Seafood Restaurant $$
Chinese   Road Map 2 B4
200 Three West Centre, 7900 Westminster Hwy, Richmond, V6X 1A5
Tel *(604) 303-8833*
Head here for regional Chinese specialties as well as amazing dim sum. Traditional decor.

Tacofino Commissary $$
Regional   Road Map 2 B4
2327 E Hastings St, V5L 1V6
Tel *(604) 253-8226*
Following up on its successful taco truck, Tacofino Commissary now runs an extremely popular restaurant serving cod, tuna, pork, and yam tacos. The banana churros make an excellent dessert.

The Teahouse Restaurant $$
North American   Road Map 2 B4
7501 Stanley Park Dr, V6G 3E2
Tel *(604) 669-3281*
Offering the city's finest sunset views, the Teahouse Restaurant boasts healthy, modern dishes featuring local game and seafood such as lamb and wild salmon.

Bishop's $$$
North American   Road Map 2 B4
2183 W 4th Ave, V6K 1N7
Tel *(604) 738-2025*
Organic ingredients determine the weekly menu here, which features local seafood and meats such as duck and beef.

CinCin $$$
Italian   Road Map 2 E1
1154 Robson St, V6E 1B5
Tel *(604) 688-7338*
CinCin's Imaginative menu emphasizes wood fire-grilled Italian specialties. Try the signature grilled sea bass stuffed with cherry tomatoes, olives, and fennel.

Farmer's Apprentice $$$
Regional   Road Map 2 B4
1535 W 6th Ave, V6J 1R1
Tel *(604) 620-2070*
The exquisite eight-course tasting menus at this place change daily to incorporate the freshest produce available. Lovely atmosphere.

The Salmon House $$$
North American   Road Map 2 B4
2229 Folkestone Way, V7S 2V6
Tel *(604) 926-3212*
House specialties at this mountainside location include excellent seafood chowder and barbecued salmon. Great wine list.

Tojo's $$$
Japanese   Road Map 2 B4
1133 W Broadway, V6H 1G1
Tel *(604) 872-8050*
A master sushi chef creates the authentic Japanese cuisine and sushi on offer here. Fixed-price *omakase* menus guarantee an imaginative meal. Varied list of fine sakes and wines.

Vij's $$$
Indian   Road Map 2 B4
1480 W 11th Ave, V6H 1L1
Tel *(604) 736-6664*
One of the city's most famous eateries, Vij's offers flavorful dishes created with various East Indian cooking styles. Try the lamb popsicles. Casual takeout is available next door.

For more information on types of restaurants *see p293*

British Columbia

COWICHAN BAY:
The Masthead $$$
Regional **Road Map** 2 B5
*1705 Cowichan Bay Rd,
V0R 1R0*
Tel *(250) 748-3714*
Housed in a historic building
dating from 1863, The Masthead's
menu is built around local
produce, seafood, and British
Columbia wines. Harbor views.

CRANBROOK: Rockies Tap
& Grill $
North American **Road Map** 2 C4
209 Van Horne St S, V1C 6R9
Tel *(250) 417-0425*
Situated inside the Prestige Rocky
Mountain Resort, beside the
railroad museum, Rockies has a
varied menu of salads, steaks,
and seafood. The adjacent bar
serves pub food.

FERNIE: The Curry Bowl $
Asian **Road Map** 2 C4
931 7th Ave, V0B 1M5
Tel *(250) 423-2695*
Ensconced in an unassuming
bungalow, The Curry Bowl
serves Thai, East Indian, and
Indonesian food. Choices range
from simple noodle dishes to
complex entrées.

GALIANO ISLAND: Galiano
Grand Central Emporium $
Café **Road Map** 2 B4
2740 Sturdies Bay Rd, V0N 1P0
Tel *(250) 539-9885*
A café filled with an eclectic
collection of furniture, typifying
the island's laid-back ambience.
Highlights on the menu include
omelets made with free-range
eggs and sandwiches.

GIBSONS: Chasters $$$
Regional **Road Map** 2 B4
*1532 Ocean Beach Esplanade,
V0N 1V5*
Tel *(604) 886-2887* **Closed** *Seasonal,
call for hours*
This intimate, casual spot offers
scenic ocean views and fresh
West Coast cuisine with an
emphasis on seasonal ingredients.
Impressive, well-chosen wine list.

GOLDEN: Eagle's Eye
Restaurant $$
Regional **Road Map** 2 C4
*1500 Kicking Horse Trail,
V0A 1H0*
Tel *(250) 439-5424*
Reached only by gondola,
this is one of North America's
highest restaurants. Contem-
porary Canadian cooking; menus
change seasonally.

KAMLOOPS: Chapters
Viewpoint $
Seafood **Road Map** 2 B4
610 W Columbia St, V2C 1L1
Tel *(250) 374-3224*
Perched on a hill above the town,
this restaurant delivers on the
stunning views. Menu features
steaks, seafood, and dishes with
New Mexican flavors.

KELOWNA: Hanna's Lounge
& Grill $
North American **Road Map** 2 B4
1352 Water St, V1Y 9P4
Tel *(250) 860-1266*
Enjoy standard favorites – pasta,
pizza, steaks, and seafood – in
a casual, family-friendly environ-
ment. Wine list leans heavily
toward local producers. Great
waterfront views.

DK Choice

KELOWNA: Old Vines
Restaurant $$$
Regional **Road Map** 2 B4
3303 Boucherie Rd, V1Z 2H3
Tel *(250) 769-2500*
At Quail's Gate Estate Winery,
high above the sparkling
Okanagan Lake, a small stone
cottage with a patio serves
as a restaurant for vineyard
visitors. The menu is filled with
contemporary dishes that can
be easily paired with sumptuous
wines. Sunday brunch is also
available. Sit by the cozy wine
bar or the fireside lounge.

NELSON: All Seasons Café $
Regional **Road Map** 2 C4
620 Herridge Ln, V1L 6A7
Tel *(250) 352-0101*
This busy bistro is housed in a
restored heritage cottage, with
a tree-canopied patio. Seasonal
West Coast menu; great wine list.
Roast dinners offered on Sundays.

NELSON: Vienna Café $
American **Road Map** 2 C4
411 Kootenay St, V1L 1K7
Tel *(250) 354-4646*
A casual café where tables are
surrounded by used books. The
simple menu includes fresh
soups, healthy smoothies, and
delicious chicken burgers.

PARKSVILLE: Cedars Restaurant
& Lounge $$
Regional **Road Map** 2 B4
1155 Resort Dr, V9P 2E5
Tel *(250) 248-2072*
This beautiful restaurant, housed in
a beachfront resort, has a seasonal
menu that emphasizes Vancouver
Island ingredients. Good wine list.

PENTICTON: Bogner's of
Penticton $$$
Regional **Road Map** 2 B4
302 W Eckhardt Ave, V2A 2A9
Tel *(250) 493-2711* **Closed** *Mon & Tue*
Located in a charming 1915
heritage house, the menu here
includes home-made pasta and
local lamb dishes.

PRINCE GEORGE:
The Twisted Cork $$
Regional **Road Map** 2 B3
1157 5th Ave, V2L 3L1
Tel *(250) 561-5550*
This restaurant uses fresh, locally
sourced ingredients in delicious
dishes such as bison and
guinness pie, wild salmon, and
cedar plank halibut. Wide range
of local craft beers.

PRINCE RUPERT: Cow Bay
Café $
Seafood **Road Map** 2 A3
205 Cow Bay Rd, V8J 1A2
Tel *(250) 627-1212* **Closed** *Sun & Mon*
A cozy restaurant, where tables
spill out onto the Prince Rupert
Harbour dock. Menu changes
daily, depending on the local
seafood and produce available.

Old Vines Restaurant at Quail's Gate Estate Winery, Kelowna, BC

**QUALICUM BEACH:
Bistro 694** $$
North American   Road Map 2 A4
694 Memorial Ave, V9K 1T7
Tel (250) 752-0301
Locally sourced ingredients
are used to produce tasty crab
cakes, burgers, and pasta dishes.
The attentive staff add to the
dining experience.

**REVELSTOKE: Woolsey
Creek Bistro** $$$
Regional   Road Map 2 C4
604 2nd St W, V0E 2S0
Tel (250) 837-5500
The eco-friendly approach at
this popular bistro emphasizes
organic and recyclable products.
Farm-to-table menu with
global touches.

**SALTSPRING ISLAND:
Hastings House** $$$
Regional   Road Map 2 B4
160 Upper Ganges Rd, V8K 2S2
Tel (250) 537-2362   Closed Nov–Feb
The three-course dinner menu
changes daily at this manor
overlooking the Ganges Harbour.
Features lamb, produce, and
wines all produced on the island.

**SOOKE: Sooke Harbour
House** $$$
Regional   Road Map 2 B5
1528 Whiffen Spit Rd, V9Z 0T4
Tel (250) 642-3421   Closed Tue & Wed
Award-winning place that serves
a daily-changing, four-course set
menu focusing on wild seafood,
free-range meat, and organic
produce. Acclaimed wine cellar.

TERRACE: Don Diego's $
Mexican   Road Map 2 A3
3212 Kalum St, V8G 2M9
Tel (250) 635-2307
This bright, busy restaurant has
a patio perfectly situated to
catch the evening sun. Tasty
Mexican offerings made with
local produce.

TOFINO: Wolf in the Fog $$
Regional   Road Map 2 A4
150 4th St, V0R 2Z0
Tel (250) 725-9653
The menu is luxurious at this sea-
facing restaurant, with foie gras
as an integral ingredient. Try
the shrimp croquettes, potato-
rusted oysters, and creole sable
fish. Impressive cocktail list.

**UCLUELET: Matterson House
Restaurant** $$
Regional   Road Map 2 A4
1682 Peninsula Rd, V0R 3A0
Tel (250) 726-2200
A small, charming eatery located
in a historic house that offers
a variety of breakfast, lunch,

The brightly lit, wooden interiors at Wolf in the Fog, Tofino, BC

and dinner selections. Seafood
dishes and home-made desserts
are the specialties.

**VERNON: Blue Heron
Waterfront Pub & Restaurant** $$
North American   Road Map 2 C4
7673 Okanagan Landing Rd, V1H 1G8
Tel (778) 475-5981   Closed Oct–May
Pub food, including fish and
chips and shepherd's pie, are the
staples at this waterfront eatery
with a sunny patio. Heartier fare
includes New York strip steak.

VICTORIA: Barb's Place $
Seafood   Road Map 2 B5
1 Dallas Rd, Fisherman's Wharf,
V8V 0B2
Tel (250) 384-6515   Closed Nov–Feb
Barb's offers alfresco dining at
picnic tables set along a dock. Fish
and chips is very popular, and seals
wait for handouts from diners.

VICTORIA: The Flying Otter Grill $
Regional   Road Map 2 B5
950 Wharf St, V8W 1T3
Tel (250) 414-4220
This floating eatery has a casual
ambience and superb views of
the busy Inner Harbor. Dishes
focus on seafood.

VICTORIA: Brasserie L'Ecole $$
French   Road Map 2 B5
1715 Government St., V8W 1Z4
Tel (250) 475-6260   Closed Sun & Mon
Seasonal, local ingredients
are cooked in classic, French-
country style at this brasserie. No
reservations, so expect to wait.

VICTORIA: OLO $$
Regional   Road Map 2 B5
509 Fisgard St, V8W 2P3
Tel (250) 590-8795
OLO gives an interesting twist to
home-made pastas, steaks, and
vegetarian sides, plus the catch
of the day. International wine list.

VICTORIA: Camille's $$$
Regional   Road Map 2 B5
45 Bastion Sq, V8W 1J1
Tel (250) 381-3433   Closed Sun & Mon
The constantly changing menu at
this charming place often features
mussels, salmon, venison, elk,
wild boar, and local produce.

VICTORIA: Il Terrazzo $$$
Italian   Road Map 2 B5
555 Johnson St, V8W 1M2
Tel (250) 361-0028
Come here to enjoy delicious
Northern Italian cuisine such as
veal marsala and grilled squid,
plus wood-fired oven specialities.
Tucked away down a narrow
alley, set in an 1890s building.

WHISTLER: Purebread $
Café   Road Map 2 B4
1040 Millar Creek Rd, V0N 1B1
Tel (604) 938-3013
Hearty sandwiches, crusty breads,
and tempting treats such as
cinnamon buns and apple cakes
make this laid-back bakery a
popular breakfast choice.

WHISTLER: Araxi $$$
Regional   Road Map 2 B4
4222 Village Square, V0N 1B4
Tel (604) 932-4540
Book ahead to enjoy the creatively
conceived menu at this romantic
fine-dining restaurant. There is a
dedicated raw bar as well.

**YOHO NATIONAL PARK: Truffle
Pigs Bistro** $$
North American   Road Map 2 C4
100 Center St, Field, V0A 1G0
Tel (250) 343-6303
A friendly little eatery and lodge,
where the kitchen emphasizes
fresh, regional ingredients in
dishes such as home-made wild
boar pâté and duck cassoulet.
Meals are paired with local craft
beers and wines.

For more information on types of restaurants see p293

SHOPPING IN THE PACIFIC NORTHWEST

Downtown districts in the Pacific Northwest provide everything from the luxury goods offered by exclusive stores to bargains that can be picked up in flea markets. Outdoor gear manufactured by world-renowned local companies is popular. Shoppers can also purchase footwear and clothing to suit every taste; many secondhand shops sell vintage clothing and accessories. Other items to shop for are antiques, books, and music from the chain stores and independents; fresh produce; smoked Pacific salmon; and first-class wines. Native American and First Nations jewelry, carvings, paintings, and other handicrafts and artwork are sold throughout the region in specialty shops, cultural centers, and galleries. Delicious Canadian maple syrup is widely available in British Columbia.

Store window filled with antiques in Portland's Sellwood District

Shopping Hours

Stores are generally open seven days a week. Standard hours are from 9 or 10am to 6pm, though many stores and malls remain open until 9pm on certain nights. Sunday hours are usually noon to 5pm. Smaller stores often open at 10am, close at 6pm, and are closed on Sundays or Mondays. The busiest shopping days of the week are Fridays and weekends.

Sales

Local newspapers are a good source of information on upcoming sales. End-of-season sales can offer as much as 70 percent off the regular price. In the days – and in some cases weeks – following Christmas, many stores offer huge discounts and specials.

Payment

Most stores accept all major credit cards, with Visa and MasterCard being the most popular. "Direct payment" with bank debit cards at point-of-sale terminals are also widely used. Traveler's checks are readily accepted with proper identification, such as a valid passport or a driver's license. In most US stores, foreign currency is not accepted, whereas many Canadian stores will accept both US and Canadian currencies. However, the exchange rate offered by stores is generally substantially lower than what a bank or currency exchange office will give, so it is

Hat store at Vancouver's Granville Island, one of many specialty shops

best to change any currency you have in advance. Personal checks are rarely accepted.

Sales Tax

Sales taxes vary depending on which state or province you are visiting, and in the US they can vary depending on where you are within a state. In Washington, taxes are in the 8 to 9 percent range (with Seattle's at 9.5 percent), though groceries are exempt. Out-of-state or foreign visitors to Seattle who have no sales tax at home are exempt, provided they show ID such as a valid driver's license. In Oregon, there is no sales tax. In British Columbia, a 7 percent provincial sales tax (PST) and a 5 percent federal Goods and Service Tax (GST) apply to most goods; the major exception is basic food items. Taxes are usually added

Glasshouse, Seattle's oldest glassblowing studio, at Pioneer Square

to the price at the time of purchase, so price tags rarely include taxes.

Returns

Be sure you understand the store's return policy before you pay. Each store sets its own return and exchange policies, which are generally to be found posted at the cash register. Some stores offer full refunds, while others maintain an all-sales-final policy or give an in-shop credit note rather than a refund.

Keep your receipt as a proof of purchase, in case you decide to return the item or find that it is in some way defective. Sale items are usually not returnable.

Fruit stall at Granville Island's public market, Vancouver

Markets

Farmers' markets held in cities and rural communities across the Pacific Northwest sell locally grown fruits and vegetables. Apples, apricots, plums, cherries, berries, tomatoes, and zucchini are common offerings. Some markets also sell seafood, baked goods, flowers, crafts, and locally made souvenirs.

Markets range from large and sheltered, such as Granville Island Public Market (see p223) in Vancouver, and Pike Place Market (see pp136–9) in Seattle, to medium-sized open-air markets, such as the Saturday Market in Portland's Old Town district (see p58), to small markets consisting of a few trucks parked in a lot or field. Many of the seafood merchants at these markets, particularly larger ones, will ship fresh fish to your home.

Wine shop at Chateau Ste. Michelle, one of Washington's top vineyards

Most of the larger markets are open year-round, whereas many of the smaller markets may be seasonal, running from early spring to late fall.

Outlet Stores

Shoppers can find great bargains at outlet malls, sometimes saving as much as 70 percent off the regular price.

Oregon is home to the Columbia Gorge Premium Outlets, east of Portland in Troutdale, and the Woodburn Premium Outlets, located south of Portland. Tanger Factory Outlet Center, the largest in the Pacific Northwest, offers tax-free shopping. Washington's 50-store Premium Outlets at North Bend is located east of Seattle.

British Columbia's outlet centers includes the Roots factory outlets in Vancouver and New Westminster, just east of Vancouver.

Fine Wines

The Pacific Northwest produces world-class rieslings, pinot noirs and chardonnays, as well as dessert wines, such as late harvest wines and flavorful ice wines made from grapes that are picked and crushed while frozen. Pinot gris and pinot blanc are also becoming increasingly important varieties.

Hundreds of wineries in Oregon's Willamette Valley (see pp102–3), Washington's Yakima Valley (see p195), the Walla Walla Valley (see pp196–7), the greater Puget Sound area, and British Columbia's Okanagan Valley (see pp262–3) offer guided tours and wine tastings. Most of the wineries also sell directly to the public.

Winegrowers' associations in Oregon, Washington, and British Columbia provide visitors with maps and guides to regional wineries, as well as information about special events, such as Washington Wine Month (March), the Oregon Wine Month (May), the Oregon Wine and Art Auction, and the Okanagan Fall Wine Festival, in British Columbia.

Kite store to suit all tastes and winds, Pacific City, Oregon

OUTDOOR ACTIVITIES

The dramatically varied terrain and beautiful landscapes of the Pacific Northwest make it an ideal region for a wide range of outdoor activities, from such peaceful pursuits as bird-watching, whale-watching, hiking, and fishing, to more exhilarating sports such as skiing, snowboarding, surfing, scuba diving, and white-water rafting. For information about particular activities, equipment rentals, instruction, and guided tours, check the websites or contact the state or provincial tourist offices.

Kite-boarding on the Hood River, off the Columbia River Gorge

Adventure Sports

The dramatic landscape of the Pacific Northwest offers countless possibilities for thrill-seekers, such as hang gliding, paragliding, kite-boarding, hot-air ballooning, and sky-diving, to name just a few.

In Oregon, both Lakeview, in the south, and Cape Kiwanda, in the north, provide ideal conditions for hang gliding and paragliding, as does **Lake Chelan** in Washington. In British Columbia, the most popular spot for these sports is Malahat, north of Victoria, offering spectacular views of the Saanich Peninsula and Strait of Georgia. For more information about hang gliding and paragliding in BC, contact the **Hang Gliding and Paragliding Association of Canada**.

Hot-air ballooning offers another exciting way to get a bird's-eye view of the region. To float over Oregon's wine country in a balloon, contact **Vista Balloon Adventures**. In Washington, you can take a balloon ride over the Methow Valley and enjoy a champagne brunch with **Morning Glory Balloon Tours**, or fly over the Woodinville area vineyards with **Over the Rainbow**.

Beaches

The shorelines of the Pacific Northwest are among the most scenic in the world. Although the waters are generally cool, swimming offers refreshment during the summer months.

The **Oregon Dunes National Recreation Area**, between Florence and Coos Bay, comprises 50 sq miles (130 sq km) of huge sand dunes, some more than 500 ft (150 m) tall. Higher than those of the Sahara Desert, these steep dunes are ideal for sandboarding. The Umpqua Scenic Dunes Trail, 30 miles (48 km) south of Florence and approximately 1 mile (1.6 km) long, skirts the tallest dunes in the area. Enjoy the breathtaking views from the boardwalk's overlook, located 24 miles (39 km) north of North Bend.

Oregon's top beaches include Bandon, **Oswald West State Park**, **Cannon Beach**, **Sunset Bay State Park** beaches, and the beaches of the **Samuel H. Boardman State Scenic Corridor**.

Deception Pass State Park beaches, in the Puget Sound area, are located in Washington's most popular

Dune buggies on Oregon's sand dunes, near Florence

state park. A 15-minute drive from downtown Seattle, **Alki Beach** (see p163) offers a panoramic view of the city's skyline and of Elliott Bay. Other particularly beautiful beaches in Washington include Dungeness Spit, the longest saltwater sand spit in North America, and the sandy and cliff-lined beaches in **Olympic National Park**.

In British Columbia, among the beaches that dot Vancouver's shoreline the most popular are English Bay, Sunset (see p224), Kitsilano, Jericho, Locarno, Spanish Banks, and the Second and Third Beaches in Stanley Park (see pp230–31). Visitors are also

Sunbathers at Kitsilano Beach on English Bay, Vancouver

Sandboarding at Oregon Dunes National Recreation Area

drawn to the tranquil and beautiful shores of the Gulf Islands *(see p259)*.

Bird-watching

Throughout the year, bird-watchers are able to sight gulls, sandpipers, plovers, and ducks along the coasts of Oregon and Washington, while British Columbia boasts important migration habitats for waterfowl, shorebirds, and hawks. Contact the local **Audubon Society** chapter for more information about birds and the many superb birding spots in the Pacific Northwest, such as Oregon's **Malheur National Wildlife Refuge** and **Ten Mile Creek Sanctuary**, Washington's Skagit River, and the **George C. Reifel Migratory Bird Sanctuary** in British Columbia.

Camping

There are numerous campsites tucked away in wilderness areas, close to cities, and near beaches. All of the region's national parks and most state and provincial parks offer excellent campgrounds.

In the high country, campgrounds are usually open from mid-June through August, and in lower elevations year-round. Space in most parks is available on a first-come, first-served basis. To reserve a spot in a state park in Oregon, call **Reservations Northwest**; in Washington, call **Washington State Parks**. In Canada, call **Parks Canada**, or to book a place in one of

British Columbia's provincial parks and campgrounds, contact the reservation service that is run by **Discover Camping**.

Canoeing and Kayaking

Canoeing and kayaking are both easy and environmentally friendly ways of seeing the Pacific Northwest's beautiful waters along with its abundant marine life.

Washington's Puget Sound and San Juan Islands are the most popular destinations for sea kayakers in the Pacific Northwest. White-water kayakers flock to the state's many rivers, and Lake Ozette in **Olympic National Park** is a hot spot for canoeists.

Off Oregon, the ocean's waters are generally too rough for kayaking, but the bays along the coast and the Lewis and Clark National Wildlife Refuge, on the Columbia River, provide calmer waters for paddlers. For listings of canoe and kayak outfitters in

the US, visit the **Arcadian Outdoor Guide** website.

For information about many canoeing and kayaking destinations in British Columbia, contact the **Recreational Canoeing Association of BC**.

Caving

Whether you are an experienced caver or simply interested in venturing into tubes of lava and limestone, there are thousands of caving possibilities in the region. Among the most popular are the Oregon Caves National Monument, Lava River Caves, and Sea Lion Caves in Oregon; Washington's Gardner Cave; and British Columbia's Cody and Horne Lake Caves.

Caves are largely unaffected by the climate outdoors, so, although it may be warm outside, temperatures inside average 50°F (10°C) year-round. Be sure to wear warm clothing and comfortable footwear. For new information about exploring the caves of the Pacific Northwest, contact the **BC Parks** or the **National Caves Association**.

Cycling

Cycling is an inexpensive and healthy way of traveling around the cities and countryside of the Pacific Northwest. Most of the parks in the region have designated cycling trails as well as rental outlets for equipment; Portland, Seattle, Vancouver, and many other large cities have cycling paths.

White-water kayaking on the fast-moving McKenzie River in Oregon

Rollerbladers, cyclists, and walkers at Green Lake, Seattle

Several companies offer long-distance cycling tours in the region. **Bicycle Adventures** offers tours through Oregon, Washington, and Western Canada. Contact state and provincial tourist offices for details on tour operators. For maps of cycling trails in Washington, contact the **Washington State Department of Transportation**; for cycling in British Columbia, contact **Cycling BC**. Most local tourist offices and bike rental shops will also have information about cycling.

Ecotourism

Several companies organize ecotours, allowing travelers to enjoy the natural beauty of the Pacific Northwest's landscape while respecting local communities and the environment. Guided wilderness cruises, kayak tours around Washington's San Juan Islands, and llama treks through Silver Falls State Park in Salem, Oregon, are among some of the ecotours available. Eco-friendly tours are increasingly popular with visitors and if you want to learn about the impact of tourism, or obtain information about ecologically and socially responsible travel options, contact the **International Ecotourism Society**.

Fishing

The Pacific Northwest is a paradise for fishing enthusiasts.

Pacific salmon, steel-head, perch, bass, trout, halibut, and sturgeon are among the region's catches.

For information on freshwater fishing in the US, contact the **Washington Department of Fish and Wildlife** or the **Oregon Department of Fish and Wildlife**. Most visitors' centers and fishing shops also provide details of local regulations.

In Canada, contact the **Sport Fishing Institute** for information about sport fishing, and **Fisheries and Oceans Canada** for information on saltwater fishing licenses.

Golfing

Within the Pacific Northwest, golfers can choose from golf courses with scenic backdrops of mountain vistas, coastal views, or cityscapes. Because of the mild climate, you can golf all year round in many areas of the region.

Most of Oregon's golf courses are clustered in the areas around Portland and Bend-Redmond; there are also several along the coast, including Bandon Dunes Golf Resort, one of the top-ranked golf resorts in North America. While a few of Washington's resorts maintain private courses, most of its cities offer public ones. British Columbia has more than 200 golf courses, from par threes to 18-hole championship courses. To obtain listings of both private and public courses, contact state, provincial, or local tourism offices.

Hiking

Hiking trails leading over mountains, through meadows and forests, and along seashores offer nature lovers everything from strenuous climbs to leisurely strolls. All the national, state, and provincial parks have well-marked trails of varying lengths and levels of difficulty. Visitors' centers and the **American Hiking Society** are good sources of information about hiking and provide detailed maps. The **Pacific Northwest Trail Association** offers information about the scenic 1,200-mile (1,931-km) trail, which runs from the Continental Divide to the Pacific Ocean.

Most of the more popular hikes in the Pacific Northwest require minimal preparation, but if you intend to venture into little-known territory, plan to travel with a trained guide.

Fishing for trout in Oregon's peaceful McKenzie River Valley

Rock Climbing and Mountaineering

The Pacific Northwest's Cascade, Coast, and Rocky Mountain systems offer innumerable possibilities for rock climbing and mountaineering.

In Oregon, **Timberline Mountain Guides** offer instruction and guided climbs on rock, snow, and ice. Rock climbers will want to visit the world-renowned Smith Rock State Park, near Redmond, to check out its 1,300 climbing routes, some of which are the toughest in the world.

Visitors to Washington can hire a guide or take lessons from outfits such as **North Cascades Mountain Guides** and **Rainier Mountaineering**. The **Peshastin Pinnacles State Park** was created especially for rock climbers.

For information about climbing and mountaineering in British Columbia, contact the **Federation of Mountain Clubs of BC** or **BC Parks**.

Water Sports

The Pacific coastline and the rivers and lakes of the Pacific Northwest attract enthusiasts of white-water rafting, scuba diving, swimming, boating, surfing, kayaking, kite-boarding, stand-up paddleboarding, and windsurfing.

White-water rafting is one of the region's most popular sports, especially in the waters of the Cascades range. Destinations in Oregon include the Deschutes, Snake, and John Day Rivers; in Washington, the Wenatchee, Skykomish, and Methow Rivers; and, in British Columbia, the Mackenzie River system. Basic training courses are usually available for inexperienced rafters. To book a rafting trip in the US, contact **River Riders** or **Wildwater River Guides** in Washington. To find out about BC's outfitters, contact **BC Parks**. **Wedge Rafting** offers rafting as well as jet-boating tours that whisk passengers close to waterfalls.

The coasts of the Pacific Northwest, and of Puget Sound

Sailboats on Burrard Inlet, with West Vancouver in the background

and the San Juan Islands in particular, offer scuba divers thousands of miles of ocean flora and fauna. Visit **3 Routes** on the Internet to access comprehensive scuba-diving directories for Oregon, Washington, and British Columbia. There are also many prime surfing spots along the Pacific coast, through the Strait of Juan de Fuca, and around the San Juan Islands.

For windsurfers, the Columbia River Gorge, a stretch of the Columbia River which forms a natural divide between Oregon and Washington, offers ideal conditions and beautiful scenery. The popular Columbia Gorge Sailpark in Oregon has a large shallow area for beginners. British Columbia's best windsurfing is near the town of Squamish, a Coast Salish word meaning "strong wind." The sport is also popular on the Sunshine Coast, in White Rock, and at Jericho Beach in Vancouver.

Whale-watching

Whale-watching is one of the most popular outdoor activities in the Pacific Northwest, particularly during the spring and summer. An off-shore show, courtesy of more than 20,000 gray whales that migrate every year from Alaska to California and Mexico, can be seen from boats or from the shores of the Pacific Ocean in Oregon, Washington, and British Columbia. A number of charter companies run whale-watching cruises.

The best vantage points in Oregon include Cape Meares, Cape Lookout, Cape Kiwanda, Devil's Punchbowl, Cape Perpetua, Sea Lion Caves, Shore Acres State Park, Face Rock Wayside, Cape Blanco, Cape Sebastian, and Harris Beach State Park.

In Washington, orcas swim around the San Juan Islands and in the waters off Puget Sound; San Juan Island's **Lime Kiln Point State Park** is the only park in the US dedicated to whale-watching.

In British Columbia, of the dozens of companies that organize boat tours, most are Victoria-based. Both **Seacoast Expeditions** and **Five-Star Whale Watching** aim to minimize the negative impact of tourism on the whale populations. The shores of Vancouver Island's **Pacific Rim National Park Reserve** are also world-famous for whale-watching, making binoculars a handy addition to the suitcase.

White-water rafting the Nahatlatch River in southwestern British Columbia

Snowboarding the challenging Mount Hood Meadows, in Oregon

Winter Sports

The Pacific Northwest boasts some of the world's best snowboarding and downhill and cross-country skiing. Oregon's Mount Bachelor offers some of the best skiing in the US, and in the summer you can snow-ski down Mount Hood at Timberline Lodge, where the US Olympic team practices. Most of Washington's 16 ski areas are in the Cascade Mountains, at locations such as Mount Baker, Stevens Pass, and Crystal Mountain *(see p190)*, though there are also a number of smaller ski areas in the eastern part of the state. In British Columbia, Whistler *(see pp260–61)* delights skiers with

North America's longest vertical run, 11 sq miles (28.5 sq km) of ski and snowboard terrain, more than 200 trails, and 12 alpine bowls. For details, contact **Tourism Whistler**.

In addition to snowboarding and skiing, other popular winter sports include ice skating, dogsledding, snowshoeing, snowmobiling, and heli-skiing (being lifted by helicopter to backcountry peaks for skiing or boarding off the beaten track).

Safety Measures

Both grizzly and black bears live in the national parks of the BC Rockies. Although bear sightings are rare, visitors should observe

DIRECTORY

Adventure Sports

Hang Gliding and Paragliding Association of Canada
Tel (877) 370-2078.
w hpac.ca

Lake Chelan
w chelanflyers.com

Morning Glory Balloon Tours
Tel (509) 997-1700.
w balloon winthrop.com

Over the Rainbow
Tel (425) 487-8611.
w letsgo ballooning.com

Vista Balloon Adventures
Tel (503) 625-7385.
w vistaballoon.com

Beaches

Alki Beach
Tel (206) 684-4075.
w seattle.gov

Cannon Beach
Tel (503) 436-2623.
w cannonbeach.org

Deception Pass State Park
Tel (360) 902-8844.
w parks.wa.gov

Olympic National Park
Tel (360) 565-3130.
w nps.gov

Oregon Dunes National Recreation Area
Tel (541) 750-7000.
w fs.usda.gov

Oswald West State Park
Tel (800) 551-6949.
w oregon.gov

Samuel H. Boardman State Scenic Corridor
Tel (800) 551-6949.
w oregon.gov

Sunset Bay State Park
Tel (800) 551-6949.
w oregon.gov

Bird-watching

Audubon Society
Tel (800) 542-2748.
w audubon.org

George C. Reifel Migratory Bird Sanctuary
Tel (604) 946-6980.
w reifelbird sanctuary.com

Malheur National Wildlife Refuge
Tel (541) 493-2612.
w fws.gov

Ten Mile Creek Sanctuary
Tel (541) 547-4227.

Camping

Discover Camping
Tel (519) 826-6850 or (800) 689-9025.
w discovercamping.ca

Parks Canada
Tel (888) 773-8888.
w pc.gc.ca

Reservations Northwest
Tel (800) 452-5687.
w oregon.gov

Washington State Parks
Tel Reservations:
(888) 226-7688.
w parks.wa.gov

Canoeing and Kayaking

Arcadian Outdoor Guide
Tel (913) 558-8525.
w thetent.com

Olympic National Park
See Beaches.

Recreational Canoeing Association of BC
w bccanoe.com

Caving

BC Parks
w env.gov.bc.ca

National Caves Association
w cavern.com

Cycling

Bicycle Adventures
Tel (425) 250-5540.
w bicycle adventures.com

Cycling BC
Tel (604) 737-3034.
w cyclingbc.net

Washington State Department of Transportation
w wsdot.wa.gov

the rules posted at campgrounds. A leaflet published by Parks Canada, entitled "You Are in Bear Country," gives safety tips for encounters with bears. The fundamental rules are: do not approach the animals, never feed them, and do not run. Bears have an excellent sense of smell, so, when camping, be sure to store food or trash properly, inside a car or in the bear-proof boxes provided.

While less alarming, insects can be irritating. Take all possible measures to repel black flies and mosquitoes. Do not drink stream or river water without thoroughly boiling it first, as it may contain parasites.

When camping and hiking, be sure to bring a map, compass, flashlight, or headlamp with spare bulbs and batteries; sunglasses and sunscreen;

a first-aid kit, including anti-histamines and bug repellent; a pocketknife; matches kept in a waterproof container, and a fire starter.

Sailing gear with flashlight, pocketknife, and other safety accessories

DIRECTORY

Ecotourism

International Ecotourism Society
Tel (202) 506-5033.
W ecotourism.org

Fishing

Fisheries and Oceans Canada
Tel (613) 993-0999.
W dfo-mpo.gc.ca

Oregon Department of Fish and Wildlife
Tel (503) 947-6000.
W dfw.state.or.us

Sport Fishing Institute
Tel (604) 270-3439.
W sportfishing.bc.ca

Washington Department of Fish and Wildlife
Tel (360) 902-2200.
W wdfw.wa.gov

Hiking

American Hiking Society
Tel (301) 565-6704.
W americanhiking.org

Pacific Northwest Trail Association
Tel (877) 854-9415.
W pnt.org

Rock Climbing and Mountaineering

BC Parks
W env.gov.bc.ca

Federation of Mountain Clubs of BC
Tel (604) 873-6096.
W mountainclubs.org

North Cascades Mountain Guides
Tel (509) 996-3194.
W ncmountainguides.com

Peshastin Pinnacles State Park
W parks.wa.gov

Rainier Mountaineering
Tel (888) 892-5462.
W rmiguides.com

Timberline Mountain Guides
Tel (541) 312-9242.
W timberlinemtguides.com

Water Sports

3 Routes
W 3routes.com

BC Parks
W env.gov.bc.ca

River Riders
Tel (800) 448-7238.
W riverrider.com

Wedge Rafting
Tel (604) 932-7171.
W wedgerafting.com

Wildwater River Guides
Tel (800) 522-9453.
W wildwater-river.com

Whale-watching

Five-Star Whale Watching
Tel (250) 388-7223.
W 5starwhales.com

Lime Kiln Point State Park
Tel (360) 902-8844.
W parks.wa.gov

Pacific Rim National Park Reserve
Tel (250) 726-3500.
W pc.gc.ca

Seacoast Expeditions
Tel (250) 383-2254.
W seacoastexpeditions.com

Winter Sports

Tourism Whistler
Tel (800) 944-7853.
W whistler.com

National Parks

Crater Lake National Park
Tel (541) 594-3000.
W nps.gov

Kootenay National Park
Tel (250) 347-9505.
W pc.gc.ca

National Park Service
Tel (510) 817-1300.
W nps.gov

North Cascades National Park
Tel (360) 854-7200.
W nps.gov

US Forest Service
Tel (800) 832-1355.
W fs.fed.us

State and Provincial Parks

Oregon State Parks
Tel (800) 551-6949.
W oregon.gov

Smith Rock State Park
Tel (800) 551-6949.
W oregon.gov

Washington State Parks
Tel (360) 902-8844.
W parks.wa.gov

SURVIVAL
GUIDE

PRACTICAL INFORMATION

The Pacific Northwest's stunning scenery attracts visitors from around the world. Booming tourism, including ecotourism, has spawned an extensive network of facilities and services for visitors: internationally acclaimed accommodations and restaurants abound, while efficient transportation by air, land, and water takes travelers virtually anywhere they want to go. The following pages provide useful information for all travelers planning a trip to this region. Personal Health and Security *(see pp320–21)* recommends a number of precautions; Banking and Currency *(see p322)* and Media and Communications *(see p323)* answer financial and media queries. There is also information on traveling to the region *(see pp324–5)* and driving once there *(see pp326–7).*

When to Go

Visitors should first determine what they would like to do. The region's winter weather is ideal for skiing and other snow sports, while warmer weather suits hiking, cycling, fishing, and watersports. (See also pp34–7 for details on seasonal events and weather in the Pacific Northwest.)

The peak tourist season extends from mid-May through September. In the metropolitan areas of Portland, Seattle, and Vancouver, spring is often quite rainy, with temperatures in the 60–69°F (16–21°C) range. Along the coast, mild summer temperatures average 77°F (25°C) and occasionally go as high as 85°F (29°C), which makes walking around these cities comfortable. Central and eastern regions can be significantly hotter than the coast.

In early September, trees at the higher elevations begin to change color, making excursions out of the cities even more scenic. In September and early October, the weather in the three major cities, particularly in Seattle, can be quite dry and sunny.

Although the weather is generally clement along the coast, rain is not uncommon in other areas. It starts to get chilly again in the fall, toward the end of October.

Except in areas catering to skiers and other snow sports enthusiasts, winter is the least popular season to visit. This makes it an ideal time of year for visitors who are looking for fewer crowds and more affordable hotel rates. Though snowfalls in the three main coastal cities are relatively rare, in the interior and eastern regions they can be frequent and heavy. If you plan to cross from west to east between late fall and early spring, inquire first about road conditions.

Visas and Passports

Due to changing US immigration laws, visitors to Washington and Oregon who are traveling from outside the US should check current entry requirements with a US embassy or consulate before leaving. All visitors must have a valid passport, and visitors from most countries must have a non-immigrant visitor's visa. Citizens of Australia, New Zealand, the UK, and many other European countries can visit the US without a visa if they plan to stay for fewer than 90 days. All travelers under the Visa Waiver Program must pre-register with the Department of Homeland Security's Electronic System for Travel Authorization (ESTA) at www.cbp.gov well in advance of their departure.

Visitors to Canada (including US citizens) must carry a valid passport (for US visitors, a US passport card or enhanced

Crystal Mountain, Washington, a perfect winter ski destination

◄ Skiers in powder snow, Whistler, British Columbia

driver's license is acceptable when crossing the border by land or sea, but not by air). A visa is not necessary for visitors from the US, EU, UK, and British Commonwealth countries. In your home country, the nearest Canadian consulate, embassy, or high commission will have current information on visa regulations. Visitors who are under the age of 18 and traveling alone must carry a letter from a parent or guardian giving them permission to do so.

All travelers who plan to stay in Canada or the US for 90 days or longer must have visas. If crossing the border by car, be prepared for customs personnel to do a search.

Canadian landed immigrants should check the regulations before traveling to the US – citizens of some Commonwealth countries that were formerly exempt from the visa requirement are now required to have a visa.

Travel Safety Advice

Visitors can get up-to-date travel safety information from the **State Department** in the US, the **Foreign and Commonwealth Office** in the UK, and the **Department of Foreign Affairs and Trade** in Australia.

Customs Allowances

Visitors 21 years of age and over are permitted to enter the US with 2 pints (1 liter) of alcohol, 200 cigarettes, 100 cigars or 4 pounds (1.8 kg) of smoking tobacco, and gifts worth up to $100. Visitors to British Columbia who are 19 years of age or older are allowed up to 3.15 pints (1.5 liters) of wine or 2.4 pints (1.14 liters) of liquor, 200 cigarettes, 50 cigars, or 0.44 lb (200 g) of tobacco, and gifts worth up to $200.

Restricted items through customs include meats, dairy products, and fresh fruits and vegetables. Travelers entering either country with large quantities of cash (more than $10,000) or traveler's checks must declare it.

Bikes and windsurfing gear in Hood River, Oregon

Tourist Information

Maps and information about sights, events, accommodations, and tours are available free of charge from the **Travel Oregon**, **Washington State Tourism**, and **Tourism British Columbia**. These agencies also provide either free reservation services for a wide range of accommodation or referrals to such services. Most communities in the Pacific Northwest also operate visitors' information centers or seasonal tourism booths, which offer information about local activities, lodgings, and restaurants.

Time Zones

There are two time zones in the Pacific Northwest: Pacific Standard Time (PST) and Mountain Standard Time (MST). Washington and most of British Columbia and Oregon lie within the Pacific time zone. Parts of Oregon, along the Idaho

"Pioneers" at the National Historic Oregon Trail Interpretive Center

border, and parts of British Columbia, along the Alberta border, lie within the mountain time zone. The clocks are turned back 1 hour in November; in March they are turned forward one hour to Daylight Savings Time.

Opening Hours and Admission Prices

Most businesses are open weekdays from 9am to 5pm, but many in Seattle's, Portland's, and Vancouver's downtown districts stay open later. Many businesses are also open on weekends. Banks open from 9 or 9:30am to 4:30 or 5pm, and some offer limited hours on Saturdays. Most attractions are open daily, except perhaps on public holidays (see p37). Opening hours can be shorter outside the summer season.

Most attractions charge an admission fee, but discounts are widely available for families, children, students, and seniors. Check tourist brochures and local papers for discount coupons.

Permits are required to access several national parks and campgrounds in the region: check before planning a visit. A **Discover Pass** provides entry to Washington's many state parks. A day-use pass costs $10, while the annual pass costs $30. It is advisable to purchase these online or at select stores in advance, as not all state parks sell them on-site. Note that this pass is for motor vehicles only.

A restaurant and wine bar in Portland's South Park Blocks

Taxes

In Oregon, hotel tax is 8–12.5 percent and there is no sales tax. Hotel tax in Seattle is 15.6 percent but varies throughout the rest of the state; and Washington's sales taxes are between 8 to 9 percent but do not apply to groceries.

In British Columbia, a 7 percent provincial sales tax (PST) and a 5 percent federal Goods and Service Tax (GST) apply to most goods and services. Hotel rooms are subject to GST, PST, and an additional 3 percent hotel tax.

Etiquette

Pacific Northwesterners' dress tends to be casual, practical, and dependent on the weather. Stricter clothing requirements apply in theaters, high-end restaurants, and other more formal places. Designated beaches allow topless and nude sunbathing.

Alcohol and Cigarettes

Alcohol is available in some grocery stores, government liquor stores, beer and wine stores, and licensed restaurants, bars, and clubs. Drinking alcohol in non-licensed public places is illegal, as is driving with an open bottle of alcohol. There are strict laws against drinking and driving.

The minimum legal drinking age in Oregon and Washington is 21; in British Columbia, 19. Younger travelers are advised to carry photo identification, such as a passport or driver's license, should they need to prove they are of legal age to enter bars or clubs or to order alcohol in restaurants.

In Oregon and Washington, cigarettes can be sold only to people 18 or older; in British Columbia, 19 or older. It is illegal to smoke in public buildings and on public transportation. Smoking in restaurants, pubs, bars, and shopping centers is prohibited.

Tipping

Tips and service charges are not usually added to restaurant bills. For service at restaurants, cafés, bars, and clubs, and for tour guides, a standard tip is 15 to 20 percent of the amount before taxes. Porters and bellhops should be tipped at least $1 per bag or suitcase; cloakroom attendants, $1 per garment; and chambermaids, a minimum of $1 to $2 per day.

Travelers with Disabilities

The Pacific Northwest has some of the world's best facilities and recreational opportunities for travelers with physical disabilities. Most public buildings, hotels (see p284), public transit, and entertainment venues are wheelchair accessible. However, some older buildings and smaller venues may not be. Taxi service is available for people with wheelchairs, and parking spaces closest to the entrance of most buildings are reserved for persons with disabilities (note that permits may be required).

The **Society for Accessible Travel and Hospitality** is an excellent source of information. To find out about barrier-free sports and recreation opportunities in British Columbia, contact **BC Disability Games**.

Senior Travelers

Reduced rates for attractions, hotels, transportation, and services are often available for seniors. Photo identification proving one's age may be required. Seniors are eligible for discounts with Amtrak and VIA rail services and with Greyhound bus services (see p324). If discounts are not advertised, inquire when purchasing tickets. Also inquire about discounts for seniors' traveling companions.

For discounts and more information about traveling as a senior, contact the **American Association of Retired Persons**, in the US or Canada. For information about learning programs for people 55 years of age and older, contact **Elderhostel**.

Women Travelers

The Pacific Northwest is generally safe for women travelers. However, caution is advisable in deserted places, and walking around alone after dark is not advisable, especially if you do not know the district very well. Keep a confident attitude, avoid telling anyone you are traveling alone, and do not hitchhike.

Petting zoo at Port Townsend's farmers' market, Washington

Oregon Museum of Science and Industry, in Portland

Traveling with Children

The Pacific Northwest is extremely child-friendly, with many attractions suited to children, including zoos and a multitude of festivals, events, and programs. The region's beaches and outdoor activities can entertain children year-round. Admission to attractions is often free for children under five who are accompanied by a parent. In most cities, children under five can also travel for free on public transportation when they are accompanied by a parent; there are often concession fares for older children.

Many hotels offer cribs, highchairs, even babysitting services, and restaurants generally welcome children. With more upscale establishments, you may wish to inquire in advance whether children are welcome. When renting a car, be sure to reserve a child's car seat in advance.

Student Travelers

An international student identity card (ISIC), administered by the **International Student Travel Confederation**, entitles full-time students to discounts on travel as well as admission to movies, galleries, museums, theaters, and many other tourist attractions. The ISIC should be purchased in the student's home country; they are available at **STA Travel** and **Travel CUTS** (in the US and Canada only).

A wide range of bus and rail *(see pp324–5)* discounts are available to students. Ask for a copy of the *ISIC Student Handbook*, for listings of places that offer discounts to cardholders, as well as travel tips.

Members of **Hostelling International** (HI) can stay at HI locations throughout the Pacific Northwest *(see p283)*. Ask about free shuttles and other amenities at HI's regional offices.

Conversion Chart

Imperial to Metric
1 inch = 2.5 centimeters
1 foot = 30 centimeters
1 mile = 1.6 kilometers
1 ounce = 28 grams
1 pound = 454 grams
1 pint = 0.6 liter
1 US pint = 0.5 liter
1 US quart = 0.9 liter
1 gallon = 4.6 liters
1 US gallon = 3.8 liters

Metric to Imperial
1 centimeter = 0.4 inch
1 meter = 3 feet 3 inches
1 kilometer = 0.6 mile
1 gram = 0.04 ounce
1 kilogram = 2.2 pounds
1 liter = 1.8 pints/1.1 US quarts

Bear in mind that 1 US pint (0.5 liter) is a smaller measure than 1 UK pint (0.6 liter).

Electricity

Electrical sockets accept two- or three-prong plugs and operate at 110 volts. You will need a plug adapter and voltage converter or power transformer to operate 220-volt appliances such as hairdryers and rechargers. Batteries are universal and are readily available.

DIRECTORY

Travel Safety Advice

Australia
Department of Foreign Affairs and Trade
w dfat.gov.au
w smartraveller.gov.au

UK
Foreign and Commonwealth Office w gov.uk/foreign-travel-advice

US
US Department of State
w travel.state.gov

Tourist Information

Tourism BC
Tel (800) 435-5622.
w hellobc.com

Travel Oregon
Tel (800) 547-7842.
w traveloregon.com

Washington State Tourism
Tel (800) 544-1800.
w experiencewa.com

Opening Hours and Admission Prices

Discover Pass
w discoverpass.wa.gov

Travelers with Disabilities

BC Disability Games
PO Box 56037, RPO Valley Center, Langley, BC, V3A 8B3. Tel (604) 530-7738.
w bcdisabilitygames.org

Society for Accessible Travel and Hospitality
347 5th Ave, Suite 605, New York, NY 10016. Tel (212) 447-7284. w sath.org

Senior Travelers

American Association of Retired Persons
601 E Street NW, Washington, DC 20049.
Tel (888) 687-2277.
w aarp.org

Elderhostel
11 Avenue de Lafayette, Boston, MA 02111.
Tel (800) 454-5768.
w roadscholar.org

Student Travelers

Hostelling International
Central Administrative Office, 8401 Colesville Rd, Suite 600, Silver Spring, MD 20910.
Tel (240) 650-2100.
w hiusa.org
w hihostels.ca

International Student Travel Confederation
w isic.org

STA Travel
Tel In US: (800) 781-4040.
w statravel.com

Travel CUTS
Tel (800) 667-2887.
w travelcuts.com

Useful Websites

Canada Border Services Agency
w cbsa.gc.ca

Canada Revenue Agency
w cra-arc.gc

Personal Health and Security

The Pacific Northwest prides itself on the safety of its towns and cities and on its welcoming attitude toward visitors. Street crime is rare, and police are a visible presence as they patrol the major cities on horseback, motorcycle, and on foot. However, it is still wise to be vigilant and to find out from your hotel or a tourist information center which parts of town should be avoided. In the open countryside, bear in mind natural dangers, such as unexpectedly inclement weather and wild animals. Always heed local warnings.

Guidelines on Safety

While traveling, it is always advisable to take a few basic precautions and at all times to remain aware of your surroundings.

Carry traveler's checks and small amounts of cash in a secure bag, purse, or pocket, and do not carry your wallet in a back pocket. Pickpockets and thieves, who are often well dressed and tend to work in pairs, target their victims in airports, malls, and other crowded areas.

Always watch your luggage carefully at airports and while checking in and out of your hotel. Although theft is rare in hotel rooms, ask at your hotel if you can store valuable items, such as jewelry, credit cards, or extra cash, in the hotel safe.

When you use an automated teller machine (ATM), choose one that is located in a well-lit, busy area and never let a stranger look over your shoulder or assist you in using your bank card.

Travelers with cars should park in well-lit garages or use valet parking if offered by the hotel, and avoid leaving valuable items in the car. Always lock the doors when you park

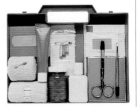

Compact first-aid kit, an essential item for travelers

the car and leave the glove compartment empty and open. It is also advisable to keep the car doors locked while driving.

Medical Matters

Most major cities in the Pacific Northwest have walk-in medical clinics, which are usually sufficient for minor injuries and ailments. Clinics and hospitals are listed in the Yellow Pages of the telephone directory. Without insurance, medical services can be expensive. Even with insurance, you may have to pay upfront for the medical treatment and seek reimbursement from your insurance company later.

Nonprescription painkillers and other medicines can be obtained from drugstores, many of which are open 24 hours a day. Prescription drugs can be dispensed only from a pharmacy. If you take a prescription drug, pack an extra supply, as well as a copy of the prescription. A first-aid kit is also recommended when camping or trekking into remote areas.

If you have HIV or AIDS, call the embassy or consulate of the country to which you are traveling to find out about regulations regarding travelers with either of these conditions. The entry requirements can change at short notice.

Emergencies

Dial 911 if the emergency requires the fire department, police, or an ambulance; if you are not in a major city, dial 0. The call can be made free of charge from any telephone. Most hospitals have a 24-hour emergency room; be prepared for a long wait. Although they may be busy, public hospitals can be much less expensive than private ones. Hospitals in British Columbia will provide treatment to anyone, regardless of health care coverage; in the US, visitors must provide payment or proof of insurance coverage before receiving treatment.

Natural Hazards

Before setting off to hike or camp, check with the appropriate state, provincial, or federal forest service for information on the conditions in the area and recommended safety precautions. Skiers and snowboarders should heed warning signs and stay on groomed runs and trails. It is always best to be accompanied when engaging in any such outdoor activity. Insects are another hazard. While black flies, which are common in the spring, are annoying, they are relatively harmless. Mosquitoes, however, which are prevalent in the summer, can be carriers of the potentially fatal West Nile virus. Ticks, which can be carriers of Lyme disease, are found in dry, wooded areas. To protect yourself, use insect repellent and wear long sleeves, long trousers, and socks. If you are bitten and develop a rash or flu-like symptoms, seek medical attention immediately.

When camping, beware of cougars, wolves, coyotes, and bears (see pp312–13). Many parks post information on recent sightings. Leaving food out can attract dangerous wildlife and is illegal in many areas, as is feeding wild animals.

Most beaches in Oregon and Washington are not patrolled by lifeguards. Heed the red-tide warnings that alert shellfish collectors to contamination. Also watch out for riptides, which are strong currents that can quickly pull swimmers away from the shore. To avoid being swept out to sea, don't fight the current and swim parallel to the shore.

Vancouver police officers on duty

Law Enforcement

The Portland and Seattle police departments are present in these cities on foot, on horseback, motorcycle, and in cars. Neighborhood security teams, made up of citizen volunteers, also patrol on foot in some areas. Outside metropolitan areas, there are county police and sheriff's offices to assist you. British Columbia is policed by the Royal Canadian Mounted Police (RCMP); some municipalities also have their own police forces. In addition, you are likely to see security officers from private security companies in airports and public places, and on Vancouver's downtown streets.

It is illegal to comment on or joke about bombs, guns, and terrorism in places such as airports, where it is possible to be arrested or removed from a flight for an off-the-cuff remark.

Drinking and driving is taken very seriously in the Pacific Northwest, and it is illegal to carry open alcohol containers in a vehicle. However, you may carry previously opened bottles of alcohol if they are inside a bag, stapled shut, and carried in your trunk. Police checks for impaired drivers are increasingly common. Narcotics users can face criminal charges, followed by moves for deportation; penalties are especially severe in the US.

Lost or Stolen Property

Although the chances of retrieving lost or stolen items are slim, it is nevertheless important to report missing items to the police as soon as possible. Be sure to obtain a copy of the police record in case you need it for an insurance claim.

Before leaving home, make photocopies of important documents such as your passport, driver's license, credit cards, and identification cards; keep one set of photocopies at home, another set with you.

Should you lose your passport, contact your nearest embassy or consulate. Visitors do not generally need a new passport if they are returning directly to their home country and so may be issued a temporary one. However, if you are traveling on to another destination, you will need to replace your permanent passport. Report lost credit cards and traveler's checks as soon as you notice them missing; **American Express**, **MasterCard**, **Visa**, and **Thomas Cook** all have toll-free call centers open 24 hours a day, seven days a week. If you have a record of the traveler's checks' numbers, replacing them should be fairly straightforward and new ones are issued within 24 hours. For items lost on public transit or in a taxi, contact the lost-and-found departments of the appropriate transit system or taxi company.

A park ranger

Travel Insurance

Travel insurance is essential when traveling. Consider purchasing insurance for health and medical emergencies, trip cancellation and interruption, theft, and loss of valuable possessions. A minimum of $1 million medical coverage is recommended, especially if you are traveling to the US. Insurance for luggage and travel documents can be arranged through a travel agent or the airline. Emergency dental, out-of-pocket, and loss-of-vacation expenses are generally covered by separate policies. Ask your travel agent or insurance company to recommend suitable insurance; also check with your credit card company (see p322).

DIRECTORY

Emergencies

Police, Fire, Ambulance
Tel In major cities call 911; elsewhere, dial 0.

Hospitals
Tel Call 411 for directory assistance.

Embassies and Consulates

Links to US Embassies and Consulates Worldwide
w usembassy.gov

Links to Canadian Embassies, Consulates, and High Commissions Worldwide
w international.gc.ca

Lost or Stolen Credit Cards and Traveler's Checks

American Express
Tel (800) 869-3016 for credit cards, (800) 528-4800 for traveler's checks.

MasterCard
Tel (800) 627-8372.

Thomas Cook
Tel (800) 223-7373

Visa
Tel (800) 847-2911 for credit cards, (800) 227-6811 for traveler's checks.

Banking and Currency

Banks and foreign currency exchanges are plentiful throughout the Pacific Northwest, with many banks extending their opening hours during the evenings and on weekends. ATMs (automated teller machines) are the most useful, though, allowing visitors to make cash withdrawals 24 hours a day. Credit cards are a more common form of payment than hard currency, especially at hotels or car rental companies, but keep some local cash on hand for tipping, public transportation, and the food trucks that are common in the cities of Portland, Seattle, and Vancouver.

An ATM, common throughout the Pacific Northwest

Banks and Foreign Currency Exchange

Most banks are open from 9 or 9:30am to 4:30 or 5pm, with many in downtown locations offering extended hours, especially on Fridays. Some banks are also open on weekends, but all are closed on statutory holidays.

Exchange rates for foreign currency are posted in banks where exchange services are offered (usually the main branches of large banks) as well as at foreign exchange brokers, **American Express** and **Travelex** being the most popular ones.

In an emergency, visitors can have cash wired from home by way of electronic money transfer services offered by American Express, **Thomas Cook**, and **Western Union**.

ATMs

Automated teller machines (ATMs, or ABMs – automated banking machines, in Canada) can be found in bank branches, shopping centers, gas stations, grocery stores, mini-marts, transit terminals, airports, and some bars and restaurants. Consult with your bank, credit union, or credit card company about which ATM systems will accept your bank card, and what fees and commissions will be charged on each transaction made outside your home country.

Credit Cards

The most widely accepted credit cards are **Visa**, **MasterCard**, and **Diners Club**, which can be used to pay for just about anything, from a cup of coffee to a hotel room. American Express and **Discover** are also accepted in some places. Credit cards are often required when checking into a hotel or renting a car – many such places will insist on taking your credit card information to use as a form of deposit.

If your credit card company offers travel insurance, keep a copy of the statement of conditions and coverage with your travel documents. Before leaving home, be sure to note all emergency contact numbers connected with your credit card in case of loss or theft.

Traveler's Checks and Currency Cards

American Express, Thomas Cook, and Visa issue traveler's checks and it is advisable to purchase them in US or Canadian currency. A passport or other photo identification is required to cash traveler's checks. Keep in mind that, in rural areas and areas less geared to tourism, traveler's checks may not be accepted.

An increasingly popular alternative to traveler's checks are prepaid currency cards, which function like debit or credit cards and can be used to withdraw money from ATMs or to pay for services in shops and restaurants. These cards are available through several providers, including Thomas Cook and Travelex, but look for one that offers fair exchange rates, no ATM fees, and no charges for purchases.

Currency

Both in the US and Canada the unit of currency is the dollar, which is divided into 100 cents. Coins include denominations of 1 cent (penny) – US only, as Canada has discontinued the penny – 5 cents (nickel), 10 cents (dime), 25 cents (quarter), and $1 (buck; in Canada it is often called a "loonie"). In Canada, there is also a $2 coin, a "toonie." Bank notes, or bills, are printed in denominations of $5, $10, $20, $50, and $100. In the US, a $2 bill is also in circulation, but it is uncommon. Plan to arrive with $50 to $100 in local currency and get small change as soon as possible for tipping, transportation, and other incidentals.

Media and Communications

The wide use of cellular telephones and the Internet has changed the communications picture in most of the world, and the Pacific Northwest is, of course, no exception. Visitors will find this region well supplied with mobile telephone stores and public access to computers and Wi-Fi. The variety of readily available local newspapers and magazines makes it easy to keep up with world news as well as the latest dining and entertainment options for each of the cities.

Many places offer free Wi-Fi access

Public Telephones

Public pay phones are becoming rarer, but they can still be found at some bars, restaurants, public buildings, gas stations, and at rest stops outside of urban areas. Some use credit cards, but most are coin-operated and take 5-, 10-, and 25-cent coins. Local calls made from pay phones in the US cost 35 cents; in Canada, 50 cents. You can buy prepaid phone cards from mini-marts and gas stations for long-distance calls.

For local calls, dial the area code followed by the seven-digit number. For long-distance calls within North America, dial 1, followed by the area code and the local number. For calls outside North America, dial 011, followed by the country code, then the city or area code, then the local telephone number; or dial 0 for the operator.

Cell Phones

Visitors who wish to use their own cell phone in the US and Canada will need a SIM card that has been set up for "roaming." However, it is essential to check with your phone provider what charges you may incur while abroad. Some companies offer "bundles" of calls and data to save costs while you are away.

Cell phones can also be rented or purchased locally in many places, from kiosks in shopping malls to stores and online, with companies such as **Cellhire**.

Internet

Almost all hotels offer the use of computers and most also have Wi-Fi, though you may have to pay. In hotels' public areas, however, Wi-Fi is often complimentary. Coffee shops, libraries, shopping malls, and university hangouts usually offer free Wi-Fi access as well. To find public Wi-Fi hot spots at your destination, go to **jiwire.com**.

Postal Services

Post offices generally open weekdays from 9am to 5pm; also on Saturdays in the US. Stamped, addressed mail can be dropped into roadside mailboxes, which are blue in the US and red in Canada. Pick-up times are listed on the boxes. Most hotels will also accept letters and postcards at the front desk.

Mail sent within the US or Canada takes from 1 to 5 business days for delivery; overseas mail, up to 7 business days. Courier companies and the priority services of the **US Postal Service** and **Canada Post** offer speedier delivery.

Newspapers, Television, and Radio

Newsstands in the Pacific Northwest carry most major international and national papers, including the *New York Times*, the *Wall Street Journal*, and *USA Today* in the US, and *The Globe and Mail* and the *National Post* in Canada. Local papers are available at sidewalk boxes, coffee shops, and convenience stores.

The US has a multitude of TV channels, provided by the four networks – ABC, CBS, Fox, and NBC – as well as many cable channels. CNN is a national 24-hour headline news station. Various radio stations in the US offer local news bulletins and weather forecasts. National Public Radio is a good source of commercial-free news and entertainment; it is usually located along the FM band.

The CBC, Canada's public broadcasting corporation, has local, national, and international television and radio programming. VTV, the Vancouver affiliate of CTV, Canada's largest private television broadcaster, airs news and other programs daily.

Area Codes

Oregon
- Portland, Salem and Astoria — 503/971
- Oregon, elsewhere — 541/458

Washington
Western Washington
- Seattle — 206/564
- Eastside — 425
- Southside, including Tacoma — 253/564
- Elsewhere — 360/564
Eastern Washington — 509

British Columbia
- Vancouver/Lower Mainland — 604/778/236
- BC, elsewhere — 250/778/236

DIRECTORY

Cell Phones

Cellhire
Tel (877) 244-7242.
W cellhire.com

Internet

Wi-Fi Hotspot Finder
W jiwire.com

Postal Services

United States Postal Service
Tel (800) 275-8777.
W usps.com

Canada Post
Tel (800) 267-1177.
W canadapost.ca

TRAVEL INFORMATION

The three major airports in the Pacific Northwest are conveniently located to serve the metropolitan areas of Portland, Oregon; Seattle, Washington; and Vancouver, British Columbia. But these urban centers can also be easily accessed by train, car, or bus on the region's excellent network of well-maintained highways. Train travel is ideal for enjoying the picturesque landscape; buses are relatively inexpensive; and driving is particularly popular, as it enables travelers to visit many locations that would otherwise be difficult to reach. Once you have arrived in the Pacific Northwest, ferries and cruises provide a scenic way of traveling between coastal communities.

Arriving by Air

Washington's major airport is **Sea-Tac International Airport** (SEA), located between Seattle and Tacoma. In Oregon, **Portland International Airport** (PDX) is just a few miles outside the city proper. Most major carriers fly into these airports, though international passengers may need to stop in Seattle and transfer to another plane to fly into Portland.

United Airlines offers flights to the major cities of the Pacific Northwest, while **Alaska Airlines** and **Horizon Air** fly to these as well as to regional destinations. **San Juan Airlines** and **Kenmore Air** fly between Seattle and the San Juan Islands.

The point of arrival for most international visitors to British Columbia is **Vancouver International Airport** (YVR), which is served by Canada's major carrier, **Air Canada**, as well as other national airlines from around the world. **WestJet** is a low-cost national alternative that links up with other major airlines. Air Canada's regional division flies to most major BC destinations; smaller airlines, such as **Harbour Air**, serving the Gulf Islands, and **Hawkair**, serving northern BC, connect the province's smaller communities.

Transportation from the Airport

Taxis and the less expensive shuttle buses are readily available at all of the three major international airports in the Pacific Northwest. Some hotels provide shuttle service; ask when booking your room. The least expensive way to get into the cities from the airports is by public transit. The **MAX** light rail system is ideal for getting into Portland; **Gray Line** also offers an airport service. Seattle's **Metro Transit** buses run from Sea-Tac Airport, and share-ride shuttles and a light rail are available. **TransLink** buses run regularly from the Vancouver airport, while the **Canada Line SkyTrain** reaches downtown Vancouver from the airport in 25 minutes.

Traveling by Bus

Although the bus may be the slowest way of getting to the Pacific Northwest, it may be the most economical. **Greyhound** has bus routes throughout the region; **Gray Line** and **Pacific Coach Lines** offer sightseeing tours. Discounts are often available for children, students, and senior citizens.

Traveling by Train

If you are traveling from within the US or Canada, the train is a good way to get to

Amtrak train, offering convenient travel and sightseeing at once

the Pacific Northwest and to travel within it. **Amtrak** offers daily services to Washington and Oregon from the Midwest and California and has daily runs between Vancouver, Seattle, Portland, and Eugene, Oregon.

In British Columbia, **VIA Rail**, Canada's national rail service, links Vancouver to Alberta and the rest of Canada. **Rocky Mountaineer®** takes a stunning scenic route to Whistler or Kamloops, continuing on to Jasper, or Lake Louise, Banff, and Calgary, in Alberta, or along the coast to Seattle. Reserve seats through a travel agent or VIA Rail directly.

Union Station, Portland's Italian Renaissance-style train depot, opened 1896

Traveling by Car

Oregon, Washington, and British Columbia maintain an extensive network of highways. The major interstate through Oregon and Washington is I-5, running north to British Columbia and south to California. The best route to eastern Washington from Seattle is I-90; the most accessible route to eastern Oregon from Portland is I-84. The Trans-Canada Highway traverses British Columbia, linking it to the rest of the country. There are no tolls on roads leading into Portland and Seattle, and all US interstate highways are free. Speed limits and seat-belt laws are strictly enforced.

Travelers driving across the Canada–US border can choose from 16 crossings. Bring your passport and a current driver's license. In some cases, an International Driving Permit will be required. Rules governing border crossings are subject to change; check with the authorities before traveling.

Washington State Ferries terminal, Port Townsend

Traveling by Ferry

Ferries are an important, and scenic, mode of transportation in the Pacific Northwest.
Washington State Ferries *(see p166)* travel regularly between Washington's mainland and the Puget Sound and San Juan Islands, as well as to Sidney, British Columbia, 17 miles (27 km) north of Victoria.

In British Columbia, **BC Ferries** travel 25 routes along the Sunshine Coast, in the Gulf Islands, the Queen Charlotte Islands, Haida Gwaii, and between the mainland and Vancouver Island. It has two terminals in the Vancouver area: one in Tsawwassen, the other in Horseshoe Bay. Unlike BC ferries, the **Victoria Clipper** provides a route to Washington. It also travels from Victoria and Seattle to the San Juan Islands.

BC and Washington ferries carry both foot passangers and vehicles, and offer discounts for students and seniors.

DIRECTORY

Airports

Portland International Airport
Tel (877) 739-4636.
W pdx.com

Sea-Tac International Airport
Tel (800) 544-1965.
W portseattle.org

Vancouver International Airport
Tel (604) 207-7077.
W yvr.ca

Airlines

Air Canada
Tel (888) 247-2262.
W aircanada.com

Alaska Airlines
Tel (800) 252-7522.
W alaskaair.com

Harbour Air
Tel (800) 665-0212.
W harbour-air.com

Hawkair
Tel (800) 487-1216.
W hawkair.ca

Horizon Air
Tel (800) 252-7522.
W alaskaair.com

Kenmore Air
Tel (866) 435-9524.
W kenmoreair.com

San Juan Airlines
Tel (800) 874-4434.
W sanjuanairlines.com

United Airlines
Tel (800) 864-8331.
W united.com

WestJet
Tel (888) 937-8538.
W westjet.com

Transportation from the Airport

Canada Line SkyTrain
Tel (604) 953-3333.
W thecanadaline.com

MAX (TriMet)
Tel (503) 238-7433.
W trimet.org

Metro Transit
Tel (206) 553-3000.
W metro.king county.gov

TransLink
Tel (604) 953-3333.
W translink.ca

Bus Companies

Gray Line
Tel In Portland & Seattle: (800) 472-9546. In Victoria: (800) 667-0882.
W grayline.com

Greyhound
Tel In US: (800) 231-2222.
In Canada: (800) 661-8747.
W greyhound.com (US);
W greyhound.ca (Can)

Pacific Coach Lines
Tel (800) 661-1725.
W pacificcoach.com

Rail Companies

Amtrak
Tel (800) 872-7245.
W amtrak.com

Rocky Mountaineer®
Tel (877) 460-3200.
W rockymountaineer. com

VIA Rail
Tel (888) 842-7245.
W viarail.ca

Ferry Companies

BC Ferries
Tel (888) 223-3779.
W bcferries.com

Victoria Clipper
Tel (800) 888-2535.
W clippervacations. com

Washington State Ferries
Tel (800) 843-3779 or (206) 464-6400 (Seattle).
W wsdot.wa.gov

Traveling by Car in the Pacific Northwest

Driving is the best way to explore the Pacific Northwest, especially if you want to enjoy the spectacular beauty of more remote areas, such as Oregon's Hells Canyon, the mountains of Washington's Olympic Peninsula, or British Columbia's Okanagan Valley. In major cities, parking may be hard to find and traffic heavy during rush hours; tune into local TV or radio news for reports on traffic and road conditions, particularly if you visit in the winter. Rental cars are widely available at airports and in the cities and towns.

Driver's License and Insurance

In the US, you do not need an International Driving Permit if you are carrying a valid driver's license from the country in which you live. You must, however, carry proof of auto insurance, vehicle registration, and, if renting a car, the rental contract.

A valid driver's license from your own country entitles you to drive for up to 6 months in British Columbia. It is advisable to carry an International Driving Permit as well, in case you run into problems.

Insurance coverage for drivers is compulsory. Before leaving home, check your own policy to see if you are covered in a rental car. Most rental agencies offer damage and liability insurance; it is a good idea to have both. Insurance can be purchased on arrival through the **British Columbia Automobile Association (BCAA)**; in the US, contact the **American Automobile Association (AAA)**.

Rules of the Road

Vehicles are driven on the right-hand side of the road in both the US and Canada. Right-hand turns on a red light are permitted after coming to a complete stop unless otherwise indicated.

Distances and speed limits are posted in miles in the US, and in kilometers in Canada. Speed limits vary from 25 mph (40 km/h) on neighborhood streets to a maximum of 65 mph (105 km/h) on major highways. Speed limits are strictly enforced. On most major highways in the Pacific Northwest, carpool lanes are available for vehicles with two or more passengers, to reduce pollution and traffic.

Four-way stops are common in the Pacific Northwest. The first car to reach the intersection has the right of way. At intersections with no stop signs, drivers must yield to the car on their right.

Coin-operated parking meter

Because traffic in and around Portland, Seattle, and Vancouver can be heavy, it is wise to avoid rush hours in these cities, generally between 7:30 and 9:30am and from 3:30 to 6pm on weekdays. On city streets, parking meters offer between 15 minutes and 2 hours of parking. Be sure to put money into the meter and to read all signs, since parking enforcement officers are especially active within city limits.

Seat belts are compulsory throughout the Pacific Northwest for both drivers and passengers, and children weighing less than 40 lb (18 kg) must be in the appropriate child seats. Cyclists and motorcyclists are required to wear helmets. Driving while intoxicated (which is defined as having a blood alcohol content of more than 0.08 percent) is a criminal offense. If you are involved in an accident, contact the local police. (In Canada, local policing may be done by the Royal Canadian Mounted Police, or RCMP, depending on where you are.)

Safety on the Road

The Pacific Northwest experiences heavy rainfall and road surfaces become very slippery when wet, which increases the risk of hydroplaning. Other potential safety hazards for drivers include heavy snowfalls, black ice, and fog, which can be particularly thick along the coast. To be safe, always carry a spare tire, and salt or sand in winter, a flashlight, jumper cables, blankets, water, some emergency food, and a shovel. Before venturing out onto back roads, be sure to inquire about road conditions and weather forecasts and to have a full tank of gas. Refill the tank fairly often along the way as an extra precaution. If you know you will be driving on dirt roads or in treacherous conditions, you may want to rent a vehicle with four-wheel drive.

During the spring and summer, wildlife such as deer, bears, elk, and moose have

The spectacular Columbia River Historic Highway, near Rowena, Oregon

Speed limit

Gas pump

Road conditions

Rest area

Wildlife

been known to rush out of the woods onto the roads. Signs will indicate where wildlife is most likely to appear; take extra care in these areas.

Car Rentals

Car rental agencies such as **Alamo**, **Avis**, **Budget**, **Enterprise**, **Hertz**, **National**, and **Thrifty** are located within the cities and towns as well as at airports. To rent a vehicle in the US or Canada, you must be 21 years of age and have a valid driver's license. If you are younger than 25, you will likely have to pay a higher insurance premium. A major credit card is usually required, even when you are prepared to make a hefty cash deposit.

Rent a car that suits your destination: a small car or sedan is appropriate for city sightseeing, but if you plan to cross mountain ranges, especially between October and April, opt for a sturdier, high-traction vehicle. Recreational vehicles (RVs) can also be rented but are more expensive and usually need to be reserved well in advance. Many outlets are reluctant to rent their cars if they know there is a risk of gravel roads chipping the paintwork, so if you plan to drive along back roads, you may be best off renting from an outlet in the backcountry.

Sign for a rental car agency

Fuel

Most vehicles in the US and Canada run on unleaded fuel, sold by the gallon in the US and by the liter in Canada. Fuel prices fluctuate, and are generally higher in Canada than in the US, although Canadian prices are still significantly lower than they are in Europe.

Service stations are usually self-serve (except in Oregon, where law prohibits self-serve), and many are closed at night. At full-serve stations, you remain in your car while an attendant fills up your gas tank and usually washes the windshield, making full-serve slightly more expensive. Be sure to keep your gas tank full when traveling through the mountains or in more remote areas.

Roadside Assistance

Emergency road service is available 24 hours a day, 365 days a year, anywhere in the US or Canada. Members of the **American Automobile Association**, **Canadian Automobile Association**, and **British Columbia Automobile Association** can call (800) 222-4357. Be prepared to give your name, membership number and expiry date, phone number, vehicle type, license plate number, exact location, and tow destination.

DIRECTORY

Reports on Road Conditions

In British Columbia
Tel (800) 550-4997.
W drivebc.ca

In Oregon
Tel (800) 977-6368.
W tripcheck.com

In Washington
Tel (206) 368-4499 or (800) 695-7623. W wsdot.wa.gov

Car Rentals

Alamo
Tel (877) 222-9075.
W alamo.com

Avis
Tel (800) 230-4898.
W avis.com

Budget
Tel (800) 527-0700.
W budget.com

Enterprise
Tel (800) 261-7331.
W enterprise.com

Hertz
Tel (800) 654-3131. W hertz.com

National
Tel (877) 222-9058.
W nationalcar.com

Thrifty
Tel (800) 847-4389.
W thrifty.com

Roadside Assistance

American Automobile Association
Tel (800) 222-4357.
W aaa.com

British Columbia Automobile Association
Tel In Lower Mainland, BC: (604) 293-2222 or cell users: *222; In other areas of Canada & US: (800) 222-4357 (all are 24-hr emergency service numbers). W bcaa.bc.ca

Canadian Automobile Association
Tel (800) 222-4357 (24-hr emergency service). W caa.ca

A gas station, one of many on major highways and in towns and cities

General Index

Acknowledgments

Dorling Kindersley and International Book Productions would like to thank the following people, whose contributions and assistance have made the preparation of this book possible.

Main Contributors

Stephen Brewer, a New York-based travel writer, is proud to have been born in Oregon, where he spends as much time as he can.

Constance Brissenden has explored beautiful British Columbia for more than 25 years. A freelance writer living in Vancouver, she has written 12 books on travel and history.

Anita Carmin, a Seattle native, specializes in travel writing. Her assignments have taken her from the ballrooms of Europe to a remote jungle lagoon on the Yucatan Peninsula.

Additional Contributors Allison Austin, Cora Lee

Additional Picture Research Rachel Barber, Rhiannon Furbear, Nigel Hicks, Gunter Marx, Ellen Root, Paul Whitfield

Additional Photography William Carleton, Frank Jenkins, Helen Townsend, Lisa Voormeij, Peter Wilson

Cartography VISUTronX, Ajax, Ontario, Canada

Proofreader Garry Bowers

Indexer Helen Peters

For Dorling Kindersley

Publishing Manager Helen Townsend
Art Editor Ian Midson
Cartographer Casper Morris
DTP Designers Jason Little, Conrad Van Dyk
Picture Researcher Claire Bowers
Proofreader Lucilla Watson

Revisions

Umesh Aggarwal, Claire Baranowski, Kate Berens, Uma Bhattacharya, Hilary Bird, Jo Cowen, Heather Douglas, Gadi Farfour, Fay Franklin, Taraneh Ghajar Jerven, Eric Grossman, Lydia Halliday, Vinod Harish, Mohammad Hassan, Andrew Hempstead, Susanne Hillen, Rose Hudson, Jacky Jackson, Jasneet Kaur, Priya Kukadia, Priyanka Harris, Rahul Kumar, Savitha Kumar, Vincent Kurien, Rachel Laidler, Maite Lantaron, Hayley Maher, Alison McGill, James McQuillen, Kate Molan, George Nimmo, Catherine Palmi, Susie Peachey, Marianne Petrou, Pete Quinlan, Rada Radojicic, Erin Richards, Marisa Renzullo, Sands Publishing Solutions, Azeem Siddiqui, Rituraj Singh, Sadie Smith, Jaynan Spengler, Helen Townsend, Nikky Twyman, Richa Verma, Hugo Wilkinson, Ed Wright, Karen Villabona, Lisa Voormeij.

Special Assistance

The publisher would also like to thank the following for their assistance: Amy Buranski, Experience Music Project; Cindy Bjorklund and Tim Manns, National Park Service; Perry Cooper, Seattle Center; Ardie Davis, Domaine Serene; Courtney Hallam; Angelika Harris; Leslie Lambert, Nathalie Levesque, and Natalie Stone, National Archives of Canada; Donald Olson; Jeffrey Richstone; Dana Selover; Tammy Walker, Walla Walla Chamber of Commerce.

Photography Permissions

The publisher would also like to thank the following for their assistance and kind permission to photograph at their establishments:

American Advertising Museum; Capilano Suspension Bridge and Park; Catch the Wind Kite Shop; Christ Church Cathedral; End of Oregon Trail; Evergreen Aviation Museum; Experience Music Project; Fraser – Fort George Regional Museum; Governor Hotel; Granville Island Public Market; Helmcken House; Klondike Gold Rush National Historic Park; Multnomah County Library; Museum of Flight; National Historic Oregon Trail Interpretive Center; Oregon Maritime Center; Oregon Museum of Science and Industry; Pacific Place; Pioneer Place; Port Townsend Farmers Market; Portland Art Museum; Powell's City of Books; Seattle Aquarium; Seattle Children's Museum; Tillamook County Creamery Association; Victoria Bay Centre; Victoria Parliament Buildings.

Picture Credits

Works of art have been reproduced with the permission of the following copyright holders:
Steve Badanes, Will Martin, Donna Walter, and Ross Whitehead *Fremont Troll*, 1990 162bl; Jonathan Barofsky *Hammering Man* 132tr; Richard Beyer *People Waiting for the Interurban* 162tl; Dale Chihuly *Benaroya Hall Silver Chandelier* 1998 133clb; City of Vancouver: *Percy Williams* by Ann McLaren 1996 217c; *Captain John Deighton (Gassy Jack)* by Vern Simpson 1970 205cr, 208tl; *The Crab* by George Norris 1968 225t; *Gate to the Northwest Passage* by Alan Chung Hung 1980 224c; *Inukshuk* by Alvin Kanak 1986 30tr; *Chinatown Millennium Gate* by Joe Y. Wai Architect, Inc. 2002. 208b; Georgia Gerber, Rachel the market pig 137bl; © Raymond Kaskey 1985 *Portlandia* 67c; Jack Mackie *Dance Steps on Broadway* 1981 157bl; Portland Art Museum: courtyard artwork 62tr; Alan Storey *Broken Column* 215c; *Logger's Culls*, c.1935, oil on canvas, Vancouver Art Gallery, VAG 39.1, photo: Trevor Mills 215t; Hai Ying Wu *The Fallen Firefighters' Memorial* 1998 126cl.

The publisher would like to thank the following individuals, companies, and picture libraries for permission to reproduce their photographs:

Ace Hotel Portland: 286bl; **Alamy Images:** Pat Canova 126cl; Danita Delimont 122cb; Mike Finn-Kelcey 216ca; ImageState/Randa Bishop 225tl; Inge Johnsson 154; Ninette Maumus 36tl; Brad Mitchell 185tc; Bernard O'Kane *Perre's Ventaglio III* by Beverly Pepper, 1967 148tl; Chuck Pefley 139; Stephen Power 140tc; PSL Images 322; Dave Robertson 323cla; travelstock44 216tl; Michael Wheatley 221cra; **Amazon.com, Inc:** 45br.

BC Archives: PDP00289 38. **BC Place:** 217tc; **Bellingham/Whatcom County Convention and Visitors Bureau:** Jim Poth 22t; Keith Lazelle 27cra; **The Boeing Company:** 45crb; **Pearl Bucknall:** photographersdirect.com 221br.

Canlis Restaurant: 299bc; **Emily Carr University of Art & Design:** 222bc; **Celilo:** Heidi Janke 296bl; **Chateau Benoit:** Ashley Smith 102bl; **Chateau Ste. Michelle:** 49b, 122b, 307tr; **The Children's Museum, Seattle:** 152tc; **City of Vancouver Archives:** Stuart Thomson photo CVA 99-2507 31br; Harry T. Devine photo LGN 1045 207br; W. Chapman photo CVA 677-441 225br; **Convention & Visitors Association of Lane County Oregon:** Lon Beale 309tl; Michael Chafron 103crb; Norm Coyer 33tl; 100tl; Dick Dietrich 310cb; Dianne Dietrick Leis 105tr; Darrel Lindblad 31cr; Sally McAleer 32cl, 100bc, 309bc; Sandland Adventures 100cr, 308tr; Sea Lion Caves 26tr; Randy Siner 310cra; **Corbis:** Walter Bibikow/JAI 210; Dave Blackney/All Canada Photos 15bc; Peter Carroll/First Light 144; Fridmar Damm 11c; Design Pics/Kevin Smith 273tr; Jon Hicks 134; Historical Picture Archive 8–9; Randy Lincks 312–13; © Museum of History and Industry/Wilse127br; Jose Fuste Raga 13tr; Tim Thompson 202; Craig Tuttle 50–51; **Courtesy of Colorado Historical Society:** CHSJ1449, William Henry Jackson 43crb; **Crystal Mountain:** Jeremy Martinson www.cascaonline.com 190b, 316b; **Crystal Springs Rhododendron Garden:** Barbara L. Darval 78cr.

Denver Public Library, Western History Collection: X- 31120 31bl; The Depot Restaurant: Beachdog.com 301tc; Domaine Serene: 102cl; Dorst, Adrian: 259cl; Dreamstime.com: Adeliepenguin. 279crb; Kushnirov Avraham 248bl; Junko Barker 23br; Nilanjan Bhattacharya 10bl; Jon Bilous 63bl; Chris Boswell 13bl; Dan Breckwoldt 46–7, 198–9; Lembi Buchanan 124; Bwendy3 32–3c; Sorin Colac 279tl; Crystal Craig 140br; James Crawford 56ca; Davidgn 53cr; Deymos 130–31; Victoria Ditkovsky 53tr; Lindsay Douglas 20; Eudaemon 280–81; Fallsview 226; Fred Goldstein 218; Lijuan Guo 174; Hitmans 12bl; Ivkovich 99br; Keeton10 56bc; Dan Klimke 14bl; Kyrylyuk 206tr; Nelugo 2–3; Kaye Eileen Oberstar 279bl; Pnwnature 64tl, 97bl; Steven Prorak 278cl; Gino Rigucci 204tr, 324br; Brandon Smith 15tr; Steve Smith 274t; Smontgom65 27tl; Yasushi Tanikado 279cra; Leszek Wrona 212.

Edgewater Hotel, Seattle: Zimmerman 285; Experience Music Project: 151bc, 151tc; Stanley Smith 150cl; Lara Swimmer 150bc.

Fairmont Hotels and Resorts, Canada: Empress Hotel Victoria 291br; Fairmont Hotel Vancouver: 214tr; Fernie Alpine Resort: 265tl, 266cla; Four Seasons Olympic Hotel: Photos by Robb Gordon 123tr, 132b.

Geiser Grand Hotel: 284tc, 297tc; Gunter Marx – Stock Photos: 26cl, 28c–29c, 29br, 35tr, 37bl, 179t, 258cr, 258bl, 259br, 260cl, 271cr, 272t, 274br, 277br, 311br; Granville Island Information Office: 303br.

Robert Harding Picture Library: Strigi Egmont/age fotostock 54; National Geographic 190tc; Hastings House Country House Hotel: 293tr; Heather Douglas Photography: 96br; Hells Canyon Adventures: Ed Riche 119bl, 119crb; Hemispheres Images: Philippe Renault 320cr; The Herbfarm: Ron Zimmerman 300tl; Higgins Restaurant: John Valls 295tr.

Inn at Abeja: Jumping Rocks 289tl; iStockphoto.com: KingWu 66cb.

John Day Fossil Beds National Monument: Courtesy of National Park Service and NWIA 115c.

Kamloops Tourism: 309cr; Koocanusa Publications: 265br.

Courtesy of Leavenworth Chamber of Commerce: 37t; L'Ecole No. 41 Winery: Brent Bergherm 196tr; Leonardo Media Ltd.: 64br.

H. R. Macmillan Space Centre: 225cr; Matt's in the Market: 298tl; Alison McGill: 32bl, 207tr, 220cl, 230br, 239bc; Medicine Wheel Website Design: 194tl; Metropolitan Grill: 293bl; Microsoft: 163bc; Miku, Vancouver: 302br; Mount St. Helens National Volcanic Monument: 24bl, 45tl, 197cl; Mscua, University of Washington Libraries: UW6991 128br, UW10921 43tl; The Museum of Flight: 163cr.

National Archives of Canada: E. Sandys C-011040 8; Theodore J. Richardson C-102057 30c–31c; William George Richardson Hind C-13978 30b; John B. Wilkinson C-150276 31tr; Robert Petley C-103553 39b; Peter Rindisbacher C-001904 40crb; Alfred Jacob Miller C-000411 40tl; Henry James Warre C-001621 41b, C-001623 42br; Charles William Jefferys C-70270 41tl; Robert William Rutherford C-09870 42bl; Lady Frances Musgrave C-35986 44tl;

Edward Roper R9266-350 215br; National Park Service: 25tc, 29cra, 112tl, 192bl, 192cl, 193bl, 193br, 193cr; © David New-Small, photo: Kenji Nagai 222cr; Northern BC Tourism Association: 273br.

Oregon Coast Aquarium: 99bl; Oregon Zoo: 74tr, 74bc, 75br, Michael Durham 77bl; Orpheum Theatre: Photo: David Blue 237tl.

Paley's Place: John Valls 296tr; Paramount Hotel: 287tr; Pike Place Market Preservation & Development Authority: 44bc, 138bl; Photolibrary: Jtb Photo Communications 213bl; Point Defiance Zoo & Aquarium: 187tl; Portland Art Museum: 52cb; Portland Streetcar: 52cla; Provenance Hotels: Hotel Lucia 282br; Hotel Max 288br.

Images Courtesy of Quails' Gate: 292bl, 304br.

Rosewood Hotel Georgia: 290tl; Royal BC Museum: 256bc, 256cb, 256clb, 256cla, 257cr, 257cra, 257tc.

Science World British Columbia: 217br; Seattle Aquarium: 26bl, 142br, 142tr, 143br, 143cra, 143tl; Bryce Mohan Photography 142cl, 143crb; Seattle Center: Photo by Carson Jones 149br; Seattle Children's Theatre: Chris Bennion 165bc; Seattle's Convention and Visitors Bureau: 142t; Sentinel Hotel: 52clb; Seres: 294br; Sitka & Spruce: Dylan + Jeni 301bl; Southwest Washington Convention & Visitors Bureau: 197cr; Superstock: Richard Cummins 60; Kelly Funk/All Canada Photos 246; Randy Lincks/All Canada Photos 11tl; Alan Majchrowicz/age fotostock 90; George Ostertag 70 /age fotostock 14tr.

Tamástslikt Cultural Institute: 115br; Terra Galleria Photography: 193tl; Tillicum Village: 185cr.

University of British Columbia Museum of Anthropology: 234bc, 234cla, 235bc, 235c.

Vancouver Art Gallery: 200tr; Logger's Culls, c.1935, oil on canvas, Vancouver Art Gallery, VAG 39.1, photo: Trevor Mills 215ct; Vancouver Opera: Tim Matheson 237bc; Viewfinders: 34bl, 35bl, 91b, 101br, 101t, 107br, 109br, 110bl, 110cla, 111br, 111t, 112bl, 112br, 113bl, 113cr, 114tl, 118bl, 118cl, 119tl, 178br, 178tr, 179bl, 179tl, 182tr, 183cra, 183tl, 187br, 195tl, 196bl, 312tr.

Walla Walla Chamber of Commerce: 195br; Wickaninnish Inn: The Pointe Restaurant 305tr; Woodland Park Zoo: Rice Brewer 161cra; Dennis Conner 160cl/cb, 161t; Jeremy Dwyer-Lindgren 161c.

Elevation relief art modified by VISUTronX from: Mountain High Maps® Copyright © 1993 Digital Wisdom Inc.

Front Endpaper
Corbis: Craig Tuttle Lbr; Dreamstime.com: Dan Breckwoldt Ltl; Dhilde Lc; Lijuan Guo Rcr; Superstock: Kelly Funk/All Canada Photos Rtc; Alan Majchrowicz/age fotostock Rbc.

Cover
Front and Spine: Alamy Images: Inge Johnsson.

All other images © Dorling Kindersley
For further information see: www.dkimages.com

Special Editions of DK Travel Guides

DK Travel Guides can be purchased in bulk quantities at discounted prices for use in promotions or as premiums. We are also able to offer special editions and personalized jackets, corporate imprints, and excerpts from all of our books, tailored specifically to meet your own needs.

To find out more, please contact:
in the US specialsales@dk.com
in the UK travelguides@uk.dk.com
in Canada specialmarkets@dk.com
in Australia penguincorporatesales@
penguinrandomhouse.com.au

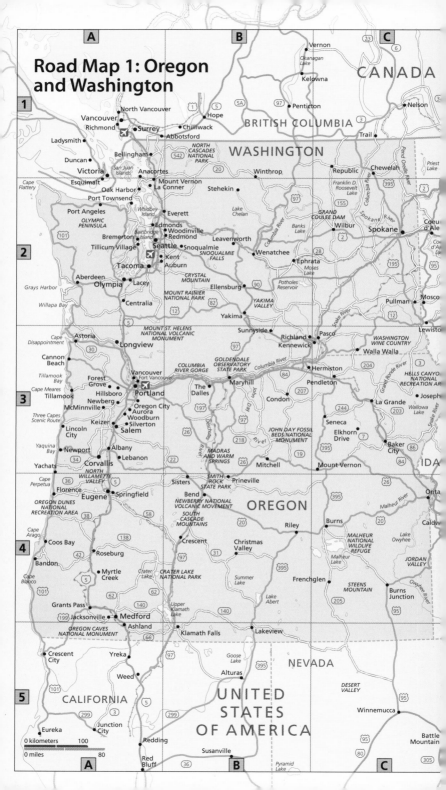